PLI Basic Training
Using VSAM, IMS and DB2

Robert Wingate

ISBN 13:   978-1720867456

Disclaimer

The contents of this book are based upon the author's understanding of and experience with the following IBM products: PLI, VSAM, IMS and DB2. Every attempt has been made to provide correct information. However, the author and publisher do not guarantee the accuracy of every detail, nor do they assume responsibility for information included in or omitted from it. All of the information in this book should be used at your own risk.

Copyright

Contents

INTRODUCTION 11

WELCOME 11
ASSUMPTIONS: 11
APPROACH TO LEARNING 11

CHAPTER ONE : PLI LANGUAGE BASICS 15

PLI LANGUAGE BASICS 15
    Programming Format 15
VARIABLES, DATA TYPES AND ASSIGNMENT 16
    Variable Declaration 16
    Data Types 16
    Data Structures 18
    Sample Program 19
SEQUENCE, SELECTION, ITERATION 21
    Sequence 21
    Selection 21
    Iteration 22
FILE I/O 25
    Pseudo Code for PLITRN3 25
    Program Listing for PLITRN3 26
REPORTING 33
    ANSI Carriage Control 33
    Report Program Sample 34
CALCULATIONS 45
EDITS AND VALIDATION 51
TABLES 63
SUB PROGRAMS 73
CHAPTER ONE REVIEW QUESTIONS 88

CHAPTER TWO: PLI PROGRAMMING WITH VSAM...91

INTRODUCTION 91
TYPES OF VSAM FILES 91
    Key Sequence Data Set (KSDS) 91
    Entry Sequence Data Set (ESDS) 92
    Relative Record Data Set (RRDS) 92
CREATING VSAM FILES 92
LOADING AND UNLOADING VSAM FILES 94
VSAM UPDATES WITH FILE MANAGER 96
APPLICATION PROGRAMMING WITH VSAM 103

PLI Program to Read Records (PLIVS1) 103
PLI Program to Add Records (PLIVS2) 105
PLI Program to Update Records (PLIVS3)...107
PLI Program to Delete Records (PLIVS4) 110
PLI Program to Retrieve Records Sequentially (PLIVS5)........................113
CREATING AND ACCESSING ALTERNATE INDEXES..115
PLI Program to Read Alternate Index (PLIVS6) 118
OTHER VSAM JCL..122
JCL to CREATE ESDS 122
JCL to CREATE RRDS 122
JCL to LIST DATASET INFORMATION 123
VSAM FILE STATUS CODES...125
CHAPTER TWO QUESTIONS 127

CHAPTER THREE: PLI PROGRAMMING WITH IMS 129

DESIGNING AND CREATING IMS DATABASES 129
Sample System Specification 129
Database Descriptor (DBD)..132
Program Specification Block   (PSB) 135
IMS APPLICATION PROGRAMMING BASICS 137
The IMS Program Interface..137
Loading an IMS Database 141
Reading a Segment (GU) 148
Reading a Database Sequentially (GN)..152
Updating a Segment (GHU/REPL) 156
Deleting a Segment (GHU/DLET)...160
Inserting Child Segments 163
Reading Child Segments Sequentially (GNP) 170
Inserting Child Segments Down the Hierarchy (3 levels) 177
Read Child Segments Down the Hierarchy (3 levels) 185
ADDITIONAL IMS PROGRAMMING FEATURES 193
Retrieve Segments Using Searchable Fields..193
Retrieve Segments Using Boolean SSAs...198
Command Codes..203
Summary of Command Codes...209
Committing and Rolling Back Changes 210
Performing Checkpoint Restart...223
IMS PROGRAMMING GUIDELINES 236
CHAPTER THREE REVIEW QUESTIONS 237

CHAPTER FOUR : PLI PROGRAMMING WITH DB2 241

BASIC z/OS TOOLS FOR DB2 241
DB2 Interactive 241
DATA MANIPULATION LANGUAGE 249

Overview...249
DML SQL Statements 250
XML...297
SPECIAL REGISTERS...307
BUILT-IN FUNCTIONS...311
TABLE Functions...320
ROW functions..322
APPLICATION PROGRAMMING WITH DB2 323
CURSORS...323
Types of Cursors...323
Error Handling 328
Dynamic versus Static SQL..334
Program Preparation...336
DATA CONCURRENCY...337
Isolation Levels & Bind Release Options 337
COMMIT, ROLLBACK, and SAVEPOINTS..340
Units of Work..344
Autonomous Transactions...344
Applications 345
Checkpoint/Restart processing...345
STORED PROCEDURES...350
Types of stored procedures..350
Examples of Stored Procedures 351
Stored Procedure Error Handling..357
More Stored Procedure Examples 360
USER DEFINED FUNCTIONS..368
Types of UDF...369
Examples of UDFs 369
TRIGGERS 379
Types of triggers...380
Timings of triggers...380
Examples of Triggers 381
REFERENTIAL INTEGRITY..387
Referential Constraints Overview 387
Adding a Foreign Key Relationship 387
Deleting a Record from the Parent Table 388
SPECIAL TABLES 390
Temporal and Archive Tables 390
Business Time Example...392
Materialized Query Tables...399
Temporary Tables...401
CHAPTER FIVE REVIEW QUESTIONS...404
ADDITIONAL RESOURCES 409

APPENDICES **411**

CHAPTER QUESTIONS AND ANSWERS 411
    Chapter One Review Questions *411*
    Chapter Two Review Questions *414*
    Chapter Three Review Questions...*418*
    Chapter Four Review Questions...*423*

INDEX **431**

OTHER TITLES BY ROBERT WINGATE **433**

ABOUT THE AUTHOR **439**

Introduction

Welcome

Congratulations on your purchase of **PLI Basic Training using VSAM, IMS and DB2.** This book will teach you the basic information and skills you need to develop applications with PLI on IBM mainframes running z/OS. The instruction, examples and sample programs in this book are a fast track to becoming productive as quickly as possible using PLI. The content is easy to read and digest, well organized and focused on honing real job skills.

This is not an "everything you need to know about PLI" book. Rather, this text will teach you what you need to know to become **productive quickly** with PLI using VSAM, IMS and DB2. For additional detail, you can download and reference the IBM manuals and Redbooks associated with these products.

Assumptions:

While I do not assume that you know a great deal about IBM mainframe programming, I do assume that you've logged into an IBM mainframe and know your way around. Also I assume that you have a working knowledge of computer programming in some language (it can be a language other than PLI). All in all, I assume you have:

1. A working knowledge of ISPF navigation and basic operations such as creating data sets.

2. A basic understanding of structured programming concepts.

3. A basic understanding of SQL.

4. Access to a mainframe computer running z/OS and DB2 (and having a PLI compiler available).

Approach to Learning

I suggest you follow along and do the examples yourself in your own test environment. There's nothing like hands-on experience. Going through the motions will help you learn faster.

If you do not have access to a mainframe system through your job, I can recommend Mathru Technologies. You can rent a mainframe account from them at a very affordable rate, and this includes access to VSAM, IMS and DB2 (at this writing they offer **DB2 version 10**). Their environment supports PLI as well. The URL to the Mathru web site is:

http://mathrutech.com/index.html

Besides the instruction and examples, I've included questions at the end of each chapter. I recommend that you answer these and then check yourself against the answers in the back of the book.

Knowledge, experience and practice questions. Will that guarantee that you'll succeed as a PLI application developer? Of course, nothing is guaranteed in life. But if you put sufficient effort into this well-rounded training plan that includes all three of the above, I believe you have a very good chance of becoming productive as an IBM Application Developer as soon as possible. This is your chance to get a quick start!

Best of luck!

Robert Wingate
IBM Certified Application Developer – DB2 11 for z/OS

Chapter One : PLI Language Basics

Introduction

PLI is an acronym for Programming Language One (sometimes it is written as PL/I, PL/1 or PL1). It is a third generation procedural language developed by IBM and has been around since 1966. At that time COBOL was the language of choice for business and FORTRAN was commonly used for science and engineering. PLI was developed as a hybrid language that would support both business and scientific/engineering users.

Although PLI never caught on as well as COBOL did, there is still plenty of PLI code out there, primarily in the engineering and manufacturing sectors where it is most popular. If you are used to programming in other languages such as C or Java, you will feel at home with PLI because the language works more like these languages than COBOL. For example, in both PLI and Java the recipient variable of a data assignment is on the left hand side of the statement (unlike in COBOL where it is on the right).

So data assignment in PLI is as simple as:

```
X = 27;
```

Having programmed in PLI for many years, I can testify that it is a very usable language. As legacy PLI programmers retire, there is still code to be maintained or converted to other languages. This chapter will help make you productive quickly.

PLI Language Basics

Programming Format
Unlike COBOL, the PLI language has few restrictions as to formatting for program code. PLI declarations and statements must be coded between positions 2 and 72 (inclusive) of each line. Position 1 of each line is reserved for operating system use. Positions 73-80 can be used for sequence numbers if you like. I prefer to clear these columns by issuing the UNNUM command on the command line.

In PLI, there are no program divisions of the sort that COBOL requires. You need only provide a program name in proper syntax and an END statement to encapsulate the program source. Everything in between follows the rules of declaring variables, defining and calling procedures. You should declare variables before they can be used, hence conventionally all global variables are declared before any procedural statements.

Variables, Data Types and Assignment

Variable Declaration

Variables are defined using the DECLARE or DCL keyword followed by a variable name, followed by a variable type and (optionally) an initial value. For example, we can declare a fixed binary variable called REC_CNTR as follows:

```
DCL REQ_CNTR FIXED BIN(31) INIT(0);
```

A character type variable that is 30 bytes long can be defined as follows:

```
DCL EMP_LAST_NAME   CHAR(30);
```

Note that for hyphenating variables and procedure names, the underscore character _ is used in PLI instead of the dash.

Data Types

You'll notice some PLI variables are defined with the PIC clause. A PICTURE (or PIC) clause is a sequence of characters, each of which represents a portion of the data item and what it may contain. For numeric variables you specify PIC 9 and the number of digits, and optionally a sign character which is S.[1] Consider the following:

```
DCL EMP_PAY_TTL 'S999999V99';
```

The EMP_PAY_TTL variable is 8 digits plus a sign character S (meaning the positive or negative sign is stored with the numeric value). We have also specified an **implied** decimal point by including a V in the picture definition. This actually does not change the storage of the variable, but tells the compiler how to align the results of computations.

Finally, note that you can specify either 'S9(6)V99' or 'S999999V99' for EMP_PAY_TTL. The meaning is the same.

Now let's look at the numeric (arithmetic), character and bit level variable types.

---

[1] The sign character can appear either before the 9's or after. The examples in this book show the S character before the 9's. For me this is easier to read, but to each their own view.

Coded Arithmetic

Fixed Binary

Fixed binary can be defined as either of the following:

```
DCL VAR1 FIXED BIN(15);  /*  2 byte signed integer */
DCL VAR2 FIXED BIN(31);  /*  4 byte signed integer */
```

FIXED BIN variables use integers and are often used for accumulators and counters. Because this is a binary format, it is very efficient for integer calculations. I recommend you use it accordingly.

Fixed Decimal

This is commonly called packed decimal. It is used for numbers that require decimal fractions, such as calculations involving money. The first number in the declaration specifies how many total decimal places. The second number indicates how many places occur to the right of the decimal point.

```
DCL REG_PAY  FIXED DEC(7,2);
DCL BON_PAY  FIXED DEC(5,2),
```

Float

Floating point variables are typically used in scientific applications where precision requires many digits. You can define floating point variables as FLOAT BINARY or as FLOAT DECIMAL.

```
DCL VAR1 FLOAT BINARY (21);
DCL VAR2 FLOAT DECIMAL (6);  /* no fractional part in float */
```

Character

Character data is alphanumeric and is defined using either the CHAR or PIC format.

```
DCL EMP_LAST_NAME CHAR(30);
```

You can also define a varying length CHAR variable by specifying the VARYING attribute. For example, we previously defined EMP_LAST_NAME as a fixed width of 30 bytes. If you assign the value "SCOTT" to EMP_LAST_NAME it will be padded with 25 spaces. On the other hand, if you define EMP_LAST_NAME with the VARYING attribute, then the length will be adjusted to the length of the value you assign to it.

```
DCL EMP_LAST_NAME CHAR(30) VARYING;
```

In the case of the above, the value 30 just designates the maximum length. The actual length is the length of the string assigned to the variable.

Bit

You can define bit level variables in PLI. They have values of either bit 0 or bit 1. That is, a bit level variable is either off (0) or on (1). You specify the value between single quotes and follow the string with the B literal. The following example declares a bit level variable and initializes it to off.

```
DCL SW_END_OF_FILE STATIC BIT(01) INIT('0'B);
```

Typically bit level variables are used for switches.

Data Structures

Data items in PLI are declared hierarchically through the use of level-numbers which indicate if a data item is part of another structure. An item with a higher level-number is subordinate to an item with a lower one. Top-level data items, with a level-number of 1 (or 01 by convention), are sometimes called records but they need not be records in the traditional sense of the word. Sometimes they are just groupings of variables.

Here are two structures:

```
DCL 01 EMP_VARIABLES,
        05  EMP_ID         FIXED BIN (31),
        05  EMP_LAST_NAME  CHAR(30),
        05  EMP_FIRST_NAME CHAR(20);

DCL 01 ERR_REC,
        05 FILLER1             CHAR(10) INIT ('SQLCODE = '),
        05 SQLCODE_VIEW        PIC '-999',
        05 ERR_EMPID           FIXED BIN (31) INIT (0),
        05 FILLER2             CHAR(01) INIT (' '),
        05 ERR_TAB             CHAR(08) INIT (' '),
        05 ERR_PARA            CHAR(15) INIT (' ');
```

Notice in the above that each element is followed by a comma, except for the last element of the structure which is terminated with a semicolon.

18

Sample Program

Okay, so let's do a PLI version of the obligatory "Hello World" program. This is even more simple than in COBOL. We'll name the program PLIHELO. We'll use the PUT SKIP LIST command (which displays to the SYSPRINT DD defined in your JCL) and the literal value "HELLO WORLD" to implement the program. Here is our code.

```
PLIHELO: PROC OPTIONS(MAIN);
/******************************************************************
* PROGRAM NAME :   PLIHELO - SAMPLE PL/1 PROGRAM                 *
******************************************************************/

    PUT SKIP LIST ('HELLO WORLD');

END PLIHELO;
```

Note that the program name PLIHELO is followed by a colon and then the word PROCEDURE or usually just PROC, and then a semi-colon. This syntax is mandatory. You also can supply the OPTIONS clause, and for a main program (as opposed to a sub-program) you would specify OPTIONS(MAIN). Also notice that PLI statements are ended with a semi-colon.

Now we must compile and link the program according to the procedures in our shop. Again, you'll need to get the correct procedure from your technical leader or supervisor. In my case I am executing a procedure named IBMZPLI which resides in a library named SYS1.PROCLIB. Your location may be different.

Now we can run the program using this JCL:

```
//USER01D JOB MSGLEVEL=(1,1),NOTIFY=&SYSUID
//*
//*  RUN A PROGRAM
//*
//STEP01  EXEC PGM=PLIHELO
//STEPLIB   DD  DSN=USER01.LOADLIB,DISP=SHR
//SYSPRINT  DD  SYSOUT=*
//SYSUDUMP  DD  SYSOUT=*
```

And we can review output on SDSF.

```
SDSF OUTPUT DISPLAY USER01D  JOB04255  DSID   101 LINE 1      COLUMNS 02- 81
 COMMAND INPUT ===>                                          SCROLL ===> CSR
HELLO WORLD
```

Ok for our next program, instead of displaying the literal "HELLO WORLD", let's declare a variable and we'll load the literal value into the variable at run time. Then we'll display the content of the variable. This program will produce exactly the same result as the PLIHELO program.

Our program name is PLITRN1 and here is the listing. We have declared a variable named WS_MESSAGE as a 12 byte container for an alphanumeric value. We copy the literal "HELLO WORLD" into WS_MESSAGE. Finally we display the value of WS_MESSAGE.

```
PLITRN1: PROCEDURE OPTIONS(MAIN) REORDER;
/*****************************************************************
* PROGRAM NAME :   PLITRN1 - HELLO WORLD USING A VARIABLE        *
*****************************************************************/


/*****************************************************************
/*              W O R K I N G    S T O R A G E                   *
*****************************************************************/

   DCL 01  WS_MESSAGE  CHAR(12) INIT (' ');

/*****************************************************************
/*              P R O G R A M    M A I N L I N E                 *
*****************************************************************/


        WS_MESSAGE = 'HELLO WORLD';
        PUT SKIP LIST (WS_MESSAGE);

END PLITRN1;
```

Compile and link the program. Then go ahead and execute it to prove that it produces the same result as the PLIHELO program. At this point we've introduced the use of variables and comments. For our next program we'll explore the program control techniques.

Sequence, Selection, Iteration

Structured programming involves writing code that controls the execution of a program. This involves the primary concepts sequence, selection and iteration.

Sequence

Sequence means that program statements are executed sequentially according to the order in which they occur (either in the main procedure of a program, or within sub-procedures). For example, assume we have two variables VARIABLE-A and VARIABLE-B already declared in a program. The following code will execute sequentially.

```
VARIABLE_A = VARIABLE_A + 1;
VARIABLE_B = VARIABLE_A * 2;
PUT SKIP DATA (VARIABLE_B);
```

The above is an example of the **sequence** control structure and it will occur throughout the program unless one of the other two control structures intervenes. You can also invoke procedures sequentially which is considered part of the sequence control structure.

```
CALL P100_INITIALIZATION;
CALL P200_MAINLINE;
CALL P300_TERMINATION;
```

We'll do that in later programs. It's a good way to structure a program.

Selection

Selection means the program will execute statements based on a condition. For example, given a variable RECORD_COUNTER, we could display the number of records if the value is greater than zero; otherwise we can display a literal if it is zero.

```
IF RECORD_COUNTER > 0 THEN
    PUT SKIP LIST ('NUMBER OF RECORDS IS ' || RECORD_COUNTER);
ELSE
    PUT SKIP LIST ('NO RECORDS WERE PROCESSED');
```

Notice above we show how to concatenate a literal and a variable in a PUT statement. The two vertical bars || indicates concatenation (one vertical bar is the symbol for the Boolean OR – don't mix these up).

You can also use IF/THEN logic for calling procedures. For example:

```
IF COUNTRY = 'USA' THEN
   CALL P100_PROCESS_DOMESTIC;
ELSE
   CALL P200_PROCESS_INTERNATIONAL;
```

Another type of selection is using the SELECT statement which implements the CASE programming construct. We'll show an example of that shortly.

Iteration

Iteration means repeating an action until some condition is met. The condition can use a counter to ensure the action is executed for a specified number of times, or it can be a switch whose value indicates a condition is true. PLI looping verbs are DO WHILE and DO UNTIL. We'll show both in the next sample program.

PLITRN2

To demonstrate rudimentary sequence, selection and iteration, our sample program PLITRN2 will do the following:

1. Show the flow of a sequential set of instructions

2. Show branching if/then and case (SELECT)

3. Show perform until (implemented as DO UNTIL)[2]

Here is our program code. We use a counter variable CNTR. We follow a sequence of statements. We use both IF/THEN and SELECT logic for branching. Finally we perform a procedure until the value of the counter reaches a certain value with a DO UNTIL loop. We invoke procedures using the CALL verb.

```
PLITRN2: PROC OPTIONS (MAIN);
/********************************************************************
* PROGRAM NAME :    PLITRN2 - PERFORM MULTI ROW INSERT TO DB2 TABLE *
********************************************************************/

/*********************************************************/
/*  PROGRAM WITH SEQUENCE, SELECTION AND ITERATION.      */
/*********************************************************/
```

---

[2] You can also use the DO WHILE (condition) such as DO WHILE (not end of file). The DO WHILE and DO UNTIL both test for their conditions at the top of the loop; however DO UNTIL always executes at least one time, whereas DO WHILE can execute zero times (if it's condition for executing is not true from the beginning). We'll use DO WHILE later in this chapter.

```
/*******************************************************************
/*                 W O R K I N G   S T O R A G E                  *
*******************************************************************/

   DCL 01  CNTR        FIXED BIN(31) INIT (0);

/*******************************************************************
/*                 P R O G R A M   M A I N L I N E                *
*******************************************************************/

   PUT SKIP LIST ('PLI WITH SEQUENCE, SELECTION AND ITERATION');

       PUT SKIP LIST ('** PROCESSING IF/THEN SELECTION');

       IF CNTR = 0 THEN
          CALL P100_ROUTINE_A;
       CNTR = CNTR + 1;

       IF CNTR > 0 THEN
          CALL P200_ROUTINE_B;

       PUT SKIP LIST ('** PROCESSING CASE TYPE SELECTION');

       CNTR = 0;

       SELECT (CNTR);
          WHEN (0) CALL P100_ROUTINE_A;
          WHEN (1) CALL P200_ROUTINE_B;
          OTHERWISE PUT SKIP LIST('NO ROUTINE TO PERFORM');
       END; /* SELECT */

       CNTR = CNTR + 1;

       SELECT (CNTR);
          WHEN (0) CALL P100_ROUTINE_A;
          WHEN (1) CALL P200_ROUTINE_B;
          OTHERWISE PUT SKIP LIST('NO ROUTINE TO PERFORM');
       END; /* SELECT */

       CNTR = CNTR + 1;

       SELECT (CNTR);
          WHEN (0) CALL P100_ROUTINE_A;
          WHEN (1) CALL P200_ROUTINE_B;
          OTHERWISE PUT SKIP LIST('NO ROUTINE TO PERFORM');
```

```
        END; /* SELECT */

        CNTR = 0;
        DO UNTIL (CNTR >= 3);
            CALL P300_ROUTINE_C;
        END; /* DO UNTIL */

P100_ROUTINE_A: PROC;

    PUT SKIP LIST('PROCESSING IN P100-ROUTINE-A');
    PUT SKIP LIST('LEAVING P100-ROUTINE-A');

END P100_ROUTINE_A;

P200_ROUTINE_B: PROC;

    PUT SKIP LIST('PROCESSING IN P200-ROUTINE-B');
    PUT SKIP LIST('LEAVING P200-ROUTINE-B');

END P200_ROUTINE_B;

P300_ROUTINE_C: PROC;

    PUT SKIP LIST('PROCESSING IN P300_ROUTINE_C');
    CNTR = CNTR + 1;
    PUT SKIP LIST('ITERATOR VALUE IS ' || CNTR);
    PUT SKIP LIST('LEAVING P300_ROUTINE_C');

END P300_ROUTINE_C;

END PLITRN2;
```

Now let's compile and link, and then run the program.

```
PLI WITH SEQUENCE, SELECTION AND ITERATION
** PROCESSING IF/THEN SELECTION
PROCESSING IN P100-ROUTINE-A
LEAVING P100-ROUTINE-A
PROCESSING IN P200-ROUTINE-B
LEAVING P200-ROUTINE-B
** PROCESSING CASE TYPE SELECTION
PROCESSING IN P100-ROUTINE-A
LEAVING P100-ROUTINE-A
PROCESSING IN P200-ROUTINE-B
LEAVING P200-ROUTINE-B
```

24

```
NO ROUTINE TO PERFORM
PROCESSING IN P300_ROUTINE_C
ITERATOR VALUE IS                1
LEAVING P300_ROUTINE_C
PROCESSING IN P300_ROUTINE_C
ITERATOR VALUE IS                2
LEAVING P300_ROUTINE_C
PROCESSING IN P300_ROUTINE_C
ITERATOR VALUE IS                3
LEAVING P300_ROUTINE_C
```

File I/O

Starting with program PLITRN3 we will do programming for a fictitious Human Resource application. Program PLITRN3 will read a file of employee pay information, reformat the data values and then write a record to an output file. This program will include the following:

- File definition

- Read file input

- Write file output

- Use a processing loop with a bit level variable as a switch

Pseudo Code for PLITRN3

Often it is helpful to pseudo code your program design before you start coding. Your pseudo code need not be extremely elaborate, but it helps you to think out the code structure. The following pseudo code specifies what the program PLITRN3 will do.

```
Announce start of program
Open Files
Do Priming Read
Do Until End of Input File
        Move Input Fields to Output Fields
        Display Pay Values
        Write Output Record
        Read Next Input Record
End Do Until
Close Files
Announce End of Program
```

Program Listing for PLITRN3

To use input and/or output files in a PLI program, you must include file names and definitions. Like COBOL, you must provide a reference to the JCL DD name of the file you are processing. Unlike COBOL, PLI does not require file descriptors. You do need to declare the file name and a few keywords such as the type of I/O (record or stream) and whether it is input or output. The file name you declare in the program is named exactly the same as the DD name identifier in the JCL that executes the program.

For example, here's the JCL we will use to run the program. Notice there is an EMPIFILE DD and an EMPOFILE DD. These are the input and output files, respectively.

```
//USER01D JOB MSGLEVEL=(1,1),NOTIFY=&SYSUID
//*
//*  RUN A PLI PROGRAM
//*
//STEP01  EXEC PGM=PLITRN3
//STEPLIB  DD  DSN=USER01.LOADLIB,DISP=SHR
//SYSOUT   DD  SYSOUT=*
//EMPIFILE DD DSN=USER01.EMPLOYEE.PAY,DISP=SHR
//EMPOFILE DD DSN=USER01.EMPLOYEE.PAYOUT,DISP=(OLD,KEEP,KEEP)
//SYSPRINT DD  SYSOUT=*
//SYSUDUMP DD  SYSOUT=*
//SYSOUT   DD  SYSOUT=*
```

To reference these files in our PLI program, we will declare the file name variables which will be named the same as the DD names of the files in the JCL.

```
DCL EMPIFILE FILE RECORD SEQL INPUT;
DCL EMPOFILE FILE RECORD SEQL OUTPUT;
```

This above means the file we refer to in the program as EMPIFILE is the file that has DD name EMPIFILE in the JCL that we use to execute the program. Similarly, the EMPOFILE in our program refers to the file with DD name EMPOFILE in the JCL. We also specify that these files will use records in sequential order.

So far, our program looks like this:

```
PLITRN3: PROCEDURE OPTIONS(MAIN);
/*****************************************************************
* PROGRAM NAME :   PLITRN3 - FILE INPUT AND OUTPUT             *
*****************************************************************/
```

```
/*********************************************************************
/*                    F I L E S    U S E D                          *
*********************************************************************/

     DCL EMPIFILE FILE RECORD SEQL INPUT;
     DCL EMPOFILE FILE RECORD SEQL OUTPUT;
```

Now we will need to define the record structure for EMPIFILE. It will be helpful to look at the actual file content. Let's say that the employee id occupies the first 4 bytes, the regular pay bytes 10 through 16, and the bonus pay bytes 19 through 24. Here is a file whose structure matches that definition.

```
BROWSE      USER01.EMPLOYEE.PAY                    Line 00000000 Col 001 080
  Command ===>                                         Scroll ===> CSR
----+----1----+----2----+----3----+----4----+----5----+----6----+----7----+----
*************************** Top of Data ***************************
1111    8700000  670000
1122    8200000  600000
3217    6500000  550000
4175    5500000  150000
4720    8000000  250000
4836    6200000  220000
6288    7000000  200000
7459    8500000  450000
9134    7500000  250000
*************************** Bottom of Data ***************************
```

Now let's code the structure which is named IN_EMPLOYEE_RECORD.

```
     DCL 01 IN_EMPLOYEE_RECORD,
            05  EMPLOYEE_ID     CHAR(04),
            05  FILLER1         CHAR(05),
            05  REGULAR_PAY     PIC '99999V99',
            05  FILLER2         CHAR(02),
            05  BONUS_PAY       PIC '9999V99',
            05  FILLER3         CHAR(56);
```

Note the use of the variable names FILLER1, FILLER2, etc. In PLI, the word FILLER is not a reserved word (like it is in COBOL), so you cannot reuse it or you will get a compiler error for a duplicated variable name. You could use any non-reserved words you like to serve the filler function as long as they are unique within the program. As a convention, we are using the word FILLER plus a sequence number.

When we want to read the file into this structure we must code the file name and the structure variable we want to read the record into.

27

```
READ FILE (EMPIFILE) INTO (IN_EMPLOYEE_RECORD);
```

Our next step is to define the output record structure in detail in working storage. Suppose we want to save some space by compressing the readable numbers into a more compact format. We can make the employee id fixed binary format, and we'll use packed decimal (FIXED DEC) for our pay variables. Here is our output structure:

```
DCL 01 OUT_EMPLOYEE_RECORD,
       05  EMP_ID_OUT     FIXED BIN(31),
       05  FILLER4        CHAR(05) INIT (' '),
       05  REG_PAY_OUT    FIXED DEC(8,2),
       05  FILLER5        CHAR(02) INIT (' '),
       05  BON_PAY_OUT    FIXED DEC(8,2),
       05  FILLER6        CHAR(59) INIT (' ');
```

Finally, we must add code to write a record to the output file by specifying the WRITE verb, the file name and the record structure. This write statement is straightforward and follows a similar pattern to our read logic. We write to the file from our output record structure as follows:

```
WRITE FILE (EMPOFILE) FROM (OUT_EMPLOYEE_RECORD);
```

Ok, let's briefly return to our pseudo code to review the roadmap of the program.

> Announce start of program
> Open Files
> Do Priming Read
> Do Until End of Input file
>   Move Input Fields to Output Fields
>   Display Pay Values
>   Write Output Record
>   Read Next Input Record
> End Do Until
> Close Files
> Announce End of Program

We need a couple more things for our program and then we'll be ready. First we need to declare a bit switch which we can use with the end-of-file condition to tell us when to stop processing the input file. First we'll define the switch and then we'll define the condition where we set it. Here is the switch:

```
DCL SW_END_OF_FILE STATIC BIT(01) INIT('0'B);
```

We have declared variable SW_END_OF_FILE STATIC at the bit level, and initialized it to off (zero). Now we are going to declare an ON CONDITION. PLI allows you to define what steps to take when certain things happen. One of those things is the ENDFILE condition which is raised when your program has read the last record in a file. Code the following somewhere in your working storage area:

```
ON ENDFILE (EMPIFILE) SW_END_OF_FILE =  '1'B;
```

The above says that when an ENDFILE condition is encountered on file EMPIFILE, then set the value of the SW_END_OF_FILE bit variable to ON (1). This is handy because we can use this bit switch as a loop control variable and it will automatically be set to ON (bit 1) when the end of the input file EMPIFILE is encountered.

Ok, here is our complete program listing.

```
PLITRN3: PROCEDURE OPTIONS (MAIN) REORDER;
 /*****************************************************************
 * PROGRAM NAME :   PLITRN3 - FILE INPUT AND OUTPUT             *
 *****************************************************************/

 /*****************************************************************
 /*              F I L E S    U S E D                           *
 *****************************************************************/

   DCL EMPIFILE FILE RECORD SEQL INPUT;
   DCL EMPOFILE FILE RECORD SEQL OUTPUT;

 /*****************************************************************
 /*              W O R K I N G    S T O R A G E                 *
 *****************************************************************/

   DCL SW_END_OF_FILE           STATIC BIT(01) INIT('0'B);

   DCL 01 IN_EMPLOYEE_RECORD,
          05  EMPLOYEE_ID   CHAR(04),
          05  FILLER1       CHAR(05),
          05  REGULAR_PAY   PIC '9999999',
          05  FILLER2       CHAR(02),
          05  BONUS_PAY     PIC '999999',
          05  FILLER3       CHAR(56);

   DCL 01 OUT_EMPLOYEE_RECORD,
          05  EMP_ID_OUT    FIXED BIN(31),
          05  FILLER4       CHAR(05) INIT (' '),
          05  REG_PAY_OUT   FIXED DEC(8,2),
```

```
               05  FILLER5        CHAR(02) INIT (' '),
               05  BON_PAY_OUT    FIXED DEC(8,2),
               05  FILLER6        CHAR(59) INIT (' ');

      DCL 01 DISPLAY_EMPLOYEE_PIC,
               05  DIS_REG_PAY    PIC '99999.99',
               05  DIS_BON_PAY    PIC '9999.99';

/*********************************************************************
/*                O N   C O N D I T I O N S                        *
*********************************************************************/

   ON ENDFILE (EMPIFILE) SW_END_OF_FILE =  '1'B;

/*********************************************************************
/*              P R O G R A M   M A I N L I N E                    *
*********************************************************************/

CALL P100_INITIALIZATION;
CALL P200_MAINLINE;
CALL P300_TERMINATION;

P100_INITIALIZATION: PROC;

   PUT SKIP LIST ('PLITRN3: INPUT AND OUTPUT');
   OPEN FILE (EMPIFILE),
        FILE (EMPOFILE);

   IN_EMPLOYEE_RECORD  = '';
   OUT_EMPLOYEE_RECORD = '';

END P100_INITIALIZATION;

P200_MAINLINE: PROC;

   /*  MAIN LOOP - READ THE INPUT FILE, LOAD THE OUTPUT
                   STRUCTURE AND WRITE THE RECORD TO OUTPUT */

       READ FILE (EMPIFILE) INTO (IN_EMPLOYEE_RECORD);

       DO WHILE (¬SW_END_OF_FILE);

       /* MOVE FIELDS */

           EMP_ID_OUT               = EMPLOYEE_ID;
           REG_PAY_OUT, DIS_REG_PAY = REGULAR_PAY;
```

30

```
                BON_PAY_OUT, DIS_BON_PAY = BONUS_PAY;

                PUT SKIP LIST ('EMP ID  ' || EMPLOYEE_ID);
                PUT SKIP LIST ('REG PAY ' || DIS_REG_PAY);
                PUT SKIP LIST ('BON PAY ' || DIS_BON_PAY);

                WRITE FILE (EMPOFILE) FROM (OUT_EMPLOYEE_RECORD);

                READ FILE (EMPIFILE) INTO (IN_EMPLOYEE_RECORD);

        END; /* DO WHILE */

 END P200_MAINLINE;

 P300_TERMINATION: PROC;

     CLOSE FILE(EMPIFILE),
           FILE(EMPOFILE);

     PUT SKIP LIST ('PLITRN3 - SUCCESSFULLY ENDED');

 END P300_TERMINATION;

 END PLITRN3;
```

Now let's compile and run the program.

```
        PLITRN3: INPUT AND OUTPUT
        EMP ID  1111
        REG PAY 87000.00
        BON PAY 6700.00
        EMP ID  1122
        REG PAY 82000.00
        BON PAY 6000.00
        EMP ID  3217
        REG PAY 65000.00
        BON PAY 5500.00
        EMP ID  4175
        REG PAY 55000.00
        BON PAY 1500.00
        EMP ID  4720
        REG PAY 80000.00
        BON PAY 2500.00
        EMP ID  4836
        REG PAY 62000.00
        BON PAY 2200.00
```

```
EMP ID  6288
REG PAY 70000.00
BON PAY 2000.00
EMP ID  7459
REG PAY 85000.00
BON PAY 4500.00
EMP ID  9134
REG PAY 75000.00
BON PAY 2500.00
PLITRN3 - SUCCESSFULLY ENDED
```

Now let's look at the output file. You'll notice it is not very readable because the data has been packed into compressed format.

```
BROWSE    USER01.EMPOFILE                          Line 00000000 Col 001 080
 Command ===>                                                 Scroll ===> CSR
----+----1----+----2----+----3----+----4----+----5----+----6----+----7----+----8
****************************** Top of Data *********************************
...j......Á.......&..
..........e.......&..
...Þ......Í.......&..
...ø......Ø.......&..
...°......ø..........
***************************** Bottom of Data ******************************
```

You can determine the actual values by issuing the HEX command on the command line. This displays the hex value for each byte.

```
BROWSE    USER01.EMPOFILE                          Line 00000000 Col 001 080
 Command ===>                                                 Scroll ===> CSR
----+----1----+----2----+----3----+----4----+----5----+----6----+----7----+----8
----+----F----+----F----+----F----+----F----+----F----+----F----+----F----+----F
----+----1----+----2----+----3----+----4----+----5----+----6----+----7----+----8
------------------------------------------------------------------------------
****************************** Top of Data *********************************


------------------------------------------------------------------------------
...j......Á.......&..
0009000000600000005004444444444444444444444444444444444444444444444444444444444
00C1000000500C000500C000000000000000000000000000000000000000000000000000000000000
------------------------------------------------------------------------------
..........e.......&..
0012000000800000005004444444444444444444444444444444444444444444444444444444444
00D3000000500C000400C000000000000000000000000000000000000000000000000000000000000
------------------------------------------------------------------------------
```

```
...Þ......Í.......&..
002A000000070000000500444444444444444444444444444444444444444444444444444444444444444
003E000000500C000200C00000000000000000000000000000000000000000000000000000000000000000
```

Turn off the hex view by issuing the command HEX OFF.

One final comment on the PLITRN3 program - strictly speaking it is not necessary to code the explicit OPEN and CLOSE statements. PLI will automatically open a file the first time you issue a read or write statement on it. However, I suggest you code the OPEN and CLOSE anyway. You never know which compiler you will use in the future, and they may not always allow the implicit file open and close.

I suggest you use the above source code for PLITRN3 as a model for input/output programs. Customize it as you see fit. That's it for the basics of file input/output in PLI. This should be enough to get you started. In the next section we'll look at creating a report from the employee data.

Reporting

There are many ways to get data from a central data source now, especially when much of the data is stored in relational databases such as DB2. However, some years ago, most reports were generated by application programs. In fact, two of the last three environments I worked in used plenty of PLI for reporting. So you'll almost certainly encounter reporting programs if you work in a PLI shop.

PLI can be used for simple or complex reports. Basically what you do is define record structures for your headers, detail lines and trailer lines (if any). Then you write an output record using the appropriate record structure. If your report tends to be more than a printed page, you'll may use line and page counters to rewrite the headers and bump up the page number at the appropriate time.

ANSI Carriage Control

At one time almost all IBM mainframe shops used printers that operated with something called ANSI Carriage Control. That means you used the first byte of each report line to control advancing the paper – line feeds, skipping to the next page, etc.

Here are the values you code in the first byte of a report line to create the desired operation for a printer that uses ANSI carriage control.

Character	Action
blank	Advance 1 line (single spacing)
1	Advance to next page (form feed)
0	Advance 2 lines (double spacing)
-	Advance 3 lines (triple spacing)
+	Do not advance any lines before printing, overstrike previous line with current line

Now having explained about ANSI carriage control, I am going to recommend that you not use it. Why? Because many printers don't use this type of carriage control anymore. This is true especially if your form of distribution is through email or by storage on a Windows or UNIX server (or on a web site). Also, your users may not intend to print the report in which case the carriage control characters would just be distracting. This is something you will need to discover in talking with your user base.

If you decide that some sort of page/header control is needed, you can create your own. If you want to skip a line, simply write a blank line. Or two lines or three lines as necessary. Use line and page counters to determine when headers need to be recreated. We'll show an example of that before we leave this section.

Report Program Sample

Ok, let's start on program PLITRN4 which will report data from the employee pay file (employee id plus salary). Let's say we still want to write an output file with binary pay information like we did in PLITRN3, so when we add the report function for PLITRN4 we'll need a second output file. Let's assume the JCL DD name will be EMPREPRT.

```
DCL EMPREPRT FILE RECORD SEQL OUTPUT;
```

Assume we want the report file to look like this:

```
EMPLOYEE ANNUAL SALARY REPORT
-----------------------------

EMP-ID    REGULAR      BONUS
------    --------    --------
  1111    87000.00    06700.00
  1122    82000.00    06000.00
  3217    65000.00    05500.00
  4175    55000.00    01500.00
  4720    80000.00    02500.00
  4836    62000.00    02200.00
  6288    70000.00    02000.00
  7459    85000.00    04500.00
  9134    75000.00    02500.00


   END OF ANNUAL SALARY REPORT
```

To accomplish this, we'll define several structures that are "lines" to be written to the report. Some are static header lines, others are detail lines where we'll fill in the employee data. Here is one way of declaring these variables.

```
DCL 01 HDR_LINE_01,
       05  FILLER7      CHAR(25) INIT (' '),
       05  FILLER8      CHAR(30)
           INIT ('EMPLOYEE ANNUAL SALARY REPORT '),
       05  FILLER9      CHAR(25) INIT (' ');

DCL 01 HDR_LINE_02,
       05  FILLER10     CHAR(25) INIT (' '),
       05  FILLER11     CHAR(30)
           INIT ('----------------------------- '),
       05  FILLER12     CHAR(25) INIT (' ');

DCL 01 SPC_LINE         CHAR(80) INIT (' ');

DCL 01 DTL_HDR01,
       05 FILLER13      CHAR(25) INIT (' '),
       05 FILLER14      CHAR(06) INIT ('EMP-ID'),
       05 FILLER15      CHAR(03) INIT (' '),
       05 FILLER16      CHAR(08) INIT ('REGULAR '),
       05 FILLER17      CHAR(04) INIT (' '),
       05 FILLER18      CHAR(08) INIT ('BONUS   '),
       05 FILLER19      CHAR(26) INIT (' ');
```

```
DCL 01 DTL_HDR02,
        05 FILLER20        CHAR(25) INIT (' '),
        05 FILLER21        CHAR(06) INIT ('------'),
        05 FILLER22        CHAR(03) INIT (' '),
        05 FILLER23        CHAR(08) INIT ('--------'),
        05 FILLER24        CHAR(04) INIT (' '),
        05 FILLER25        CHAR(08) INIT ('-------'),
        05 FILLER26        CHAR(26) INIT (' ');

DCL 01 DTL_LINE,
        05 FILLER27        CHAR(27) INIT (' '),
        05 RPT_EMP_ID      PIC '9999',
        05 FILLER28        CHAR(03) INIT (' '),
        05 RPT_REG_PAY     PIC '99999.99',
        05 FILLER29        CHAR(04) INIT (' '),
        05 RPT_BON_PAY     PIC '99999.99',
        05 FILLER30        CHAR(26) INIT (' ');

DCL 01 TRLR_LINE_01,
        05  FILLER31       CHAR(26) INIT (' '),
        05  FILLER32       CHAR(30)
            INIT (' END OF ANNUAL SALARY REPORT  '),
        05  FILLER33       CHAR(24) INIT (' ');
              VALUE ' END OF ANNUAL SALARY REPORT  '.
```

When we add these structures to the previous program, we get PLITRN4 and here is the
full listing. Notice that we write the headers in the initialization routine, and the footer in
the termination routine.

```
PLITRN4: PROCEDURE OPTIONS(MAIN) REORDER;
/***************************************************************
* PROGRAM NAME :  PLITRN4 - FILE INPUT AND OUTPUT, AND REPORT    *
***************************************************************/


/***************************************************************
/*              F I L E S   U S E D                            *
***************************************************************/

   DCL EMPIFILE FILE RECORD SEQL INPUT;
   DCL EMPOFILE FILE RECORD SEQL OUTPUT;
   DCL EMPREPRT FILE RECORD SEQL OUTPUT;


/***************************************************************
/*          W O R K I N G   S T O R A G E                      *
***************************************************************/
```

```
DCL SW_END_OF_FILE              STATIC BIT(01) INIT('0'B);

DCL 01 IN_EMPLOYEE_RECORD,
       05  EMPLOYEE_ID   CHAR(04),
       05  FILLER1       CHAR(05),
       05  REGULAR_PAY   PIC '9999999',
       05  FILLER2       CHAR(02),
       05  BONUS_PAY     PIC '999999',
       05  FILLER3       CHAR(56);

DCL 01 OUT_EMPLOYEE_RECORD,
       05  EMP_ID_OUT    FIXED BIN(31),
       05  FILLER4       CHAR(05) INIT (' '),
       05  REG_PAY_OUT   FIXED DEC(8,2),
       05  FILLER5       CHAR(02) INIT (' '),
       05  BON_PAY_OUT   FIXED DEC(8,2),
       05  FILLER6       CHAR(59) INIT (' ');

DCL 01 DISPLAY_EMPLOYEE_PIC,
       05  DIS_REG_PAY   PIC '99999.99',
       05  DIS_BON_PAY   PIC '9999.99';

DCL 01 HDR_LINE_01,
       05  FILLER7       CHAR(25) INIT (' '),
       05  FILLER8       CHAR(30)
           INIT ('EMPLOYEE ANNUAL SALARY REPORT '),
       05  FILLER9       CHAR(25) INIT (' ');

DCL 01 HDR_LINE_02,
       05  FILLER10      CHAR(25) INIT (' '),
       05  FILLER11      CHAR(30)
           INIT ('---------------------------- '),
       05  FILLER12      CHAR(25) INIT (' ');

DCL 01 SPC_LINE         CHAR(80) INIT (' ');

DCL 01 DTL_HDR01,
       05 FILLER13       CHAR(25) INIT (' '),
       05 FILLER14       CHAR(06) INIT ('EMP-ID'),
       05 FILLER15       CHAR(03) INIT (' '),
       05 FILLER16       CHAR(08) INIT ('REGULAR '),
       05 FILLER17       CHAR(04) INIT (' '),
       05 FILLER18       CHAR(08) INIT ('BONUS   '),
       05 FILLER19       CHAR(26) INIT (' ');
```

```
DCL 01 DTL_HDR02,
        05 FILLER20        CHAR(25) INIT (' '),
        05 FILLER21        CHAR(06) INIT ('------'),
        05 FILLER22        CHAR(03) INIT (' '),
        05 FILLER23        CHAR(08) INIT ('--------'),
        05 FILLER24        CHAR(04) INIT (' '),
        05 FILLER25        CHAR(08) INIT ('--------'),
        05 FILLER26        CHAR(26) INIT (' ');

DCL 01 DTL_LINE,
        05 FILLER27        CHAR(27) INIT (' '),
        05 RPT_EMP_ID      PIC '9999',
        05 FILLER28        CHAR(03) INIT (' '),
        05 RPT_REG_PAY     PIC '99999.99',
        05 FILLER29        CHAR(04) INIT (' '),
        05 RPT_BON_PAY     PIC '99999.99',
        05 FILLER30        CHAR(26) INIT (' ');
DCL 01 TRLR_LINE_01,
        05  FILLER31       CHAR(26) INIT (' '),
        05  FILLER32       CHAR(30)
            INIT (' END OF ANNUAL SALARY REPORT  '),
        05  FILLER33       CHAR(24) INIT (' ');

/********************************************************************
/*              O N   C O N D I T I O N S                        *
********************************************************************/

   ON ENDFILE (EMPIFILE) SW_END_OF_FILE =  '1'B;

/********************************************************************
/*              P R O G R A M   M A I N L I N E                  *
********************************************************************/

CALL P100_INITIALIZATION;
CALL P200_MAINLINE;
CALL P300_TERMINATION;

P100_INITIALIZATION: PROC;

   PUT SKIP LIST ('PLITRN3: INPUT AND OUTPUT');
   OPEN FILE (EMPIFILE),
        FILE (EMPOFILE),
        FILE (EMPREPRT);

   IN_EMPLOYEE_RECORD  = '';
   OUT_EMPLOYEE_RECORD = '';
```

```
        WRITE FILE (EMPREPRT) FROM (HDR_LINE_01);
        WRITE FILE (EMPREPRT) FROM (HDR_LINE_02);
        WRITE FILE (EMPREPRT) FROM (SPC_LINE);
        WRITE FILE (EMPREPRT) FROM (DTL_HDR01);
        WRITE FILE (EMPREPRT) FROM (DTL_HDR02);

END P100_INITIALIZATION;

P200_MAINLINE: PROC;

    /*  MAIN LOOP - READ THE INPUT FILE, LOAD THE OUTPUT
                   STRUCTURE AND WRITE THE RECORD TO OUTPUT.
                   ALSO WRITE OUT THE REPORT LINES.          */

        READ FILE (EMPIFILE) INTO (IN_EMPLOYEE_RECORD);

        DO WHILE (¬SW_END_OF_FILE);

        /* MOVE FIELDS */

            EMP_ID_OUT, RPT_EMP_ID               = EMPLOYEE_ID;
            REG_PAY_OUT, DIS_REG_PAY, RPT_REG_PAY = REGULAR_PAY;
            BON_PAY_OUT, DIS_BON_PAY, RPT_BON_PAY = BONUS_PAY;

            PUT SKIP LIST ('EMP ID  ' || EMPLOYEE_ID);
            PUT SKIP LIST ('REG PAY ' || DIS_REG_PAY);
            PUT SKIP LIST ('BON PAY ' || DIS_BON_PAY);

            WRITE FILE (EMPOFILE) FROM (OUT_EMPLOYEE_RECORD);
            WRITE FILE (EMPREPRT) FROM (DTL_LINE);

            READ FILE (EMPIFILE) INTO (IN_EMPLOYEE_RECORD);

        END; /* DO WHILE */

END P200_MAINLINE;

P300_TERMINATION: PROC;

    WRITE FILE (EMPREPRT) FROM (SPC_LINE);
    WRITE FILE (EMPREPRT) FROM (SPC_LINE);
    WRITE FILE (EMPREPRT) FROM (TRLR_LINE_01);

    CLOSE FILE(EMPIFILE),
          FILE(EMPOFILE);
```

```
        PUT SKIP LIST ('PLITRN4 - SUCCESSFULLY ENDED');

  END P300_TERMINATION;

  END PLITRN4;
```

This program works, but for a longer report with more data you might need to use page breaks and page numbers. This can be done fairly easily with a line counter and page counter. Let's go ahead and revise our program to use the counters.

Since we only have a few records for our example, let's say we want to see a maximum of 6 detail lines per page. We'll code the line and page counters, and here is the revised program listing. Notice we have broken the header writing logic into its own routine. Again, I recommend that you use this as a logic model for your report programs.

```
PLITRN4: PROCEDURE OPTIONS(MAIN) REORDER;
/*****************************************************************
* PROGRAM NAME :   PLITRN4 - FILE INPUT AND OUTPUT, AND REPORT     *
*****************************************************************/

/*****************************************************************
/*              F I L E S    U S E D                           *
*****************************************************************/

   DCL EMPIFILE FILE RECORD SEQL INPUT;
   DCL EMPOFILE FILE RECORD SEQL OUTPUT;
   DCL EMPREPRT FILE RECORD SEQL OUTPUT;

/*****************************************************************
/*            W O R K I N G    S T O R A G E                   *
*****************************************************************/

   DCL SW_END_OF_FILE          STATIC BIT(01) INIT('0'B);

   DCL 01 IN_EMPLOYEE_RECORD,
          05  EMPLOYEE_ID   CHAR(04),
          05  FILLER1       CHAR(05),
          05  REGULAR_PAY   PIC '9999999',
          05  FILLER2       CHAR(02),
          05  BONUS_PAY     PIC '999999',
          05  FILLER3       CHAR(56);

   DCL 01 OUT_EMPLOYEE_RECORD,
          05  EMP_ID_OUT    FIXED BIN(31),
          05  FILLER4       CHAR(05) INIT (' '),
          05  REG_PAY_OUT   FIXED DEC(8,2),
          05  FILLER5       CHAR(02) INIT (' '),
          05  BON_PAY_OUT   FIXED DEC(8,2),
```

```
            05  FILLER6        CHAR(59) INIT (' ');

DCL 01 DISPLAY_EMPLOYEE_PIC,
            05  DIS_REG_PAY    PIC '99999.99',
            05  DIS_BON_PAY    PIC '9999.99';

DCL 01 HDR_LINE_01,
            05  FILLER7        CHAR(25) INIT (' '),
            05  FILLER8        CHAR(30)
                INIT ('EMPLOYEE ANNUAL SALARY REPORT '),
            05  FILLER9        CHAR(05) INIT ('PAGE-'),
            05  R_PAGE_NO      PIC 'Z9',
            05  FILLER9X       CHAR(18) INIT (' ');

DCL 01 HDR_LINE_02,
            05  FILLER10       CHAR(25) INIT (' '),
            05  FILLER11       CHAR(38)
                INIT ('---------------------------------- '),
            05  FILLER12       CHAR(17) INIT (' ');

DCL 01 SPC_LINE            CHAR(80) INIT (' ');

DCL 01 DTL_HDR01,
            05 FILLER13        CHAR(25) INIT (' '),
            05 FILLER14        CHAR(06) INIT ('EMP-ID'),
            05 FILLER15        CHAR(03) INIT (' '),
            05 FILLER16        CHAR(08) INIT ('REGULAR '),
            05 FILLER17        CHAR(04) INIT (' '),
            05 FILLER18        CHAR(08) INIT ('BONUS   '),
            05 FILLER19        CHAR(26) INIT (' ');

DCL 01 DTL_HDR02,
            05 FILLER20        CHAR(25) INIT (' '),
            05 FILLER21        CHAR(06) INIT ('------'),
            05 FILLER22        CHAR(03) INIT (' '),
            05 FILLER23        CHAR(08) INIT ('--------'),
            05 FILLER24        CHAR(04) INIT (' '),
            05 FILLER25        CHAR(08) INIT ('--------'),
            05 FILLER26        CHAR(26) INIT (' ');

DCL 01 DTL_LINE,
            05 FILLER27        CHAR(27) INIT (' '),
            05 RPT_EMP_ID      PIC '9999',
            05 FILLER28        CHAR(03) INIT (' '),
            05 RPT_REG_PAY     PIC '99999.99',
            05 FILLER29        CHAR(04) INIT (' '),
            05 RPT_BON_PAY     PIC '99999.99',
            05 FILLER30        CHAR(26) INIT (' ');

DCL 01 TRLR_LINE_01,
            05  FILLER31       CHAR(26) INIT (' '),
            05  FILLER32       CHAR(30)
                INIT (' END OF ANNUAL SALARY REPORT  '),
```

41

```
        05  FILLER33      CHAR(24) INIT (' ');

  DCL  C_MAX_LINES     FIXED BIN(15) INIT (6);

  DCL  01 ACCUMULATORS,
          05 A_PAGE_CTR  FIXED BIN(15) INIT (0),
          05 A_LINE_CTR  FIXED BIN(15) INIT (0);

/**********************************************************************
/*             O N   C O N D I T I O N S                             *
**********************************************************************/

   ON ENDFILE (EMPIFILE) SW_END_OF_FILE = '1'B;

/**********************************************************************
/*             P R O G R A M   M A I N L I N E                       *
**********************************************************************/

CALL P100_INITIALIZATION;
CALL P200_MAINLINE;
CALL P300_TERMINATION;

P100_INITIALIZATION: PROC;

    PUT SKIP LIST ('PLITRN3: INPUT AND OUTPUT');
    OPEN FILE (EMPIFILE),
         FILE (EMPOFILE),
         FILE (EMPREPRT);

    IN_EMPLOYEE_RECORD  = '';
    OUT_EMPLOYEE_RECORD = '';

    CALL P1000_WRITE_HEADERS;

END P100_INITIALIZATION;

P200_MAINLINE: PROC;

    /*  MAIN LOOP - READ THE INPUT FILE, LOAD THE OUTPUT
                    STRUCTURE AND WRITE THE RECORD TO OUTPUT.
                    ALSO WRITE OUT THE REPORT LINES.          */

       READ FILE (EMPIFILE) INTO (IN_EMPLOYEE_RECORD);

       DO WHILE (¬SW_END_OF_FILE);

       /* MOVE FIELDS */

          EMP_ID_OUT, RPT_EMP_ID            = EMPLOYEE_ID;
          REG_PAY_OUT, DIS_REG_PAY, RPT_REG_PAY = REGULAR_PAY;
          BON_PAY_OUT, DIS_BON_PAY, RPT_BON_PAY = BONUS_PAY;

          PUT SKIP LIST ('EMP ID  ' || EMPLOYEE_ID);
```

```
                PUT SKIP LIST ('REG PAY ' || DIS_REG_PAY);
                PUT SKIP LIST ('BON PAY ' || DIS_BON_PAY);

                WRITE FILE (EMPOFILE) FROM (OUT_EMPLOYEE_RECORD);

                A_LINE_CTR = A_LINE_CTR + 1;
                IF A_LINE_CTR > C_MAX_LINES THEN
                   CALL P1000_WRITE_HEADERS;

                WRITE FILE (EMPREPRT) FROM (DTL_LINE);

                READ FILE (EMPIFILE) INTO (IN_EMPLOYEE_RECORD);

            END; /* DO WHILE */

END P200_MAINLINE;

P300_TERMINATION: PROC;

    WRITE FILE (EMPREPRT) FROM (SPC_LINE);
    WRITE FILE (EMPREPRT) FROM (SPC_LINE);
    WRITE FILE (EMPREPRT) FROM (TRLR_LINE_01);

    CLOSE FILE(EMPIFILE),
          FILE(EMPOFILE);

    PUT SKIP LIST ('PLITRN4 - SUCCESSFULLY ENDED');

END P300_TERMINATION;

P1000_WRITE_HEADERS: PROC;

    WRITE FILE (EMPREPRT) FROM (SPC_LINE);
    A_PAGE_CTR = A_PAGE_CTR + 1;
    R_PAGE_NO = A_PAGE_CTR;
    WRITE FILE (EMPREPRT) FROM (HDR_LINE_01);
    WRITE FILE (EMPREPRT) FROM (HDR_LINE_02);
    WRITE FILE (EMPREPRT) FROM (SPC_LINE);
    WRITE FILE (EMPREPRT) FROM (DTL_HDR01);
    WRITE FILE (EMPREPRT) FROM (DTL_HDR02);

    A_LINE_CTR = 0;

END P1000_WRITE_HEADERS;

END PLITRN4;
```

When we run this revised program, here is the output:

```
    PLITRN4: INPUT AND OUTPUT
    EMP ID  1111
    REG PAY 87000.00
```

```
BON PAY 6700.00
EMP ID  1122
REG PAY 82000.00
BON PAY 6000.00
EMP ID  3217
REG PAY 65000.00
BON PAY 5500.00
EMP ID  4175
REG PAY 55000.00
BON PAY 1500.00
EMP ID  4720
REG PAY 80000.00
BON PAY 2500.00
EMP ID  4836
REG PAY 62000.00
BON PAY 2200.00
EMP ID  6288
REG PAY 70000.00
BON PAY 2000.00
EMP ID  7459
REG PAY 85000.00
BON PAY 4500.00
EMP ID  9134
REG PAY 75000.00
BON PAY 2500.00
PLITRN4 - SUCCESSFULLY ENDED
```

And here is the report file content:

```
EMPLOYEE ANNUAL SALARY REPORT PAGE- 1
-------------------------------------

EMP-ID    REGULAR       BONUS
------    --------      --------
  1111    87000.00      06700.00
  1122    82000.00      06000.00
  3217    65000.00      05500.00
  4175    55000.00      01500.00
  4720    80000.00      02500.00
  4836    62000.00      02200.00


EMPLOYEE ANNUAL SALARY REPORT PAGE- 2
-------------------------------------

EMP-ID    REGULAR       BONUS
```

```
------    --------    --------
 6288    70000.00    02000.00
 7459    85000.00    04500.00
 9134    75000.00    02500.00


      END OF ANNUAL SALARY REPORT
```

If you prefer you can include a continuation trailer record for all except the last page. This record would state something like 'REPORT CONTINUED ON NEXT PAGE'. I'm sure you'll have some other ideas of how to improve the report image and usefulness. In concluding this section, let's remember you'll find plenty of PLI code that generates reports in the world of legacy IBM mainframe systems. Be prepared for it.

Calculations

Like all programming languages, PLI does computations and assigns the results to a value on the left hand side of the computation equation. So for example we could code

```
VARIABLE2 = VARIABLE1 * 5;
```

Or you could code with parenthesis:

```
VARIABLE2 = (VARIABLE1 * 5);
```

Let's look at how we could do calculations in our employee pay program. Assume we want to give each employee a 10% raise. First we need a few arithmetic variables. We'll use FIXED DEC variables and here they are:

```
DCL 01 PAY_RAISE_VARS,
       05 REG_PAY_PKD      FIXED DEC(7,2) INIT(0),
       05 PAY_RAISE_PKD    FIXED DEC(7,2) INIT(0),
       05 NEW_PAY_PKD      FIXED DEC(7,2) INIT(0);
```

Since we are dealing with money, we coded FIXED DEC(7,2) which means a total of 7 digits with two digits to the right of the decimal point. Now we can code the calculation as follows:

```
REG_PAY_PKD = REGULAR_PAY;
NEW_PAY_PKD = (REG_PAY_PKD + (REG_PAY_PKD * 0.10));
```

We'll need to add some field assignments, and also we will change both the output data file and the report file to include the new calculated regular pay. Here is the program listing.

```
PLITRN5: PROCEDURE OPTIONS(MAIN) REORDER;
/*******************************************************************
* PROGRAM NAME :   PLITRN5 - FILE INPUT AND OUTPUT, AND REPORT.   *
*                            ALSO CALCULATE A PAY RAISE.           *
*******************************************************************/
/*******************************************************************
/*                  F I L E S   U S E D                           *
*******************************************************************/
   DCL EMPIFILE FILE RECORD SEQL INPUT;
   DCL EMPOFILE FILE RECORD SEQL OUTPUT;
   DCL EMPREPRT FILE RECORD SEQL OUTPUT;


/*******************************************************************
/*                W O R K I N G   S T O R A G E                   *
*******************************************************************/

   DCL SW_END_OF_FILE          STATIC BIT(01) INIT('0'B);

   DCL 01 IN_EMPLOYEE_RECORD,
          05  EMPLOYEE_ID   CHAR(04),
          05  FILLER1       CHAR(05),
          05  REGULAR_PAY   PIC '99999V99',
          05  FILLER2       CHAR(02),
          05  BONUS_PAY     PIC '9999V99',
          05  FILLER3       CHAR(56);

   DCL 01 OUT_EMPLOYEE_RECORD,
          05  EMP_ID_OUT    FIXED BIN(31),
          05  FILLER4       CHAR(05) INIT (' '),
          05  REG_PAY_OUT   FIXED DEC(7,2),
          05  FILLER5       CHAR(02) INIT (' '),
          05  BON_PAY_OUT   FIXED DEC(7,2),
          05  FILLER5A      CHAR(02) INIT (' '),
          05  NEW_PAY_OUT   FIXED DEC(7,2),
          05  FILLER6       CHAR(55) INIT (' ');

   DCL 01 DISPLAY_EMPLOYEE_PIC,
          05 DIS_REG_PAY  PIC '99999V.99',
          05 DIS_BON_PAY  PIC '99999V.99',
          05 DIS_NEW_PAY  PIC '99999V.99';

   DCL 01 HDR_LINE_01,
          05  FILLER7       CHAR(25) INIT (' '),
          05  FILLER8       CHAR(30)
              INIT ('EMPLOYEE ANNUAL SALARY REPORT '),
          05  FILLER9       CHAR(25) INIT (' ');
```

```
DCL 01 HDR_LINE_02,
     05  FILLER10      CHAR(25) INIT (' '),
     05  FILLER11      CHAR(30)
         INIT ('--------------------------- '),
     05  FILLER12      CHAR(25) INIT (' ');

DCL 01 SPC_LINE        CHAR(80) INIT (' ');

DCL 01 DTL_HDR01,
     05 FILLER13       CHAR(19) INIT (' '),
     05 FILLER14       CHAR(06) INIT ('EMP-ID'),
     05 FILLER15       CHAR(03) INIT (' '),
     05 FILLER16       CHAR(08) INIT ('REGULAR '),
     05 FILLER17       CHAR(04) INIT (' '),
     05 FILLER18       CHAR(08) INIT ('BONUS   '),
     05 FILLER18A      CHAR(04) INIT (' '),
     05 FILLER18B      CHAR(08) INIT ('NEW PAY '),
     05 FILLER19       CHAR(20) INIT (' ');

DCL 01 DTL_HDR02,
     05 FILLER20       CHAR(19) INIT (' '),
     05 FILLER21       CHAR(06) INIT ('------'),
     05 FILLER22       CHAR(03) INIT (' '),
     05 FILLER23       CHAR(08) INIT ('--------'),
     05 FILLER24       CHAR(04) INIT (' '),
     05 FILLER24A      CHAR(08) INIT ('--------'),
     05 FILLER24B      CHAR(04) INIT (' '),
     05 FILLER25       CHAR(08) INIT ('--------'),
     05 FILLER26       CHAR(20) INIT (' ');

DCL 01 DTL_LINE,
     05 FILLER27       CHAR(21) INIT (' '),
     05 RPT_EMP_ID     PIC '9999',
     05 FILLER28       CHAR(03) INIT (' '),
     05 RPT_REG_PAY    PIC '99999V.99',
     05 FILLER29       CHAR(04) INIT (' '),
     05 RPT_BON_PAY    PIC '99999V.99',
     05 FILLER29A      CHAR(04) INIT (' '),
     05 RPT_NEW_PAY    PIC '99999V.99',
     05 FILLER30       CHAR(20) INIT (' ');

DCL 01 TRLR_LINE_01,
     05  FILLER31      CHAR(26) INIT (' '),
     05  FILLER32      CHAR(30)
         INIT (' END OF ANNUAL SALARY REPORT  '),
```

```
              05  FILLER33      CHAR(24) INIT (' ');

   DCL 01 PAY_RAISE_VARS,
          05 REG_PAY_PKD      FIXED DEC(7,2) INIT(0),
          05 PAY_RAISE_PKD    FIXED DEC(7,2) INIT(0),
          05 NEW_PAY_PKD      FIXED DEC(7,2) INIT(0);



/***********************************************************************
/*              O N   C O N D I T I O N S                      *
************************************************************************/
   ON ENDFILE (EMPIFILE) SW_END_OF_FILE =  '1'B;

/***********************************************************************
/*              P R O G R A M   M A I N L I N E                *
************************************************************************/

CALL P100_INITIALIZATION;
CALL P200_MAINLINE;
CALL P300_TERMINATION;

P100_INITIALIZATION: PROC;

     PUT SKIP LIST ('PLITRN5: INPUT AND OUTPUT, CALCULATION, REPORT');
     OPEN FILE (EMPIFILE),
          FILE (EMPOFILE),
          FILE (EMPREPRT);

     IN_EMPLOYEE_RECORD  = '';
     OUT_EMPLOYEE_RECORD = '';

     WRITE FILE (EMPREPRT) FROM (HDR_LINE_01);
     WRITE FILE (EMPREPRT) FROM (HDR_LINE_02);
     WRITE FILE (EMPREPRT) FROM (SPC_LINE);
     WRITE FILE (EMPREPRT) FROM (DTL_HDR01);
     WRITE FILE (EMPREPRT) FROM (DTL_HDR02);

END P100_INITIALIZATION;

P200_MAINLINE: PROC;

     /*  MAIN LOOP - READ THE INPUT FILE, LOAD THE OUTPUT
                     STRUCTURE AND WRITE THE RECORD TO OUTPUT.
                     ALSO WRITE OUT THE REPORT LINES.          */

        READ FILE (EMPIFILE) INTO (IN_EMPLOYEE_RECORD);
```

48

```
                DO WHILE (¬SW_END_OF_FILE);

            /* MOVE FIELDS */

                REG_PAY_PKD = REGULAR_PAY;
                NEW_PAY_PKD = (REG_PAY_PKD + (REG_PAY_PKD * 0.10));

                EMP_ID_OUT, RPT_EMP_ID = EMPLOYEE_ID;
                REG_PAY_OUT, DIS_REG_PAY, RPT_REG_PAY = REGULAR_PAY;
                BON_PAY_OUT, DIS_BON_PAY, RPT_BON_PAY = BONUS_PAY;
                NEW_PAY_OUT, RPT_NEW_PAY, DIS_NEW_PAY = NEW_PAY_PKD;

                PUT SKIP LIST ('EMP ID ' || EMPLOYEE_ID);
                PUT SKIP LIST ('REG PAY ' || DIS_REG_PAY);
                PUT SKIP LIST ('BON PAY ' || DIS_BON_PAY);
                PUT SKIP LIST ('NEW PAY ' || DIS_NEW_PAY);

                WRITE FILE (EMPOFILE) FROM (OUT_EMPLOYEE_RECORD);
                WRITE FILE (EMPREPRT) FROM (DTL_LINE);

                READ FILE (EMPIFILE) INTO (IN_EMPLOYEE_RECORD);

            END; /* DO WHILE */

END P200_MAINLINE;

P300_TERMINATION: PROC;

    WRITE FILE (EMPREPRT) FROM (SPC_LINE);
    WRITE FILE (EMPREPRT) FROM (SPC_LINE);
    WRITE FILE (EMPREPRT) FROM (TRLR_LINE_01);

    CLOSE FILE(EMPIFILE),
          FILE(EMPOFILE);

    PUT SKIP LIST ('PLITRN5 - SUCCESSFULLY ENDED');

END P300_TERMINATION;

END PLITRN5;
```

Here is the output from the program.

```
    PLITRN5: INPUT AND OUTPUT, CALCULATION, REPORT
    EMP ID  1111
```

```
                REG PAY 87000.00
                BON PAY 06700.00
                NEW PAY 95700.00
                EMP ID  1122
                REG PAY 82000.00
                BON PAY 06000.00
                NEW PAY 90200.00
                EMP ID  3217
                REG PAY 65000.00
                BON PAY 05500.00
                NEW PAY 71500.00
                EMP ID  4175
                REG PAY 55000.00
                BON PAY 01500.00
                NEW PAY 60500.00
                EMP ID  4720
                REG PAY 80000.00
                BON PAY 02500.00
                NEW PAY 88000.00
                EMP ID  4836
                REG PAY 62000.00
                BON PAY 02200.00
                NEW PAY 68200.00
                EMP ID  6288
                REG PAY 70000.00
                BON PAY 02000.00
                NEW PAY 77000.00
                EMP ID  7459
                REG PAY 85000.00
                BON PAY 04500.00
                NEW PAY 93500.00
                EMP ID  9134
                REG PAY 75000.00
                BON PAY 02500.00
                NEW PAY 82500.00
                PLITRN5 - SUCCESSFULLY ENDED
```

And here is the updated report file content:

```
        EMPLOYEE ANNUAL SALARY REPORT
        -----------------------------


EMP-ID   REGULAR      BONUS         NEW PAY
------   --------     --------      --------
  1111   87000.00     06700.00      95700.00
  1122   82000.00     06000.00      90200.00
  3217   65000.00     05500.00      71500.00
```

```
4175    55000.00    01500.00    60500.00
4720    80000.00    02500.00    88000.00
4836    62000.00    02200.00    68200.00
6288    70000.00    02000.00    77000.00
7459    85000.00    04500.00    93500.00
9134    75000.00    02500.00    82500.00

        END OF ANNUAL SALARY REPORT
```

Edits and Validation

So far the data we processed in our training programs did not have any errors, and we haven't yet coded for any. Obviously in the real world you have to code for errors, both those that can cause your program to abend, as well as those that don't. The latter are sometimes worse because it can allow bad data to corrupt your client's business information.

For PLITRN6, we will start with our previous program PLITRN5 and we will change our data to create some obvious errors. Let's say we have these rules:

1. Employee id must be numeric and greater than zero

2. Regular Pay must be numeric and greater than zero

3. Bonus Pay must be numeric and greater than zero

And let's modify our pay file to create a couple of errors. In this case, the first record has a non-numeric regular pay, and the second has a zero value for regular pay.

```
    ----+----1----+----2----+----3

    * * * * * * * * * * * * * * * * * * * * * * * * *
    1111    8700GGG    670000
    1122    0000000    600000
    3217    6500000    550000
    4175    5500000    150000
    4720    8000000    250000
    4836    6200000    220000
    6288    7000000    200000
    7459    8500000    450000
    9134    7500000    250000
    * * * * * * * * * * * * * * * * * * * * * * * * *
```

We should check these fields to ensure all values are valid. Also, we must decide whether to continue editing once an error is found. Errors can sometimes cascade (one error leads to another) and you may eventually force an unwanted abend. For example if we check the employee id for a numeric value and it is not numeric, and then we check further to see if the value is greater than zero, this will force a data exception. So we should code around these sorts of problems.

Obviously you would want to check your values for numeric first so as to avoid the data exception. But how to stop doing additional edits when an error is encountered? There are several ways to do this. A classic way is to create a label at the end of the procedure and use a GOTO statement to transfer control to the end of the procedure. That is a way that would work, but it is not consistent with good structured programming.

Another way is to set an error flag and then to include a check of the flag as part of each edit. If an error has been detected, do not perform any other edits. If there are no previous errors, then perform the current edit. I rather prefer this method and will use it here.

So you could set up an edit/validation procedure that is called from the main procedure. Your main procedure would check to see if any errors were found. Here's a bit of pseudo code that details what we want to do.

```
MAIN PROCEDURE

CALL ERROR CHECKING PROCEDURE

IF ERROR SWTICH IS NO THEN
    PROCESS SUCCESSFULLY EDITED RECORD
ELSE
    DO ERROR PROCESSING


ERROR CHECKING PROCEDURE

SET ERROR SWITCH TO NO

IF VAR1 IS NUMERIC THEN
    CONTINUE
ELSE
    SET ERROR SWITCH TO YES
    ASSIGN ERROR MESSAGE
END IF

IF ERROR SWITCH IS NO THEN
```

```
        IF VAR2 IS NUMERIC THEN
            CONTINUE
        ELSE
            SET ERROR SWITCH TO YES
            ASSIGN ERROR MESSAGE
        END IF
    END IF

    IF ERROR SWITCH IS NO THEN
        IF VAR1 IS GREATER THAN ZERO THEN
            CONTINUE
        ELSE
            SET ERROR SWITCH TO YES
            ASSIGN ERROR MESSAGE

        END IF
    END IF

    IF VAR1 IS GREATER THAN ZERO THEN
        IF VAR2 IS NUMERIC THEN
            CONTINUE
        ELSE
            SET ERROR SWITCH TO YES
             ASSIGN ERROR MESSAGE
        END IF
    END IF
```

Of course you're routine could be much more elaborate than that. But this is how we will implement our edits and validations in PLITRN6.

First let us add a flag called SW_HAS_ERROR.

```
    DCL SW_HAS_ERROR     STATIC BIT(01) INIT('0'B);
```

Next we must code a check for numeric values. Unlike COBOL, PLI does not have an IS NUMERIC builtin function. So we will check for numeric values using a string variable that contains 0 thru 9, and the VERIFY function. First let's declare the valid numeric values as a character string as follows.

```
    DCL 01 NUMERICS      CHAR(10) INIT('0123456789');
```

Now we can check any variable content for numeric by specifying:

```
    IF VERIFY(variable name, NUMERICS) = 0 THEN
```

The verify determines whether all values in the first parameter **<variable name>** are part of the subset defined by NUMERICS which in this case is the second parameter. If so, then the value zero is returned. If one or more characters in **<variable name>** is not part of the subset NUMERICS, then it returns the position of the first value that is not. So we need a statement such as this to test whether a value is numeric::

```
IF VERIFY(EMPLOYEE_ID,NUMERICS) = 0 THEN
```

Now let's code an error-checking routine based on the pseudo code above. Note that in PLI the NOT Boolean is represented with the symbol ¬ and not all keyboards will show this symbol. You may need to customize your 3270 emulator to allow for it. In my case I map the ¬ symbol to the { keyboard character since I don't use the latter.

```
P1000_EDIT_RECORD: PROC;

    SW_HAS_ERROR = SW_NO;

    IF VERIFY(EMPLOYEE_ID,NUMERICS) = 0 THEN
       EMP_ID_BIN = EMPLOYEE_ID;
    ELSE
       DO;
          SW_HAS_ERROR = SW_YES;
          PUT SKIP LIST ('EMP ID IS NOT NUMERIC '
             || EMPLOYEE_ID);
       END;

    ELSE; /* NO ACTION */


    IF (¬SW_HAS_ERROR) THEN
       IF EMP_ID_BIN <= 0 THEN
          DO;
             SW_HAS_ERROR = SW_YES;
             PUT SKIP LIST ('EMP ID CANNOT BE ZERO '
                || EMPLOYEE_ID);
          END;
    ELSE; /* NO ACTION */

    IF (¬SW_HAS_ERROR) THEN
       IF VERIFY(REGULAR_PAY,NUMERICS) = 0 THEN
          REG_PAY_PKD = REGULAR_PAY;
       ELSE
          DO;
             SW_HAS_ERROR = SW_YES;
```

54

```
                  PUT SKIP LIST ('REG PAY IS NOT NUMERIC '
                     || REGULAR_PAY);
            END;
         ELSE; /* NO ACTION */

         IF (¬SW_HAS_ERROR) THEN
            IF REG_PAY_PKD <= 0 THEN
               DO;
                  SW_HAS_ERROR = SW_YES;
                  PUT SKIP LIST ('REG PAY CANNOT BE ZERO '
                     || REGULAR_PAY);
               END;
            ELSE; /* NO ACTION */
         ELSE; /* NO ACTION */


         IF (¬SW_HAS_ERROR) THEN
            IF VERIFY(BONUS_PAY,NUMERICS) = 0 THEN
               BON_PAY_PKD = BONUS_PAY;
            ELSE
               DO;
                  PUT SKIP LIST ('BON PAY IS NOT NUMERIC '
                     || BONUS_PAY);
                  SW_HAS_ERROR = SW_YES;
               END;
         ELSE; /* NO ACTION */

         IF (¬SW_HAS_ERROR) THEN
            IF BON_PAY_PKD <= 0 THEN
               DO;
                  SW_HAS_ERROR = SW_YES;
                  PUT SKIP LIST ('BON PAY CANNOT BE ZERO '
                     || BONUS_PAY);
               END;
            ELSE; /* NO ACTION */
         ELSE; /* NO ACTION */

         IF SW_HAS_ERROR THEN
            PUT SKIP LIST ('** RECORD DISCARDED --> ' || EMPLOYEE_ID);

      END P1000_EDIT_RECORD;
```

Now as you can see, each error is checked only if an error has not already been found. We could compact this further by nesting our IF/THEN to three levels, adding another IF/THEN/ELSE to check for the greater than zero condition. To take the employee id field as an example:

```
        IF (¬SW_HAS_ERROR) THEN
           IF VERIFY(EMPLOYEE_ID,NUMERICS) = 0 THEN
              IF EMP_ID_BIN > 0 THEN
                 EMP_ID_BIN = EMPLOYEE_ID;
              ELSE
                 DO;
                    SW_HAS_ERROR = SW_YES;
                    PUT SKIP LIST ('EMP ID CANNOT BE ZERO '
                       || EMPLOYEE_ID);
                 END;
           ELSE
              DO;
                 SW_HAS_ERROR = SW_YES;
                 PUT SKIP LIST ('EMP ID IS NOT NUMERIC '
                    || EMPLOYEE_ID);
              END;
        ELSE; /* NO ACTION */
```

That's definitely more compact, and I kind of prefer this nesting. Still, for our PLITRN6 program we'll only nest to two levels.

Ok here is our complete program listing, and notice that in the main procedure we are checking to make sure the edit routine found no errors before mapping our data fields and writing records.

```
PLITRN6: PROCEDURE OPTIONS(MAIN) REORDER;
/*******************************************************************
* PROGRAM NAME :   PLITRN5 - FILE INPUT AND OUTPUT, AND REPORT.   *
*                            ALSO CALCULATE A PAY RAISE. ALSO      *
*                            PERFORMS FIELD EDITS.                 *
*******************************************************************/


/*******************************************************************
/*              F I L E S   U S E D                                *
*******************************************************************/

   DCL EMPIFILE FILE RECORD SEQL INPUT;
   DCL EMPOFILE FILE RECORD SEQL OUTPUT;
   DCL EMPREPRT FILE RECORD SEQL OUTPUT;


/*******************************************************************
/*              W O R K I N G   S T O R A G E                      *
*******************************************************************/

   DCL SW_END_OF_FILE          STATIC BIT(01) INIT('0'B);
```

56

```
DCL SW_HAS_ERROR              STATIC BIT(01) INIT('0'B);
DCL SW_YES                    STATIC BIT(01) INIT('1'B);
DCL SW_NO                     STATIC BIT(01) INIT('0'B);


DCL 01 IN_EMPLOYEE_RECORD,
       05  EMPLOYEE_ID   CHAR(04),
       05  FILLER1       CHAR(05),
       05  REGULAR_PAY   PIC '99999V99',
       05  FILLER2       CHAR(02),
       05  BONUS_PAY     PIC '9999V99',
       05  FILLER3       CHAR(56);

DCL 01 OUT_EMPLOYEE_RECORD,
       05  EMP_ID_OUT    FIXED BIN(31),
       05  FILLER4       CHAR(05) INIT (' '),
       05  REG_PAY_OUT   FIXED DEC(7,2),
       05  FILLER5       CHAR(02) INIT (' '),
       05  BON_PAY_OUT   FIXED DEC(7,2),
       05  FILLER5A      CHAR(02) INIT (' '),
       05  NEW_PAY_OUT   FIXED DEC(7,2),
       05  FILLER6       CHAR(55) INIT (' ');

DCL 01 DISPLAY_EMPLOYEE_PIC,
       05 DIS_REG_PAY   PIC '99999V.99',
       05 DIS_BON_PAY   PIC '99999V.99',
       05 DIS_NEW_PAY   PIC '99999V.99';

DCL 01 HDR_LINE_01,
       05  FILLER7       CHAR(25) INIT (' '),
       05  FILLER8       CHAR(30)
           INIT ('EMPLOYEE ANNUAL SALARY REPORT '),
       05  FILLER9       CHAR(25) INIT (' ');

DCL 01 HDR_LINE_02,
       05  FILLER10      CHAR(25) INIT (' '),
       05  FILLER11      CHAR(30)
           INIT ('--------------------------- '),
       05  FILLER12      CHAR(25) INIT (' ');

DCL 01 SPC_LINE           CHAR(80) INIT (' ');

DCL 01 DTL_HDR01,
       05 FILLER13       CHAR(19) INIT (' '),
       05 FILLER14       CHAR(06) INIT ('EMP-ID'),
       05 FILLER15       CHAR(03) INIT (' '),
```

```
          05  FILLER16         CHAR(08) INIT ('REGULAR '),
          05  FILLER17         CHAR(04) INIT ('    '),
          05  FILLER18         CHAR(08) INIT ('BONUS   '),
          05  FILLER18A        CHAR(04) INIT ('    '),
          05  FILLER18B        CHAR(08) INIT ('NEW PAY '),
          05  FILLER19         CHAR(20) INIT ('    ');

   DCL  01  DTL_HDR02,
          05  FILLER20         CHAR(19) INIT ('    '),
          05  FILLER21         CHAR(06) INIT ('------'),
          05  FILLER22         CHAR(03) INIT ('    '),
          05  FILLER23         CHAR(08) INIT ('--------'),
          05  FILLER24         CHAR(04) INIT ('    '),
          05  FILLER24A        CHAR(08) INIT ('--------'),
          05  FILLER24B        CHAR(04) INIT ('    '),
          05  FILLER25         CHAR(08) INIT ('--------'),
          05  FILLER26         CHAR(20) INIT ('    ');

   DCL  01  DTL_LINE,
          05  FILLER27         CHAR(21) INIT ('    '),
          05  RPT_EMP_ID       PIC '9999',
          05  FILLER28         CHAR(03) INIT ('    '),
          05  RPT_REG_PAY      PIC '99999V.99',
          05  FILLER29         CHAR(04) INIT ('    '),
          05  RPT_BON_PAY      PIC '99999V.99',
          05  FILLER29A        CHAR(04) INIT ('    '),
          05  RPT_NEW_PAY      PIC '99999V.99',
          05  FILLER30         CHAR(20) INIT ('    ');

   DCL  01  TRLR_LINE_01,
          05  FILLER31         CHAR(26) INIT ('    '),
          05  FILLER32         CHAR(30)
              INIT (' END OF ANNUAL SALARY REPORT  '),
          05  FILLER33         CHAR(24) INIT ('    ');

   DCL  01  PAY_RAISE_VARS,
          05  REG_PAY_PKD      FIXED DEC(7,2) INIT(0),
          05  PAY_RAISE_PKD    FIXED DEC(7,2) INIT(0),
          05  BON_PAY_PKD      FIXED DEC(7,2) INIT(0),
          05  NEW_PAY_PKD      FIXED DEC(7,2) INIT(0);

   DCL  01  NUMERICS           CHAR(10) INIT('0123456789');

/****************************************************************
/*                O N   C O N D I T I O N S                    *
 ****************************************************************/
```

58

```
        ON ENDFILE (EMPIFILE) SW_END_OF_FILE =  '1'B;

/**********************************************************************
/*                 P R O G R A M   M A I N L I N E              *
 **********************************************************************/

CALL P100_INITIALIZATION;
CALL P200_MAINLINE;
CALL P300_TERMINATION;

P100_INITIALIZATION: PROC;

    PUT SKIP LIST ('PLITRN6: I/O, CALC, REPORT, ERROR HANDLING');
    OPEN FILE (EMPIFILE),
         FILE (EMPOFILE),
         FILE (EMPREPRT);

    IN_EMPLOYEE_RECORD  = '';
    OUT_EMPLOYEE_RECORD = '';

    WRITE FILE (EMPREPRT) FROM (HDR_LINE_01);
    WRITE FILE (EMPREPRT) FROM (HDR_LINE_02);
    WRITE FILE (EMPREPRT) FROM (SPC_LINE);
    WRITE FILE (EMPREPRT) FROM (DTL_HDR01);
    WRITE FILE (EMPREPRT) FROM (DTL_HDR02);

END P100_INITIALIZATION;

P200_MAINLINE: PROC;

    /*  MAIN LOOP - READ THE INPUT FILE, LOAD THE OUTPUT
                    STRUCTURE AND WRITE THE RECORD TO OUTPUT.
                    ALSO WRITE OUT THE REPORT LINES.          */

        READ FILE (EMPIFILE) INTO (IN_EMPLOYEE_RECORD);

        DO WHILE (¬SW_END_OF_FILE);
           CALL P1000_EDIT_RECORD;
           IF SW_HAS_ERROR THEN; /* NO ACTION */
           ELSE
              DO;
        /* MOVE FIELDS */

                 REG_PAY_PKD = REGULAR_PAY;
                 NEW_PAY_PKD = (REG_PAY_PKD + (REG_PAY_PKD * 0.10));
```

59

```
                    EMP_ID_OUT, RPT_EMP_ID
                      = EMPLOYEE_ID;
                    REG_PAY_OUT, DIS_REG_PAY, RPT_REG_PAY
                      = REGULAR_PAY;
                    BON_PAY_OUT, DIS_BON_PAY, RPT_BON_PAY = BONUS_PAY;
                    NEW_PAY_OUT, RPT_NEW_PAY, DIS_NEW_PAY
                      = NEW_PAY_PKD;

                    PUT SKIP LIST ('EMP ID ' || EMPLOYEE_ID);
                    PUT SKIP LIST ('REG PAY ' || DIS_REG_PAY);
                    PUT SKIP LIST ('BON PAY ' || DIS_BON_PAY);
                    PUT SKIP LIST ('NEW PAY ' || DIS_NEW_PAY);

                    WRITE FILE (EMPOFILE) FROM (OUT_EMPLOYEE_RECORD);

                    WRITE FILE (EMPREPRT) FROM (DTL_LINE);

                END; /* IF SW_HAS_ERROR */

              READ FILE (EMPIFILE) INTO (IN_EMPLOYEE_RECORD);

          END; /* DO WHILE */

END P200_MAINLINE;

P300_TERMINATION: PROC;

    WRITE FILE (EMPREPRT) FROM (SPC_LINE);
    WRITE FILE (EMPREPRT) FROM (SPC_LINE);
    WRITE FILE (EMPREPRT) FROM (TRLR_LINE_01);

    CLOSE FILE(EMPIFILE),
          FILE(EMPOFILE);

    PUT SKIP LIST ('PLITRN6 - SUCCESSFULLY ENDED');

END P300_TERMINATION;

P1000_EDIT_RECORD: PROC;

    SW_HAS_ERROR = SW_NO;

    IF VERIFY(EMPLOYEE_ID,NUMERICS) = 0 THEN
        EMP_ID_BIN = EMPLOYEE_ID;
    ELSE
```

```
        DO;
            SW_HAS_ERROR = SW_YES;
            PUT SKIP LIST ('EMP ID IS NOT NUMERIC '
                || EMPLOYEE_ID);
        END;

IF (¬SW_HAS_ERROR) THEN
    IF EMP_ID_BIN <= 0 THEN
        DO;
            SW_HAS_ERROR = SW_YES;
            PUT SKIP LIST ('EMP ID CANNOT BE ZERO '
                || EMPLOYEE_ID);
        END;
ELSE; /* NO ACTION */


IF (¬SW_HAS_ERROR) THEN
    IF VERIFY(REGULAR_PAY,NUMERICS) = 0 THEN
        REG_PAY_PKD = REGULAR_PAY;
    ELSE
        DO;
            SW_HAS_ERROR = SW_YES;
            PUT SKIP LIST ('REG PAY IS NOT NUMERIC '
                || REGULAR_PAY);
        END;
ELSE; /* NO ACTION */

IF (¬SW_HAS_ERROR) THEN
    IF REG_PAY_PKD <= 0 THEN
        DO;
            SW_HAS_ERROR = SW_YES;
            PUT SKIP LIST ('REG PAY CANNOT BE ZERO '
                || REGULAR_PAY);
        END;
    ELSE; /* NO ACTION */
ELSE; /* NO ACTION */


IF (¬SW_HAS_ERROR) THEN
    IF VERIFY(BONUS_PAY,NUMERICS) = 0 THEN
        BON_PAY_PKD = BONUS_PAY;
    ELSE
        DO;
            PUT SKIP LIST ('BON PAY IS NOT NUMERIC '
                || BONUS_PAY);
            SW_HAS_ERROR = SW_YES;
```

```
              END;
          ELSE; /* NO ACTION */

          IF (¬SW_HAS_ERROR) THEN
              IF BON_PAY_PKD <= 0 THEN
                  DO;
                      SW_HAS_ERROR = SW_YES;
                      PUT SKIP LIST ('BON PAY CANNOT BE ZERO '
                          || BONUS_PAY);
                  END;
              ELSE; /* NO ACTION */
          ELSE; /* NO ACTION */

          IF SW_HAS_ERROR THEN
              PUT SKIP LIST ('** RECORD DISCARDED --> ' || EMPLOYEE_ID);

  END P1000_EDIT_RECORD;

  END PLITRN6;
```

Here is our program output:

```
    PLITRN6: I/O, CALC, REPORT, ERROR HANDLING
    REG PAY IS NOT NUMERIC 8700GGG
    ** RECORD DISCARDED --> 1111
    REG PAY CANNOT BE ZERO 0000000
    **· RECORD DISCARDED --> 1122
    EMP ID  3217
    REG PAY 65000.00
    BON PAY 05500.00
    NEW PAY 71500.00
    EMP ID  4175
    REG PAY 55000.00
    BON PAY 01500.00
    NEW PAY 60500.00
    EMP ID  4720
    REG PAY 80000.00
    BON PAY 02500.00
    NEW PAY 88000.00
    EMP ID  4836
    REG PAY 62000.00
    BON PAY 02200.00
    NEW PAY 68200.00
    EMP ID  6288
    REG PAY 70000.00
    BON PAY 02000.00
    NEW PAY 77000.00
    EMP ID  7459
    REG PAY 85000.00
```

```
BON PAY 04500.00
NEW PAY 93500.00
EMP ID  9134
REG PAY 75000.00
BON PAY 02500.00
NEW PAY 82500.00
PLITRN6 - SUCCESSFULLY ENDED
```

Of course there are many ways to code error handling routines. For the numeric edit you could capture the value of the first nonnumeric digit to make it easier for the programmer to find the error. You could also add an exception report and have it routed to someone whose job it is to review and correct errors. Or you could abend the program to make sure the error gets attention.

Tables

There are many reasons to use internal tables in an application program.[3] For example you may have an external flat file that contains valid values for a field edit. Putting this information into an internal table makes it easily searchable to perform the validation. Another example is when you want to accumulate complex statistics for raw data – a table can be perfect for this. A third example is when you need to combine data from multiple files to create a composite file.

In our case, we are going to do use the third example – to combine employee-related data elements from two files to produce a combined file that contains all the elements. Let's look at our files in detail.

We have an employee profile file that contains employee id, last and first name, years of service and the data of the employee's last promotion.

```
----+----1----+----2----+----3----+----4----+----5----+----6----+----7----+----8
***************************** Top of Data *****************************
1111 VEREEN                    CHARLES           12 2017-01-01
1122 JENKINS                   DEBORAH            5 2017-01-01
3217 JOHNSON                   EDWARD             4 2017-01-01
4175 TURNBULL                  FRED               1 2016-12-01
4720 SCHULTZ                   TIM                9 2017-01-01
4836 SMITH                     SANDRA             3 2017-01-01
6288 WILLARD                   JOE                6 2016-01-01
7459 STEWART                   BETTY              7 2016-07-31
9134 FRANKLIN                  BRIANNA            0 2016-10-01
***************************** Bottom of Data *****************************
```

---

[3] For PLI we'll use the terms table and array interchangeably. Unlike COBOL, PLI doesn't have a separate variable type for tables versus arrays. Both terms mean array in PLI.

The second file is the pay file we have been working with, and it looks like this:

```
----+----1----+----2----+----3----+----4----+----5----+----6----+----7----+----8
***************************** Top of Data *********************************
1111    8700000  670000
1122    8200000  600000
3217    6500000  550000
4175    5500000  150000
4720    8000000  250000
4836    6200000  220000
6288    7000000  200000
7459    8500000  450000
9134    7500000  250000
**************************** Bottom of Data *******************************
```

Here's what we are going to do:

1. Declare an array in the program that includes both the profile and the pay fields for each employee

2. Read the pay file and load the pay data into the table

3. Read the employee profile file and load the data into the table (locating the appropriate table entry by searching on employee id)

4. Write the data in the employee table to a master file

Ok our program id is PLITRN7. We'll need file declarations for the pay file, the employee profile file, and the master file that will used for output.

```
DCL EMPPAYFL FILE RECORD SEQL INPUT;
DCL EMPLOYIN FILE RECORD SEQL INPUT;
DCL EMPLMAST FILE RECORD SEQL OUTPUT;
```

We'll of course need record structures as well. Here are the structures for each of the three files:

```
DCL 01  IN_EMPPAYFL_RECORD,
        05  EMPLOYEE_ID   CHAR(04),
        05  FILLER1       CHAR(05),
        05  REGULAR_PAY   PIC '99999V99',
        05  FILLER2       CHAR(02),
        05  BONUS_PAY     PIC '9999V99',
        05  FILLER3       CHAR(56);

DCL 01 IN_EMPLOYIN_RECORD,
        05  EMPL_ID_IN    CHAR(04),
        05  FILLER4       CHAR(01),
```

```
    05   EMPL_LNAME      CHAR(30),
    05   FILLER5         CHAR(01),
    05   EMPL_FNAME      CHAR(20),
    05   FILLER6         CHAR(01),
    05   EMPL_YRS_SRV    CHAR(02),
    05   FILLER7         CHAR(01),
    05   EMPL_PRM_DTE    CHAR(10),
    05   FILLER8         CHAR(10);

DCL 01 OUT_EMPLMAST_RECORD,
    05   EMPLMAST_EMP_ID    CHAR(04),
    05   FILLER9            CHAR(01) INIT (' '),
    05   EMPLMAST_LNAME     CHAR(30),
    05   EMPLMAST_FNAME     CHAR(20),
    05   FILLER10           CHAR(01) INIT (' '),
    05   EMPLMAST_YRS_SRV   CHAR(02),
    05   FILLER11           CHAR(01) INIT (' '),
    05   EMPLMAST_PRM_DTE   CHAR(10),
    05   FILLER12           CHAR(01) INIT (' '),
    05   EMPLMAST_REG_PAY   PIC '99999V99',
    05   FILLER13           CHAR(01) INIT (' '),
    05   EMPLMAST_BON_PAY   PIC '9999V99',
    05   FILLER14           CHAR(01) INIT (' ');
```

Next we'll need to declare our table. In PLI a table is simply an array – there is no difference between table and array, just two words for the same thing. For this example, we are going to assume that we know beforehand exactly how many entries we need for the table (looking at our files, we know we need 9 entries), and that is how many we will build the table with. Here's how to define it in PLI:

```
DCL 01 EMP_MASTER_TBL,
    05 EMP_DATA (9),
        10 EMP_ID          CHAR(04),
        10 EMP_LAST_NAME   CHAR(30),
        10 EMP_FIRST_NAME  CHAR(20),
        10 EMP_YRS_SERVICE PIC '99',
        10 EMP_PROM_DATE   CHAR(10),
        10 EMP_REG_PAY     PIC '99999V99',
        10 EMP_BON_PAY     PIC '9999V99';

DCL 01 EMP_NDX FIXED BIN(31) INIT(0);
```

We declared an 01 level structure, with an 05 level named EMP_DATA (9) whereby the number indicates that this is an array of size 9. We've also established a counter variable to use for an index which we named EMP_NDX.

To refer to an entry or element in the table, use the EMP_NDX index. You can set the index to a particular value by simply assigning the value as in:

```
    EMP_NDX = 1;
```

To bump the index to the next higher value, code:

```
    EMP_NDX = EMP_NDX + 1;
```

To bump the index to the next lower value, code:

```
    EMP_NDX = EMP_NDX - 1;
```

Finally, to search for a value in the table, we can set up a "found" flag, and then loop through the table until we either find the right key, or we reach the maximum number of entries in the table. If we do find the employee id, then we'll add the fields from the record to our table. Here's the logic.

```
    DO EMP_NDX = 1 TO 9 WHILE (¬SW_FOUND);
        IF EMPL_ID_IN = EMP_ID(EMP_NDX) THEN
            DO;
                /* MAP EMPLOYEE FIELDS TO THE TABLE */
                EMP_LAST_NAME(EMP_NDX)   = EMPL_LNAME;
                EMP_FIRST_NAME(EMP_NDX)  = EMPL_FNAME;
                EMP_YRS_SERVICE(EMP_NDX) = EMPL_YRS_SRV;
                EMP_PROM_DATE(EMP_NDX)   = EMPL_PRM_DTE;

                PUT SKIP LIST
                    (' EMP ID   : ' || EMP_ID(EMP_NDX));
                PUT SKIP LIST
                    (' LNAME    : ' || EMP_LAST_NAME(EMP_NDX));
                PUT SKIP LIST (' FNAME    : ' ||
                    EMP_FIRST_NAME(EMP_NDX));
                PUT SKIP LIST
                    (' YRS SVC  : ' ||
                    EMP_YRS_SERVICE(EMP_NDX));
                PUT SKIP LIST
                    (' PROM DTE : ' || EMP_PROM_DATE(EMP_NDX));
                PUT SKIP LIST
                    (' REG PAY  : ' || EMP_REG_PAY(EMP_NDX));
                PUT SKIP LIST
                    (' BONUS PAY: ' || EMP_BON_PAY(EMP_NDX));

                SW_FOUND = SW_YES;

            END; /* IF */

        ELSE;

    END; /* DO EMP_NDX = 1 TO 9 */

    IF (¬SW_FOUND) THEN
```

```
                     PUT SKIP LIST ('RECORD NOT FOUND ' || EMPL_ID_IN);
```

When we are ready to unload the table to create a record for the output file, we'll use a loop that cycles through the table varying the EMP_NDX value.

```
DO EMP_NDX = 1 TO 9;
    EMPLMAST_EMP_ID  = EMP_ID (EMP_NDX);
    EMPLMAST_LNAME   = EMP_LAST_NAME (EMP_NDX);
    EMPLMAST_FNAME   = EMP_FIRST_NAME(EMP_NDX);
    EMPLMAST_YRS_SRV = EMP_YRS_SERVICE(EMP_NDX);
    EMPLMAST_PRM_DTE = EMP_PROM_DATE(EMP_NDX);
    EMPLMAST_REG_PAY = EMP_REG_PAY(EMP_NDX);
    EMPLMAST_BON_PAY = EMP_BON_PAY(EMP_NDX);

    WRITE FILE (EMPLMAST) FROM (OUT_EMPLMAST_RECORD);

END; /* DO */
```

The DO X = 1 to Y logic is very handy. I expect you will find many other uses for this in your programming. Ok, here is the complete program listing.

```
PLITRN7: PROCEDURE OPTIONS(MAIN) REORDER;
/************************************************************
* PROGRAM NAME :   PLITRN5 - FILE INPUT AND OUTPUT, TABLES USED   *
*                           TO MERGE TWO DIFFERENT FILES.         *
************************************************************/

/************************************************************
/*                F I L E S    U S E D                      *
************************************************************/

    DCL EMPPAYFL FILE RECORD SEQL INPUT;
    DCL EMPLOYIN FILE RECORD SEQL INPUT;
    DCL EMPLMAST FILE RECORD SEQL OUTPUT;

/************************************************************
/*               W O R K I N G    S T O R A G E            *
************************************************************/

    DCL SW_END_OF_FILE            STATIC BIT(01) INIT('0'B);
    DCL SW_FOUND                  STATIC BIT(01) INIT('0'B);
    DCL SW_YES                    STATIC BIT(01) INIT('1'B);
    DCL SW_NO                     STATIC BIT(01) INIT('0'B);

    DCL 01 IN_EMPPAYFL_RECORD,
           05  EMPLOYEE_ID    CHAR(04),
           05  FILLER1        CHAR(05),
           05  REGULAR_PAY    PIC '99999V99',
           05  FILLER2        CHAR(02),
           05  BONUS_PAY      PIC '9999V99',
           05  FILLER3        CHAR(56);
```

67

```
DCL 01 IN_EMPLOYIN_RECORD,
        05  EMPL_ID_IN     CHAR(04),
        05  FILLER4        CHAR(01),
        05  EMPL_LNAME     CHAR(30),
        05  FILLER5        CHAR(01),
        05  EMPL_FNAME     CHAR(20),
        05  FILLER6        CHAR(01),
        05  EMPL_YRS_SRV   CHAR(02),
        05  FILLER7        CHAR(01),
        05  EMPL_PRM_DTE   CHAR(10),
        05  FILLER8        CHAR(10);

DCL 01 OUT_EMPLMAST_RECORD,
        05  EMPLMAST_EMP_ID    CHAR(04),
        05  FILLER9            CHAR(01) INIT (' '),
        05  EMPLMAST_LNAME     CHAR(30),
        05  EMPLMAST_FNAME     CHAR(20),
        05  FILLER10           CHAR(01) INIT (' '),
        05  EMPLMAST_YRS_SRV   CHAR(02),
        05  FILLER11           CHAR(01) INIT (' '),
        05  EMPLMAST_PRM_DTE   CHAR(10),
        05  FILLER12           CHAR(01) INIT (' '),
        05  EMPLMAST_REG_PAY   PIC '99999V99',
        05  FILLER13           CHAR(01) INIT (' '),
        05  EMPLMAST_BON_PAY   PIC '9999V99',
        05  FILLER14           CHAR(01) INIT (' ');

DCL 01 EMP_MASTER_TBL,
        05 EMP_DATA (9),
           10 EMP_ID          CHAR(04),
           10 EMP_LAST_NAME   CHAR(30),
           10 EMP_FIRST_NAME  CHAR(20),
           10 EMP_YRS_SERVICE PIC '99',
           10 EMP_PROM_DATE   CHAR(10),
           10 EMP_REG_PAY     PIC '99999V99',
           10 EMP_BON_PAY     PIC '9999V99';

DCL 01 EMP_NDX FIXED BIN(31) INIT(0);

/*****************************************************************
/*              O N   C O N D I T I O N S                       *
*****************************************************************/

   ON ENDFILE (EMPPAYFL) SW_END_OF_FILE =  '1'B;
   ON ENDFILE (EMPLOYIN) SW_END_OF_FILE =  '1'B;

/*****************************************************************
/*            P R O G R A M   M A I N L I N E                   *
*****************************************************************/
```

```
CALL P100_INITIALIZATION;
CALL P200_MAINLINE;
CALL P300_TERMINATION;

P100_INITIALIZATION: PROC;

    PUT SKIP LIST ('PLITRN6: I/O, CALC, REPORT, ERROR HANDLING');
    OPEN FILE (EMPPAYFL),
         FILE (EMPLOYIN),
         FILE (EMPLMAST);

    IN_EMPPAYFL_RECORD  = '';
    IN_EMPLOYIN_RECORD  = '';

    EMP_DATA(*) = '';

END P100_INITIALIZATION;

P200_MAINLINE: PROC;

    CALL P1000_LOAD_PAY_DATA;
    CALL P1100_LOAD_EMPLOYEE_DATA;
    CALL P1200_WRITE_EMPLOYEE_MSTR_FILE;

END P200_MAINLINE;

P300_TERMINATION: PROC;

    CLOSE FILE(EMPPAYFL),
          FILE(EMPLOYIN),
          FILE(EMPLMAST);

    PUT SKIP LIST ('PLITRN7 - SUCCESSFULLY ENDED');

END P300_TERMINATION;

P1000_LOAD_PAY_DATA: PROC;

    SW_END_OF_FILE = SW_NO;
    EMP_NDX = 0;

    READ FILE (EMPPAYFL) INTO (IN_EMPPAYFL_RECORD);

    DO WHILE (¬SW_END_OF_FILE);

       /* MOVE FIELDS */

       EMP_NDX = EMP_NDX + 1;

       EMP_ID(EMP_NDX)      = EMPLOYEE_ID;
       EMP_REG_PAY(EMP_NDX) = REGULAR_PAY;
       EMP_BON_PAY(EMP_NDX) = BONUS_PAY;
```

```
            PUT SKIP LIST ('EMP ID  ' || EMP_ID(EMP_NDX));
            PUT SKIP LIST ('REG PAY ' || EMP_REG_PAY(EMP_NDX));
            PUT SKIP LIST ('BON PAY ' || EMP_BON_PAY(EMP_NDX));

            READ FILE (EMPPAYFL) INTO (IN_EMPPAYFL_RECORD);

        END; /* DO WHILE */

END P1000_LOAD_PAY_DATA;

P1100_LOAD_EMPLOYEE_DATA: PROC;

    SW_END_OF_FILE = SW_NO;

    READ FILE (EMPLOYIN) INTO (IN_EMPLOYIN_RECORD);

    DO WHILE (¬SW_END_OF_FILE);

        /* SEARCH FOR EMP_ID */

        SW_FOUND = SW_NO;

        DO EMP_NDX = 1 TO 9 WHILE (¬SW_FOUND);
            IF EMPL_ID_IN = EMP_ID(EMP_NDX) THEN
                DO;

                    /* MAP EMPLOYEE FIELDS TO THE TABLE */

                    EMP_LAST_NAME(EMP_NDX)   = EMPL_LNAME;
                    EMP_FIRST_NAME(EMP_NDX)  = EMPL_FNAME;
                    EMP_YRS_SERVICE(EMP_NDX) = EMPL_YRS_SRV;
                    EMP_PROM_DATE(EMP_NDX)   = EMPL_PRM_DTE;

                    PUT SKIP LIST
                        (' EMP ID   : ' || EMP_ID(EMP_NDX));
                    PUT SKIP LIST
                        (' LNAME    : ' || EMP_LAST_NAME(EMP_NDX));
                    PUT SKIP LIST
                        (' FNAME    : ' || EMP_FIRST_NAME(EMP_NDX));
                    PUT SKIP LIST
                        (' YRS SVC  : ' || EMP_YRS_SERVICE(EMP_NDX));
                    PUT SKIP LIST
                        (' PROM DTE : ' || EMP_PROM_DATE(EMP_NDX));
                    PUT SKIP LIST
                        (' REG PAY  : ' || EMP_REG_PAY(EMP_NDX));
                    PUT SKIP LIST
                        (' BONUS PAY: ' || EMP_BON_PAY(EMP_NDX));

                    SW_FOUND = SW_YES;

                END; /* IF */

            ELSE;
```

70

```
            END; /* DO EMP_NDX = 1 TO 9 */

        IF (¬SW_FOUND) THEN
            PUT SKIP LIST ('RECORD NOT FOUND ' || EMPL_ID_IN);

        READ FILE (EMPLOYIN) INTO (IN_EMPLOYIN_RECORD);

    END; /* DO WHILE */

END P1100_LOAD_EMPLOYEE_DATA;

P1200_WRITE_EMPLOYEE_MSTR_FILE: PROC;

    DO EMP_NDX = 1 TO 9;

        EMPLMAST_EMP_ID  = EMP_ID (EMP_NDX);
        EMPLMAST_LNAME   = EMP_LAST_NAME (EMP_NDX);
        EMPLMAST_FNAME   = EMP_FIRST_NAME (EMP_NDX);
        EMPLMAST_YRS_SRV = EMP_YRS_SERVICE (EMP_NDX);
        EMPLMAST_PRM_DTE = EMP_PROM_DATE (EMP_NDX);
        EMPLMAST_REG_PAY = EMP_REG_PAY (EMP_NDX);
        EMPLMAST_BON_PAY = EMP_BON_PAY (EMP_NDX);

        WRITE FILE (EMPLMAST) FROM (OUT_EMPLMAST_RECORD);

    END; /* DO */

END P1200_WRITE_EMPLOYEE_MSTR_FILE;

END PLITRN7;
```

Ok here is the output from the program:

```
PLITRN7: I/O, CALC, REPORT, ERRORS, TABLES
EMP ID  1111
REG PAY 8700000
BON PAY 670000
EMP ID  1122
REG PAY 8200000
BON PAY 600000
EMP ID  3217
REG PAY 6500000
BON PAY 550000
EMP ID  4175
REG PAY 5500000
BON PAY 150000
EMP ID  4720
REG PAY 8000000
BON PAY 250000
EMP ID  4836
REG PAY 6200000
BON PAY 220000
```

```
EMP ID  6288
REG PAY 7000000
BON PAY 200000
EMP ID  7459
REG PAY 8500000
BON PAY 450000
EMP ID  9134
REG PAY 7500000
BON PAY 250000


EMP ID    : 1111
LNAME     : VEREEN
FNAME     : CHARLES
YRS SVC   : 12
PROM DTE : 2017-01-01
REG PAY   : 8700000
BONUS PAY: 670000
EMP ID    : 1122
LNAME     : JENKINS
FNAME     : DEBORAH
YRS SVC   : 05
PROM DTE : 2017-01-01
REG PAY   : 8200000
BONUS PAY: 600000
EMP ID    : 3217
LNAME     : JOHNSON
FNAME     : EDWARD
YRS SVC   : 04
PROM DTE : 2017-01-01
REG PAY   : 6500000
BONUS PAY: 550000
EMP ID    : 4175
LNAME     : TURNBULL
FNAME     : FRED
YRS SVC   : 01
PROM DTE : 2016-12-01
REG PAY   : 5500000
BONUS PAY: 150000
EMP ID    : 4720
LNAME     : SCHULTZ
FNAME     : TIM
YRS SVC   : 09
PROM DTE : 2017-01-01
REG PAY   : 8000000
BONUS PAY: 250000
EMP ID    : 4836
LNAME     : SMITH
FNAME     : SANDRA
YRS SVC   : 03
PROM DTE : 2017-01-01
REG PAY   : 6200000
BONUS PAY: 220000
```

```
EMP ID    : 6288
LNAME     : WILLARD
FNAME     : JOE
YRS SVC   : 06
PROM DTE  : 2016-01-01
REG PAY   : 7000000
BONUS PAY: 200000
EMP ID    : 7459
LNAME     : STEWART
FNAME     : BETTY
YRS SVC   : 07
PROM DTE  : 2016-07-31
REG PAY   : 8500000
BONUS PAY: 450000
EMP ID    : 9134
LNAME     : FRANKLIN
FNAME     : BRIANNA
YRS SVC   : 00
PROM DTE  : 2016-10-01
REG PAY   : 7500000
BONUS PAY: 250000
PLITRN7 - SUCCESSFULLY ENDED
```

And here is the content of the master file.

```
1111  VEREEN          CHARLES          12 2017-01-01 8700000 670000
1122  JENKINS         DEBORAH          05 2017-01-01 8200000 600000
3217  JOHNSON         EDWARD           04 2017-01-01 6500000 550000
4175  TURNBULL        FRED             01 2016-12-01 5500000 150000
4720  SCHULTZ         TIM              09 2017-01-01 8000000 250000
4836  SMITH           SANDRA           03 2017-01-01 6200000 220000
6288  WILLARD         JOE              06 2016-01-01 7000000 200000
7459  STEWART         BETTY            07 2016-07-31 8500000 450000
9134  FRANKLIN        BRIANNA          00 2016-10-01 7500000 250000
```

That's it for the basics of tables. For our last introductory topic with PLI, we will briefly visit sub programs.

Sub Programs

A sub program then is simply a program that can be called by another program. Sub programs are a way of reusing code because they allow multiple programs to perform the same logic or function by issuing a simple invocation statement. In PLI a sub program is invoked with the CALL verb and the program name (and usually a parameter list).

I've worked in an environment that never used sub programs, and then in another environment that nested sub programs six and seven levels deep. I hope your environment is somewhere in between. Anyway let's look at the basics of subprograms and how they work.

Subprograms can be loaded statically or dynamically. A static load means that the subprogram is linked with the calling program at compile time, hence the sub program object module is included in the final load module for the calling program. Subsequent changes to the sub program will not be reflected in the calling program until/unless the calling program is recompiled/linked.

A dynamic load means the subprogram is not statically linked with the calling program at compile time. Rather the sub program is resolved and loaded dynamically at run time. This means you get the most current version of that subprogram from the load library. We'll show both statically and dynamically loaded sub programs in the following example.

Let's create two programs: a subprogram named PLIELVL and a calling program PLITRN8. The PLIELVL program will accept an integer which represents the years of service for the employee. The subprogram will return a string value representing the employee's "level" of service from ENTRY to ADVANCED to SENIOR depending on how many years of service. Less than one year is ENTRY, 1 year through 5 years is ADVANCED and more than 5 years is SENIOR.

We'll first need to establish a way to pass the years of service from the calling program to the sub program, and then to pass the employee level of service back to the calling program. Unlike COBOL which has an explicit Linkage Section for this, you can declare your PLI variables anywhere in your storage. Here is our declaration:

```
DCL 01 LK_EMP_VARIABLES,
       10  LK_YEARS            FIXED BIN(31),
       10  LK_EMP_LEVEL        CHAR(10);
```

In order for this structure to be linked with the calling program, you must include the structure name as a parameter in the program definition. Here is the name of the program, the required PROC keyword, and in parentheses we include our linkage structure variable. This is how it is done.

```
PLIELVL: PROC(LK_EMP_VARIABLES);
```

Now the calling program must declare a similar structure and pass it to the subprogram as a parameter. We'll see that in a few minutes when we code the calling program. Meanwhile, the PLIELVL program will find the passed years of service in the LK_YEARS variable. PLIELVL will then load the employee level of service value to the LK_EMP_LEVEL variable.

So we will need some logic to determine the employee level of service based on years of service. We could code this using IF/THEN logic as follows:

```
IF LK_YEARS < 1 THEN
   LK_EMP_LEVEL = 'ENTRY     ';
ELSE
   IF LK_YEARS <= 5 THEN
      LK_EMP_LEVEL = 'ADVANCED  ';
   ELSE
       LK_EMP_LEVEL = 'SENIOR    ';
```

This would work, but let's use a somewhat more elegant technique that implements the CASE construct. We'll use the PLI SELECT verb. Here's what it looks like:

```
SELECT(LK_YEARS);

   WHEN (0)         LK_EMP_LEVEL = 'ENTRY';
   WHEN (1,2,3,4,5) LK_EMP_LEVEL = 'ADVANCED';
   OTHERWISE        LK_EMP_LEVEL = 'SENIOR';

END; /* SELECT */
```

I like this code better. For one thing it is easier to read. It also allows for a lot more possible value ranges without having to use nesting (as you would have to do if you used the IF/THEN). I suggest using the SELECT verb when you are branching on the value of one variable and there are more than two branches.

Ok, here is our program code.

```
PLIELVL: PROC(LK_EMP_VARIABLES);

/**************************************************************
* PROGRAM NAME :   PLIELVL - ACCEPT AN INTEGER NUMBER OF YEARS    *
*                         AND RETURN AN EMPLOYEE'S SENIORITY.   *
**************************************************************/
/**************************************************************
/*              W O R K I N G   S T O R A G E              *
**************************************************************/

   DCL 01 LK_EMP_VARIABLES,
          10  LK_YEARS          FIXED BIN(31),
          10  LK_EMP_LEVEL      CHAR(10);


/**************************************************************
/*              P R O G R A M   M A I N L I N E           *
```

```
******************************************************************/

      /* DETERMINE AN EMPLOYEE SERVICE LEVEL BASED
         ON YEARS OF SERVICE */

      SELECT(LK_YEARS);

          WHEN (0)          LK_EMP_LEVEL = 'ENTRY';
          WHEN (1,2,3,4)    LK_EMP_LEVEL = 'ADVANCED';
          OTHERWISE         LK_EMP_LEVEL = 'SENIOR';

      END; /* SELECT */

   END PLIELVL;
```

Now we need a program to call the subprogram. Let's write PLITRN8 to pass the years of service to the subprogram, and then display the return value. Here's our code:

```
PLITRN8: PROCEDURE OPTIONS(MAIN) REORDER;
/**********************************************************************
* PROGRAM NAME :   PLITRN8 - CALLS A SUBPROGRAM PLIELVL PASSING      *
*                            YEARS OF SERVICE TO OBTAIN THE          *
*                            THE EMPLOYEE'S SERVICE LEVEL.           *
**********************************************************************/

/**********************************************************************
/*              F I L E S    U S E D                                 *
**********************************************************************/

   DCL EMPLMAST FILE RECORD SEQL INPUT;

/**********************************************************************
/*              E X T E R N A L    E N T R I E S                     *
**********************************************************************/

   DCL PLIELVL EXTERNAL ENTRY;

/**********************************************************************
/*              W O R K I N G    S T O R A G E                       *
**********************************************************************/

   DCL SW_END_OF_FILE          STATIC BIT(01) INIT('0'B);
   DCL SW_YES                  STATIC BIT(01) INIT('1'B);
   DCL SW_NO                   STATIC BIT(01) INIT('0'B);
```

```
      DCL 01 IN_EMPLMAST_RECORD,
              05  EMPLMAST_EMP_ID   CHAR(04),
              05  FILLER1           CHAR(01) INIT (' '),
              05  EMPLMAST_LNAME    CHAR(30),
              05  EMPLMAST_FNAME    CHAR(20),
              05  FILLER2           CHAR(01) INIT (' '),
              05  EMPLMAST_YRS_SRV  CHAR(02),
              05  FILLER3           CHAR(01) INIT (' '),
              05  EMPLMAST_PRM_DTE  CHAR(10),
              05  FILLER4           CHAR(01) INIT (' '),
              05  EMPLMAST_REG_PAY  PIC '99999V99',
              05  FILLER5           CHAR(01) INIT (' '),
              05  EMPLMAST_BON_PAY  PIC '9999V99',
              05  FILLER6           CHAR(01) INIT (' ');

      DCL 01 EMP_LINK_DATA,
              05 EMP_ID_BIN         FIXED BIN(31),
              05 EMP_LEVEL          CHAR(10);


/**********************************************************************
/*               O N   C O N D I T I O N S                      *
**********************************************************************/

   ON ENDFILE (EMPLMAST) SW_END_OF_FILE = '1'B;


/**********************************************************************
/*               P R O G R A M   M A I N L I N E                *
**********************************************************************/

CALL P100_INITIALIZATION;
CALL P200_MAINLINE;
CALL P300_TERMINATION;

P100_INITIALIZATION: PROC;

   PUT SKIP LIST ('PLITRN8: I/O AND CALLING A SUB-PROGRAM');
   OPEN FILE (EMPLMAST);

   IN_EMPLMAST_RECORD  = '';

END P100_INITIALIZATION;

P200_MAINLINE: PROC;

   SW_END_OF_FILE = SW_NO;
```

```
        READ FILE (EMPLMAST) INTO (IN_EMPLMAST_RECORD);

     DO WHILE (¬SW_END_OF_FILE);

        /* GET THE EMPLOYEE SERVICE LEVEL */

        EMP_ID_BIN = EMPLMAST_YRS_SRV;
        EMP_LEVEL  = ' ';

        CALL PLIELVL (EMP_LINK_DATA);

        PUT SKIP LIST (' EMP ID: ' || EMPLMAST_EMP_ID);
        PUT SKIP LIST (' YEARS : ' || EMPLMAST_YRS_SRV);
        PUT SKIP LIST (' LEVEL : ' || EMP_LEVEL);

        READ FILE (EMPLMAST) INTO (IN_EMPLMAST_RECORD);

     END; /* DO WHILE */

 END P200_MAINLINE;

 P300_TERMINATION: PROC;

     CLOSE FILE(EMPLMAST);

     PUT SKIP LIST ('PLITRN8 - SUCCESSFULLY ENDED');

 END P300_TERMINATION;

 END PLITRN8;
```

Now let's focus for a minute on the call to PLIELVL:

```
        CALL PLIELVL (EMP_LINK_DATA);
```

Notice a couple of things with the code. One is that we use the EMP_LINK_DATA
structure to pass data back and forth between PLITRN8 and PLIELVL. This is required.
The other thing to notice is that we did not place the program name in quote marks like
we did in COBOL. Instead we declared it as an external entry and then we call it by
name:

```
        DCL PLIELVL EXTERNAL ENTRY;
```

This declaration is required so that the linker can locate and resolve the call to this program. `PLIELVL` will be linked into the `PLITRN8` load module when `PLITRN8` is compiled. To see what the result looks like, you can use File Manager to browse the load module. Select File Manager from your ISPF menu, then from the following screen, select **Utilities.**

```
File Manager                    Primary Option Menu
Command ===>

0    Settings       Set processing options            User ID . : USER01
1    View           View data                         System ID : MATE
2    Edit           Edit data                         Appl ID . : FMN
3    Utilities      Perform utility functions         Version . : 11.1.0
4    Tapes          Tape specific functions           Terminal. : 3278
5    Disk/VSAM      Disk track and VSAM CI functions  Screen. . : 1
6    OAM            Work with OAM objects             Date. . . : 2018/02/06
7    Templates      Template and copybook utilities   Time. . . : 05:27
8    HFS            Access Hierarchical File System
9    WebSphere MQ   List, view and edit MQ data
X    Exit           Terminate File Manager
```

From the next screen select LOADLIB

```
File Manager                    Utility Functions
Command ===>

0    DBCS           Set DBCS data format for print
1    Create         Create data
2    Print          Print data
3    Copy           Copy data
4    Dslist         Catalog services
5    VTOC           Work with VTOC
6    Find/Change    Search for and change data
7    AFP            Browse AFP data
8    Storage        Browse user storage
9    Printdsn       Browse File Manager print data set
10   Loadlib        Load module utility functions
11   Compare        Compare data
12   Audit trail    Print audit trail report
13   Copybook       View and Print
14   WebSphere MQ   List WebSphere MQ managers and queues
```

Now select option 1 (View).

```
File Manager              Load module utility functions
Command ===>

1  View          View load module information
2  Compare       Compare load modules
```

Finally, enter the library name and member name PLITRN8, and press Enter.

```
File Manager              Load Module Information
Command ===>

Input:
   Data set name . . . . . 'USER01.LOADLIB'
   Member  . . . . . . . . PLITRN8      (Blank or pattern for member list)
   Volume serial . . . . .              (If not cataloged)


Processing Options:

   Order CSECTs by                  Output to
   1   1. Address                   1   1. Display
       2. Name                          2. Printer

   Enter "/" to select option
      YY/MM/DD date format (default: YYYY.DDD)
      Batch execution                    Advanced member selection
                                         Skip member name list
```

Notice that both `PLITRN8` and `PLIELVL` are present in the `PLITRN8` load module.

```
File Manager                Load Module Information        Row 00001 of 00128
Command ===>                                                     Scroll PAGE

 Load Library   USER01.LOADLIB
 Load Module    PLITRN8
       Linked on 2018.037 at 11:44:09 by PROGRAM BINDER 5695-PMB V1R1
             EPA 000000 Size 0002370 TTR 002A1A SSI          AC 00 AM 31  RM ANY

Address CSECT name         Type Size    AMODE RMODE Compiler 1 Date 1   Compil ±
        *                  *    *        *     *     *          *        *
<---+-> <---+----10---+-> <--> <---+-> <---> <---> <---+----> <---+--> <---+>
0000000 CEESTART           SD   000007C MIN   ANY   PL/I V4R2 2018.037
0000000 CEESTART.CEESTART  LD   000007C MIN   ANY   PL/I V4R2 2018.037
0000080 PLITRN81           SD   0000A90 MIN   ANY   PL/I V4R2 2018.037
0000080 PLITRN81.PLITRN81  LD   0000A90 MIN   ANY   PL/I V4R2 2018.037
00000C8 PLITRN81.PLITRN8   LD   0000A90 MIN   ANY   PL/I V4R2 2018.037
0000B10 PLITRN82           SD   00000C4 MIN   ANY   PL/I V4R2 2018.037
0000B10 PLITRN82.PLITRN82  LD   00000C4 MIN   ANY   PL/I V4R2 2018.037
0000BD8 @PLITRN8           SD   0000004 MIN   ANY   PL/I V4R2 2018.037
0000BD8 @PLITRN8.@PLITRN8  LD   0000004 MIN   ANY   PL/I V4R2 2018.037
0000CD0 IBMCYRT.IBMCYRT    LD   0000200 MIN   ANY   PL/I V3R9 2011.074
0000ED0 IBMPOFCX           SD   0000074 MIN   ANY   PL/I V3R9 2011.074
0000ED0 IBMPOFCX           ID   0000074 MIN   ANY   PL/I V3R9 2011.074
0000ED0 IBMPOFCX.IBMPOFCX  LD   0000074 MIN   ANY   PL/I V3R9 2011.074
0000F48 IBMQOFOP           SD   0000014 MIN   ANY   HLASM V1R6 2011.074
0000F48 IBMQOFOP           ID   0000014 MIN   ANY   HLASM V1R6 2011.074
0000F48 IBMQOFOP.IBMQOFOP  LD   0000014 MIN   ANY   HLASM V1R6 2011.074
0000F60 PLIELVL1           SD   0000230 MIN   ANY   PL/I V4R2 2018.017
0000F60 PLIELVL1.PLIELVL1  LD   0000230 MIN   ANY   PL/I V4R2 2018.017
0000FA8 PLIELVL1.PLIELVL   LD   0000230 MIN   ANY   PL/I V4R2 2018.017
```

Now let's run the program and view the output.

```
        PLITRN8: I/O AND CALLING A SUB-PROGRAM
         EMP ID: 1111
         YEARS : 12
         LEVEL : SENIOR
         EMP ID: 1122
         YEARS : 05
         LEVEL : SENIOR
         EMP ID: 3217
         YEARS : 04
         LEVEL : ADVANCED
         EMP ID: 4175
         YEARS : 01
         LEVEL : ADVANCED
```

```
            EMP ID: 4720
            YEARS : 09
            LEVEL : SENIOR
            EMP ID: 4836
            YEARS : 03
            LEVEL : ADVANCED
            EMP ID: 6288
         YEARS : 06
          LEVEL : SENIOR
          EMP ID: 7459
          YEARS : 07
          LEVEL : SENIOR
          EMP ID: 9134
          YEARS : 00
          LEVEL : ENTRY
        PLITRN8 - SUCCESSFULLY ENDED
```

Now let's look at how to call the PLIELVL program dynamically. You must make one small change to PLIELVL to define it as a sub program. You must change the OPTIONS(MAIN) to OPTIONS(FETCHABLE). Then you must make one small change to the PLITRN8 program to load the PLIELVL program dynamically using the keyword FETCH.

Here is the revised PLIELVL program source. Only one thing has changed which is on the first line where we added OPTIONS(FETCHABLE).

```
PLIELVL: PROC(LK_EMP_VARIABLES) OPTIONS(FETCHABLE);
/********************************************************************
 * PROGRAM NAME :   PLIELVL - ACCEPT AN INTEGER NUMBER OF YEARS    *
 *                            AND RETURN AN EMPLOYEE'S SENIORITY.  *
 ********************************************************************/

/********************************************************************
/*             W O R K I N G   S T O R A G E                       *
 ********************************************************************/

   DCL 01 LK_EMP_VARIABLES,
          10  LK_YEARS          FIXED BIN(31),
          10  LK_EMP_LEVEL      CHAR(10);

/********************************************************************
/*             P R O G R A M   M A I N L I N E                     *
 ********************************************************************/

/* DETERMINE AN EMPLOYEE SERVICE LEVEL BASED ON YEARS OF SERVICE */
```

```
        SELECT(LK_YEARS);

           WHEN (0)          LK_EMP_LEVEL = 'ENTRY';
           WHEN (1,2,3,4)    LK_EMP_LEVEL = 'ADVANCED';
           OTHERWISE         LK_EMP_LEVEL = 'SENIOR';

        END; /* SELECT */

    END PLIELVL;
```

Finally we must code the statement **FETCH PLIELVL** somewhere in the PLITRN8 source. You could put it anywhere, but I suggest putting it after the external entry declaration so it will be clear we are loading PLIELVL dynamically. Here is our revised source now.

```
PLITRN8: PROCEDURE OPTIONS(MAIN) REORDER;
 /******************************************************************
 * PROGRAM NAME :   PLITRN8 - CALLS A SUBPROGRAM PLIELVL PASSING  *
 *                            YEARS OF SERVICE TO OBTAIN THE       *
 *                            THE EMPLOYEE'S SERVICE LEVEL.        *
 ******************************************************************/

 /******************************************************************
 /*              F I L E S   U S E D                              *
 ******************************************************************/

    DCL EMPLMAST FILE RECORD SEQL INPUT;

 /******************************************************************
 /*            E X T E R N A L   E N T R I E S                    *
 ******************************************************************/

    DCL PLIELVL EXTERNAL ENTRY;
    FETCH PLIELVL;

 /******************************************************************
 /*              W O R K I N G   S T O R A G E                    *
 ******************************************************************/

    DCL SW_END_OF_FILE          STATIC BIT(01) INIT('0'B);
    DCL SW_YES                  STATIC BIT(01) INIT('1'B);
    DCL SW_NO                   STATIC BIT(01) INIT('0'B);

    DCL 01 IN_EMPLMAST_RECORD,
           05  EMPLMAST_EMP_ID  CHAR(04),
```

83

```
         05  FILLER1          CHAR(01) INIT (' '),
         05  EMPLMAST_LNAME   CHAR(30),
         05  EMPLMAST_FNAME   CHAR(20),
         05  FILLER2          CHAR(01) INIT (' '),
         05  EMPLMAST_YRS_SRV CHAR(02),
         05  FILLER3          CHAR(01) INIT (' '),
         05  EMPLMAST_PRM_DTE CHAR(10),
         05  FILLER4          CHAR(01) INIT (' '),
         05  EMPLMAST_REG_PAY PIC '99999V99',
         05  FILLER5          CHAR(01) INIT (' '),
         05  EMPLMAST_BON_PAY PIC '9999V99',
         05  FILLER6          CHAR(01) INIT (' ');

  DCL 01 EMP_LINK_DATA,
         05 EMP_ID_BIN       FIXED BIN(31),
         05 EMP_LEVEL        CHAR(10);

/********************************************************************
/*              O N   C O N D I T I O N S                         *
********************************************************************/

   ON ENDFILE (EMPLMAST) SW_END_OF_FILE =  '1'B;

/********************************************************************
/*              P R O G R A M   M A I N L I N E                   *
********************************************************************/

CALL P100_INITIALIZATION;
CALL P200_MAINLINE;
CALL P300_TERMINATION;

P100_INITIALIZATION: PROC;

   PUT SKIP LIST ('PLITRN8: I/O AND CALLING A SUB-PROGRAM');
   OPEN FILE (EMPLMAST);

   IN_EMPLMAST_RECORD  = '';

END P100_INITIALIZATION;

P200_MAINLINE: PROC;

   SW_END_OF_FILE = SW_NO;

   READ FILE (EMPLMAST) INTO (IN_EMPLMAST_RECORD);
```

```
      DO WHILE (¬SW_END_OF_FILE);

          /* GET THE EMPLOYEE SERVICE LEVEL */

          EMP_ID_BIN = EMPLMAST_YRS_SRV;
          EMP_LEVEL  = ' ';

          CALL PLIELVL (EMP_LINK_DATA);

          PUT SKIP LIST (' EMP ID: ' || EMPLMAST_EMP_ID);
          PUT SKIP LIST (' YEARS : ' || EMPLMAST_YRS_SRV);
          PUT SKIP LIST (' LEVEL : ' || EMP_LEVEL);
          READ FILE (EMPLMAST) INTO (IN_EMPLMAST_RECORD);

      END; /* DO WHILE */

  END P200_MAINLINE;

  P300_TERMINATION: PROC;

      CLOSE FILE(EMPLMAST);

      PUT SKIP LIST ('PLITRN8 - SUCCESSFULLY ENDED');

  END P300_TERMINATION;

  END PLITRN8;
```

Now let's compile the program and look at the load module. When we view it using File Manager, you can see the PLIELVL module is no longer there. Instead it will be loaded into memory at run time.`

```
File Manager                 Load Module Information        Row 00001 of 0012
Command ===>                                                   Scroll PAGE

 Load Library   USER01.LOADLIB
 Load Module    PLITRN8
     Linked on 2018.037 at 12:05:49 by PROGRAM BINDER 5695-PMB V1R1
           EPA 000000 Size 00021E8 TTR 002D0A SSI          AC 00 AM 31  RM A

Address CSECT name         Type Size    AMODE RMODE Compiler 1 Date 1   Compil
        *                  *    *        *    *     *         *         *
<---+-> <---+----10---+-> <--> <---+-> <---> <---> <---+----> <---+--> <---+>
0000000 CEESTART           SD   000007C MIN   ANY   PL/I  V4R2 2018.037
0000000 CEESTART.CEESTART  LD   000007C MIN   ANY   PL/I  V4R2 2018.037
0000080 PLITRN81           SD   0000B10 MIN   ANY   PL/I  V4R2 2018.037
0000080 PLITRN81.PLITRN81  LD   0000B10 MIN   ANY   PL/I  V4R2 2018.037
```

```
00000C8 PLITRN81.PLITRN8      LD  0000B10 MIN   ANY    PL/I   V4R2 2018.037
0000B90 PLITRN82              SD  00000D4 MIN   ANY    PL/I   V4R2 2018.037
0000B90 PLITRN82.PLITRN82     LD  00000D4 MIN   ANY    PL/I   V4R2 2018.037
0000C68 @PLITRN8              SD  0000004 MIN   ANY    PL/I   V4R2 2018.037
0000C68 @PLITRN8.@PLITRN8     LD  0000004 MIN   ANY    PL/I   V4R2 2018.037
0000C70 CEEMAIN               SD  000000C MIN   ANY    PL/I   V4R2 2018.037
0000C70 CEEMAIN.CEEMAIN       LD  000000C MIN   ANY    PL/I   V4R2 2018.037
0002088 IBMQOFCN              ID  0000014 MIN   ANY    HLASM  V1R6 2011.074
0002088 IBMQOFCN.IBMQOFCN     LD  0000014 MIN   ANY    HLASM  V1R6 2011.074
00020A0 IBMQOFCI              SD  0000014 MIN   ANY    HLASM  V1R6 2011.074
00020A0 IBMQOFCI              ID  0000014 MIN   ANY    HLASM  V1R6 2011.074
00020A0 IBMQOFCI.IBMQOFCI     LD  0000014 MIN   ANY    HLASM  V1R6 2011.074
00020B8 CEESG003              SD  000012B MIN   ANY    HLASM  V1R6 2011.077
00020B8 CEESG003.CEESG003     LD  000012B MIN   ANY    HLASM  V1R6 2011.077
```

To prove that we will load the most recent version of PLIELVL dynamically, let's make a small change to it, just to add a display statement. Let's add this to PLIELVL:

```
PUT SKIP LIST ('MESSAGE FROM PLIELVL BEING CALLED DYNAMICALLY');
```

Now let's recompile PLIELVL and then run PLITRN8 (without recompiling PLITRN8). Here is the result of executing PLITRN8, and notice the message from PLIELVL. This simply demonstrates that you can change PLIELVL at any time and the changes will be in effect immediately because you are loading the PLIELVL program dynamically.

```
PLITRN8: I/O AND CALLING A SUB-PROGRAM
MESSAGE FROM PLIELVL BEING CALLED DYNAMICALLY
 EMP ID: 1111
 YEARS : 12
 LEVEL : SENIOR
MESSAGE FROM PLIELVL BEING CALLED DYNAMICALLY
 EMP ID: 1122
 YEARS : 05
 LEVEL : SENIOR
MESSAGE FROM PLIELVL BEING CALLED DYNAMICALLY
 EMP ID: 3217
 YEARS : 04
 LEVEL : ADVANCED
MESSAGE FROM PLIELVL BEING CALLED DYNAMICALLY
 EMP ID: 4175
 YEARS : 01
 LEVEL : ADVANCED
MESSAGE FROM PLIELVL BEING CALLED DYNAMICALLY
 EMP ID: 4Review Questions0
 YEARS : 09
 LEVEL : SENIOR
```

```
MESSAGE FROM PLIELVL BEING CALLED DYNAMICALLY
  EMP ID: 4836
  YEARS : 03
  LEVEL : ADVANCED
MESSAGE FROM PLIELVL BEING CALLED DYNAMICALLY
  EMP ID: 6288
  YEARS : 06
  LEVEL : SENIOR
MESSAGE FROM PLIELVL BEING CALLED DYNAMICALLY
  EMP ID: 7459
  YEARS : 07
  LEVEL : SENIOR
MESSAGE FROM PLIELVL BEING CALLED DYNAMICALLY
  EMP ID: 9134
  YEARS : 00
  LEVEL : ENTRY
PLITRN8 - SUCCESSFULLY ENDED
```

The benefit of calling sub programs dynamically should be obvious. Suppose you have 10 programs that call a sub program. If you use the static approach, a change to the subprogram requires recompiling not only the sub program, but also all 10 calling programs. However, if you are calling the sub program dynamically you need only compile the subprogram. Since a dynamic call loads the current version of the sub program, you will always get the latest. [4]

---

[4] There are some exceptions to this, such as with IMS and CICS where programs are loaded into a different run time library when first used. In that case you must either cycle the online environment or issue a reload command that is specific to the product and environment. This is not a developer task. Typically either a DBA or system administrator will perform these tasks upon request.

Chapter One Review Questions

1. If you are performing arithmetic calculations, which data type usually performs best?

2. What is an example of an ON condition and what it is used for?

3. What verb is used to implement the case control structure in a PL/1 program?

4. What is the difference between a DO WHILE control structure and a DO UNTIL control structure?

5. How would one use the VERIFY function?

6. How do you include a copybook?

7. How do you concatenate two string variables in PLI?

8. If you want to declare an array of 100 elements of CHAR(04) and call the array TABLE1, how would you code it?

9. What does the FETCHABLE attribute mean?

10. What is the basic syntax to declare a file named TESTFILE for record type input?

11. What carriage control character would you use to skip to the top of the next page?

12. If you are performing arithmetic calculations, which data type usually performs best?

13. What is an example of an ON condition and what it is used for?

14. What verb is used to implement the case control structure in a PL/1 program?

15. What is the difference between a DO WHILE control structure and a DO UNTIL control structure?

16. How would one use the VERIFY function?

17. How do you include a copybook?

18. How do you concatenate two string variables in PLI?

19. If you want to declare an array of 100 elements of CHAR(04) and call the array TABLE1, how would you code it?

20. What does the FETCHABLE attribute mean?

21. What is the basic syntax to declare a file named TESTFILE for record type input?

22. What carriage control character would you use to skip to the top of the next page?

23. What are the two ways a procedure can end normally?

24. What statement specifies the action to be taken in a SELECT statement if none of the WHEN conditions is satisfied?

Chapter Two: PLI Programming with VSAM

Introduction

Virtual Storage Access Method (VSAM) is an IBM DASD (direct access storage device) file storage access method. It has been used for many years, including with the Multiple Virtual Storage (MVS) architecture and now in z/OS. VSAM offers four data set organizations:

- Key Sequenced Data Set (KSDS)

- Entry Sequenced Data Set (ESDS)

- Relative Record Data Set (RRDS)

- Linear Data Set (LDS)

The KSDS, RRDS and ESDS organizations all are record-based. The LDS organization uses a sequence of pages without a predefined record structure.

VSAM records are either fixed or variable length. Records are organized in fixed-size blocks called Control Intervals (CIs). The CI's are organized into larger structures called Control Areas (CAs). Control Interval sizes are measured in bytes — for example 4 kilobytes — while Control Area sizes are measured in disk tracks or cylinders. When a VSAM file is read, a complete Control Interval is transferred to memory.

The Access Method Services utility program IDCAMS is used to define and delete VSAM data sets. In addition, you can write custom programs in COBOL, PLI and Assembler to access VSAM datasets using Data Definition (DD) statements in Job Control Language (JCL), or via dynamic allocation or in online regions such as in Customer Information Control System (CICS).

Types of VSAM Files

Key Sequence Data Set (KSDS)

This organization type is the most commonly used. Each record has one or more key fields and a record can be retrieved (or inserted) by key value. This provides random access to data. Records are of variable length. IMS uses KSDS files (as we'll see in the next chapter).

Entry Sequence Data Set (ESDS)

This organization keeps records in the order in which they were entered. Records must be accessed sequentially. This organization is used by IMS for overflow datasets.

Relative Record Data Set (RRDS)

This organization is based on record retrieval number; record 1, record 2, etc. This provides random access but the program must have a way of knowing which record number it is looking for.

Linear Data Set (LDS)

This organization is a byte-stream data set. It is rarely used by application programs.

We'll focus on KSDS files because they are the most commonly used and the most useful.

A KSDS cluster consists of following two components:

- **Index** – The index component of the KSDS cluster is comprised of the list of key values for the records in the cluster with pointers to the corresponding records in the data component. The index component relates the key of each record to the record's relative location in the data set. When a record is added or deleted, this index is updated.

- **Data** – The data component of the KSDS cluster contains the actual data. Each record in the data component of a KSDS cluster contains a key field with same number of characters and occur in the same relative position in each record.

Creating VSAM Files

You create VSAM files using the IDCAMS utility. Here is the meaning of the keywords in the control statement, followed by an example.

NAME	The cluster name which is then extended one node for the data and index physical files. See example below.
RECSZ	The record length.
TRK	The space allocated for the file. It can be in tracks or cylinders.
FREESPACE	How much free space to leave on each control interval.
KEYS	The length and displacement of the key field.

CISZ	The Control Interval Size specified in bytes
VOLUMES	The DASD volume(s) which will physically store the data.
INDEX	The data set name of the index file.
DATA	The data set name that houses the data records.

Here is sample JCL:

```
//USER01D JOB MSGLEVEL=(1,1),NOTIFY=&SYSUID
//*
//*************************************************
//* DEFINE VSAM KSDS CLUSTER
//*************************************************
//JS010    EXEC PGM=IDCAMS
//SYSUDUMP DD SYSOUT=*
//SYSPRINT DD SYSOUT=*
//SYSOUT   DD SYSOUT=*
//SYSIN    DD  *
  DEFINE CLUSTER(NAME(USER01.EMPLOYEE)   -
  RECSZ(80 80)       -
  TRK(2,1)           -
  FREESPACE(5,10) -
  KEYS(4,0)          -
  CISZ(4096)         -
  VOLUMES(DEVHD1) -
  INDEXED)           -
  INDEX(NAME(USER01.EMPLOYEE.INDEX)) -
  DATA(NAME(USER01.EMPLOYEE.DATA))
/*
//SYSPRINT DD SYSOUT=*
//SYSUDUMP DD SYSOUT=*
```

This creates a catalog entry with two datasets, one for the record data and one for the index.

```
DSLIST - Data Sets Matching USER01.EMPLOYEE             Row 1 of 11
Command ===>                                     Scroll ===> CSR

Command - Enter "/" to select action         Message       Volume
-------------------------------------------------------------------------
        USER01.EMPLOYEE                                    *VSAM*
        USER01.EMPLOYEE.DATA                               DEVHD1
        USER01.EMPLOYEE.INDEX                              DEVHD1
*************************** End of Data Set list ***************************
```

Loading and Unloading VSAM Files

You can add data to a VSAM KSDS in several ways:

1. Copying data from a flat file

2. Using File Manager

3. Using an application program

We'll show examples of all three. First, let us design a VSAM file. For purposes of this text book, we will be creating and maintaining a simple employee file for a fictitious human resource department. Here are the columns and data types for our file which we will name EMPLOYEE.

Field Name	Type
EMP_ID (primary key)	Numeric 4 bytes
EMP_LAST_NAME	Character(30)
EMP_FIRST_NAME	Character(20)
EMP_SERVICE_YEARS	Numeric 2 bytes
EMP_PROMOTION_DATE	Date in format YYYY-MM-DD

Now let's say we have created a simple text file in this format with the data for our VSAM file. We can browse it:

```
BROWSE    USER01.EMPLOYEE.LOAD                      Line 00000000 Col 001 080
 Command ===>                                            Scroll ===> CSR
----+----1----+----2----+----3----+----4----+----5----+----6----+----7----+----8
******************************* Top of Data ********************************
3217JOHNSON                     EDWARD              042017-01-01
7459STEWART                     BETTY               072016-07-31
9134FRANKLIN                    BRIANNA             032016-10-01
4720SCHULTZ                     TIM                 092017-01-01
6288WILLARD                     JOE                 062016-01-01
1122JENKINS                     DEBORAH             052016-09-01
```

We can use this text file to load our VSAM file. Note however that before we load, we need to sort the records into key sequence. Otherwise IDCAMS will give us an error when we try to load. You can edit the file and on the command line issue a SORT 1 4 command (space between 1 and 4) to sort the records.

```
BROWSE    USER01.EMPLOYEE.LOAD                      Line 00000000 Col 001 080
 Command ===>                                            Scroll ===> CSR
----+----1----+----2----+----3----+----4----+----5----+----6----+----7----+----8
****************************** Top of Data ******************************
1122JENKINS                    DEBORAH                052016-09-01
3217JOHNSON                    EDWARD                 042017-01-01
4720SCHULTZ                    TIM                    092017-01-01
6288WILLARD                    JOE                    062016-01-01
7459STEWART                    BETTY                  072016-07-31
9134FRANKLIN                   BRIANNA                032016-10-01
```

Save the file to apply the changes. Now we are ready. We can use the following IDCAMS JCL to load the VSAM file. The INDATASET is our input file, and the OUTDATASET is the VSAM file. Note that we specify the VSAM file cluster name in this job, not the DATA or INDEX file names.

```
//USER01D JOB 'NAME',MSGLEVEL=(1,1),NOTIFY=&SYSUID
//*
//*************************************************************
//* REPRO/COPY DATA FROM PS TO VSAM KSDS
//*************************************************************
//STEP90   EXEC PGM=IDCAMS
//SYSPRINT DD SYSOUT=*
//SYSOUT   DD SYSOUT=*
//SYSUDUMP DD SYSOUT=*
//SYSIN    DD *
  REPRO -
  INDATASET (USER01.EMPLOYEE.LOAD) -
  OUTDATASET(USER01.EMPLOYEE)
/*
//*
```

Once loaded, we can view the data using the ISPF BROWSE function. If this doesn't work on your system, you'll need to use IBM File Manager or another tool which allows you to browse/edit VSAM files.

```
Browse              USER01.EMPLOYEE.DATA                    Top of 6
Command ===>                                                Scroll PAGE
                        Type DATA      RBA                  Format CHAR
                                         Col 1
----+----10---+----2----+----3----+----4----+----5----+----6----+----7----+----
****  Top of data  ****
1122JENKINS                     DEBORAH                052016-09-01
3217JOHNSON                     EDWARD                 042017-01-01
4720SCHULTZ                     TIM                    092017-01-01
6288WILLARD                     JOE                    062016-01-01
7459STEWART                     BETTY                  072016-07-31
9134FRANKLIN                    BRIANNA                032016-10-01
****  End of data  ****
```

To edit the data you will need to use a tool such as File Manager. Let's do this next.

VSAM Updates with File Manager

You can perform adds, changes and deletes to data records in File Manager. First, it will be useful if we create a file layout to assist us with viewing and updating data. Let's create a PLI layout as follows.

```
/************************************************
* PLI DECLARATION FOR VSAM FILE EMPLOYEE       *
************************************************/
 DCL 01 EMPLOYEE,
      05 EMP_ID               PIC '9999',
      05 EMP_LAST_NAME        CHAR(30),
      05 EMP_FIRST_NAME       CHAR(20),
      05 EMP_SERVICE_YEARS    PIC '99',
      05 EMP_PROMOTION_DATE   CHAR(10),
      05 EMP_SSN              CHAR(09),
      05 FILLER               CHAR(05);
```

Save this in your copylib library. You can use member name EMPLOYEE.

Now let's go to File Manager. Select File Manager from your ISPF menu (it may be different on your system). Below is the main FM menu. Select the EDIT option.

```
File Manager                      Primary Option Menu
Command ===>

0   Settings      Set processing options            User ID . : USER01
1   View          View data                         System ID : MATE
2   Edit          Edit data                         Appl ID . : FMN
3   Utilities     Perform utility functions         Version . : 11.1.0
4   Tapes         Tape specific functions           Terminal. : 3278
5   Disk/VSAM     Disk track and VSAM CI functions  Screen. . : 2
6   OAM           Work with OAM objects             Date. . . : 2018/03/07
7   Templates     Template and copybook utilities   Time. . . : 02:41
8   HFS           Access Hierarchical File System
9   WebSphere MQ  List, view and edit MQ data
X   Exit          Terminate File Manager
```

Enter your file name, copybook file name, and select the processing option 1.

```
File Manager                      Edit Entry Panel
Command ===>

Input Partitioned, Sequential or VSAM Data Set, or HFS file:
   Data set/path name 'USER01.EMPLOYEE'                         +
   Member . . . . . .            (Blank or pattern for member list)
   Volume serial  . .            (If not cataloged)
   Start position . .                                  +
   Record limit . . .            Record sampling
   Inplace edit . . .            (Prevent inserts and deletes)
Copybook or Template:
   Data set name  . . 'USER01.COPYLIB(EMPLOYEE)'
   Member . . . . . .            (Blank or pattern for member list)
Processing Options:
 Copybook/template   Start position type   Enter "/" to select option
1  1. Above          1. Key                   Edit template   Type (1,2,S)
   2. Previous        2. RBA                   Include only selected records
   3. None            3. Record number         Binary mode, reclen 80
   4. Create dynamic  4. Formatted key         Create audit trail
```

Now you will see this screen. Notice the format is TABL which shows the data in list format. If you want to change it to show one record at a time, type over the TABL with SNGL (which means single record).

```
Edit                USER01.EMPLOYEE                          Top of 6
Command ===>                                                Scroll PAGE
      Key                     Type KSDS      RBA            Format TABL
         EMP-ID EMP-LAST-NAME                EMP-FIRST-NAME EMP-SERVICE-
            #2 #3                            #4                       #5
         ZD 1:4 AN 5:30                      AN 35:20          ZD 55:2
         <--->  <---+----1----+----2----+----> <---+----1----+----> <->
****** **** Top of data ****
000001  1122 JENKINS                       DEBORAH                 5
000002  3217 JOHNSON                       EDWARD                  4
000003  4720 SCHULTZ                       TIM                     9
000004  6288 WILLARD                       JOE                     6
000005  7459 STEWART                       BETTY                   7
000006  9134 FRANKLIN                      BRIANNA                 3
****** **** End of data ****
```

Now you can edit each field on the record except the key. You cannot change the key, although you can specify a different key to bring up a different record. Let's bring up employee 6288.

```
Edit                USER01.EMPLOYEE                          Rec 1 of 6
Command ===>                                                Scroll PAGE
Key 1122                    Type KSDS      RBA 0            Format SNGL
                                              Top Line is 1    of 6
Current 01: EMPLOYEE                          Length 80
Field                  Data
EMP-ID                  1122
EMP-LAST-NAME          JENKINS
EMP-FIRST-NAME         DEBORAH
EMP-SERVICE-YEARS        5
EMP-PROMOTION-DATE    2016-09-01
FILLER
***  End of record  ***
```

Now we can change this record. Let's modify the years of service by changing it to 8.

```
Edit              USER01.EMPLOYEE                      Rec 4 of 6
Command ===>                                             Scroll PAGE
Key 6288                    Type KSDS     RBA 240        Format SNGL
                                             Top Line is 1   of 6
Current 01: EMPLOYEE                                    Length 80
Field                 Data
EMP-ID                  6288
EMP-LAST-NAME         WILLARD
EMP-FIRST-NAME        JOE
EMP-SERVICE-YEARS       6
EMP-PROMOTION-DATE    2016-01-01
FILLER
***   End of record ***
```

Now you can either type SAVE on the command line or simply PF3 to exit from the record. In this case, let's press PF3 to exit the Edit screen. You will be notified that the record was updated by the message on the upper right portion of the screen.

```
File Manager               Edit Entry Panel        1 record(s) updated
Command ===>

Input Partitioned, Sequential or VSAM Data Set, or HFS file:
   Data set/path name 'USER01.EMPLOYEE'                              +
   Member . . . . . .           (Blank or pattern for member list)
   Volume serial  . .           (If not cataloged)
   Start position . .                              +
   Record limit . . .           Record sampling
   Inplace edit . . .           (Prevent inserts and deletes)
Copybook or Template:
   Data set name  . . 'USER01.COPYLIB(EMPLOYEE)'
   Member . . . . . .           (Blank or pattern for member list)
Processing Options:
 Copybook/template   Start position type   Enter "/" to select option
 1  1. Above            1. Key              Edit template    Type (1,2,S)
    2. Previous         2. RBA              Include only selected records
    3. None             3. Record number    Binary mode, reclen 80
    4. Create dynamic   4. Formatted key    Create audit trail
```

Now let's see how we can insert and delete records. Actually it is pretty simple. If you are in table mode, you just use the I(nsert) command to insert a record, or the D(elete) command to delete one. Let's add a record for employee 1111 who is Sandra Smith with 9 years of service and a promotion date of 01/01/2017. To do this, type I on the first line of detail.

```
Edit                USER01.EMPLOYEE                              Rec 1 of 6
Command ===>                                                    Scroll PAGE
     Key 1122                  Type KSDS      RBA 0             Format TABL
         EMP-ID EMP-LAST-NAME                 EMP-FIRST-NAME    EMP-SERVICE-
           #2 #3                               #4                        #5
         ZD 1:4 AN 5:30                        AN 35:20             ZD 55:2
         <--->  <---+----1----+----2----+----> <---+----1----+----->   <->
I00001   1122 JENKINS                          DEBORAH                    5
000002   3217 JOHNSON                          EDWARD                     4
000003   4720 SCHULTZ                          TIM                        9
000004   6288 WILLARD                          JOE                        8
000005   7459 STEWART                          BETTY                      7
000006   9134 FRANKLIN                         BRIANNA                    3
****** ****   End of data   ****
```

Now you can enter the data. You will need to scroll to the right (PF11) to add the
correct years of service and promotion date.

```
Edit                USER01.EMPLOYEE                              Rec 1 of 7
Command ===>                                                    Scroll PAGE
     Key 1122                  Type KSDS      RBA 0             Format TABL
         EMP-ID EMP-LAST-NAME                 EMP-FIRST-NAME    EMP-SERVICE-
           #2 #3                               #4                        #5
         ZD 1:4 AN 5:30                        AN 35:20             ZD 55:2
         <--->  <---+----1----+----2----+----> <---+----1----+----->   <->
000001   1122 JENKINS                          DEBORAH                    5
000002   1111 SMITH                            SANDRA                     0
000003   3217 JOHNSON                          EDWARD                     4
000004   4720 SCHULTZ                          TIM                        9
000005   6288 WILLARD                          JOE                        8
000006   7459 STEWART                          BETTY                      7
000007   9134 FRANKLIN                         BRIANNA                    3
****** ****   End of data   ****
```

You could also switch to SNGL mode to make it easier to enter the data on one page.

```
Edit                USER01.EMPLOYEE                              Rec 1 of 7
Command ===>                                                    Scroll PAGE
Key 1111                      Type KSDS      RBA 0             Format SNGL
                                              Top Line is 1      of 6
Current 01: EMPLOYEE                          Length 80
Field                Data
EMP-ID                1111
EMP-LAST-NAME        SMITH
EMP-FIRST-NAME       SANDRA
EMP-SERVICE-YEARS      9
EMP-PROMOTION-DATE   2017-01-01
FILLER
***  End of record  ***
```

Now type SAVE on the command line.

```
Edit                USER01.EMPLOYEE                         Rec 1 of 7
Command ===>         SAVE                                    Scroll PAGE
Key 1111                      Type KSDS     RBA 0           Format SNGL
                                                 Top Line is 1    of 6
Current 01: EMPLOYEE                                        Length 80
Field                 Data
EMP-ID                 1111
EMP-LAST-NAME         SMITH
EMP-FIRST-NAME        SANDRA
EMP-SERVICE-YEARS       9
EMP-PROMOTION-DATE    2017-01-01
FILLER
***  End of record  ***
```

When you press Enter you can verify the record was saved.

```
Edit                USER01.EMPLOYEE                1 record(s) updated
Command ===>                                            Scroll PAGE
Key 1111                      Type KSDS     RBA 0           Format SNGL
                                                 Top Line is 1    of 6
Current 01: EMPLOYEE                                       Length 80
Field                 Data
EMP-ID                 1111
EMP-LAST-NAME         SMITH
EMP-FIRST-NAME        SANDRA
EMP-SERVICE-YEARS       9
EMP-PROMOTION-DATE    2017-01-01
FILLER
***  End of record  ***
```

Finally, to delete a record, just go to TABL mode, find the record you want to delete, and use a D action. Let's delete the record we just added.

```
Edit                USER01.EMPLOYEE                          Rec 1 of 7
Command ===>                                               Scroll PAGE
       Key 1111                  Type KSDS    RBA 0        Format TABL
         EMP-ID EMP-LAST-NAME                 EMP-FIRST-NAME  EMP-SERVICE-
            #2 #3                             #4                       #5
            ZD 1:4 AN 5:30                    AN 35:20          ZD 55:2
            <--->  <---+----1----+----2----+----> <---+----1----+----> <->
D00001   1111 SMITH                        SANDRA                     9
000002   1122 JENKINS                      DEBORAH                    5
000003   3217 JOHNSON                      EDWARD                     4
000004   4720 SCHULTZ                      TIM                        9
000005   6288 WILLARD                      JOE                        8
000006   7459 STEWART                      BETTY                      7
000007   9134 FRANKLIN                     BRIANNA                    3
****** ****  End of data   ****
```

When you press Enter, the record will disappear from the list. You can either type SAVE on the command line, or simply exit the file and the delete action will be saved.

```
Edit                USER01.EMPLOYEE                1 record(s) updated
Command ===>                                               Scroll PAGE
       Key 1122                  Type KSDS    RBA 80       Format TABL
         EMP-ID EMP-LAST-NAME                 EMP-FIRST-NAME  EMP-SERVICE-
            #2 #3                             #4                       #5
            ZD 1:4 AN 5:30                    AN 35:20          ZD 55:2
            <--->  <---+----1----+----2----+----> <---+----1----+----> <->
000001   1122 JENKINS                      DEBORAH                    5
000002   3217 JOHNSON                      EDWARD                     4
000003   4720 SCHULTZ                      TIM                        9
000004   6288 WILLARD                      JOE                        8
000005   7459 STEWART                      BETTY                      7
000006   9134 FRANKLIN                     BRIANNA                    3
****** ****  End of data   ****
```

Application Programming with VSAM

PLI Program to Read Records (PLIVS1)

Now it's time to use VSAM in an application program. A program to retrieve a record is not much different from reading a flat file. The main difference is that with VSAM you specify the key value of the record you want to retrieve. Let's name our first program PLIVS1.

In our file definition, we must reference the JCL DD name of the VSAM cluster name. In PLI we define the VSAM file by specifying DIRECT INPUT KEYED and additionally ENV(VSAM). We also intercept certain PLI oncodes to detect conditions such as **record not found**, and **duplicate record**. We specify the record key in PLI using the READ statement.

```
READ FILE (EMPVSFIL) INTO (EMPLOYEE) KEY(EMP_ID);
```

Here is the PLI source code:

```
PLIVS1: PROC OPTIONS(MAIN) REORDER;
/******************************************************************
* PROGRAM NAME :  PROGRAM TO READ A RECORD FROM A VSAM FILE.     *
******************************************************************/

/******************************************************************
/*              F I L E S    U S E D                             *
******************************************************************/

   DCL EMPVSFIL FILE RECORD DIRECT INPUT KEYED ENV(VSAM);

/******************************************************************
/*              W O R K I N G    S T O R A G E                   *
******************************************************************/

   DCL SW_END_OF_FILE            STATIC BIT(01) INIT('0'B);


   DCL 01  EMPLOYEE,
           05 EMP_ID             PIC'9999',
           05 EMP_LAST_NAME      CHAR (30),
           05 EMP_FIRST_NAME     CHAR (20),
           05 EMP_SERVICE_YEARS  PIC  '99',
           05 EMP_PROMOTION_DATE CHAR (10),
           05 FILLER             CHAR (14);

/******************************************************************
/*              O N    C O N D I T I O N S                       *
******************************************************************/
```

103

```
    ON ENDFILE (EMPVSFIL) SW_END_OF_FILE =  '1'B;

    ON KEY(EMPVSFIL) BEGIN;
       IF ONCODE=51 THEN PUT SKIP LIST ('NOT FOUND ' || EMP_ID);
       IF ONCODE=52 THEN PUT SKIP LIST ('DUPLICATE ' || EMP_ID);
    END;

/**********************************************************************
/*                 P R O G R A M   M A I N L I N E                  *
 *********************************************************************/

CALL P100_INITIALIZATION;
CALL P200_MAINLINE;
CALL P300_TERMINATION;

P100_INITIALIZATION: PROC;

    PUT SKIP LIST ('PLIVS1: VSAM FILE INPUT');
    OPEN FILE (EMPVSFIL);
    EMPLOYEE = '';

END P100_INITIALIZATION;

P200_MAINLINE: PROC;

    /*  READ THE INPUT FILE, AND WRITE THE RECORD TO OUTPUT */

    EMP_ID = '3217';
    READ FILE (EMPVSFIL) INTO (EMPLOYEE) KEY(EMP_ID);
    PUT SKIP DATA (EMPLOYEE);

END P200_MAINLINE;

P300_TERMINATION: PROC;

    CLOSE FILE(EMPVSFIL);
    PUT SKIP LIST ('PLIVS1 - SUCCESSFULLY ENDED');

END P300_TERMINATION;

END PLIVS1;
```

Compile and link (according to the procedures in your installation), and then run the program. Here is our output:

```
PLIVS1: VSAM FILE INPUT
EMPLOYEE.EMP_ID=3217    EMPLOYEE.EMP_LAST_NAME='JOHNSON                    '
EMPLOYEE.EMP_FIRST_NAME='EDWARD           '  EMPLOYEE.EMP_SERVICE_YEARS=04
EMPLOYEE.EMP_PROMOTION_DATE='2017-01-01'     EMPLOYEE.FILLER='493082938      '
PLIVS1 - SUCCESSFULLY ENDED
```

PLI Program to Add Records (PLIVS2)

Now let's do a program `PLIVS2` to add a record. Let's add employee 1111 who is Sandra Smith with 9 years of service and a promotion date of 01/01/2017.

To add records, we must define the file for output. Then we simply load the record structure, and then do the WRITE. Also we've set an **ON KEY** condition to trap a duplicate record condition (oncode 52). If a dup is encountered then we set an error switch. Here's how the add program will look.

```
PLIVS2: PROC OPTIONS(MAIN) REORDER;
/***************************************************************
* PROGRAM NAME :   PROGRAM TO ADD A RECORD TO A VSAM FILE.     *
****************************************************************/

    DCL ONCODE BUILTIN;

/***************************************************************
/*                F I L E S    U S E D                         *
****************************************************************/

    DCL EMPVSFIL FILE RECORD DIRECT OUTPUT KEYED ENV(VSAM);

/***************************************************************
/*            W O R K I N G    S T O R A G E                   *
****************************************************************/

    DCL SW_END_OF_FILE          STATIC BIT(01) INIT('0'B);

    DCL SW__IO_ERROR            STATIC BIT(01) INIT('0'B);

    DCL 01   EMPLOYEE,
             05 EMP_ID                PIC'9999',
             05 EMP_LAST_NAME         CHAR (30),
             05 EMP_FIRST_NAME        CHAR (20),
             05 EMP_SERVICE_YEARS     PIC  '99',
             05 EMP_PROMOTION_DATE    CHAR (10),
             05 FILLER                CHAR (14);
/***************************************************************
/*            O N    C O N D I T I O N S                       *
****************************************************************/

    ON ENDFILE (EMPVSFIL) SW_END_OF_FILE =  '1'B;

    ON KEY(EMPVSFIL) BEGIN;
       SELECT(ONCODE);
          WHEN (51)
             DO;
                PUT SKIP LIST ('KEY NOT FOUND ' || EMP_ID);
                SW_IO_ERROR = '1'B;
             END;
```

```
            WHEN (52)
               DO;
                   PUT SKIP LIST ('DUPLICATE KEY ' || EMP_ID);
                   SW_IO_ERROR = '1'B;
               END;
            OTHERWISE;

         END; /* SELECT */

      END; /*  ON KEY  */

/*******************************************************************
/*              P R O G R A M   M A I N L I N E             *
*******************************************************************/

CALL P100_INITIALIZATION;
CALL P200_MAINLINE;
CALL P300_TERMINATION;

P100_INITIALIZATION: PROC;

    PUT SKIP LIST ('PLIVS2: VSAM FILE ADD');
    OPEN FILE (EMPVSFIL);
    EMPLOYEE = '';
    SW_ERROR =  '0'B;

END P100_INITIALIZATION;

P200_MAINLINE: PROC;

    /*  WRITE THE RECORD TO OUTPUT */

    EMP_ID = '1111';
    EMP_LAST_NAME   = 'SMITH';
    EMP_FIRST_NAME  = 'SANDRA';
    EMP_SERVICE_YEARS = '09';
    EMP_PROMOTION_DATE = '2017-01-01';

    WRITE FILE (EMPVSFIL) FROM (EMPLOYEE) KEYFROM(EMP_ID);

    IF SW_IO_ERROR THEN
       PUT SKIP LIST ('ADD FAILED FOR EMPLOYEE ' || EMP_ID);
    ELSE
       PUT SKIP LIST ('SUCCESSFUL ADD FOR EMPLOYEE ' || EMP_ID);

END P200_MAINLINE;

P300_TERMINATION: PROC;

    CLOSE FILE(EMPVSFIL);

    PUT SKIP LIST ('PLIVS2 - SUCCESSFULLY ENDED');
```

```
END P300_TERMINATION;

END PLIVS2;
```

And here is the result:

```
PLIVS2: VSAM FILE INPUT
SUCCESSFUL ADD FOR RECORD 1111
PLIVS2 - SUCCESSFULLY ENDED
```

We can verify that the record was added by checking File Manager.

```
View              USER01.EMPLOYEE                       Top of 7
Command ===>                                            Scroll PAGE
    Key                     Type KSDS   RBA             Format TABL
      EMP-ID EMP-LAST-NAME               EMP-FIRST-NAME EMP-SERVICE-
          #2 #3                          #4                       #5
          ZD 1:4 AN 5:30                 AN 35:20        ZD 55:2
          <---> <---+----1----+----2----+----> <---+----1----+----> <->
****** **** Top of data   ****
000001    1111 SMITH                     SANDRA                   9
000002    1122 JENKINS                   DEBORAH                  5
000003    3217 JOHNSON                   EDWARD                   4
000004    4720 SCHULTZ                   TIM                      9
000005    6288 WILLARD                   JOE                      8
000006    7459 STEWART                   BETTY                    7
000007    9134 FRANKLIN                  BRIANNA                  3
****** ****   End of data   ****
```

We can also test the duplicate record logic by running the program a second time. This time, our output is as follows:

```
PLIVS2: VSAM FILE ADD
DUPLICATE KEY 1111
ADD FAILED FOR EMPLOYEE 1111
PLIVS2 - SUCCESSFULLY ENDED
```

Great, it correctly reported the error. Always test your error logic to make sure it works!

PLI Program to Update Records (PLIVS3)

For PLIVS3 we will update a record. To do that we must first read the record into the record structure, make modifications and then REWRITE the record. Let's say we need to change the years of service for Sandra Smith from 9 to 10. Here is a program that would do this. Notice we define the VSAM file for update.

```
PLIVS3: PROC OPTIONS(MAIN) REORDER;
/*********************************************************************
* PROGRAM NAME :  PLIVS3 PROGRAM TO UPDATE A RECORD ON A VSAM FILE.*
**********************************************************************/

/*********************************************************************
/*               F I L E S   U S E D                              *
**********************************************************************/

   DCL EMPVSFIL FILE RECORD DIRECT UPDATE KEYED ENV(VSAM);

/*********************************************************************
/*               W O R K I N G   S T O R A G E                    *
**********************************************************************/

   DCL ONCODE                 BUILTIN;

   DCL SW_IO_ERROR            STATIC BIT(01) INIT('0'B);

   DCL 01   EMPLOYEE,
            05 EMP_ID               PIC'9999',
            05 EMP_LAST_NAME        CHAR (30),
            05 EMP_FIRST_NAME       CHAR (20),
            05 EMP_SERVICE_YEARS    PIC  '99',
            05 EMP_PROMOTION_DATE   CHAR (10),
            05 FILLER               CHAR (14);

/*********************************************************************
/*               O N   C O N D I T I O N S                        *
**********************************************************************/

   ON KEY(EMPVSFIL) BEGIN;
      SELECT(ONCODE);
         WHEN (51)
            DO;
               PUT SKIP LIST ('KEY NOT FOUND ' || EMP_ID);
               SW_IO_ERROR = '1'B;
            END;
         WHEN (52)
            DO;
               PUT SKIP LIST ('DUPLICATE KEY ' || EMP_ID);
               SW_IO_ERROR = '1'B;
            END;
         OTHERWISE;

      END; /* SELECT */

   END; /* ON KEY */

/*********************************************************************
/*               P R O G R A M   M A I N L I N E                  *
**********************************************************************/
```

108

```
CALL P100_INITIALIZATION;
CALL P200_MAINLINE;
CALL P300_TERMINATION;

P100_INITIALIZATION: PROC;

    PUT SKIP LIST ('PLIVS3: VSAM FILE UPDATE');
    OPEN FILE (EMPVSFIL);
    EMPLOYEE = '';

END P100_INITIALIZATION;

P200_MAINLINE: PROC;

    /*  WRITE THE RECORD TO OUTPUT */

    EMP_ID = '1111';
    READ FILE (EMPVSFIL) INTO (EMPLOYEE) KEY(EMP_ID);

    IF SW_IO_ERROR THEN
       DO;
           PUT SKIP LIST ('ERROR - RECORD NOT UPDATED');
           RETURN;
       END;

    EMP_SERVICE_YEARS = '10';

    REWRITE FILE (EMPVSFIL) FROM(EMPLOYEE) KEY(EMP_ID);

    IF SW_IO_ERROR THEN
       PUT SKIP LIST ('ERROR - RECORD NOT UPDATED');
    ELSE
       PUT SKIP LIST ('SUCCESSFUL REWRITE FOR EMPLOYEE '
           || EMP_ID);

END P200_MAINLINE;

P300_TERMINATION: PROC;

    CLOSE FILE(EMPVSFIL);

    PUT SKIP LIST ('PLIVS3 - SUCCESSFULLY ENDED');

END P300_TERMINATION;

END PLIVS3;
```

Now let's compile, link and run. Here's the output.

```
PLIVS3: VSAM FILE UPDATE
SUCCESSFUL UPDATE FOR RECORD 1111
EMPLOYEE.EMP_ID=1111    EMPLOYEE.EMP_LAST_NAME='SMITH                 '
```

And we can verify that the change took place by checking in File Manager.

```
View              USER01.EMPLOYEE                      Rec 1 of 7
 Command ===>                                          Scroll PAGE
 Key 1111                  Type KSDS    RBA 0          Format SNGL
                                          Top Line is 1    of 6
 Current 01: EMPLOYEE                               Length 80
 Field             Data
 EMP-ID              1111
 EMP-LAST-NAME       SMITH
 EMP-FIRST-NAME      SANDRA
 EMP-SERVICE-YEARS   10
 EMP-PROMOTION-DATE  2017-01-01
 FILLER              ..............
 ***  End of record  ***
```

PLI Program to Delete Records (PLIVS4)

Now let's write program PLIVS4 to delete the Sandra Smith record we just worked with. Actually it will be similar to the update program, except we don't have to first retrieve the record before deleting. And of course we will use the verb DELETE instead of REWRITE.

```
PLIVS4: PROC OPTIONS(MAIN) REORDER;
/*****************************************************************
* PROGRAM NAME :  PROGRAM TO DELETE A RECORD ON A VSAM FILE.     *
*****************************************************************/

/*****************************************************************
/*              F I L E S    U S E D                             *
*****************************************************************/

   DCL EMPVSFIL FILE RECORD DIRECT UPDATE KEYED ENV(VSAM);

/*****************************************************************
/*              W O R K I N G    S T O R A G E                   *
*****************************************************************/

   DCL ONCODE                 BUILTIN;
   DCL SW_IO_ERROR            STATIC BIT(01) INIT('0'B);
   DCL SW_END_OF_FILE         STATIC BIT(01) INIT('0'B);

   DCL 01  EMPLOYEE,
           05 EMP_ID              PIC'9999',
           05 EMP_LAST_NAME       CHAR (30),
           05 EMP_FIRST_NAME      CHAR (20),
           05 EMP_SERVICE_YEARS   PIC '99',
           05 EMP_PROMOTION_DATE  CHAR (10),
           05 FILLER              CHAR (14);
```

110

```
/*******************************************************************
/*                    O N   C O N D I T I O N S                   *
*******************************************************************/

   ON KEY(EMPVSFIL) BEGIN;
      SELECT(ONCODE);
         WHEN (51)
            DO;
            PUT SKIP LIST ('KEY NOT FOUND ' || EMP_ID);
            SW_IO_ERROR = '1'B;
            END;
         WHEN (52)
            DO;
               PUT SKIP LIST ('DUPLICATE KEY ' || EMP_ID);
               SW_IO_ERROR = '1'B;
            END;

         OTHERWISE;

      END; /* SELECT */

   END; /* ON KEY */

/*******************************************************************
/*                  P R O G R A M   M A I N L I N E               *
*******************************************************************/

CALL P100_INITIALIZATION;
CALL P200_MAINLINE;
CALL P300_TERMINATION;

P100_INITIALIZATION: PROC;

   PUT SKIP LIST ('PLIVS4: VSAM FILE DELETE');
   OPEN FILE (EMPVSFIL);
   EMPLOYEE = '';

END P100_INITIALIZATION;

P200_MAINLINE: PROC;

   /* SET THE RECORD KEY AND THEN DELETE THE RECORD */

   EMP_ID = '1111';
   DELETE FILE(EMPVSFIL) KEY(EMP_ID);

   IF SW_IO_ERROR THEN
      PUT SKIP LIST ('ERROR - RECORD NOT DELETED');
   ELSE
      PUT SKIP LIST ('SUCCESSFUL DELETE OF EMPLOYEE '
         || EMP_ID);

END P200_MAINLINE;
```

```
P300_TERMINATION: PROC;

    CLOSE FILE(EMPVSFIL);

    PUT SKIP LIST ('PLIVS4 - SUCCESSFULLY ENDED');

END P300_TERMINATION;

END PLIVS4;
```

And here is the output.

```
PLIVS4: VSAM FILE DELETE
SUCCESSFUL DELETE OF EMPLOYEE 1111
PLIVS4 - SUCCESSFULLY ENDED
```

And we can verify that the record was deleted by checking in File Manager. As we can see, there is no longer an employee 1111.

```
View            USER01.EMPLOYEE                         Rec 1 of 6
Command ===>                                            Scroll PAGE
    Key 1122               Type KSDS     RBA 0          Format TABL
        EMP-ID EMP-LAST-NAME                 EMP-FIRST-NAME  EMP-SERVICE-
           #2 #3                             #4                    #5
        ZD 1:4 AN 5:30                       AN 35:20         ZD 55:2
        <---> <---+----1----+----2----+----> <---+----1----+---->   <->
000001   1122 JENKINS                        DEBORAH               5
000002   3217 JOHNSON                        EDWARD                4
000003   4720 SCHULTZ                        TIM                   9
000004   6288 WILLARD                        JOE                   8
000005   7459 STEWART                        BETTY                 7
000006   9134 FRANKLIN                       BRIANNA               3
****** ****  End of data   ****
```

Let's test the error logic by running the delete a second time. This branches to the ONCODE logic that sets an error switch and announces that the delete was not successful.

```
PLIVS4: VSAM FILE DELETE
KEY NOT FOUND 1111
ERROR - RECORD NOT DELETED
PLIVS4 - SUCCESSFULLY ENDED
```

The delete error logic works. Let's also go back and check the update error logic in PLIVS3 that updates the same record. As with the delete action, the update should now fail because the record is not there.

```
PLIVS3: VSAM FILE UPDATE
KEY NOT FOUND 1111
ERROR - RECORD NOT UPDATED
```

If course, you could do more by stating that file status 23 means a requested record was not found. You could even define the various file status codes in working storage with a description (see table at the end of this chapter), and display the text as an error message.

All is working, great. Let's move on!

PLI Program to Retrieve Records Sequentially (PLIVS5)

Now let's read all of the records sequentially with program PLIVS5. We will need to define the file for sequential access, and we'll use a loop which will stop when we reach end of file.

```
PLIVS5: PROC OPTIONS(MAIN) REORDER;
 /***********************************************************************
 * PROGRAM NAME :   PROGRAM TO READ SEQUENTIALLY FROM A VSAM FILE.    *
 ***********************************************************************/

 /***********************************************************************
 /*                  F I L E S    U S E D                             *
 ***********************************************************************/

    DCL EMPVSFIL FILE RECORD SEQUENTIAL INPUT KEYED ENV(VSAM);

 /***********************************************************************
 /*                W O R K I N G    S T O R A G E                    *
 ***********************************************************************/

    DCL ONCODE                    BUILTIN;

    DCL SW_END_OF_FILE            STATIC BIT(01) INIT('0'B);

    DCL 01   EMPLOYEE,
             05 EMP_ID            PIC'9999',
             05 EMP_LAST_NAME     CHAR (30),
             05 EMP_FIRST_NAME    CHAR (20),
             05 EMP_SERVICE_YEARS PIC  '99',
             05 EMP_PROMOTION_DATE CHAR (10),
             05 FILLER            CHAR (14);

 /***********************************************************************
 /*                O N    C O N D I T I O N S                        *
 ***********************************************************************/

    ON ENDFILE (EMPVSFIL) SW_END_OF_FILE = '1'B;

 /***********************************************************************
 /*                P R O G R A M    M A I N L I N E                  *
 ***********************************************************************/
```

113

```
CALL P100_INITIALIZATION;
CALL P200_MAINLINE;
CALL P300_TERMINATION;

P100_INITIALIZATION: PROC;

    PUT SKIP LIST ('PLIVS5: VSAM READ LOOP');
    OPEN FILE (EMPVSFIL);
    EMPLOYEE = '';

END P100_INITIALIZATION;

P200_MAINLINE: PROC;

    /*  DO PRIMING READ THE INPUT FILE */

    READ FILE (EMPVSFIL) INTO (EMPLOYEE);

    IF SW_END_OF_FILE THEN
       PUT SKIP LIST ('NO RECORDS IN FILE');
    ELSE
       DO WHILE (¬SW_END_OF_FILE);

          /*  DISPLAY THE DATA VALUES */

          PUT SKIP DATA (EMPLOYEE);

          READ FILE (EMPVSFIL) INTO (EMPLOYEE);

          IF SW_END_OF_FILE THEN
             PUT SKIP LIST ('END OF FILE ENCOUNTERED');

       END; /* DO UNTIL */

END P200_MAINLINE;

P300_TERMINATION: PROC;

    CLOSE FILE(EMPVSFIL);

    PUT SKIP LIST ('PLIVS5 - SUCCESSFULLY ENDED');

END P300_TERMINATION;

END PLIVS5;
```

Compile, link, run, and here is the output:

```
PLIVS5: VSAM READ LOOP
EMPLOYEE.EMP_ID=1122     EMPLOYEE.EMP_LAST_NAME='JENKINS              '
EMPLOYEE.EMP_FIRST_NAME='DEBORAH             '  EMPLOYEE.EMP_SERVICE_YEARS=05
EMPLOYEE.EMP_PROMOTION_DATE='2016-09-01'        EMPLOYEE.FILLER='034658724    '
EMPLOYEE.EMP_ID=3217     EMPLOYEE.EMP_LAST_NAME='JOHNSON              '
```

```
EMPLOYEE.EMP_FIRST_NAME='EDWARD              '  EMPLOYEE.EMP_SERVICE_YEARS=04
EMPLOYEE.EMP_PROMOTION_DATE='2017-01-01'         EMPLOYEE.FILLER='493082938      '
EMPLOYEE.EMP_ID=4720    EMPLOYEE.EMP_LAST_NAME='SCHULTZ                       '
EMPLOYEE.EMP_FIRST_NAME='TIM                 '  EMPLOYEE.EMP_SERVICE_YEARS=09
EMPLOYEE.EMP_PROMOTION_DATE='2017-01-01'         EMPLOYEE.FILLER='209482059      '
EMPLOYEE.EMP_ID=6288    EMPLOYEE.EMP_LAST_NAME='WILLARD                       '
EMPLOYEE.EMP_FIRST_NAME='JOE                 '  EMPLOYEE.EMP_SERVICE_YEARS=08
EMPLOYEE.EMP_PROMOTION_DATE='2016-01-01'         EMPLOYEE.FILLER='030467384      '
EMPLOYEE.EMP_ID=7459    EMPLOYEE.EMP_LAST_NAME='STEWART                       '
EMPLOYEE.EMP_FIRST_NAME='BETTY               '  EMPLOYEE.EMP_SERVICE_YEARS=07
EMPLOYEE.EMP_PROMOTION_DATE='2016-07-31'         EMPLOYEE.FILLER='991837283      '
EMPLOYEE.EMP_ID=9134    EMPLOYEE.EMP_LAST_NAME='FRANKLIN                      '
EMPLOYEE.EMP_FIRST_NAME='BRIANNA             '  EMPLOYEE.EMP_SERVICE_YEARS=03
EMPLOYEE.EMP_PROMOTION_DATE='2016-10-01'         EMPLOYEE.FILLER='333073948      '
END OF FILE ENCOUNTERED
PLIVS5 - SUCCESSFULLY ENDED
```

This is a model you can use whenever you need to cycle through a VSAM file sequentially. It should prove useful.

Creating and Accessing Alternate Indexes

So far we've dealt with a VSAM file that has a single index which is associated with the key. Suppose however that you need another index on a file? That is, you need to randomly access your data using another field from the file? You can do this with VSAM, and you can access the data via the alternate index in application programs.

Suppose we want to add a social security number field to our EMPLOYEE file, and that we want an alternate index on it. To do this we will do the following:

1. Modify our file layout to include a social security number field named EMP-SSN.

2. Reload the EMPLOYEE VSAM file to include the social security numbers.

3. Create the alternate index which will be named EMPSSN.

4. Build and test the alternate index.

First, let's update our file layout in the EMPLOYEE copybook. Here it is with the EMP_SSN added.

```
DCL 01  EMPLOYEE,
        05 EMP_ID              PIC'9999',
        05 EMP_LAST_NAME       CHAR (30),
        05 EMP_FIRST_NAME      CHAR (20),
        05 EMP_SERVICE_YEARS   PIC  '99',
        05 EMP_PROMOTION_DATE  CHAR (10),
        05 EMP_SSN             CHAR (09),
        05 FILLER              CHAR (05);
```

115

Then we could add the social security numbers through File Manager. Another alternative is to unload the data first into a flat file, add the social security number values to the flat file, and then scratch and recreate the VSAM file (using the revised unload file. If you want to do the unload, here is some sample JCL.

```
//USER01D JOB 'WINGATE',MSGLEVEL=(1,1),NOTIFY=&SYSUID
//*
//***********************************************************
//* UNLOAD DATA FROM VSAM KSDS TO PS DATA SET
//***********************************************************
//JS010     EXEC PGM=IDCAMS
//SYSPRINT DD SYSOUT=*
//SYSOUT    DD SYSOUT=*
//DD1       DD DSN=USER01.EMPLOYEE,DISP=SHR
//DD2       DD DSN=USER01.EMPLOYEE.UNLOAD,
//             DISP=(NEW,CATLG,DELETE),
//             SPACE=(TRK,(1,1),RLSE),
//             UNIT=SYSDA,VOL=SER=DEVHD1,
//             DCB=(DSORG=PS,RECFM=FB,LRECL=80,BLKSIZE=27920)
//SYSIN     DD *
  REPRO -
  INFILE(DD1) -
  OUTFILE(DD2)
/*
```

I'm going to use File Manager instead. Here's the first record. I am of course adding random nine digit numbers here, not real social security numbers.

```
Edit              USER01.EMPLOYEE                    Rec 1 of 6
Command ===>                                         Scroll PAGE
Key 1122              Type KSDS     RBA 0            Format SNGL
                                          Top Line is 1   of 7
Current 01: EMPLOYEE                                 Length 80
Field               Data
EMP-ID              1122
EMP-LAST-NAME       JENKINS
EMP-FIRST-NAME      DEBORAH
EMP-SERVICE-YEARS    5
EMP-PROMOTION-DATE  2016-09-01
EMP_SSN             034658724
FILLER
*** End of record  ***
```

Once I've finished adding SSNs, I will verify that all six records have them.

```
   Edit              USER01.EMPLOYEE                      Rec 1 of 6
   Command ===>                                           Scroll PAGE
        Key 1122              Type KSDS     RBA 0          Format TABL
        EMP-SERVICE-YEARS EMP-PROMOTION-DATE EMP_SSN    FILLER
                   #5 #6                      #7         #8
                   ZD 55:2 AN 57:10           AN 67:9    AN 76:5
                   <-> <---+---->             <---+---> <--->
   000001              5 2016-09-01           034658724
   000002              4 2017-01-01           493082938
   000003              9 2017-01-01           209482059
   000004              8 2016-01-01           030467384
   000005              7 2016-07-31           991837283
   000006              3 2016-10-01           333073948
   ****** ****   End of data   ****
```

Now, it's time to build the alternate index. First, we give it a file name and establish the other attributes. We'll give the index file name USER01.EMPLOYEE.ALX. And we will define the key as 9 bytes beginning at displacement 66. That's where the social security number is. We also indicate that it is related to the USER01.EMPLOYEE cluster.

DEFINE PATH is used to relate the alternate index to the base cluster. While defining path we specify the name of the path and the alternate index to which this path is related. This is the actual link between the VSAM cluster and the alternate index.

Finally, the BLDINDEX command is used to build the alternate index. BLDINDEX reads all the records in the VSAM indexed data set (base cluster) and extracts the data needed to build the alternate index.

```
//USER01D JOB 'WINGATE',MSGLEVEL=(1,1),NOTIFY=&SYSUID
//*
//*************************************************************
//* DEFINE ALTERNAME INDEX
//*************************************************************
//JS010    EXEC PGM=IDCAMS
//SYSPRINT DD SYSOUT=*
//SYSOUT   DD SYSOUT=*
//SYSIN    DD  *
  DEFINE AIX  -
  (NAME(USER01.EMPLOYEE.ALX) -
  RELATE(USER01.EMPLOYEE)      -
  CISZ(4096) -
  KEYS(9,66) -
  UNIQUEKEY -
  UPGRADE -
  RECORDSIZE(80,80) -
  TRK(2,1) -
  FREESPACE(10,20) -
  VOLUMES(DEVHD1)    -
```

```
        )
/*
//*
//****************************************************************
//* DEFINE PATH
//****************************************************************
//JS020     EXEC PGM=IDCAMS
//SYSPRINT DD SYSOUT=*
//SYSOUT   DD SYSOUT=*
//SYSIN    DD  *
  DEFINE PATH (NAME(USER01.EMPLOYEE.PATH) -
               PATHENTRY(USER01.EMPLOYEE.ALX) UPDATE
/*
//*
//****************************************************************
//* BUILD INDEX
//****************************************************************
//JS030     EXEC PGM=IDCAMS
//SYSPRINT DD SYSOUT=*
//SYSOUT   DD SYSOUT=*
//SYSIN    DD *
  BLDINDEX -
       INDATASET (USER01.EMPLOYEE) -
       OUTDATASET(USER01.EMPLOYEE.ALX)
/*
//*
```

PLI Program to Read Alternate Index (PLIVS6)

Now we can use this alternate index to randomly access the data using the EMP_SSN field. We'll write program PLIVS6 to demonstrate this. Suppose for example we want to retrieve the record with SSN value 209482059 which is Tim Shultz. We can clone the first program PLIVS1 into PLIVS6. We do need to change a few things.

First our JCL must include a DD name for the PATH associated with the alternate index. When you use an alternate index, the DD name for the PATH must be the same as the DD name for the cluster except that the PATH DD name must have a 1 at the end of it. Since a DD identifier can be a maximum of 8 bytes, we must shorten the DD name of our EMPLOYEE VSAM file (in the program and JCL) to 7 bytes to so we can include a corresponding DD name for the PATH.

We will shorten our cluster DD name to EMPVSFL. We can then define the PATH DD name as EMPVSFL1. Here's our JCL.

```
//USER01D JOB MSGLEVEL=(1,1),NOTIFY=&SYSUID
//*
//*  RUN A PLI PROGRAM
//*
//STEP01  EXEC PGM=PLIVS6
```

```
//STEPLIB  DD  DSN=USER01.LOADLIB,DISP=SHR
//SYSOUT   DD  SYSOUT=*
//EMPVSFL  DD  DSN=USER01.EMPLOYEE,DISP=SHR
//EMPVSFL1 DD  DSN=USER01.EMPLOYEE.PATH,DISP=SHR
//SYSPRINT DD  SYSOUT=*
//SYSUDUMP DD  SYSOUT=*
//SYSOUT   DD  SYSOUT=*
```

Second we need to change the file definition to match the DD name change we made to the JCL (you do not need to declare the main file, but you do need to declare the PATH DD). Here is the code change.

```
DCL EMPVSFL1 FILE RECORD DIRECT INPUT KEYED ENV(VSAM);
```

Finally, we need to establish that the alternate key is to be used in the READ. We specify **KEY(EMP_SSN)** to use the alternate key.

```
READ FILE (EMPVSFL1) INTO (EMPLOYEE) KEY (EMP_SSN);
```

Here is the final program listing with these features:

```
PLIVS6: PROC OPTIONS(MAIN) REORDER;
/****************************************************************
* PROGRAM PURPOSE: PROGRAM TO RETRIEVE RECORD ON A VSAM FILE    *
*                  USING AN ALTERNATE INDEX.                    *
****************************************************************/

/****************************************************************
/*               F I L E S   U S E D                            *
****************************************************************/

   DCL EMPVSFL1 FILE RECORD DIRECT INPUT KEYED ENV(VSAM);

/****************************************************************
/*           W O R K I N G   S T O R A G E                      *
****************************************************************/

   DCL ONCODE                 BUILTIN;

   DCL SW_IO_ERROR            STATIC BIT(01) INIT('0'B);

   DCL 01  EMPLOYEE,
           05 EMP_ID               PIC'9999',
           05 EMP_LAST_NAME        CHAR (30),
           05 EMP_FIRST_NAME       CHAR (20),
           05 EMP_SERVICE_YEARS    PIC  '99',
           05 EMP_PROMOTION_DATE   CHAR (10),
           05 EMP_SSN              CHAR (09),
           05 FILLER               CHAR (05);
```

```
/********************************************************************
/*                  O N   C O N D I T I O N S                      *
********************************************************************/

   ON KEY(EMPVSFL1) BEGIN;
      SELECT(ONCODE);
         WHEN (51)
            DO;
               PUT SKIP LIST ('KEY NOT FOUND ' || EMP_SSN);
               SW_IO_ERROR = '1'B;
            END;
         WHEN (52)
            DO;
               PUT SKIP LIST ('DUPLICATE KEY ' || EMP_SSN);
               SW_IO_ERROR = '1'B;
            END;
         OTHERWISE;

      END; /* SELECT */

   END; /* ON KEY */

/********************************************************************
/*                 P R O G R A M   M A I N L I N E                 *
********************************************************************/

CALL P100_INITIALIZATION;
CALL P200_MAINLINE;
CALL P300_TERMINATION;

P100_INITIALIZATION: PROC;

   PUT SKIP LIST ('PLIVS6: VSAM FILE READ USING ALTERNATE KEY');
   OPEN FILE (EMPVSFL1);
   EMPLOYEE = '';

END P100_INITIALIZATION;

P200_MAINLINE: PROC;

   /*  WRITE THE RECORD TO OUTPUT */

   EMP_SSN = '209482059';
   READ FILE (EMPVSFL1) INTO (EMPLOYEE) KEY (EMP_SSN);

   IF SW_IO_ERROR THEN
      PUT SKIP LIST ('ERROR - RECORD NOT READ');
   ELSE
      DO;
         PUT SKIP LIST ('SUCCESSFUL READ OF EMPLOYEE SSN ' || EMP_SSN);
         PUT SKIP DATA (EMPLOYEE);
      END;
```

120

```
END P200_MAINLINE;

P300_TERMINATION: PROC;

    CLOSE FILE(EMPVSFL1);

    PUT SKIP LIST ('PLIVS6 - SUCCESSFULLY ENDED');

END P300_TERMINATION;

END PLIVS6;
```

Now compile, link, and execute the program. Here's our output.

```
PLIVS6: VSAM FILE READ USING ALTERNATE KEY
SUCCESSFUL READ OF EMPLOYEE SSN 209482059
EMPLOYEE.EMP_ID=4720    EMPLOYEE.EMP_LAST_NAME='SCHULTZ                    '
EMPLOYEE.EMP_FIRST_NAME='TIM              '  EMPLOYEE.EMP_SERVICE_YEARS=09
EMPLOYEE.EMP_PROMOTION_DATE='2017-01-01'     EMPLOYEE.EMP_SSN='209482059'
PLIVS6 - SUCCESSFULLY ENDED
```

Alternate keys give you tremendous flexibility when using VSAM. You can have more than one or more alternate keys on a file and you can specify more than one key in your application programs.

Other VSAM JCL

We haven't gone into much detail about the other file organizations because KSDS is the most common. However, here is some sample JCL for creating the ESDS and RRDS formats.

JCL to CREATE ESDS

```
//****************************************************************
//* DEFINE VSAM ESDS CLUSTER
//****************************************************************
//STEP30   EXEC PGM=IDCAMS
//SYSPRINT DD SYSOUT=*
//SYSOUT   DD SYSOUT=*
//SYSIN    DD  *
  DEFINE CLUSTER(NAME(USER01.TEST.ESDS.CLUSTER)  -
  RECORDSIZE(45,45)     -
  CYLINDERS(2,1)        -
  CISZ(4096)            -
  VOLUMES(DEVHD1)       -
  NONINDEXED)           -
  DATA(NAME(USER01.TEST.ESDS.DATA))
/*
//*
```

JCL to CREATE RRDS

```
//*
//****************************************************************
//* DEFINE VSAM RRDS CLUSTER
//****************************************************************
//STEP40   EXEC PGM=IDCAMS
//SYSPRINT DD SYSOUT=*
//SYSOUT   DD SYSOUT=*
//SYSIN    DD  *
  DEFINE CLUSTER(NAME(USER01.TEST.RRDS.CLUSTER)  -
  RECORDSIZE(45,45)     -
  CYLINDERS(2,1)        -
  NUMBERED)             -
  DATA(NAME(USER01.TEST.RRDS.DATA))
/*
```

JCL to LIST DATASET INFORMATION

```
//USER01L JOB 'WINGATE',MSGLEVEL=(1,1),NOTIFY=&SYSUID
//*
//************************************************************
//* LISTCAT COMMAND
//************************************************************
//STEP110  EXEC PGM=IDCAMS
//SYSPRINT DD SYSOUT=*
//SYSOUT   DD SYSOUT=*
//SYSIN    DD  *
     LISTCAT ENTRIES(USER01.EMPLOYEE) ALL
/*
//*
```

```
IDCAMS  SYSTEM SERVICES                                      TIME: 08:05:59
     LISTCAT ENTRIES(USER01.EMPLOYEE) ALL
CLUSTER ------- USER01.EMPLOYEE
     IN-CAT --- CATALOG.Z113.MASTER
     HISTORY
        DATASET-OWNER-----(NULL)      CREATION--------2018.064
        RELEASE----------------2      EXPIRATION------0000.000
        CA-RECLAIM---------(YES)
        EATTR------------(NULL)
        BWO STATUS--------(NULL)      BWO TIMESTAMP-----(NULL)
        BWO--------------(NULL)
     PROTECTION-PSWD-----(NULL)       RACF---------------(NO)
     ASSOCIATIONS
        DATA-----USER01.EMPLOYEE.DATA
        INDEX----USER01.EMPLOYEE.INDEX
        AIX------USER01.EMPLOYEE.ALX
   DATA ------- USER01.EMPLOYEE.DATA
     IN-CAT --- CATALOG.Z113.MASTER
     HISTORY
DATASET-OWNER-----(NULL)       CREATION--------2018.064
        RELEASE----------------2      EXPIRATION------0000.000
        ACCOUNT-INFO--------------------------------(NULL)
     PROTECTION-PSWD-----(NULL)       RACF---------------(NO)
     ASSOCIATIONS
        CLUSTER--USER01.EMPLOYEE
     ATTRIBUTES
        KEYLEN----------------4       AVGLRECL-------------80       BUFSPACE-------
        RKP-------------------0       MAXLRECL-------------80       EXCPEXIT-------
        SHROPTNS(1,3)  RECOVERY       UNIQUE         NOERASE        INDEXED      N
        NONSPANNED
     STATISTICS  (* - VALUE MAY BE INCORRECT)
        REC-TOTAL-------------7*      SPLITS-CI-------------0*      EXCPS----------
        REC-DELETED-----------9*      SPLITS-CA-------------0*      EXTENTS-------
        REC-INSERTED----------3*      FREESPACE-%CI----------5      SYSTEM-TIMESTAM
        REC-UPDATED----------11*      FREESPACE-%CA---------10          X'D3FD7137
        REC-RETRIEVED-------191*      FREESPC-----------45056*
     ALLOCATION
```

```
      SPACE-TYPE--------TRACK        HI-A-RBA-----------49152
      SPACE-PRI--------------1       HI-U-RBA-----------49152
      SPACE-SEC--------------1
   VOLUME
      VOLSER-----------DEVHD1        PHYREC-SIZE---------4096      HI-A-RBA-------
      DEVTYPE------X'3010200F'       PHYRECS/TRK-----------12      HI-U-RBA-------
      VOLFLAG-----------PRIME        TRACKS/CA--------------1
      EXTENTS:
      LOW-CCHH-----X'00AF000E'       LOW-RBA----------------0      TRACKS---------
      HIGH-CCHH----X'00AF000E'       HIGH-RBA-----------49151
   INDEX ------ USER01.EMPLOYEE.INDEX
      IN-CAT --- CATALOG.Z113.MASTER
      HISTORY
         DATASET-OWNER-----(NULL)    CREATION--------2018.064
         RELEASE---------------2     EXPIRATION------0000.000
      PROTECTION-PSWD-----(NULL)     RACF---------------(NO)
      ASSOCIATIONS
         CLUSTER--USER01.EMPLOYEE
      ATTRIBUTES
         KEYLEN----------------4     AVGLRECL---------------0      BUFSPACE-------
         RKP-------------------0     MAXLRECL-----------4089       EXCPEXIT-------
         SHROPTNS(1,3)   RECOVERY    UNIQUE            NOERASE     NOWRITECHK
      STATISTICS  (* - VALUE MAY BE INCORRECT)
         REC-TOTAL-------------1*    SPLITS-CI--------------0*     EXCPS----------
         REC-DELETED-----------0*    SPLITS-CA--------------0*     EXTENTS--------
         REC-INSERTED----------0*    FREESPACE-%CI----------0      SYSTEM-TIMESTAM
         REC-UPDATED-----------0*    FREESPACE-%CA----------0          X'D3FD7137
         REC-RETRIEVED---------4*    FREESPC-----------45056*
      ALLOCATION
         SPACE-TYPE--------TRACK     HI-A-RBA-----------49152
         SPACE-PRI-------------1     HI-U-RBA------------4096
         SPACE-SEC-------------1
      VOLUME
         VOLSER-----------DEVHD1     PHYREC-SIZE---------4096      HI-A-RBA-------
         DEVTYPE------X'3010200F'    PHYRECS/TRK-----------12      HI-U-RBA-------
         VOLFLAG-----------PRIME     TRACKS/CA--------------1
         EXTENTS:
         LOW-CCHH-----X'00B60007'    LOW-RBA----------------0      TRACKS---------
         HIGH-CCHH----X'00B60007'    HIGH-RBA-----------49151
IDCAMS  SYSTEM SERVICES                                    TIME: 08:05:59
         THE NUMBER OF ENTRIES PROCESSED WAS:
                      AIX -------------------0
                      ALIAS -----------------0
                      CLUSTER ---------------1
                      DATA ------------------1
                      GDG -------------------0
                      INDEX -----------------1
                      NONVSAM ---------------0
                      PAGESPACE -------------0
                      PATH ------------------0
                      SPACE -----------------0
                      USERCATALOG -----------0
                      TAPELIBRARY -----------0
                      TAPEVOLUME ------------0
                      TOTAL -----------------3
           THE NUMBER OF PROTECTED ENTRIES SUPPRESSED WAS 0
IDC0001I FUNCTION COMPLETED, HIGHEST CONDITION CODE WAS 0


IDC0002I IDCAMS PROCESSING COMPLETE. MAXIMUM CONDITION CODE WAS 0
```

VSAM File Status Codes

Here is a list of the VSAM status codes you might encounter.

Code	Description
00	Operation completed successfully
02	Non-Unique Alternate Index duplicate key found
04	Invalid fixed length record
05	While performing OPEN File and file is not present
10	End of File encountered
14	Attempted to READ a relative record outside file boundary
20	Invalid Key for VSAM KSDS or RRDS
21	Sequence error while performing WRITE or changing key on REWRITE
22	Primary duplicate Key found
23	Record not found or File not found
24	Key outside boundary of file
30	Permanent I/O Error
34	Record outside file boundary
35	While performing OPEN File and file is not present
37	OPEN file with wrong mode
38	Tried to OPEN a Locked file
39	OPEN failed because of conflicting file attributes

41 Tried to OPEN a file that is already open

42 Tried to CLOSE a file that is not OPEN

43 Tried to REWRITE without READing a record first

44 Tried to REWRITE a record of a different length

46 Tried to READ beyond End-of-file

47 Tried to READ from a file that was not opened I-O or INPUT

48 Tried to WRITE to a file that was not opened I-O or OUTPUT

49 Tried to DELETE or REWRITE to a file that was not opened I-O

91 Password or authorization failed

92 Logic Error

93 Resources are not available

94 Sequential record unavailable or concurrent OPEN error

95 File Information invalid or incomplete

96 No DD statement for the file

97 OPEN successful and file integrity verified

98 File is Locked - OPEN failed

99 Record Locked - record access failed

Chapter Two Questions

1. What are the three types of VSAM datasets?

2. How are records stored in an ESDS (entry sequenced) dataset?

3. What VSAM feature enables you to access the records in a KSDS dataset based on a key that is different than the file's primary key?

4. What is the general purpose utility program that provides services for VSAM files?

5. Which AMS function lists information about datasets?

6. If you are mostly going to use a KSDS file for sequential access, should you define a larger or smaller control interval when creating the file?

7. What is the basic AMS command to create a VSAM file?

8. To use the REWRITE command in PLI, the VSAM file must be opened in what mode?

9. When you define an alternate index, what is the function of the RELATE parameter?

10. When you define a path using DEFINE PATH, what does the PATHENTRY parameter do?

11. After you've defined an alternate index and path, what AMS command must you issue to actually populate the alternate index?

12. After you've created a VSAM file, if you need to add additional DASD volumes that can be used with that file, what command would you use?

13. If you want to set a VSAM file to read- only status, what command would you use?

14. What are some ways you can improve the performance of a KSDS file?

15. Do primary key values in a KSDS have to be unique?

16. Is there a performance penalty for using an alternate index compared to using the primary key?

Chapter Three: PLI Programming with IMS

Introduction

IMS is a hierarchical database management system (DBMS) that has been around since the 1960's. Although relational DBMSs are more common now, there is still an installed base of IMS users and IBM provides robust support for it. IMS is highly tuned for transaction management and generally provides excellent performance for that environment.

This text book deals with IMS DB, the IMS database manager. IMS also has a transaction manager called IMS DC. We will be covering IMS DB in this volume, and IMS DC in later volume.

There are two modes of running IMS programs. One is DLI which runs within its own address space. There is also Batch Mode Processing (BMP) which runs under the IMS online control region. The practical difference between the 2 concerns programs that update the database. A program requires exclusive use of the database if running in DLI mode. If run in BMP mode, a program does not require exclusive use of the database because it is run in the shared IMS online environment. The IMS online system "referees" the shared online environment.

I need to point out that records are called "segments" in IMS. I'll use the terms segment and record more or less interchangeably throughout the chapter. There are usually multiple segment types in an IMS database, although not always.

Designing and Creating IMS Databases

Sample System Specification

We're going to create a hierarchical database for a fictitious human resource system that will involve employees. In fact the database will be named EMPLOYEE and the root segment will also be named EMPLOYEE. This segment will include information such as name, years of service and social security number.

The EMPLOYEE segment will have a child segment that stores details about the employee's pay. The segment will be named EMPPAY and include the effective date, annual pay and bonus pay.

The EMPPAY segment will have a child segment named EMPPAYHS that includes details about each paycheck an employee received.

Note: there can be multiple EMPPAY under each EMPLOYEE, and there can be multiple EMPPAYHS under each EMPPAY. The following diagram depicts our EMPLOYEE database visually as a hierarchy.

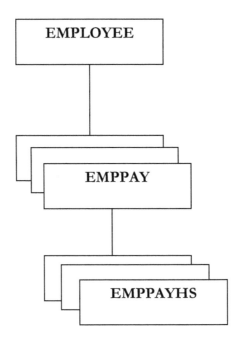

The following shows the detailed fields we will be using to organize the three record types. Note that the EMP_ID key field is only required on the root segment. You cannot access the child segments except through the root, so this makes sense.

EMPLOYEE Segment

Field Name	Type
EMP_ID	**INTEGER**
EMP_LAST_NAME	VARCHAR(30)
EMP_FIRST_NAME	VARCHAR(20)
EMP_SERVICE_YEARS	INTEGER
EMP_PROMOTION_DATE	DATE

EMPPAY segment (key is EFF_DATE):

Field Name	Type
EFF_DATE	**DATE**
EMP_REGULAR_PAY	DECIMAL
EMP_BONUS_PAY	DECIMAL
EMP_SEMIMTH_PAY	DECIMAL

EMPPAYHS segment (key is PAY_DATE):

Field Name	Type
PAY_DATE	**DATE**
ANNUAL_PAY	DECIMAL
PAY_CHECK_AMT	DECIMAL

Having decided the content of our segment types, we can create a record layout for each of these. Here's the layout for the EMPLOYEE segment:

```
DCL 01 IO_EMPLOYEE_RECORD,
       05   EMPL_ID_IN        CHAR(04),
       05   FILLER1           CHAR(01),
       05   EMPL_LNAME        CHAR(30),
       05   FILLER2           CHAR(01),
       05   EMPL_FNAME        CHAR(20),
       05   FILLER3           CHAR(01),
       05   EMPL_YRS_SRV      CHAR(02),
       05   FILLER4           CHAR(01),
       05   EMPL_PRM_DTE      CHAR(10),
       05   FILLER5           CHAR(10);
```

We've provided a bit of filler between fields, and we've left 10 bytes at the end (yes later we will be adding a field so we need some free space). Our total is 80 bytes for this segment type. The record will be keyed on **EMP_ID** which is the first four bytes of the record. We'll need this information when we define the database.

Next, the EMPPAY segment layout is as follows:

```
DCL 01 IO_EMPPAY_RECORD,
       05   PAY_EFF_DATE     CHAR(8),
       05   PAY_REG_PAY      FIXED DEC (8,2),
       05   PAY_BON_PAY      FIXED DEC (8,2),
       05   SEMIMTH_PAY      FIXED DEC (8,2),
       05   FILLER55         CHAR(57);
```

Notice there is no EMP_ID field. As mentioned earlier, child segments do not need to repeat the parent segment key. The hierarchical structure of the database makes this unnecessary. The PAY_EFF_DATE field will be the key for the EMPPAY segment, and it is 8 bytes. The format will be YYYYMMDD.

Also notice that we padded the record with filler to total 80 bytes. We didn't have to do this. The DBD will specify 23 bytes for this segment type, which is the actual record length. But often it's a convenience to leave space in the IO layout for future expansion.

Finally, here is the layout for the EMPPAYHS segment. Out key will be PAY-DATE and it will be formatted as YYYYMMDD.

```
DCL 01 IO_EMPPAYHS_RECORD.
       05  PAY_DATE            CHAR(8),
       05  PAY_ANN_PAY         FIXED DEC (8,2),
       05  PAY_AMT             FIXED DEC (8,2),
       05  FILLER65            CHAR(62);
```

Now we are ready to build the data base descriptor!

Database Descriptor (DBD)

A database descriptor is required to have an IMS database. The descriptor specifies the name of the database, plus the various segment types. Typically a database administrator will create and maintain DBDs. You should still understand how to read the DBD code to understand the structure of the database.

Here's the DBD code for our EMPLOYEE database.

```
PRINT NOGEN
DBD NAME=EMPLOYEE,ACCESS=HISAM
DATASET DD1=EMPLOYEE,OVFLW=EMPLFLW
SEGM NAME=EMPLOYEE,PARENT=0,BYTES=80
FIELD NAME=(EMPID,SEQ,U),BYTES=04,START=1,TYPE=C
SEGM NAME=EMPPAY,PARENT=EMPLOYEE,BYTES=23
FIELD NAME=(EFFDATE,SEQ,U),START=1,BYTES=8,TYPE=C
SEGM  NAME=EMPPAYHS,PARENT=EMPPAY,BYTES=18
FIELD NAME=(PAYDATE,SEQ,U),START=1,BYTES=8,TYPE=C
DBDGEN
FINISH
END
```

The code above specifies the name of the database which is EMPLOYEE, as well as an access method of HISAM (Hierarchical Indexed Sequential Access Method).

HISAM database records are stored in two data sets: a primary data set and an overflow data set. The primary dataset is always a VSAM KSDS and the overflow dataset is a VSAM ESDS.

Looking at the DBD code, we see that the DATASET DD1 and OVFLW keywords define the DD names of the primary cluster and the overflow dataset, respectively. We defined these values as EMPLOYEE and EMPLFLW, respectively. Later when we run batch jobs against the database, the DD name in our JCL must be EMPLOYEE for the KSDS file. To refer to the overflow dataset, we will use EMPLFLW.

132

Next, we define our segment types using the SEGM NAME= keywords. We also define the parent of each segment unless it is the root segment in which we specify PARENT=0. Next you specify the length of the segment. We've defined the length as the total of the fields we mapped out earlier in the PLI layouts.

For each segment, if you have any searchable fields (such as keys), they must be defined with the FIELD NAME= keywords. In our case, we will only specify the key fields for each segment. We specify the field name, that the records are to be ordered sequentially (SEQ), and that the field content must be unique(U). Then we specify how many bytes in length the field is, and it's displacement in the segment. We also specify C for character data – the actual data we store can be of any type but we specify C to indicate the default type is character data.

Here's an example of defining the employee id in the DBD from above:

```
FIELD NAME=(EMPID,SEQ,U),BYTES=04,START=1,TYPE=C
```

Finally, you conclude the DBD with

```
DBDGEN
FINISH
END
```

Now you are ready to run your installation's JCL to generate a DBD. Most likely you will ask a DBA to do this. Here's the JCL I run. It will be different for your installation.

```
//USER01D JOB MSGLEVEL=(1,1),NOTIFY=&SYSUID
//*
//PLIB     JCLLIB ORDER=SYS1.IMS.PROCLIB
//DGEN     EXEC DBDGEN,
//              MEMBER=EMPLOYEE,           <= DBD SOURCE MEMBER
//              SRCLIB=USER01.IMS.SRCLIB,  <= DBD SOURCE LIBRARY
//              DBDLIB=USER01.IMS.DBDLIB   <= DBD LIBRARY
//*
```

More information about designing, coding and generating DBDs is available on the IBM product web site.

Supporting VSAM Files

Now that we have a DBD generated, we can create the physical files for the database. Actually it can be done in either order, but you do need to know the maximum record size for all segments in order to build the IDCAMS JCL. For IMS datasets we use a VSAM key sequenced data set (KSDS).

The JCL for creating our EMPLOYEE IMS database is below. Notice that we specify a RECORDSIZE that is 8 bytes longer than the logical record size that we defined in the DBD. And although the key is the first logical byte of each record, we specify the key displacement at byte 6. The IMS system reserves the first 5 bytes of each record for its own purposes, so this is required.

Finally, note that we have a second job step to repro a dummy file to our VSAM cluster name to initialize it. This is required. Otherwise we will get an abend the first time we try to access it. Go ahead and run the JCL or ask your DBA to create the physical files.

```
//USER01D JOB MSGLEVEL=(1,1),NOTIFY=&SYSUID
//*
//************************************************************
//* DEFINE VSAM KSDS CLUSTER FOR EMPLOYEE DATABASE
//************************************************************
//VDEF     EXEC PGM=IDCAMS
//SYSPRINT DD SYSOUT=*
//SYSIN    DD  *
  DEFINE CLUSTER(NAME(USER01.IMS.EMPLOYEE.CLUSTER)   -
                INDEXED                              -
                KEYS(4,6)                            -
                RECORDSIZE(88,88)                    -
                TRACKS(2,1)                          -
                CISZ(2048)                           -
                VOLUMES(DEVHD1)                      -
                )                                    -
        DATA(NAME(USER01.IMS.EMPLOYEE.DATA))
//*
//************************************************************
//* INITIALIZE THE VSAM FILE TO PLACE EOF MARK
//************************************************************
//VINIT    EXEC PGM=IDCAMS
//SYSPRINT DD SYSOUT=*
//INF      DD  DUMMY
//OUTF     DD  DSN=USER01.IMS.EMPLOYEE.CLUSTER,DISP=SHR
//SYSIN    DD  *
  REPRO INFILE(INF) OUTFILE(OUTF)
/*
//*
```

Next, here is the JCL for creating the overflow dataset. When your KSDS is full, new records will be placed in the overflow dataset. Again, specify RECORDSIZE 88 (not 80). You must also specify NONINDEXED file to get an ESDS.

```
//USER01D JOB MSGLEVEL=(1,1),NOTIFY=&SYSUID
//*
//*************************************************************
//* DEFINE VSAM ESDS CLUSTER FOR IMS DATA BASE
//*************************************************************
//VDEF     EXEC PGM=IDCAMS
//SYSPRINT DD SYSOUT=*
//SYSOUT   DD SYSOUT=*
//SYSIN    DD  *
  DEFINE CLUSTER(NAME(USER01.IMS.EMPLFLW.CLUSTER)  -
                 NONINDEXED                         -
                 RECORDSIZE(88,88)                  -
                 TRACKS(2,1)                        -
                 CISZ(2048)                         -
                 VOLUMES(DEVHD1)                    -
                 )                                  -
        DATA(NAME(USER01.IMS.EMPLFLW.DATA))
/*
```

Ok, time to move on to our next IMS entity which is a PSB.

Program Specification Block (PSB)

A Program Specification Block (PSB) is an IMS authorization entity that specifies which segments and operations can be performed on one or more databases using this particular PSB authority. PSBs consist of one or more Program Communication Blocks (PCB) which are logical views of a database. It is typical for each IMS application program to have a separate PSB defined for it, but this is convention, not an IMS requirement. For our programming examples we will mostly use only one PSB, but we will modify it a few times. Here is the code for the PSB that we will be using for most of the examples.

```
PRINT NOGEN
PCB   TYPE=DB,NAME=EMPLOYEE,KEYLEN=20,PROCOPT=AP
SENSEG NAME=EMPLOYEE,PARENT=0
SENSEG NAME=EMPPAY,PARENT=EMPLOYEE
SENSEG NAME=EMPPAYHS,PARENT=EMPPAY
PSBGEN LANG=PL/I,PSBNAME=EMPLOYEE
END
```

Here's the meaning of each keyword for defining the PCB.

PCB – this is where you define a pointer to your database.

TYPE - typically this value is "DB" to indicate a database PCB. There is also a terminal (TP) PCB that is used for teleprocessing calls in IMS DC, but we won't be doing IMS DC in this text.

NAME - identifies the database to be accessed.

PROCOPT - Processing options. This value specifies which operations can be performed such as read, update or delete. The following are the most common options:

G	Get
I	Insert
R	Replace
D	Delete
A	All Options (G, I, R, D)
L	Load Function (Initial Loading)
LS	Load Function (Loading Sequentially)
K	Key Function - Access only key of the segment.
O	Used with G option to indicate that HOLD is not allowed.
P	Path Function (Used during Path Calls)

The PROCOPT can be defined for the entire PCB or it can be more granular by applying it to specific segments. If specified at the segment level, it overrides any PROCOPT at the PCB level.

KEYLEN – specifies the length of the concatenated key. Concatenated key is the maximum length of all the segment keys added up. This needs to be calculated by adding the longest segment key in each level from top to bottom.

In our case we have specified PROCOPT=AP for the entire PSB. That is powerful. It means All (G, I, R, D) plus authority to do path calls.

SENSEG means sensitive segment, which means you can access that segment via this PSB. You can specify which segments you want to access. You might not always want all segments to be accessed. In our case we do, so we define a SENSEG for each segment type.

You must then execute a PSBGEN (or ask your DBA to) to create the PSB. Here is the JCL I use, and note that the member name I stored the PSB source under is EMPPSB. Your JCL will be different and specific to the installation:

```
//USER01D JOB MSGLEVEL=(1,1),NOTIFY=&SYSUID
//*
//PLIB    JCLLIB ORDER=SYS1.IMS.PROCLIB
//PGEN    EXEC PSBGEN,
//            MEMBER=EMPPSB,              <= PSB SOURCE MEMBER
//            SRCLIB=USER01.IMS.SRCLIB,  <= PSB SOURCE LIBRARY
//            PSBLIB=USER01.IMS.PSBLIB   <= PSB LIBRARY
//*
```

Now you have the basic building blocks of IMS – a database descriptor (DBD), the physical VSAM files to support the database, and a PSB that provides permissions to access the data within the database. We are ready to start programming.

IMS Application Programming Basics

The IMS Program Interface

To request IMS data services in an application program, you must call the IMS interface program for that programming language. The interface program for PLI is PLITDLI. This program is called with several parameters which vary depending on the operation being requested. The call also needs to tell PLITDLI how many parameters are being passed, so we'll declare some constants in our program for that.

```
DCL THREE              FIXED BIN (31) INIT(3);
DCL FOUR               FIXED BIN (31) INIT(4);
DCL FIVE               FIXED BIN (31) INIT(5);
DCL SIX                FIXED BIN (31) INIT(6);
```

Let's take an example where you want to retrieve an EMPLOYEE segment from the EMPLOYEE database, and you want employee number 3217. Here is the call with appropriate parameters. We'll discuss each of these in turn.

```
CALL PLITDLI (FOUR,
              DLI_FUNCGU,
              PCB_MASK,
              SEG_IO_AREA,
              EMP_QUALIFIED_SSA);
```

The first parameter specifies the number of parameters being passed. In the case of the above call, the number would be four.

The second parameter is the call type. The following are the common IMS calls used to insert, retrieve, modify and delete data in an IMS database. There are some other calls we'll introduce later such as for checkpointing and rolling back data changes.

DLET	The Delete (DLET) call is used to remove a segment and its dependents from the database.
GN/GHN	The Get Next (GN) call is used to retrieve segments sequentially from the database. The Get Hold Next (GHN) is the hold form for a GN call.
GNP/GHNP	The Get Next in Parent (GNP) call retrieves dependents sequentially. The Get Hold Next in Parent (GHNP) call is the hold form of the GNP call.
GU/GHU	The Get Unique (GU) call is used to directly retrieve segments and to establish a starting position in the database for sequential processing. The Get Hold Unique (GHU) is the hold form for a GU call.
ISRT	The Insert (ISRT) call is used to load a database and to add one or more segments to the database. You can use ISRT to add a record to the end of a GSAM database or for an alternate PCB that is set up for IAFP processing.
REPL	The Replace (REPL) call is used to change the values of one or more fields in a segment.

It is a common practice to define a set of constants in your program that specify the value of the specific IMS calls. Here's the PLI code for this purpose.

```
DCL 01 DLI_FUNCTIONS,
       05 DLI_FUNCISRT      CHAR(04) INIT ('ISRT'),
       05 DLI_FUNCGU        CHAR(04) INIT ('GU  '),
       05 DLI_FUNCGN        CHAR(04) INIT ('GN  '),
       05 DLI_FUNCGHU       CHAR(04) INIT ('GHU '),
       05 DLI_FUNCGNP       CHAR(04) INIT ('GNP '),
       05 DLI_FUNCREPL      CHAR(04) INIT ('REPL'),
       05 DLI_FUNCDLET      CHAR(04) INIT ('DLET'),
       05 DLI_FUNCXRST      CHAR(04) INIT ('XRST'),
       05 DLI_FUNCCHKP      CHAR(04) INIT ('CHKP'),
       05 DLI_FUNCROLL      CHAR(04) INIT ('ROLL');
```

As you can see from the call above and the constant definitions, we are doing a Get Unique (GU) call. The DLI_FUNCGU specifies it.

The next parameter is a PCB data area that we defined as PCB_MASK. This returns various information from IMS after the database call. You must define this structure in your program since it is passing data back and forth from the PLITDLI interface program.

138

```
DCL 01 PCB_MASK              BASED(DB_PTR_PCB),
       05 DBD_NAME           CHAR(08),
       05 SEG_LEVEL          CHAR(02),
       05 STATUS_CODE        CHAR(02),
       05 PROC_OPT           CHAR(04),
       05 FILLER6            FIXED BIN (31),
       05 SEG_NAME           CHAR(08),
       05 KEY_FDBK           FIXED BIN (31),
       05 NUM_SENSEG         FIXED BIN (31),
       05 KEY_FDBK_AREA,
          10 EMPLOYEE_ID     CHAR(04);
```

One of the most important data elements in the PCB_MASK is the two byte status code
returned by the call, the STATUS_CODE.   A blank status code means that the call was
successful. Other status codes indicate the reason why the call failed. Here is a subset of
the status codes you may encounter.

IMS Status Codes

PCB Status Code	Description
AC	Hierarchic error in SSAs.
AD	Function parameter incorrect. Only applies to full-function DEQ calls.
AI	Data management OPEN error.
AJ	Incorrect parameter format in I/O area; incorrect SSA format; incorrect command used to insert a logical child segment. I/O area length in AIB is invalid; incorrect class parameter specified in Fast Path Q command code.
AK	Invalid SSA field name.
AM	Call function not compatible with processing option, segment sensitivity, transaction code, definition, or program type.
AU	SSAs too long.
DA	Segment key field or nonreplaceable field has been changed.
DJ	No preceding successful GHU or GHN call or an SSA supplied at a level not retrieved.
FT	Too many SSAs on call.
GB	End of database.
GE	Segment not found.
GG	Segment contains invalid pointer.
GP	No parentage established.
II	Segment already exists.

In your application program control is passed from IMS through an entry point. Your
entry point must refer to the PCBs in the order in which they have been defined in the

139

PSB. When you code each DL/I call, you must provide the PCB you want to use for that call.

The next parameter is the segment I/O area. This is where IMS returns the data segment you requested, or where you load data to be inserted/updated on an insert or replace command. For the EMPLOYEE record, we will define the I/O area in PLI as:

```
DCL 01 IO_EMPLOYEE_RECORD,
       05  EMPL_ID_IN          CHAR(04),
       05  FILLER1             CHAR(01),
       05  EMPL_LNAME          CHAR(30),
       05  FILLER2             CHAR(01),
       05  EMPL_FNAME          CHAR(20),
       05  FILLER3             CHAR(01),
       05  EMPL_YRS_SRV        CHAR(02),
       05  FILLER4             CHAR(01),
       05  EMPL_PRM_DTE        CHAR(10),
       05  FILLER5             CHAR(10);
```

The last parameter in our call is a Segment Search Argument (SSA). This is where we specify the type of segment we want and the key value. It is also possible to simply request the next record of a particular segment type without regard to key value. When we specify a key, that means we are using a "qualified" SSA. When we don't specify a key, it means we are using an unqualified SSA.

Here's the PLI definition for the unqualified SSA for the EMPLOYEE segment.

```
DCL 01 EMP_UNQUALIFIED_SSA,
       05  SEGNAME             CHAR(08) INIT ('EMPLOYEE'),
       05  FILLER7             CHAR(01) INIT (' ');
```

And here's the PLI definition for the qualified SSA for the EMPLOYEE segment.

```
DCL 01 EMP_QUALIFIED_SSA,
       05  SEGNAME             CHAR(08) INIT('EMPLOYEE'),
       05  FILLER8             CHAR(01) INIT('('),
       05  FIELD               CHAR(08) INIT('EMPID'),
       05  OPER                CHAR(02) INIT(' ='),
       05  EMP_ID_VAL          CHAR(04) INIT('    '),
       05  FILLER9             CHAR(01) INIT(')');
```

Both qualified and unqualified SSAs must specify the segment type or name. You specify the key for the qualified SSA in the field we've named EMP_ID_VAL. We'll show many examples of SSAs in the program examples, including the use of Boolean SSA values.

Loading an IMS Database

Ok, finally to our first program. We're going to load the IMS database with a few records from a flat file (a.k.a. a flat file). Here is the data file contents:

```
----+----1----+----2----+----3----+----4----+----5----+----6----+----7----+----8
******************************** Top of Data *********************************
1111 VEREEN            CHARLES         12 2017-01-01 937253058
1122 JENKINS           DEBORAH         05 2017-01-01 435092366
3217 JOHNSON           EDWARD          04 2017-01-01 397342007
4175 TURNBULL          FRED            01 2016-12-01 542083017
4720 SCHULTZ           TIM             09 2017-01-01 650450254
4836 SMITH             SANDRA          03 2017-01-01 028374669
6288 WILLARD           JOE             06 2016-01-01 209883920
7459 STEWART           BETTY           07 2016-07-31 019572830
9134 FRANKLIN          BRIANNA         00 2016-10-01 937293598
```

As you can see, we've formatted the records exactly like we want them to be applied to the database. Of course, your input layout could be different than the eventual IMS segment layout, but using the same layout makes it easier to program because you don't have to do field assignments in the program.

Now let's create a program to load the data called PLIIMS1. We'll define the input file of course. Let's assume that the DD name for the employee load file is EMPIFILE.

```
DCL EMPIFILE FILE RECORD SEQL INPUT;
```

We've specified a SEG_IO_AREA to read the input file into and to write the IMS record from. We could have used the IO_EMPLOYEE_RECORD for the insert instead (and we will later), but I first want to demonstrate the value of having your input records structured the same as the IMS segment. When you do this, it really simplifies the coding such that you can both read and write using use a one element structure like SEG_IO_AREA.

Next we'll code a few needed things including:

- An end of file switch for the loop we'll create to load the records.

- The DLI call constants.

- The Employee segment I/O structure.

- The Employee segment SSA.

```
DCL SW_END_OF_FILE          STATIC BIT(01) INIT('0'B);
DCL ONCODE                  BUILTIN;
DCL DB_PTR_PCB              POINTER;
```

```
        DCL PLITDLI                    EXTERNAL ENTRY;

        DCL 01 DLI_FUNCTIONS,
                05 DLI_FUNCISRT        CHAR(04) INIT ('ISRT'),
                05 DLI_FUNCGU          CHAR(04) INIT ('GU  '),
                05 DLI_FUNCGN          CHAR(04) INIT ('GN  '),
                05 DLI_FUNCGHU         CHAR(04) INIT ('GHU '),
                05 DLI_FUNCGNP         CHAR(04) INIT ('GNP '),
                05 DLI_FUNCREPL        CHAR(04) INIT ('REPL'),
                05 DLI_FUNCDLET        CHAR(04) INIT ('DLET'),
                05 DLI_FUNCXRST        CHAR(04) INIT ('XRST'),
                05 DLI_FUNCCHKP        CHAR(04) INIT ('CHKP'),
                05 DLI_FUNCROLL        CHAR(04) INIT ('ROLL');

        DCL 01 IN_EMPLOYEE_RECORD,
                05  EMPL_ID_IN         CHAR(04),
                05  FILLER1            CHAR(01),
                05  EMPL_LNAME         CHAR(30),
                05  FILLER2            CHAR(01),
                05  EMPL_FNAME         CHAR(20),
                05  FILLER3            CHAR(01),
                05  EMPL_YRS_SRV       CHAR(02),
                05  FILLER4            CHAR(01),
                05  EMPL_PRM_DTE       CHAR(10),
                05  FILLER5            CHAR(10);


        DCL 01 EMP_UNQUALIFIED_SSA,
                05  SEGNAME            CHAR(08) INIT ('EMPLOYEE'),
                05  FILLER7            CHAR(01) INIT (' ');

        DCL 01 EMP_QUALIFIED_SSA,
                05  SEGNAME            CHAR(08) INIT('EMPLOYEE'),
                05  FILLER8            CHAR(01) INIT('('),
                05  FIELD              CHAR(08) INIT('EMPID'),
                05  OPER               CHAR(02) INIT(' ='),
                05  EMP_ID_VAL         CHAR(04) INIT('    '),
                05  FILLER9            CHAR(01) INIT(')');

        DCL SEG_IO_AREA                CHAR(80) INIT (' ');

        DCL THREE                      FIXED BIN (31) INIT(3);
        DCL FOUR                       FIXED BIN (31) INIT(4);
        DCL FIVE                       FIXED BIN (31) INIT(5);
        DCL SIX                        FIXED BIN (31) INIT(6);
```

Finally, we'll code the PCB mask.

```
        DCL 01 PCB_MASK                BASED(DB_PTR_PCB),
                05 DBD_NAME            CHAR(08),
                05 SEG_LEVEL           CHAR(02),
                05 STATUS_CODE         CHAR(02),
```

```
         05 PROC_OPT              CHAR(04),
         05 FILLER6               FIXED BIN (31),
         05 SEG_NAME              CHAR(08),
         05 KEY_FDBK              FIXED BIN (31),
         05 NUM_SENSEG            FIXED BIN (31),
         05 KEY_FDBK_AREA,
            10 EMPLOYEE_ID        CHAR(04);
```

We'll work on the executable code next, which will complete the program. Let's talk about the actual database call. Here's what we'll use:

```
         CALL PLITDLI (FOUR,
                       DLI_FUNCISRT,
                       PCB_MASK,
                       SEG_IO_AREA,
                       EMP_UNQUALIFIED_SSA);
```

This is similar to the example we gave earlier with a couple of differences. One difference of course is that we are doing an ISRT call, so we specify the constant DLI-FUNCISRT. The other difference is that we will use an unqualified SSA. On an insert operation, IMS will always establish the record key from the I/O area and therefore it does not use a qualified SSA.

To be clear, any time you are inserting a record, you will use an **unqualified** SSA at the level of the record you are inserting. So if you are inserting a root segment, you will always use an unqualified SSA. If you are inserting a child segment under a root, you will use a qualified SSA on the root segment, and then an unqualified SSA for the child segment. If this seems a bit cryptic now, it should make more sense in later examples where we use child segments and multiple SSAs.

Ok, here's our complete program code. See what you think.

```
PLIIMS1: PROCEDURE (DB_PTR_PCB) OPTIONS(MAIN);
/********************************************************************
* PROGRAM NAME :   PLIIMS1 - INSERT RECORDS INTO IMS EMPLOYEE DB   *
********************************************************************/

/********************************************************************
/*                F I L E S    U S E D                             *
********************************************************************/

   DCL EMPIFILE FILE RECORD SEQL INPUT;

/********************************************************************
/*              W O R K I N G    S T O R A G E                     *
********************************************************************/

   DCL SW_END_OF_FILE            STATIC BIT(01) INIT('0'B);
```

143

```
DCL ONCODE                      BUILTIN;
DCL DB_PTR_PCB                  POINTER;

DCL PLITDLI                     EXTERNAL ENTRY;

DCL 01 DLI_FUNCTIONS,
       05 DLI_FUNCISRT          CHAR(04) INIT ('ISRT'),
       05 DLI_FUNCGU            CHAR(04) INIT ('GU  '),
       05 DLI_FUNCGN            CHAR(04) INIT ('GN  '),
       05 DLI_FUNCGHU           CHAR(04) INIT ('GHU '),
       05 DLI_FUNCGNP           CHAR(04) INIT ('GNP '),
       05 DLI_FUNCREPL          CHAR(04) INIT ('REPL'),
       05 DLI_FUNCDLET          CHAR(04) INIT ('DLET'),
       05 DLI_FUNCXRST          CHAR(04) INIT ('XRST'),
       05 DLI_FUNCCHKP          CHAR(04) INIT ('CHKP'),
       05 DLI_FUNCROLL          CHAR(04) INIT ('ROLL');

DCL 01 IN_EMPLOYEE_RECORD,
       05  EMPL_ID_IN           CHAR(04),
       05  FILLER1              CHAR(01),
       05  EMPL_LNAME           CHAR(30),
       05  FILLER2              CHAR(01),
       05  EMPL_FNAME           CHAR(20),
       05  FILLER3              CHAR(01),
       05  EMPL_YRS_SRV         CHAR(02),
       05  FILLER4              CHAR(01),
       05  EMPL_PRM_DTE         CHAR(10),
       05  FILLER5              CHAR(10);

DCL 01 PCB_MASK                 BASED(DB_PTR_PCB),
       05 DBD_NAME              CHAR(08),
       05 SEG_LEVEL             CHAR(02),
       05 STATUS_CODE           CHAR(02),
       05 PROC_OPT              CHAR(04),
       05 FILLER6               FIXED BIN (31),
       05 SEG_NAME              CHAR(08),
       05 KEY_FDBK              FIXED BIN (31),
       05 NUM_SENSEG            FIXED BIN (31),
       05 KEY_FDBK_AREA,
          10 EMPLOYEE_ID        CHAR(04);

DCL 01 EMP_UNQUALIFIED_SSA,
       05  SEGNAME              CHAR(08) INIT ('EMPLOYEE'),
       05  FILLER7              CHAR(01) INIT (' ');

DCL 01 EMP_QUALIFIED_SSA,
       05  SEGNAME              CHAR(08) INIT('EMPLOYEE'),
       05  FILLER8              CHAR(01) INIT('('),
       05  FIELD                CHAR(08) INIT('EMPID'),
       05  OPER                 CHAR(02) INIT(' ='),
       05  EMP_ID_VAL           CHAR(04) INIT('    '),
       05  FILLER9              CHAR(01) INIT(')');
```

```
   DCL SEG_IO_AREA                CHAR(80) INIT (' ');

   DCL THREE                      FIXED BIN (31) INIT(3);
   DCL FOUR                       FIXED BIN (31) INIT(4);
   DCL FIVE                       FIXED BIN (31) INIT(5);
   DCL SIX                        FIXED BIN (31) INIT(6);

/*********************************************************************
/*              O N   C O N D I T I O N S                           *
*********************************************************************/

   ON ENDFILE (EMPIFILE) SW_END_OF_FILE = '1'B;

/*********************************************************************
/*              P R O G R A M   M A I N L I N E                     *
*********************************************************************/

CALL P100_INITIALIZATION;
CALL P200_MAINLINE;
CALL P300_TERMINATION;

P100_INITIALIZATION: PROC;

   PUT SKIP LIST ('PLIIMS1: INSERT RECORDS');
   OPEN FILE (EMPIFILE);

   IN_EMPLOYEE_RECORD  = '';
   PCB_MASK = '';

END P100_INITIALIZATION;

P200_MAINLINE: PROC;

   /*  MAIN LOOP _ READ THE INPUT FILE, LOAD THE OUTPUT
                   STRUCTURE AND WRITE THE RECORD TO OUTPUT */

   READ FILE (EMPIFILE) INTO (IN_EMPLOYEE_RECORD);

   DO WHILE (¬SW_END_OF_FILE);

      SEG_IO_AREA = STRING(IN_EMPLOYEE_RECORD);

      CALL PLITDLI (FOUR,
                    DLI_FUNCISRT,
                    PCB_MASK,
                    SEG_IO_AREA,
                    EMP_UNQUALIFIED_SSA);

      IF STATUS_CODE = ' ' THEN
         PUT SKIP LIST ('SUCCESSFUL INSERT-REC:' || SEG_IO_AREA);
      ELSE
         DO;
            CALL P400_DISPLAY_ERROR;
```

145

```
            RETURN;
        END;

      READ FILE (EMPIFILE) INTO (IN_EMPLOYEE_RECORD);

    END; /* DO WHILE */

END P200_MAINLINE;

P300_TERMINATION: PROC;

    CLOSE FILE(EMPIFILE);

    PUT SKIP LIST ('PLIIMS1 - SUCCESSFULLY ENDED');

END P300_TERMINATION;

P400_DISPLAY_ERROR: PROC;

    PUT SKIP LIST ('ERROR ENCOUNTERED - DETAIL FOLLOWS');
    PUT SKIP LIST ('SEG_IO_AREA     :' || SEG_IO_AREA);
    PUT SKIP LIST ('DBD_NAME1:' || DBD_NAME);
    PUT SKIP LIST ('SEG_LEVEL1:' || SEG_LEVEL);
    PUT SKIP LIST ('STATUS_CODE:' || STATUS_CODE);
    PUT SKIP LIST ('PROC_OPT1 :' || PROC_OPT);
    PUT SKIP LIST ('SEG_NAME1 :' || SEG_NAME);
    PUT SKIP LIST ('KEY_FDBK1 :' || KEY_FDBK);
    PUT SKIP LIST ('NUM_SENSEG1:' || NUM_SENSEG);
    PUT SKIP LIST ('KEY_FDBK_AREA1:' || KEY_FDBK_AREA);

END P400_DISPLAY_ERROR;

END PLIIMS1;
```

Now we can compile and link the program. You'll need to ask your supervisor or teammate for the compile procedure.

Finally, one time only you must create and use a special PSB for the initial load of the database. The PSB can be identical to the one we already created except it must specify a PROCOPT of **LS** which means Load Sequential. Let's clone EMPPSB into member EMPPSBL:

```
PRINT NOGEN
PCB    TYPE=DB,NAME=EMPLOYEE,KEYLEN=20,PROCOPT=LS
SENSEG NAME=EMPLOYEE,PARENT=0
SENSEG NAME=EMPPAY,PARENT=EMPLOYEE
SENSEG NAME=EMPPAYHS,PARENT=EMPPAY
SENSEG NAME=EMPDEP,PARENT=EMPLOYEE
PSBGEN LANG=PL/I,PSBNAME=EMPLOYEE
END
```

Generate this PSB, and then let's execute the program. Execution JCL will look something like this (yours will be whatever you use at your installation). Note that we **MUST** include DD statements for the IMS database and its overflow dataset. Also we include the input file.

```
//USER01D JOB MSGLEVEL=(1,1),NOTIFY=&SYSUID
//*
//* TO RUN A IMS COBOL PROGRAM
//*
//PLIB    JCLLIB ORDER=SYS1.IMS.PROCLIB
//RUN     EXEC IMSPLIGO,
//             MBR=PLIIMS1,                  <= COBOL PROGRAM NAME
//             LOADLIB=USER01.IMS.LOADLIB,   <= LOAD LIBRARY
//             PSB=EMPPSB,         <= PSB NAME
//             PSBLIB=USER01.IMS.PSBLIB,     <= PSB LIBRARY
//             DBDLIB=USER01.IMS.DBDLIB      <= DBD LIBRARY
//*
//** FLAT FILES IF ANY  **********************
//GO.EMPIFILE DD DSN=USER01.EMPIFILE,DISP=SHR
//*
//** IMS DATABASES (VSAM)  ********************
//GO.EMPLOYEE DD DSN=USER01.IMS.EMPLOYEE.CLUSTER,DISP=SHR
//GO.EMPLFLW DD DSN=USER01.IMS.EMPLFLW.CLUSTER,DISP=SHR
//GO.SYSPRINT DD SYSOUT=*
//GO.SYSUDUMP DD SYSOUT=*
//GO.PLIDUMP DD SYSOUT=*
```

And here are the results of the run:

```
PLIIMS1: INSERT RECORDS
SUCCESSFUL INSERT-REC:1111 VEREEN          CHARLES         1
SUCCESSFUL INSERT-REC:1122 JENKINS         DEBORAH         0
SUCCESSFUL INSERT-REC:3217 JOHNSON         EDWARD          0
SUCCESSFUL INSERT-REC:4175 TURNBULL        FRED            0
SUCCESSFUL INSERT-REC:4720 SCHULTZ         TIM             0
SUCCESSFUL INSERT-REC:4836 SMITH           SANDRA          0
SUCCESSFUL INSERT-REC:6288 WILLARD         JOE             0
SUCCESSFUL INSERT-REC:7459 STEWART         BETTY           0
SUCCESSFUL INSERT-REC:9134 FRANKLIN        BRIANNA         0
PLIIMS1 - SUCCESSFULLY ENDED
```

You can browse the data using whatever tool you have such as File Manager IMS. Or you can simply browse the DATA file of the VSAM data set.

```
Browse            USER01.IMS.EMPLOYEE.DATA          Top of 9
Command ===>                                        Scroll PAGE
                      Type DATA      RBA            Format CHAR
```

147

```
                                             Col 1
----+----10---+----2----+----3---+----4---+----5---+----6---+----7----+----
**** Top of data ****
......1111 VEREEN           CHARLES           12 2017-01-01 93
......1122 JENKINS          DEBORAH           05 2017-01-01 43
......3217 JOHNSON          EDWARD            04 2017-01-01 39
......4175 TURNBULL         FRED              01 2016-12-01 54
......4720 SCHULTZ          TIM               09 2017-01-01 65
......4836 SMITH            SANDRA            03 2017-01-01 02
......6288 WILLARD          JOE               06 2016-01-01 20
......7459 STEWART          BETTY             07 2016-07-31 01
......9134 FRANKLIN         BRIANNA           00 2016-10-01 93
**** End of data ****
```

Reading a Segment (GU)

Our next program will be named PLIIMS2, and the purpose is simply to retrieve a record from the EMPLOYEE database. In this case, we want the record for employee 3217.

Our basic program structure will be similar to the load program except we will need to perform a Get Unique (GU) call, and we'll use a qualified SSA. Remember our qualified SSA structure looks like this:

```
DCL 01 EMP_QUALIFIED_SSA,
       05  SEGNAME          CHAR(08) INIT('EMPLOYEE'),
       05  FILLER8          CHAR(01) INIT('('),
       05  FIELD            CHAR(08) INIT('EMPID'),
       05  OPER             CHAR(02) INIT(' ='),
       05  EMP_ID_VAL       CHAR(04) INIT('    '),
       05  FILLER9          CHAR(01) INIT(')');
```

So we must load the EMP_ID_VAL with character value 3217. And our call will look like this:

```
CALL PLITDLI (FOUR,
              DLI_FUNCGU,
              PCB_MASK,
              IO_EMPLOYEE_RECORD,
              EMP_QUALIFIED_SSA);
```

Now we can code the entire program. We don't need a loop because we are retrieving a single record. So the program is quite simple. Not that we check for a blank status code after each IMS call, and we report an error if it is not blank. Here is the program listing.

```
PLIIMS2: PROCEDURE (DB_PTR_PCB) OPTIONS(MAIN);
 /*************************************************************
```

```
* PROGRAM NAME :   PLIIMS2 - RETRIEVE A RECORD FROM EMPLOYEE DB     *
********************************************************************/

/********************************************************************
/*                W O R K I N G   S T O R A G E                     *
********************************************************************/
   DCL ONCODE                  BUILTIN;
   DCL DB_PTR_PCB              POINTER;
   DCL PLITDLI                 EXTERNAL ENTRY;

   DCL 01 DLI_FUNCTIONS,
          05 DLI_FUNCISRT       CHAR(04) INIT ('ISRT'),
          05 DLI_FUNCGU         CHAR(04) INIT ('GU  '),
          05 DLI_FUNCGN         CHAR(04) INIT ('GN  '),
          05 DLI_FUNCGHU        CHAR(04) INIT ('GHU '),
          05 DLI_FUNCGNP        CHAR(04) INIT ('GNP '),
          05 DLI_FUNCREPL       CHAR(04) INIT ('REPL'),
          05 DLI_FUNCDLET       CHAR(04) INIT ('DLET'),
          05 DLI_FUNCXRST       CHAR(04) INIT ('XRST'),
          05 DLI_FUNCCHKP       CHAR(04) INIT ('CHKP'),
          05 DLI_FUNCROLL       CHAR(04) INIT ('ROLL');

   DCL 01 IO_EMPLOYEE_RECORD,
          05  EMPL_ID_IN        CHAR(04),
          05  FILLER1           CHAR(01),
          05  EMPL_LNAME        CHAR(30),
          05  FILLER2           CHAR(01),
          05  EMPL_FNAME        CHAR(20),
          05  FILLER3           CHAR(01),
          05  EMPL_YRS_SRV      CHAR(02),
          05  FILLER4           CHAR(01),
          05  EMPL_PRM_DTE      CHAR(10),
          05  FILLER5           CHAR(10);

   DCL 01 PCB_MASK              BASED(DB_PTR_PCB),
          05 DBD_NAME           CHAR(08),
          05 SEG_LEVEL          CHAR(02),
          05 STATUS_CODE        CHAR(02),
          05 PROC_OPT           CHAR(04),
          05 FILLER6            FIXED BIN (31),
          05 SEG_NAME           CHAR(08),
          05 KEY_FDBK           FIXED BIN (31),
          05 NUM_SENSEG         FIXED BIN (31),
          05 KEY_FDBK_AREA,
             10 EMPLOYEE_ID     CHAR(04);

   DCL 01 EMP_UNQUALIFIED_SSA,
          05  SEGNAME           CHAR(08) INIT ('EMPLOYEE'),
          05  FILLER7           CHAR(01) INIT (' ');

   DCL 01 EMP_QUALIFIED_SSA,
          05  SEGNAME           CHAR(08) INIT('EMPLOYEE'),
          05  FILLER8           CHAR(01) INIT('('),
```

149

```
           05  FIELD            CHAR(08) INIT('EMPID'),
           05  OPER             CHAR(02) INIT(' ='),
           05  EMP_ID_VAL       CHAR(04) INIT('    '),
           05  FILLER9          CHAR(01) INIT(')');

     DCL THREE                   FIXED BIN (31) INIT(3);
     DCL FOUR                    FIXED BIN (31) INIT(4);
     DCL FIVE                    FIXED BIN (31) INIT(5);
     DCL SIX                     FIXED BIN (31) INIT(6);

 /*********************************************************************
 /*               P R O G R A M   M A I N L I N E                    *
 *********************************************************************/

 CALL P100_INITIALIZATION;
 CALL P200_MAINLINE;
 CALL P300_TERMINATION;

 P100_INITIALIZATION: PROC;

     PUT SKIP LIST ('PLIIMS2: RETRIEVE RECORD FROM EMPLOYEE DB');
     IO_EMPLOYEE_RECORD  = '';

 END P100_INITIALIZATION;

 P200_MAINLINE: PROC;

    /*  SET THE EMPLOYEE SEGMENT SEARCH ARGUMENT AND CALL PLITDLI */

    EMP_ID_VAL = '3217';

    CALL PLITDLI (FOUR,
                  DLI_FUNCGU,
                  PCB_MASK,
                  IO_EMPLOYEE_RECORD,
                  EMP_QUALIFIED_SSA);

    IF STATUS_CODE = '  ' THEN
       DO;
          PUT SKIP LIST ('SUCCESSFUL RETRIEVAL :');
          PUT SKIP DATA(IO_EMPLOYEE_RECORD);
       END;
    ELSE
       CALL P400_DISPLAY_ERROR;

 END P200_MAINLINE;

 P300_TERMINATION: PROC;

    PUT SKIP LIST ('PLIIMS2 - ENDED SUCCESSFULLY');

 END P300_TERMINATION;
```

```
P400_DISPLAY_ERROR: PROC;

    PUT SKIP LIST ('ERROR ENCOUNTERED - DETAIL FOLLOWS');
    PUT SKIP LIST ('SEG_IO_AREA      :' || SEG_IO_AREA);
    PUT SKIP LIST ('DBD_NAME1:' || DBD_NAME);
    PUT SKIP LIST ('SEG_LEVEL1:' || SEG_LEVEL);
    PUT SKIP LIST ('STATUS_CODE:' || STATUS_CODE);
    PUT SKIP LIST ('PROC_OPT1 :' || PROC_OPT);
    PUT SKIP LIST ('SEG_NAME1 :' || SEG_NAME);
    PUT SKIP LIST ('KEY_FDBK1 :' || KEY_FDBK);
    PUT SKIP LIST ('NUM_SENSEG1:' || NUM_SENSEG);
    PUT SKIP LIST ('KEY_FDBK_AREA1:' || KEY_FDBK_AREA);

END P400_DISPLAY_ERROR;

END PLIIMS2;
```

And here is the output for retrieving employee 3217.

```
PLIIMS2: RETRIEVE RECORD FROM EMPLOYEE DB
SUCCESSFUL RETRIEVAL :
IO_EMPLOYEE_RECORD.EMPL_ID_IN='3217'            IO_EMPLOYEE_RECORD.FILLER1=' '
IO_EMPLOYEE_RECORD.EMPL_LNAME='JOHNSON                  '          IO_EMPLO
IO_EMPLOYEE_RECORD.EMPL_FNAME='EDWARD               '          IO_EMPLO
IO_EMPLOYEE_RECORD.EMPL_YRS_SRV='04'            IO_EMPLOYEE_RECORD.FILLER4=' '
IO_EMPLOYEE_RECORD.EMPL_PRM_DTE='2017-01-01'    IO_EMPLOYEE_RECORD.FILLER5=' 397
PLIIMS2 - ENDED SUCCESSFULLY
```

You'll use GU processing anytime you have a need to access data in the database for read-only. Also, we need to test a case where we try to retrieve an employee number which doesn't exist. Let's modify the program to look for EMP_ID 3218, then recompile and re-execute the program. Here's the result:

```
PLIIMS2: RETRIEVE RECORD FROM EMPLOYEE DB
ERROR ENCOUNTERED - DETAIL FOLLOWS
SEG_IO_AREA    :
DBD_NAME1:EMPLOYEE
SEG_LEVEL1:00
STATUS_CODE:GE
PROC_OPT1 :AP
SEG_NAME1 :
KEY_FDBK1 :          0
NUM_SENSEG1:        4
KEY_FDBK_AREA1:
PLIIMS2 - ENDED SUCCESSFULLY
```

Excellent, we captured and reported the error. IMS returned a GE return code which means the record was not found.

Reading a Database Sequentially (GN)

Now let's get just a bit more complex. Our next program PLIIMS3 will read the entire database sequentially. This scenario isn't unusual (a payroll program might process the database sequentially to generate pay checks) so you'll want to have a model of how to carry it out.

Basically we are going to create a loop that will walk through the database sequentially getting each EMPLOYEE segment using Get Next (GN) calls. We'll need a switch to indicate a stopping point which will be the end of the database (IMS code GB). We'll also use an unqualified SSA since we don't need to know the key of each record to traverse the database. Here is the code.

```
PLIIMS3: PROCEDURE (DB_PTR_PCB) OPTIONS(MAIN);
/*******************************************************************
* PROGRAM NAME: PLIIMS3 - WALK THROUGH THE EMPLOYEE (ROOT)        *
*                         SEGMENTS OF THE EMPLOYEE IMS DATABASE.  *
*******************************************************************/

/*******************************************************************
/*                 W O R K I N G   S T O R A G E                  *
*******************************************************************/

    DCL SW_END_OF_DB            STATIC BIT(01) INIT('0'B);
    DCL ONCODE                  BUILTIN;
    DCL DB_PTR_PCB              POINTER;

    DCL PLITDLI                 EXTERNAL ENTRY;

    DCL 01 DLI_FUNCTIONS,
           05 DLI_FUNCISRT      CHAR(04) INIT ('ISRT'),
           05 DLI_FUNCGU        CHAR(04) INIT ('GU  '),
           05 DLI_FUNCGN        CHAR(04) INIT ('GN  '),
           05 DLI_FUNCGHU       CHAR(04) INIT ('GHU '),
           05 DLI_FUNCGNP       CHAR(04) INIT ('GNP '),
           05 DLI_FUNCREPL      CHAR(04) INIT ('REPL'),
           05 DLI_FUNCDLET      CHAR(04) INIT ('DLET'),
           05 DLI_FUNCXRST      CHAR(04) INIT ('XRST'),
           05 DLI_FUNCCHKP      CHAR(04) INIT ('CHKP'),
           05 DLI_FUNCROLL      CHAR(04) INIT ('ROLL');

    DCL 01 IO_EMPLOYEE_RECORD,
           05  EMPL_ID_IN       CHAR(04),
           05  FILLER1          CHAR(01),
           05  EMPL_LNAME       CHAR(30),
           05  FILLER2          CHAR(01),
           05  EMPL_FNAME       CHAR(20),
           05  FILLER3          CHAR(01),
           05  EMPL_YRS_SRV     CHAR(02),
           05  FILLER4          CHAR(01),
```

```
                 05   EMPL_PRM_DTE          CHAR(10),
                 05   FILLER5               CHAR(10);

        DCL 01 PCB_MASK                BASED(DB_PTR_PCB),
                 05 DBD_NAME               CHAR(08),
                 05 SEG_LEVEL              CHAR(02),
                 05 STATUS_CODE            CHAR(02),
                 05 PROC_OPT               CHAR(04),
                 05 FILLER6                FIXED BIN (31),
                 05 SEG_NAME               CHAR(08),
                 05 KEY_FDBK                FIXED BIN (31),
                 05 NUM_SENSEG             FIXED BIN (31),
                 05 KEY_FDBK_AREA,
                    10 EMPLOYEE_ID         CHAR(04);

        DCL 01 EMP_UNQUALIFIED_SSA,
                 05  SEGNAME               CHAR(08) INIT ('EMPLOYEE'),
                 05  FILLER7               CHAR(01) INIT (' ');

        DCL 01 EMP_QUALIFIED_SSA,
                 05  SEGNAME               CHAR(08) INIT('EMPLOYEE'),
                 05  FILLER8               CHAR(01) INIT('('),
                 05  FIELD                 CHAR(08) INIT('EMPID'),
                 05  OPER                  CHAR(02) INIT(' ='),
                 05  EMP_ID_VAL            CHAR(04) INIT('    '),
                 05  FILLER9               CHAR(01) INIT(')');


        DCL THREE                      FIXED BIN (31) INIT(3);
        DCL FOUR                       FIXED BIN (31) INIT(4);
        DCL FIVE                       FIXED BIN (31) INIT(5);
        DCL SIX                        FIXED BIN (31) INIT(6);

/*********************************************************************
/*                  P R O G R A M   M A I N L I N E                 *
 ********************************************************************/

CALL P100_INITIALIZATION;
CALL P200_MAINLINE;
CALL P300_TERMINATION;

P100_INITIALIZATION: PROC;

    PUT SKIP LIST ('PLIIMS3: TRAVERSE EMPLOYEE DATABASE ROOT SEGS');
    PCB_MASK = '';
    IO_EMPLOYEE_RECORD  = '';

 /* DO INITIAL DB READ FOR FIRST EMPLOYEE RECORD */

    CALL PLITDLI (FOUR,
                  DLI_FUNCGN,
                  PCB_MASK,
                  IO_EMPLOYEE_RECORD,
```

```
                    EMP_UNQUALIFIED_SSA);

      IF STATUS_CODE = '   ' THEN;
      ELSE
          IF STATUS_CODE = 'GB' THEN
              DO;
                  SW_END_OF_DB = '1'B;
                  PUT SKIP LIST ('** END OF DATABASE');
              END;
          ELSE
              DO;
                  CALL P400_DISPLAY_ERROR;
                  RETURN;
              END;

END P100_INITIALIZATION;

P200_MAINLINE: PROC;

      /*  MAIN LOOP - CYCLE THROUGH ALL ROOT SEGMENTS IN THE DB,
                     DISPLAYING THE DATA RETRIEVED              */

          IF SW_END_OF_DB THEN
              PUT SKIP LIST ('NO RECORDS TO PROCESS!!');
          ELSE
              DO WHILE (¬SW_END_OF_DB);
                  PUT SKIP LIST ('SUCCESSFUL READ :'
                      || IO_EMPLOYEE_RECORD);

                  CALL PLITDLI (FOUR,
                                DLI_FUNCGN,
                                PCB_MASK,
                                IO_EMPLOYEE_RECORD,
                                EMP_UNQUALIFIED_SSA);

                  IF STATUS_CODE = '   ' THEN;
                  ELSE
                      IF STATUS_CODE = 'GB' THEN
                          DO;
                              SW_END_OF_DB = '1'B;
                              PUT SKIP LIST ('** END OF DATABASE');
                          END;
                      ELSE
                          DO;
                              CALL P400_DISPLAY_ERROR;
                              RETURN;
                          END;

              END; /* DO WHILE */

          PUT SKIP LIST ('FINISHED PROCESSING IN P200_MAINLINE');

END P200_MAINLINE;
```

```
P300_TERMINATION: PROC;

    CLOSE FILE(EMPIFILE);

    PUT SKIP LIST ('PLIIMS3 - SUCCESSFULLY ENDED');

END P300_TERMINATION;

P400_DISPLAY_ERROR: PROC;

    PUT SKIP LIST ('ERROR ENCOUNTERED - DETAIL FOLLOWS');
    PUT SKIP LIST ('SEG_IO_AREA      :' || SEG_IO_AREA);
    PUT SKIP LIST ('DBD_NAME1:' || DBD_NAME);
    PUT SKIP LIST ('SEG_LEVEL1:' || SEG_LEVEL);
    PUT SKIP LIST ('STATUS_CODE:' || STATUS_CODE);
    PUT SKIP LIST ('PROC_OPT1 :' || PROC_OPT);
    PUT SKIP LIST ('SEG_NAME1 :' || SEG_NAME);
    PUT SKIP LIST ('KEY_FDBK1 :' || KEY_FDBK);
    PUT SKIP LIST ('NUM_SENSEG1:' || NUM_SENSEG);
    PUT SKIP LIST ('KEY_FDBK_AREA1:' || KEY_FDBK_AREA);

END P400_DISPLAY_ERROR;

END PLIIMS3;
```

Now let's compile and link, and then execute PLIIMS3. Here's the run output.

```
PLIIMS3: TRAVERSE EMPLOYEE DATABASE ROOT SEGS
SUCCESSFUL READ :1111   SUCCESSFUL READ :      SUCCESSFUL READ :VEREEN
SUCCESSFUL READ :CHARLES                       SUCCESSFUL READ :      SUCCESSF
SUCCESSFUL READ :2017-01-01                    SUCCESSFUL READ : 937253058
SUCCESSFUL READ :1122   SUCCESSFUL READ :      SUCCESSFUL READ :JENKINS
SUCCESSFUL READ :DEBORAH                        SUCCESSFUL READ :      SUCCESSF
SUCCESSFUL READ :2017-01-01                    SUCCESSFUL READ : 435092366
SUCCESSFUL READ :3217   SUCCESSFUL READ :      SUCCESSFUL READ :JOHNSON
SUCCESSFUL READ :EDWARD                         SUCCESSFUL READ :      SUCCESSF
SUCCESSFUL READ :2017-01-01                    SUCCESSFUL READ : 397342007
SUCCESSFUL READ :4175   SUCCESSFUL READ :      SUCCESSFUL READ :TURNBULL
SUCCESSFUL READ :FRED                           SUCCESSFUL READ :      SUCCESSF
SUCCESSFUL READ :2016-12-01                    SUCCESSFUL READ : 542083017
SUCCESSFUL READ :4720   SUCCESSFUL READ :      SUCCESSFUL READ :SCHULTZ
SUCCESSFUL READ :TIM                            SUCCESSFUL READ :      SUCCESSF
SUCCESSFUL READ :2017-01-01                    SUCCESSFUL READ : 650450254
SUCCESSFUL READ :4836   SUCCESSFUL READ :      SUCCESSFUL READ :SMITH
SUCCESSFUL READ :SANDRA                         SUCCESSFUL READ :      SUCCESSF
SUCCESSFUL READ :2017-01-01                    SUCCESSFUL READ : 028374669
SUCCESSFUL READ :6288   SUCCESSFUL READ :      SUCCESSFUL READ :WILLARD
SUCCESSFUL READ :JOE                            SUCCESSFUL READ :      SUCCESSF
SUCCESSFUL READ :2016-01-01                    SUCCESSFUL READ : 209883920
SUCCESSFUL READ :7459   SUCCESSFUL READ :      SUCCESSFUL READ :STEWART
SUCCESSFUL READ :BETTY                          SUCCESSFUL READ :      SUCCESSF
SUCCESSFUL READ :2016-07-31                    SUCCESSFUL READ : 019572830
SUCCESSFUL READ :9134   SUCCESSFUL READ :      SUCCESSFUL READ :FRANKLIN
SUCCESSFUL READ :BRIANNA                        SUCCESSFUL READ :      SUCCESSF
SUCCESSFUL READ :2016-10-01                    SUCCESSFUL READ : 937293598
** END OF DATABASE
```

155

```
FINISHED PROCESSING IN P200_MAINLINE
PLIIMS3 - SUCCESSFULLY ENDED
```

You now have a model for any kind of sequential processing you want to do on root segments. Processing child segments is a bit more involved, but not much. We'll show an example of that later.

Updating a Segment (GHU/REPL)

In PLIIMS4 we will update a record. Updating (either changing or deleting a record) always involves two steps in IMS. You must first get and lock the record you are operating on so that no other process can make updates to it. Second you issue the REPL or DLET call.

A Get Hold Unique (GHU) call prevents any other process from making modifications to the record until you are finished with it. Similar calls are Get Hold Next (GHN) and Get Hold Next in Parent (GHNP).

Let's change the promotion date on employee 9134 to Sept 1, 2016. To do that we need a GHU call with a qualified SSA that we have loaded with the employee id value of 9134.

```
EMP_ID_VAL = '9134';
```

Here is the IMS call, and notice we are using IO_EMPLOYEE_RECORD as our segment I/O area. This is because it has the full record layout with all the fields which makes it easy to change the promotion date by field assignment.

```
CALL PLITDLI (FOUR,
              DLI_FUNCGHU,
              PCB_MASK,
              IO_EMPLOYEE_RECORD,
              EMP_QUALIFIED_SSA);
```

Once you've done the GHU call you can change the value of the promotion date.

```
EMPL_PRM_DTE = '2016-09-01';
```

Finally you issue the REPL call. A REPL does not use any SSA, it simply uses the segment I/O area to perform the update to the database. Notice you only have three parameters. A REPL or DLET call does not use SSAs since the record is already held in memory.

```
CALL PLITDLI (THREE,
              DLI_FUNCREPL,
              PCB_MASK,
              IO_EMPLOYEE_RECORD);
```

Here is the entire program listing for PLIIMS4.

```
 PLIIMS4: PROCEDURE (DB_PTR_PCB) OPTIONS(MAIN);
/*******************************************************************
* PROGRAM NAME :   PLIIMS4 - UPDATE A RECORD FROM EMPLOYEE DB    *
*******************************************************************/

/*******************************************************************
/*                W O R K I N G   S T O R A G E                  *
*******************************************************************/

   DCL ONCODE                  BUILTIN;
   DCL DB_PTR_PCB              POINTER;
   DCL PLITDLI                 EXTERNAL ENTRY;

   DCL 01 DLI_FUNCTIONS,
          05 DLI_FUNCISRT      CHAR(04) INIT ('ISRT'),
          05 DLI_FUNCGU        CHAR(04) INIT ('GU  '),
          05 DLI_FUNCGN        CHAR(04) INIT ('GN  '),
          05 DLI_FUNCGHU       CHAR(04) INIT ('GHU '),
          05 DLI_FUNCGNP       CHAR(04) INIT ('GNP '),
          05 DLI_FUNCREPL      CHAR(04) INIT ('REPL'),
          05 DLI_FUNCDLET      CHAR(04) INIT ('DLET'),
          05 DLI_FUNCXRST      CHAR(04) INIT ('XRST'),
          05 DLI_FUNCCHKP      CHAR(04) INIT ('CHKP'),
          05 DLI_FUNCROLL      CHAR(04) INIT ('ROLL');

   DCL 01 IO_EMPLOYEE_RECORD,
          05  EMPL_ID_IN       CHAR(04),
          05  FILLER1          CHAR(01),
          05  EMPL_LNAME       CHAR(30),
          05  FILLER2          CHAR(01),
          05  EMPL_FNAME       CHAR(20),
          05  FILLER3          CHAR(01),
          05  EMPL_YRS_SRV     CHAR(02),
          05  FILLER4          CHAR(01),
          05  EMPL_PRM_DTE     CHAR(10),
          05  FILLER5          CHAR(10);

   DCL 01 PCB_MASK             BASED(DB_PTR_PCB),
          05 DBD_NAME          CHAR(08),
          05 SEG_LEVEL         CHAR(02),
          05 STATUS_CODE       CHAR(02),
          05 PROC_OPT          CHAR(04),
          05 FILLER6           FIXED BIN (31),
          05 SEG_NAME          CHAR(08),
          05 KEY_FDBK          FIXED BIN (31),
          05 NUM_SENSEG        FIXED BIN (31),
          05 KEY_FDBK_AREA,
             10 EMPLOYEE_ID    CHAR(04);

   DCL 01 EMP_UNQUALIFIED_SSA,
          05  SEGNAME          CHAR(08) INIT ('EMPLOYEE'),
```

```
             05  FILLER7              CHAR(01) INIT (' ');

    DCL 01 EMP_QUALIFIED_SSA,
             05  SEGNAME              CHAR(08) INIT('EMPLOYEE'),
             05  FILLER8              CHAR(01) INIT('('),
             05  FIELD                CHAR(08) INIT('EMPID'),
             05  OPER                 CHAR(02) INIT(' ='),
             05  EMP_ID_VAL           CHAR(04) INIT('    '),
             05  FILLER9              CHAR(01) INIT(')');

    DCL THREE                         FIXED BIN (31) INIT(3);
    DCL FOUR                          FIXED BIN (31) INIT(4);
    DCL FIVE                          FIXED BIN (31) INIT(5);
    DCL SIX                           FIXED BIN (31) INIT(6);

/********************************************************************
/*               P R O G R A M   M A I N L I N E               *
********************************************************************/

CALL P100_INITIALIZATION;
CALL P200_MAINLINE;
CALL P300_TERMINATION;

P100_INITIALIZATION: PROC;

    PUT SKIP LIST ('PLIIMS4: UPDATE RECORD FROM EMPLOYEE DB');
    IO_EMPLOYEE_RECORD = '';
    PCB_MASK = '';

END P100_INITIALIZATION;

P200_MAINLINE: PROC;

   /*  SET THE EMPLOYEE SEGMENT SEARCH ARGUMENT AND CALL PLITDLI */

    EMP_ID_VAL = '9134';

    CALL PLITDLI (FOUR,
                  DLI_FUNCGHU,
                  PCB_MASK,
                  IO_EMPLOYEE_RECORD,
                  EMP_QUALIFIED_SSA);

    IF STATUS_CODE = '  ' THEN
       DO;
           PUT SKIP LIST ('SUCCESSFUL GET-HOLD CALL :');
           PUT SKIP DATA(IO_EMPLOYEE_RECORD);

      /*  NOW MAKE THE CHANGE AND REPLACE THE SEGMENT */

           EMPL_PRM_DTE = '2016-09-01';

           CALL PLITDLI (THREE,
```

158

```
                            DLI_FUNCREPL,
                            PCB_MASK,
                            IO_EMPLOYEE_RECORD);

            IF STATUS_CODE = '  ' THEN
                DO;
                    PUT SKIP LIST ('SUCCESSFUL REPLACE CALL :');
                    PUT SKIP DATA(IO_EMPLOYEE_RECORD);
                END;
            ELSE
                DO;
                    PUT SKIP LIST ('ERROR IN REPLACE: ' || STATUS_CODE);
                    CALL P400_DISPLAY_ERROR;
                END;

        END;

    ELSE
        DO;
            PUT SKIP LIST ('ERROR IN GET HOLD :' || STATUS_CODE);
            CALL P400_DISPLAY_ERROR;
        END;

END P200_MAINLINE;

P300_TERMINATION: PROC;

    PUT SKIP LIST ('PLIIMS4 - ENDED SUCCESSFULLY');

END P300_TERMINATION;

P400_DISPLAY_ERROR: PROC;

    PUT SKIP LIST ('ERROR ENCOUNTERED - DETAIL FOLLOWS');
    PUT SKIP LIST ('SEG_IO_AREA     :' || SEG_IO_AREA);
    PUT SKIP LIST ('DBD_NAME1:' ||  DBD_NAME);
    PUT SKIP LIST ('SEG_LEVEL1:' || SEG_LEVEL);
    PUT SKIP LIST ('STATUS_CODE:' || STATUS_CODE);
    PUT SKIP LIST ('PROC_OPT1 :' || PROC_OPT);
    PUT SKIP LIST ('SEG_NAME1 :' || SEG_NAME);
    PUT SKIP LIST ('KEY_FDBK1 :' || KEY_FDBK);
    PUT SKIP LIST ('NUM_SENSEG1:' || NUM_SENSEG);
    PUT SKIP LIST ('KEY_FDBK_AREA1:' || KEY_FDBK_AREA);

END P400_DISPLAY_ERROR;

END PLIIMS4;
```

Now let's compile and link, and then run the program.

```
PLIIMS4: UPDATE RECORD FROM EMPLOYEE DB
SUCCESSFUL GET-HOLD CALL :
```

159

```
IO_EMPLOYEE_RECORD.EMPL_ID_IN='9134'                IO_EMPLOYEE_RECORD.FILLER1=' '
IO_EMPLOYEE_RECORD.EMPL_LNAME='FRANKLIN            '              IO_EMPLO
IO_EMPLOYEE_RECORD.EMPL_FNAME='BRIANNA               '              IO_EMPLO
IO_EMPLOYEE_RECORD.EMPL_YRS_SRV='00'                IO_EMPLOYEE_RECORD.FILLER4=' '
IO_EMPLOYEE_RECORD.EMPL_PRM_DTE='2016-10-01'        IO_EMPLOYEE_RECORD.FILLER5=' 937
SUCCESSFUL REPLACE CALL :
IO_EMPLOYEE_RECORD.EMPL_ID_IN='9134'                IO_EMPLOYEE_RECORD.FILLER1=' '
IO_EMPLOYEE_RECORD.EMPL_LNAME='FRANKLIN            '              IO_EMPLO
IO_EMPLOYEE_RECORD.EMPL_FNAME='BRIANNA               '              IO_EMPLO
IO_EMPLOYEE_RECORD.EMPL_YRS_SRV='00'                IO_EMPLOYEE_RECORD.FILLER4=' '
IO_EMPLOYEE_RECORD.EMPL_PRM_DTE='2016-09-01'        IO_EMPLOYEE_RECORD.FILLER5=' 937
PLIIMS4 - ENDED SUCCESSFULLY
```

This is the basic model for doing updates to a database. The next program example is just a slight variation.

Deleting a Segment (GHU/DLET)

For PLIIMS5 we are going to delete a record. Basically the code is exactly the same as PLIIMS4 except we are deleting instead of updating a record. Let's delete employee 9134, the one we just updated. You can simply copy the PLIIMS4 code and make modifications to turn it into a delete program.

Here's the source code.

```
PLIIMS5: PROCEDURE (DB_PTR_PCB) OPTIONS(MAIN);
/*****************************************************************
* PROGRAM NAME :   PLIIMS5 - DELETE A RECORD FROM EMPLOYEE DB      *
******************************************************************/

/*****************************************************************
/*               W O R K I N G   S T O R A G E                   *
******************************************************************/

    DCL ONCODE                  BUILTIN;
    DCL DB_PTR_PCB              POINTER;
    DCL PLITDLI                 EXTERNAL ENTRY;

    DCL 01 DLI_FUNCTIONS,
           05 DLI_FUNCISRT      CHAR(04) INIT ('ISRT'),
           05 DLI_FUNCGU        CHAR(04) INIT ('GU  '),
           05 DLI_FUNCGN        CHAR(04) INIT ('GN  '),
           05 DLI_FUNCGHU       CHAR(04) INIT ('GHU '),
           05 DLI_FUNCGNP       CHAR(04) INIT ('GNP '),
           05 DLI_FUNCREPL      CHAR(04) INIT ('REPL'),
           05 DLI_FUNCDLET      CHAR(04) INIT ('DLET'),
           05 DLI_FUNCXRST      CHAR(04) INIT ('XRST'),
           05 DLI_FUNCCHKP      CHAR(04) INIT ('CHKP'),
           05 DLI_FUNCROLL      CHAR(04) INIT ('ROLL');

    DCL 01 IO_EMPLOYEE_RECORD,
           05  EMPL_ID          CHAR(04),
```

```
        05  FILLER1              CHAR(01),
        05  EMPL_LNAME           CHAR(30),
        05  FILLER2              CHAR(01),
        05  EMPL_FNAME           CHAR(20),
        05  FILLER3              CHAR(01),
        05  EMPL_YRS_SRV         CHAR(02),
        05  FILLER4              CHAR(01),
        05  EMPL_PRM_DTE         CHAR(10),
        05  FILLER5              CHAR(10);

 DCL 01 PCB_MASK                 BASED(DB_PTR_PCB),
        05 DBD_NAME              CHAR(08),
        05 SEG_LEVEL             CHAR(02),
        05 STATUS_CODE           CHAR(02),
        05 PROC_OPT              CHAR(04),
        05 FILLER6               FIXED BIN (31),
        05 SEG_NAME              CHAR(08),
        05 KEY_FDBK              FIXED BIN (31),
        05 NUM_SENSEG            FIXED BIN (31),
        05 KEY_FDBK_AREA,
           10 EMPLOYEE_ID        CHAR(04);

 DCL 01 EMP_UNQUALIFIED_SSA,
        05  SEGNAME              CHAR(08) INIT ('EMPLOYEE'),
        05  FILLER7              CHAR(01) INIT (' ');

 DCL 01 EMP_QUALIFIED_SSA,
        05  SEGNAME              CHAR(08) INIT('EMPLOYEE'),
        05  FILLER8              CHAR(01) INIT('('),
        05  FIELD                CHAR(08) INIT('EMPID'),
        05  OPER                 CHAR(02) INIT(' ='),
        05  EMP_ID_VAL           CHAR(04) INIT ('    '),
        05  FILLER9              CHAR(01) INIT(')');

 DCL THREE                       FIXED BIN (31) INIT(3);
 DCL FOUR                        FIXED BIN (31) INIT(4);
 DCL FIVE                        FIXED BIN (31) INIT(5);
 DCL SIX                         FIXED BIN (31) INIT(6);

/********************************************************************
/*              P R O G R A M   M A I N L I N E                    *
*********************************************************************/

CALL P100_INITIALIZATION;
CALL P200_MAINLINE;
CALL P300_TERMINATION;

P100_INITIALIZATION: PROC;

    PUT SKIP LIST ('PLIIMS5: DELETE RECORD FROM EMPLOYEE DB');
    IO_EMPLOYEE_RECORD  = '';
    PCB_MASK = '';
```

161

```
END P100_INITIALIZATION;

P200_MAINLINE: PROC;

    /*  SET THE EMPLOYEE SEGMENT SEARCH ARGUMENT AND CALL PLITDLI */

    EMP_ID_VAL = '9134';

    CALL PLITDLI (FOUR,
                  DLI_FUNCGHU,
                  PCB_MASK,
                  IO_EMPLOYEE_RECORD,
                  EMP_QUALIFIED_SSA);

    IF STATUS_CODE = '  ' THEN
       DO;
           PUT SKIP LIST ('SUCCESSFUL GET-HOLD CALL :');
           PUT SKIP DATA(IO_EMPLOYEE_RECORD);

      /*  NOW DELETE THE SEGMENT */

           CALL PLITDLI (THREE,
                         DLI_FUNCDLET,
                         PCB_MASK,
                         IO_EMPLOYEE_RECORD);

           IF STATUS_CODE = '  ' THEN
              DO;
                 PUT SKIP LIST ('SUCCESSFUL DELETE CALL :');
                 PUT SKIP LIST ('EMPLOYEE ' || EMPL_ID);
              END;
           ELSE
              DO;
                 PUT SKIP LIST ('ERROR IN DELETE: ' || STATUS_CODE);
                 CALL P400_DISPLAY_ERROR;
              END;

       END;

    ELSE
       DO;
          PUT SKIP LIST ('ERROR IN GET HOLD :' || STATUS_CODE);
          CALL P400_DISPLAY_ERROR;
       END;

END P200_MAINLINE;

P300_TERMINATION: PROC;

    PUT SKIP LIST ('PLIIMS5 - ENDED SUCCESSFULLY');

END P300_TERMINATION;
```

```
P400_DISPLAY_ERROR: PROC;

    PUT SKIP LIST ('ERROR ENCOUNTERED - DETAIL FOLLOWS');
    PUT SKIP LIST ('SEG_IO_AREA      :' || SEG_IO_AREA);
    PUT SKIP LIST ('DBD_NAME1:' ||  DBD_NAME);
    PUT SKIP LIST ('SEG_LEVEL1:' || SEG_LEVEL);
    PUT SKIP LIST ('STATUS_CODE:' || STATUS_CODE);
    PUT SKIP LIST ('PROC_OPT1 :' || PROC_OPT);
    PUT SKIP LIST ('SEG_NAME1 :' || SEG_NAME);
    PUT SKIP LIST ('KEY_FDBK1 :' || KEY_FDBK);
    PUT SKIP LIST ('NUM_SENSEG1:' || NUM_SENSEG);
    PUT SKIP LIST ('KEY_FDBK_AREA1:' || KEY_FDBK_AREA);

END P400_DISPLAY_ERROR;

END PLIIMS5;
```

Now compile, link and run:

```
PLIIMS5: DELETE RECORD FROM EMPLOYEE DB
SUCCESSFUL GET-HOLD CALL :
IO_EMPLOYEE_RECORD.EMPL_ID='9134'              IO_EMPLOYEE_RECORD.FILLER1=' '
IO_EMPLOYEE_RECORD.EMPL_LNAME='FRANKLIN                   '           IO_EMPLO
IO_EMPLOYEE_RECORD.EMPL_FNAME='BRIANNA              '              IO_EMPLO
IO_EMPLOYEE_RECORD.EMPL_YRS_SRV='00'           IO_EMPLOYEE_RECORD.FILLER4=' '
IO_EMPLOYEE_RECORD.EMPL_PRM_DTE='2016-09-01'   IO_EMPLOYEE_RECORD.FILLER5=' 937
SUCCESSFUL DELETE CALL :
EMPLOYEE 9134
PLIIMS5 - ENDED SUCCESSFULLY
```

As you can see, the record was deleted. Now let's move on to performing operations for records that are children of the root level in the database hierarchy.

Inserting Child Segments

So far we've only dealt with root segments. That was pretty straightforward. Now let's introduce child segments. In COBIMS6 we are going to create an EMPPAY segment under each EMPLOYEE root segment. This will be similar to how we inserted root segments except we need to specify which root segment to insert the child segment under.

First, let's look at our input file:

```
----+----1----+----2----+----3----+----4----+----5
*************************** Top of Data ****
1111    8700000   670000   362500   20170101
1122    8200000   600000   341666   20170101
3217    6500000   550000   270833   20170101
4175    5500000   150000   229166   20170101
4720    8000000   250000   333333   20170101
4836    6200000   220000   258333   20170101
6288    7000000   200000   291666   20170101
```

```
7459      8500000  450000  354166  20170101
9134      7500000  250000  312500  20170101
```

To decrypt here a little, the file contains employee id numbers with annual salary, annual bonus pay, twice-per-month paycheck dollar and cents amount, and the effective date for all this information. Let's create a record structure in COBOL for this file.

```
DCL 01 IN_EMPPAY_RECORD,
       05  EMP_ID_IN          CHAR(04),
       05  FILLER1            CHAR(05),
       05  REG_PAY_IN         PIC '99999V99',
       05  FILLER2            CHAR(02),
       05  BON_PAY_IN         PIC '9999V99',
       05  FILLER3            CHAR(02),
       05  SEMIMTH_IN         PIC '9999V99',
       05  FILLER4            CHAR(02),
       05  EFF_DATE_IN        CHAR(08),
       05  FILLER5            CHAR(38);
```

We'll also need an IMS I/O area for the EMPPAY segment. How about this one? We'll map data from the input record into this I/O area before we do the ISRT action. Note that we are using packed data fields for the IMS segment. This will save some space.

```
DCL 01 IO_EMPPAY_RECORD,
       05  PAY_EFF_DATE       CHAR(8),
       05  PAY_REG_PAY        FIXED DEC (8,2),
       05  PAY_BON_PAY        FIXED DEC (8,2),
       05  SEMIMTH_PAY        FIXED DEC (8,2),
       05  FILLER55           CHAR(57);
```

Finally, we need our SSA structures. We'll be using the unqualified EMPPAY SSA, but we'll go ahead and add both the qualified and unqualified SSAs to the program.

```
DCL 01 EMPPAY_UNQUALIFIED_SSA,
       05  SEGNAME            CHAR(08) INIT('EMPPAY  '),
       05  FILLER10           CHAR(01) INIT(' ');

DCL 01 EMPPAY_QUALIFIED_SSA,
       05  SEGNAME            CHAR(08) INIT('EMPPAY  '),
       05  FILLER11           CHAR(01) INIT('('),
       05  FIELD              CHAR(08) INIT('EFFDATE '),
       05  OPER               CHAR(02) INIT(' ='),
       05  EFFDATE_VAL        CHAR(08) INIT('        '),
       05  FILLER12           CHAR(01) INIT(')');
```

So given this information, our ISRT call should look like this. Notice that we use a qualified SSA for the EMPLOYEE root segment, and an unqualified SSA for the EMPPAY segment.

```
CALL PLITDLI (FIVE,
             DLI_FUNCISRT,
             PCB_MASK,
             IO_EMPPAY_RECORD,
             EMP_QUALIFIED_SSA,
             EMPPAY_UNQUALIFIED_SSA);
```

Of course we will need a loop for reading the input pay file, and we'll need code to map the input fields to the EMPPAY fields. And we must move the employee id on the input file to the EMPLOYEE qualified SSA. Finally, recall that we deleted employee 9134, but there is a record in the input file for 9134. Have we coded to handle this error? We'll soon see.

Here is our completed code for PLIIMS6.

```
PLIIMS6: PROCEDURE (DB_PTR_PCB) OPTIONS(MAIN);
/******************************************************************
* PROGRAM NAME :   PLIIMS6 - INSERT EMPLOYEE PAY RECORDS INTO THE  *
*                  EMPLOYEE IMS DB. ROOT KEY MUST BE SPECIFIED.    *
******************************************************************/

/******************************************************************
/*               F I L E S    U S E D                            *
******************************************************************/

   DCL EMPPAYFL FILE RECORD SEQL INPUT;

/******************************************************************
/*             W O R K I N G    S T O R A G E                    *
******************************************************************/

   DCL SW_END_OF_FILE            STATIC BIT(01) INIT('0'B);
   DCL ONCODE                    BUILTIN;
   DCL DB_PTR_PCB                POINTER;

   DCL PLITDLI                   EXTERNAL ENTRY;

   DCL 01 DLI_FUNCTIONS,
          05 DLI_FUNCISRT        CHAR(04) INIT ('ISRT'),
          05 DLI_FUNCGU          CHAR(04) INIT ('GU  '),
          05 DLI_FUNCGN          CHAR(04) INIT ('GN  '),
          05 DLI_FUNCGHU         CHAR(04) INIT ('GHU '),
          05 DLI_FUNCGNP         CHAR(04) INIT ('GNP '),
          05 DLI_FUNCREPL        CHAR(04) INIT ('REPL'),
          05 DLI_FUNCDLET        CHAR(04) INIT ('DLET'),
```

```
          05  DLI_FUNCXRST         CHAR(04) INIT ('XRST'),
          05  DLI_FUNCCHKP         CHAR(04) INIT ('CHKP'),
          05  DLI_FUNCROLL         CHAR(04) INIT ('ROLL');

  DCL 01 IN_EMPPAY_RECORD,
          05  EMP_ID_IN            CHAR(04),
          05  FILLER1              CHAR(05),
          05  REG_PAY_IN           PIC '99999V99',
          05  FILLER2              CHAR(02),
          05  BON_PAY_IN           PIC '9999V99',
          05  FILLER3              CHAR(02),
          05  SEMIMTH_IN           PIC '9999V99',
          05  FILLER4              CHAR(02),
          05  EFF_DATE_IN          CHAR(08),
          05  FILLER5              CHAR(38);

  DCL 01 IO_EMPPAY_RECORD,
          05  PAY_EFF_DATE         CHAR(8),
          05  PAY_REG_PAY          FIXED DEC (8,2),
          05  PAY_BON_PAY          FIXED DEC (8,2),
          05  SEMIMTH_PAY          FIXED DEC (8,2),
          05  FILLER55             CHAR(57);

  DCL 01 PCB_MASK                  BASED(DB_PTR_PCB),
          05  DBD_NAME             CHAR(08),
          05  SEG_LEVEL            CHAR(02),
          05  STATUS_CODE          CHAR(02),
          05  PROC_OPT             CHAR(04),
          05  FILLER6              FIXED BIN (31),
          05  SEG_NAME             CHAR(08),
          05  KEY_FDBK             FIXED BIN (31),
          05  NUM_SENSEG           FIXED BIN (31),
          05  KEY_FDBK_AREA,
          10 EMPLOYEE_ID           CHAR(04),
          10 EMP_PAY_DATE          CHAR(08);

  DCL 01 EMP_UNQUALIFIED_SSA,
          05  SEGNAME              CHAR(08) INIT ('EMPLOYEE'),
          05  FILLER7              CHAR(01) INIT (' ');

  DCL 01 EMP_QUALIFIED_SSA,
          05  SEGNAME              CHAR(08) INIT('EMPLOYEE'),
          05  FILLER8              CHAR(01) INIT('('),
          05  FIELD                CHAR(08) INIT('EMPID'),
          05  OPER                 CHAR(02) INIT(' ='),
          05  EMP_ID_VAL           CHAR(04) INIT('    '),
          05  FILLER9              CHAR(01) INIT(')');

  DCL 01 EMPPAY_UNQUALIFIED_SSA,
          05  SEGNAME              CHAR(08) INIT('EMPPAY  '),
          05  FILLER10             CHAR(01) INIT(' ');

  DCL 01 EMPPAY_QUALIFIED_SSA,
```

```
        05  SEGNAME              CHAR(08) INIT('EMPPAY  '),
        05  FILLER11             CHAR(01) INIT('('),
        05  FIELD                CHAR(08) INIT('EFFDATE '),
        05  OPER                 CHAR(02) INIT(' ='),
        05  EFFDATE_VAL          CHAR(08) INIT('        '),
        05  FILLER12             CHAR(01) INIT(')');

   DCL SEG_IO_AREA               CHAR(80) INIT (' ');

   DCL THREE                     FIXED BIN (31) INIT(3);
   DCL FOUR                      FIXED BIN (31) INIT(4);
   DCL FIVE                      FIXED BIN (31) INIT(5);
   DCL SIX                       FIXED BIN (31) INIT(6);

/*********************************************************************
/*                O N   C O N D I T I O N S                         *
*********************************************************************/

   ON ENDFILE (EMPIFILE) SW_END_OF_FILE =  '1'B;

/*********************************************************************
/*                P R O G R A M   M A I N L I N E                   *
*********************************************************************/

CALL P100_INITIALIZATION;
CALL P200_MAINLINE;
CALL P300_TERMINATION;

P100_INITIALIZATION: PROC;

   PUT SKIP LIST ('PLIIMS6: INSERT RECORDS');
   OPEN FILE (EMPPAYFL);

   IN_EMPPAY_RECORD  = '';
   PCB_MASK = '';

END P100_INITIALIZATION;

P200_MAINLINE: PROC;

   /*  MAIN LOOP - READ THE INPUT FILE, LOAD THE OUTPUT
                   STRUCTURE AND WRITE PAY RECORD TO OUTPUT */

   READ FILE (EMPPAYFL) INTO (IN_EMPPAY_RECORD);

   DO WHILE (¬SW_END_OF_FILE);

      /* ASSIGN KEY FOR EMPLOYEE LEVEL SSA */

      EMP_ID_VAL   = EMP_ID_IN;

      /* ASSIGN PAY FIELDS */
```

167

```
               PAY_EFF_DATE = EFF_DATE_IN;
               PAY_REG_PAY  = REG_PAY_IN;
               PAY_BON_PAY  = BON_PAY_IN;
               SEMIMTH_PAY  = SEMIMTH_IN;

               CALL PLITDLI (FIVE,
                             DLI_FUNCISRT,
                             PCB_MASK,
                             IO_EMPPAY_RECORD,
                             EMP_QUALIFIED_SSA,
                             EMPPAY_UNQUALIFIED_SSA);

          IF STATUS_CODE = '  ' THEN
               DO;
                    PUT SKIP LIST ('SUCCESSFUL INSERT PAY REC:');
                    PUT SKIP DATA (IO_EMPPAY_RECORD);
               END;
          ELSE
               DO;
                    CALL P400_DISPLAY_ERROR;
                    RETURN;
               END;

          READ FILE (EMPPAYFL) INTO (IN_EMPPAY_RECORD);

     END; /* DO WHILE */

END P200_MAINLINE;

P300_TERMINATION: PROC;

     CLOSE FILE(EMPPAYFL);

     PUT SKIP LIST ('PLIIMS6 - SUCCESSFULLY ENDED');

END P300_TERMINATION;

P400_DISPLAY_ERROR: PROC;

     PUT SKIP LIST ('ERROR ENCOUNTERED - DETAIL FOLLOWS');
     PUT SKIP DATA (IO_EMPPAY_RECORD);
     PUT SKIP LIST ('DBD_NAME1:' || DBD_NAME);
     PUT SKIP LIST ('SEG_LEVEL1:' || SEG_LEVEL);
     PUT SKIP LIST ('STATUS_CODE:' || STATUS_CODE);
     PUT SKIP LIST ('PROC_OPT1 :' || PROC_OPT);
     PUT SKIP LIST ('SEG_NAME1 :' || SEG_NAME);
     PUT SKIP LIST ('KEY_FDBK1 :' || KEY_FDBK);
     PUT SKIP LIST ('NUM_SENSEG1:' || NUM_SENSEG);
     PUT SKIP LIST ('KEY_FDBK_AREA1:' || KEY_FDBK_AREA);

END P400_DISPLAY_ERROR;

END PLIIMS6;
```

Compile and link, and then run the program. Here is the output.

```
PLIIMS6: INSERT RECORDS
SUCCESSFUL INSERT PAY REC:
IO_EMPPAY_RECORD.PAY_EFF_DATE='20170101'        IO_EMPPAY_RECORD.PAY_REG_PAY=
IO_EMPPAY_RECORD.PAY_BON_PAY=    6700.00         IO_EMPPAY_RECORD.SEMIMTH_PAY=
IO_EMPPAY_RECORD.FILLER55='                      " &           6Y
SUCCESSFUL INSERT PAY REC:
IO_EMPPAY_RECORD.PAY_EFF_DATE='20170101'        IO_EMPPAY_RECORD.PAY_REG_PAY=
IO_EMPPAY_RECORD.PAY_BON_PAY=    6000.00         IO_EMPPAY_RECORD.SEMIMTH_PAY=
IO_EMPPAY_RECORD.FILLER55='                      " &           6Y
SUCCESSFUL INSERT PAY REC:
IO_EMPPAY_RECORD.PAY_EFF_DATE='20170101'        IO_EMPPAY_RECORD.PAY_REG_PAY=
IO_EMPPAY_RECORD.PAY_BON_PAY=    5500.00         IO_EMPPAY_RECORD.SEMIMTH_PAY=
IO_EMPPAY_RECORD.FILLER55='                      " &           6Y
SUCCESSFUL INSERT PAY REC:
IO_EMPPAY_RECORD.PAY_EFF_DATE='20170101'        IO_EMPPAY_RECORD.PAY_REG_PAY=
IO_EMPPAY_RECORD.PAY_BON_PAY=    1500.00         IO_EMPPAY_RECORD.SEMIMTH_PAY=
IO_EMPPAY_RECORD.FILLER55='                      " &           6Y
SUCCESSFUL INSERT PAY REC:
IO_EMPPAY_RECORD.PAY_EFF_DATE='20170101'        IO_EMPPAY_RECORD.PAY_REG_PAY=
IO_EMPPAY_RECORD.PAY_BON_PAY=    2500.00         IO_EMPPAY_RECORD.SEMIMTH_PAY=
IO_EMPPAY_RECORD.FILLER55='                      " &           6Y
SUCCESSFUL INSERT PAY REC:
IO_EMPPAY_RECORD.PAY_EFF_DATE='20170101'        IO_EMPPAY_RECORD.PAY_REG_PAY=
IO_EMPPAY_RECORD.PAY_BON_PAY=    2200.00         IO_EMPPAY_RECORD.SEMIMTH_PAY=
IO_EMPPAY_RECORD.FILLER55='                      " &           6Y
SUCCESSFUL INSERT PAY REC:
IO_EMPPAY_RECORD.PAY_EFF_DATE='20170101'        IO_EMPPAY_RECORD.PAY_REG_PAY=
IO_EMPPAY_RECORD.PAY_BON_PAY=    2000.00         IO_EMPPAY_RECORD.SEMIMTH_PAY=
IO_EMPPAY_RECORD.FILLER55='                      " &           6Y
SUCCESSFUL INSERT PAY REC:
IO_EMPPAY_RECORD.PAY_EFF_DATE='20170101'        IO_EMPPAY_RECORD.PAY_REG_PAY=
IO_EMPPAY_RECORD.PAY_BON_PAY=    4500.00         IO_EMPPAY_RECORD.SEMIMTH_PAY=
IO_EMPPAY_RECORD.FILLER55='                      " &           6Y
ERROR ENCOUNTERED - DETAIL FOLLOWS
IO_EMPPAY_RECORD.PAY_EFF_DATE='20170101'        IO_EMPPAY_RECORD.PAY_REG_PAY=
IO_EMPPAY_RECORD.PAY_BON_PAY=    2500.00         IO_EMPPAY_RECORD.SEMIMTH_PAY=
IO_EMPPAY_RECORD.FILLER55='                      " &           6Y
DBD_NAME1:
SEG_LEVEL1:00
STATUS_CODE:GE
PROC_OPT1 :
SEG_NAME1 :
KEY_FDBK1 :              0
NUM_SENSEG1:             0
KEY_FDBK_AREA1:          KEY_FDBK_AREA1:20170101
PLIIMS6 - SUCCESSFULLY ENDED
```

The bolded text above shows that our error code caught the missing root segment and reported it. In this case we took a "soft landing" by not terminating the program. In the real world we might have forced an abend.[5] Or we might possibly have written the record to an exception report for someone to review and correct.

[5] You can force an abend with a memory dump by calling LE program CEE3DMP. Details for how to do

You have a model for inserting new data to child segments in an IMS database.

Reading Child Segments Sequentially (GNP)

Now let's create PLIIMS7 to read back the records we just added to the database. We can traverse the database using GN for the root segments and GNP calls for the children. So we'll borrow the code from COBIMS3 for walking through the root segments. And then we'll add code for retrieving GNP.

Keep in mind that we've only added a single EMPPAY child under each root segment. If there were more than one child, our code would need to allow for that. But for now, our spec will ask us to simply get a root and then get the first child under that root. Then display the pay information for the employee.

We already know how to traverse the root segment. So once we get a root segment, we need to take the EMP_ID returned in the IO-EMPLOYEE-RECORD and use it to set the qualified SSA for EMPLOYEE. We'll use the unqualified SSA for the EMPPAY segment. And we'll load the segment data into the IO_EMPPAY_RECORD I/O area. This is what our call will look like.

```
CALL PLITDLI (FIVE,
              DLI_FUNCGNP,
              PCB_MASK,
              IO_EMPPAY_RECORD,
              EMP_QUALIFIED_SSA,
              EMPPAY_UNQUALIFIED_SSA);
```

Other than that, our program doesn't need to use any new techniques. Here is the completed program listing.

```
PLIIMS7: PROCEDURE (DB_PTR_PCB) OPTIONS(MAIN);
  /*********************************************************************
  * PROGRAM NAME: PLIIMS7 - WALK THROUGH THE EMPLOYEE AND EMPPAY      *
  *                         SEGMENTS OF THE EMPLOYEE IMS DATABASE.    *
  *********************************************************************/
```

that are available in the IBM Knowledge Center. We will only take soft abends in this text, so we won't abend with CEE3DMP.

```
/**********************************************************************
/*                 W O R K I N G   S T O R A G E                     *
/*******************************************************************/

    DCL SW_END_OF_DB              STATIC BIT(01) INIT('0'B);
    DCL SW_NO_MORE_SEGS           STATIC BIT(01) INIT('0'B);
    DCL ONCODE                    BUILTIN;
    DCL DB_PTR_PCB                POINTER;

    DCL PLITDLI                   EXTERNAL ENTRY;

    DCL 01 DLI_FUNCTIONS,
           05 DLI_FUNCISRT        CHAR(04) INIT ('ISRT'),
           05 DLI_FUNCGU          CHAR(04) INIT ('GU  '),
           05 DLI_FUNCGN          CHAR(04) INIT ('GN  '),
           05 DLI_FUNCGHU         CHAR(04) INIT ('GHU '),
           05 DLI_FUNCGNP         CHAR(04) INIT ('GNP '),
           05 DLI_FUNCREPL        CHAR(04) INIT ('REPL'),
           05 DLI_FUNCDLET        CHAR(04) INIT ('DLET'),
           05 DLI_FUNCXRST        CHAR(04) INIT ('XRST'),
           05 DLI_FUNCCHKP        CHAR(04) INIT ('CHKP'),
           05 DLI_FUNCROLL        CHAR(04) INIT ('ROLL');

    DCL 01 IO_EMPLOYEE_RECORD,
           05  EMPL_ID            CHAR(04),
           05  FILLER1            CHAR(01),
           05  EMPL_LNAME         CHAR(30),
           05  FILLER2            CHAR(01),
           05  EMPL_FNAME         CHAR(20),
           05  FILLER3            CHAR(01),
           05  EMPL_YRS_SRV       CHAR(02),
           05  FILLER4            CHAR(01),
           05  EMPL_PRM_DTE       CHAR(10),
           05  FILLER5            CHAR(10);

    DCL 01 IO_EMPPAY_RECORD,
           05  PAY_EFF_DATE       CHAR(8),
           05  PAY_REG_PAY        FIXED DEC (8,2),
           05  PAY_BON_PAY        FIXED DEC (8,2),
           05  SEMIMTH_PAY        FIXED DEC (8,2),
           05  FILLER6            CHAR(57);

    DCL 01 IO_EMPPAYHS_RECORD.
           05  PAY_DATE           CHAR(8),
           05  PAY_ANN_PAY        FIXED DEC (8,2),
           05  PAY_AMT            FIXED DEC (8,2),
           05  FILLER65           CHAR(62);

    DCL 01 PCB_MASK               BASED(DB_PTR_PCB),
           05 DBD_NAME            CHAR(08),
           05 SEG_LEVEL           CHAR(02),
           05 STATUS_CODE         CHAR(02),
```

```
          05 PROC_OPT              CHAR(04),
          05 FILLER99              FIXED BIN (31),
          05 SEG_NAME              CHAR(08),
          05 KEY_FDBK              FIXED BIN (31),
          05 NUM_SENSEG            FIXED BIN (31),
          05 KEY_FDBK_AREA,
             10 EMPLOYEE_ID        CHAR(04);

     DCL 01 EMP_UNQUALIFIED_SSA,
          05  SEGNAME              CHAR(08) INIT ('EMPLOYEE'),
          05  FILLER7              CHAR(01) INIT (' ');

     DCL 01 EMP_QUALIFIED_SSA,
          05  SEGNAME              CHAR(08) INIT('EMPLOYEE'),
          05  FILLER8              CHAR(01) INIT('('),
          05  FIELD                CHAR(08) INIT('EMPID'),
          05  OPER                 CHAR(02) INIT(' ='),
          05  EMP_ID_VAL           CHAR(04) INIT('    '),
          05  FILLER9              CHAR(01) INIT(')');

     DCL 01 EMPPAY_UNQUALIFIED_SSA,
          05  SEGNAME              CHAR(08) INIT('EMPPAY  '),
          05  FILLER10             CHAR(01) INIT(' ');

     DCL 01 EMPPAY_QUALIFIED_SSA,
          05  SEGNAME              CHAR(08) INIT('EMPPAY  '),
          05  FILLER11             CHAR(01) INIT('('),
          05  FIELD                CHAR(08) INIT('EFFDATE '),
          05  OPER                 CHAR(02) INIT(' ='),
          05  EFFDATE_VAL          CHAR(08) INIT('        '),
          05  FILLER12             CHAR(01) INIT(')');

     DCL THREE                     FIXED BIN (31) INIT(3);
     DCL FOUR                      FIXED BIN (31) INIT(4);
     DCL FIVE                      FIXED BIN (31) INIT(5);
     DCL SIX                       FIXED BIN (31) INIT(6);

/********************************************************************
/*              P R O G R A M   M A I N L I N E                    *
********************************************************************/

CALL P100_INITIALIZATION;
CALL P200_MAINLINE;
CALL P300_TERMINATION;

P100_INITIALIZATION: PROC;

    PUT SKIP LIST ('PLIIMS7: TRAVERSE EMPLOYEE DATABASE PAY SEGS');
    PUT SKIP LIST ('PROCESSING IN P100-INITIALIZATION');

    PCB_MASK = '';
    IO_EMPLOYEE_RECORD  = '';
    IO_EMPPAY_RECORD  = '';
```

172

```
    /* DO INITIAL DB READ FOR FIRST EMPLOYEE RECORD */

    CALL PLITDLI (FOUR,
                  DLI_FUNCGN,
                  PCB_MASK,
                  IO_EMPLOYEE_RECORD,
                  EMP_UNQUALIFIED_SSA);

    IF STATUS_CODE = '  ' THEN;
    ELSE
       IF STATUS_CODE = 'GB' THEN
          DO;
             SW_END_OF_DB = '1'B;
             PUT SKIP LIST ('** END OF DATABASE');
          END;
       ELSE
          DO;
             CALL P400_DISPLAY_ERROR;
             RETURN;
          END;

END P100_INITIALIZATION;

P200_MAINLINE: PROC;

    /*  MAIN LOOP - CYCLE THROUGH ALL ROOT SEGMENTS IN THE DB,
                    DISPLAYING THE DATA RETRIEVED              */

        IF SW_END_OF_DB THEN
           PUT SKIP LIST ('NO RECORDS TO PROCESS!!');
        ELSE
           DO WHILE (¬SW_END_OF_DB);
              PUT SKIP LIST ('SUCCESSFUL EMPLOYEE READ : ' ||
              EMPL_ID);

              SW_NO_MORE_SEGS = '0'B;

              DO WHILE (¬SW_END_OF_DB & ¬SW_NO_MORE_SEGS);
                 CALL P500_GET_PAY_SEG;
              END; /* DO WHILE */

              CALL PLITDLI (FOUR,
                            DLI_FUNCGN,
                            PCB_MASK,
                            IO_EMPLOYEE_RECORD,
                            EMP_UNQUALIFIED_SSA);

              IF STATUS_CODE = '  ' THEN;
              ELSE
                 IF STATUS_CODE = 'GB' THEN
                    DO;
                       SW_END_OF_DB = '1'B;
```

```
                                PUT SKIP LIST ('** END OF DATABASE');
                        END;
                    ELSE
                        DO;
                            CALL P400_DISPLAY_ERROR;
                            RETURN;
                        END;

            END; /* DO WHILE */

        PUT SKIP LIST ('FINISHED PROCESSING IN P200_MAINLINE');

END P200_MAINLINE;

P300_TERMINATION: PROC;

    CLOSE FILE(EMPIFILE);

    PUT SKIP LIST ('PLIIMS7 - SUCCESSFULLY ENDED');

END P300_TERMINATION;

P400_DISPLAY_ERROR: PROC;

    PUT SKIP LIST ('ERROR ENCOUNTERED - DETAIL FOLLOWS');
    PUT SKIP LIST ('SEG_IO_AREA      :' || SEG_IO_AREA);
    PUT SKIP LIST ('DBD_NAME1:' || DBD_NAME);
    PUT SKIP LIST ('SEG_LEVEL1:' || SEG_LEVEL);
    PUT SKIP LIST ('STATUS_CODE:' || STATUS_CODE);
    PUT SKIP LIST ('PROC_OPT1 :' || PROC_OPT);
    PUT SKIP LIST ('SEG_NAME1 :' || SEG_NAME);
    PUT SKIP LIST ('KEY_FDBK1 :' || KEY_FDBK);
    PUT SKIP LIST ('NUM_SENSEG1:' || NUM_SENSEG);
    PUT SKIP LIST ('KEY_FDBK_AREA1:' || KEY_FDBK_AREA);

END P400_DISPLAY_ERROR;

P500_GET_PAY_SEG: PROC;

    PUT SKIP LIST ('PROCESSING IN P500_GET_PAY_SEG');
    EMP_ID_VAL  = EMPL_ID;
    EFFDATE_VAL = '20170101';

    CALL PLITDLI (FIVE,
                    DLI_FUNCGNP,
                    PCB_MASK,
                    IO_EMPPAY_RECORD,
                    EMP_QUALIFIED_SSA,
                    EMPPAY_QUALIFIED_SSA);

    SELECT (STATUS_CODE);

        WHEN (' ')
```

```
            DO;
                PUT SKIP LIST ('SUCCESSFUL EMPPAY RETRIEVAL');
                PUT SKIP LIST ('PAY_EFF_DATE ' || PAY_EFF_DATE);
                PUT SKIP LIST ('PAY_REG_PAY  ' || PAY_REG_PAY);
                PUT SKIP LIST ('PAY_BON_PAY  ' || PAY_BON_PAY);
                PUT SKIP LIST ('SEMIMTH_PAY  ' || SEMIMTH_PAY);
            END;

        WHEN ('GE')
            DO;
                SW_NO_MORE_SEGS = '1'B;
                PUT SKIP LIST ('** NO MORE PAY SEGMENTS');
            END;

        WHEN ('GB')
            DO;
                SW_END_OF_DB = '1'B;
                PUT SKIP LIST ('** END OF DATABASE');
            END;
        OTHERWISE
            CALL P400_DISPLAY_ERROR;

    END; /* SELECT */


 END P500_GET_PAY_SEG;

 END PLIIMS7;
```

Once again, let's compile and link, and then run the program. Here is the output showing both root and child segments.

```
PLIIMS7: TRAVERSE EMPLOYEE DATABASE PAY SEGS
PROCESSING IN P100-INITIALIZATION
SUCCESSFUL EMPLOYEE READ : 1111
PROCESSING IN P500_GET_PAY_SEG
SUCCESSFUL EMPPAY RETRIEVAL
PAY_EFF_DATE 20170101
PAY_REG_PAY     87000.00
PAY_BON_PAY      6700.00
SEMIMTH_PAY      3625.00
PROCESSING IN P500_GET_PAY_SEG
** NO MORE PAY SEGMENTS
SUCCESSFUL EMPLOYEE READ : 1122
PROCESSING IN P500_GET_PAY_SEG
SUCCESSFUL EMPPAY RETRIEVAL
PAY_EFF_DATE 20170101
PAY_REG_PAY     82000.00
PAY_BON_PAY      6000.00
SEMIMTH_PAY      3416.66
PROCESSING IN P500_GET_PAY_SEG
** NO MORE PAY SEGMENTS
```

```
SUCCESSFUL EMPLOYEE READ : 3217
PROCESSING IN P500_GET_PAY_SEG
SUCCESSFUL EMPPAY RETRIEVAL
PAY_EFF_DATE 20170101
PAY_REG_PAY      65000.00
PAY_BON_PAY       5500.00
SEMIMTH_PAY       2708.33
PROCESSING IN P500_GET_PAY_SEG
** NO MORE PAY SEGMENTS
SUCCESSFUL EMPLOYEE READ : 4175
PROCESSING IN P500_GET_PAY_SEG
SUCCESSFUL EMPPAY RETRIEVAL
PAY_EFF_DATE 20170101
PAY_REG_PAY      55000.00
PAY_BON_PAY       1500.00
SEMIMTH_PAY       2291.66
PROCESSING IN P500_GET_PAY_SEG
** NO MORE PAY SEGMENTS
SUCCESSFUL EMPLOYEE READ : 4720
PROCESSING IN P500_GET_PAY_SEG
SUCCESSFUL EMPPAY RETRIEVAL
PAY_EFF_DATE 20170101
PAY_REG_PAY      80000.00
PAY_BON_PAY       2500.00
SEMIMTH_PAY       3333.33
PROCESSING IN P500_GET_PAY_SEG
** NO MORE PAY SEGMENTS
SUCCESSFUL EMPLOYEE READ : 4836
PROCESSING IN P500_GET_PAY_SEG
SUCCESSFUL EMPPAY RETRIEVAL
PAY_EFF_DATE 20170101
PAY_REG_PAY      62000.00
PAY_BON_PAY       2200.00
SEMIMTH_PAY       2583.33
PROCESSING IN P500_GET_PAY_SEG
** NO MORE PAY SEGMENTS
SUCCESSFUL EMPLOYEE READ : 6288
PROCESSING IN P500_GET_PAY_SEG
SUCCESSFUL EMPPAY RETRIEVAL
PAY_EFF_DATE 20170101
PAY_REG_PAY      70000.00
PAY_BON_PAY       2000.00
SEMIMTH_PAY       2916.66
PROCESSING IN P500_GET_PAY_SEG
** NO MORE PAY SEGMENTS
SUCCESSFUL EMPLOYEE READ : 7459
PROCESSING IN P500_GET_PAY_SEG
SUCCESSFUL EMPPAY RETRIEVAL
PAY_EFF_DATE 20170101
PAY_REG_PAY      85000.00
PAY_BON_PAY       4500.00
SEMIMTH_PAY       3541.66
PROCESSING IN P500_GET_PAY_SEG
```

```
** NO MORE PAY SEGMENTS
** END OF DATABASE
FINISHED PROCESSING IN P200_MAINLINE
PLIIMS7 - SUCCESSFULLY ENDED
```

And you now have a model for traversing the database hierarchy from root to child. What remains is to demonstrate navigation through 3 levels of the hierarchy, and then reading it all back where there are multiple child segments.

Inserting Child Segments Down the Hierarchy (3 levels)

Ok, I think we have a pretty good handle on the adding and retrieving of child segments. But just to be sure, let's work with the EMPPAYHS segment, adding and retrieving records. That's slightly different that what we've done already, but not that much.

For PLIIMS8, let's add a pay history segment EMPPAYHS for all employees using pay date January 15, 2017, and using the twice-monthly pay information from the EMPPAY segment. So we need to position ourselves at the EMPPAY child segment under each EMPLOYEE root segment, and then ISRT an EMPPAYHS segment.

I think we've covered all the techniques required to write this program. Why don't you give it a try first, and then we'll get back together and compare our code? Take a good break and then code up your version.

. . . .

Ok, I'm back with a good cup of tea. Here's my version of the code. I added the segment I/O and SSAs for the EMPPAYHS segment. The INSERT call for the EMPPAYHS segment is as follows:

```
CALL PLITDLI (SIX,
              DLI_FUNCISRT,
              PCB_MASK,
              IO_EMPPAYHS_RECORD,
              EMP_QUALIFIED_SSA,
              EMPPAY_QUALIFIED_SSA,
              EMPPAYHS_UNQUALIFIED_SSA);
```

Should be no surprises there. Just a bit more navigation and slightly different database calls. Here's the full program.

```
PLIIMS8: PROCEDURE (DB_PTR_PCB) OPTIONS(MAIN);
/******************************************************************
* PROGRAM NAME :    PLIIMS8 - INSERT EMPLOYEE HISTORY PAY RECORDS  *
*                   UNDER THEIR EMPPAY PARENTS. QUALIFIED SSA'S     *
*                   MUST BE PROVIDED FOR BOTH THE EMPLOYEE AND      *
*                   EMPPAY SEGMENTS.                                *
******************************************************************/

/******************************************************************
/*                 W O R K I N G   S T O R A G E                  *
******************************************************************/

    DCL SW_END_OF_DB            STATIC BIT(01) INIT('0'B);
    DCL ONCODE                  BUILTIN;
    DCL DB_PTR_PCB              POINTER;

    DCL PLITDLI                 EXTERNAL ENTRY;

    DCL 01 DLI_FUNCTIONS,
          05 DLI_FUNCISRT       CHAR(04) INIT ('ISRT'),
          05 DLI_FUNCGU         CHAR(04) INIT ('GU  '),
          05 DLI_FUNCGN         CHAR(04) INIT ('GN  '),
          05 DLI_FUNCGHU        CHAR(04) INIT ('GHU '),
          05 DLI_FUNCGNP        CHAR(04) INIT ('GNP '),
          05 DLI_FUNCREPL       CHAR(04) INIT ('REPL'),
          05 DLI_FUNCDLET       CHAR(04) INIT ('DLET'),
          05 DLI_FUNCXRST       CHAR(04) INIT ('XRST'),
          05 DLI_FUNCCHKP       CHAR(04) INIT ('CHKP'),
          05 DLI_FUNCROLL       CHAR(04) INIT ('ROLL');

    DCL 01 IO_EMPLOYEE_RECORD,
          05  EMPL_ID           CHAR(04),
          05  FILLER1           CHAR(01),
          05  EMPL_LNAME        CHAR(30),
          05  FILLER2           CHAR(01),
          05  EMPL_FNAME        CHAR(20),
          05  FILLER3           CHAR(01),
          05  EMPL_YRS_SRV      CHAR(02),
          05  FILLER4           CHAR(01),
          05  EMPL_PRM_DTE      CHAR(10),
          05  FILLER5           CHAR(10);

    DCL 01 IO_EMPPAY_RECORD,
          05  PAY_EFF_DATE      CHAR(8),
          05  PAY_REG_PAY       FIXED DEC (8,2),
          05  PAY_BON_PAY       FIXED DEC (8,2),
          05  SEMIMTH_PAY       FIXED DEC (8,2),
          05  FILLER55          CHAR(57);

    DCL 01 IO_EMPPAYHS_RECORD,
          05  PAY_DATE          CHAR(8),
          05  PAY_ANN_PAY       FIXED DEC (8,2),
          05  PAY_AMT           FIXED DEC (8,2),
```

178

```
        05   FILLER65            CHAR(62);

DCL 01 PCB_MASK                  BASED(DB_PTR_PCB),
        05   DBD_NAME            CHAR(08),
        05   SEG_LEVEL           CHAR(02),
        05   STATUS_CODE         CHAR(02),
        05   PROC_OPT            CHAR(04),
        05   FILLER6             FIXED BIN (31),
        05   SEG_NAME            CHAR(08),
        05   KEY_FDBK            FIXED BIN (31),
        05   NUM_SENSEG          FIXED BIN (31),
        05   KEY_FDBK_AREA,
        10 EMPLOYEE_ID           CHAR(04),
        10 EMP_PAY_DATE          CHAR(08);

DCL 01 EMP_UNQUALIFIED_SSA,
        05   SEGNAME             CHAR(08) INIT ('EMPLOYEE'),
        05   FILLER7             CHAR(01) INIT (' ');

DCL 01 EMP_QUALIFIED_SSA,
        05   SEGNAME             CHAR(08) INIT('EMPLOYEE'),
        05   FILLER8             CHAR(01) INIT('('),
        05   FIELD               CHAR(08) INIT('EMPID'),
        05   OPER                CHAR(02) INIT(' ='),
        05   EMP_ID_VAL          CHAR(04) INIT('    '),
        05   FILLER9             CHAR(01) INIT(')');

DCL 01 EMPPAY_UNQUALIFIED_SSA,
        05   SEGNAME             CHAR(08) INIT('EMPPAY  '),
        05   FILLER10            CHAR(01) INIT(' ');

DCL 01 EMPPAY_QUALIFIED_SSA,
        05   SEGNAME             CHAR(08) INIT('EMPPAY  '),
        05   FILLER11            CHAR(01) INIT('('),
        05   FIELD               CHAR(08) INIT('EFFDATE '),
        05   OPER                CHAR(02) INIT(' ='),
        05   EFFDATE_VAL         CHAR(08) INIT('        '),
        05   FILLER12            CHAR(01) INIT(')');

DCL 01 EMPPAYHS_UNQUALIFIED_SSA,
        05   SEGNAME             CHAR(08) INIT('EMPPAYHS'),
        05   FILLER13            CHAR(01) INIT(' ');

DCL WS_PAY_DATE                  CHAR(08) INIT ('20170228');

DCL SEG_IO_AREA                  CHAR(80) INIT (' ');

DCL THREE                        FIXED BIN (31) INIT(3);
DCL FOUR                         FIXED BIN (31) INIT(4);
DCL FIVE                         FIXED BIN (31) INIT(5);
DCL SIX                          FIXED BIN (31) INIT(6);
```

```
/******************************************************************
/*                P R O G R A M   M A I N L I N E              *
******************************************************************/

CALL P100_INITIALIZATION;
CALL P200_MAINLINE;
CALL P300_TERMINATION;

P100_INITIALIZATION: PROC;

    PUT SKIP LIST ('PLIIMS8: INSERT RECORDS');
    PUT SKIP LIST ('PROCESSING IN P100_INITIALIZATION');

    IO_EMPLOYEE_RECORD  = '';
    IO_EMPPAY_RECORD  = '';
    IO_EMPPAYHS_RECORD  = '';
    PCB_MASK = '';

    /* DO INITIAL DB READ FOR FIRST EMPLOYEE RECORD */

    CALL PLITDLI (FOUR,
                  DLI_FUNCGN,
                  PCB_MASK,
                  IO_EMPLOYEE_RECORD,
                  EMP_UNQUALIFIED_SSA);

    IF STATUS_CODE = '  ' THEN;
    ELSE
       IF STATUS_CODE = 'GB' THEN
          DO;
              SW_END_OF_DB = '1'B;
              PUT SKIP LIST ('** END OF DATABASE');
          END;
       ELSE
          DO;
              CALL P9000_DISPLAY_ERROR;
              RETURN;
          END;

END P100_INITIALIZATION;

P200_MAINLINE: PROC;

    /*  MAIN LOOP - WALK THROUGH THE DATABASE GETTING EMPLOYEE
                    PAY HISTORY SEGMENTS.                       */

    IF SW_END_OF_DB THEN
       PUT SKIP LIST ('NO RECORDS TO PROCESS!!');
    ELSE
       DO WHILE (¬SW_END_OF_DB);

           PUT SKIP LIST ('SUCCESSFUL READ OF EMPLOYEE ' || EMPL_ID);
```

```
/* ASSIGN KEY FOR EMPLOYEE LEVEL SSA AND GET EMPPAY SEG */

EMP_ID_VAL = EMPL_ID;
CALL P2000_GET_EMPPAY;
IF STATUS_CODE ¬= ' ' THEN
   DO;
      PUT SKIP LIST ('ERROR READING EMPPAY');
      CALL P9000_DISPLAY_ERROR;
      RETURN;
   END;
ELSE
   DO;
      PUT SKIP LIST ('SUCCESSFUL PAY READ : '
         || IO_EMPPAY_RECORD);

      /* ASSIGN KEY FOR EMPPAY LEVEL SSA FOR SEG */

      EFFDATE_VAL = PAY_EFF_DATE;

      PAY_DATE    = WS_PAY_DATE;
      PAY_ANN_PAY = PAY_REG_PAY;
      PAY_AMT     = SEMIMTH_PAY;

      CALL P3000_INSERT_EMPPAYHS;
      IF STATUS_CODE ¬= ' ' THEN
         DO;
            CALL P9000_DISPLAY_ERROR;
            RETURN;
         END;
      ELSE
         DO;
            PUT SKIP LIST ('SUCCESSFUL INSERT EMPPAYHS : '
               || EMP_ID_VAL);
            PUT SKIP LIST ('SUCCESSFUL INSERT VALUES   : ' );
            PUT SKIP DATA (IO_EMPPAYHS_RECORD);
         END;

      CALL P1000_GET_NEXT_ROOT;
      IF STATUS_CODE = 'GB' THEN
         DO;
            SW_END_OF_DB = '1'B;
            PUT SKIP LIST ('** END OF DATABASE');
         END;
      ELSE
         IF STATUS_CODE = ' ' THEN;
         ELSE
            DO;
               CALL P9000_DISPLAY_ERROR;
               RETURN;
            END;

   END; /* SUCCESSFULLY RETRIEVED PAY SEG */
```

```
          END; /* DO WHILE */

      PUT SKIP LIST ('FINISHED PROCESSING IN P200_MAINLINE');

END P200_MAINLINE;

P300_TERMINATION: PROC;

      PUT SKIP LIST ('PLIIMS8 - SUCCESSFULLY ENDED');

END P300_TERMINATION;

P1000_GET_NEXT_ROOT: PROC;

   PUT SKIP LIST ('PROCESSING IN P1000_GET_NEXT_ROOT');

   CALL PLITDLI (FOUR,
                 DLI_FUNCGN,
                 PCB_MASK,
                 IO_EMPLOYEE_RECORD,
                 EMP_UNQUALIFIED_SSA);

END P1000_GET_NEXT_ROOT;

P2000_GET_EMPPAY: PROC;

   PUT SKIP LIST ('PROCESSING IN P2000_GET_EMPPAY');

   CALL PLITDLI (FIVE,
                 DLI_FUNCGNP,
                 PCB_MASK,
                 IO_EMPPAY_RECORD,
                 EMP_QUALIFIED_SSA,
                 EMPPAY_UNQUALIFIED_SSA);

END P2000_GET_EMPPAY;

P3000_INSERT_EMPPAYHS: PROC;

   PUT SKIP LIST ('PROCESSING IN P3000-INSERT-EMPPAYHS');

   CALL PLITDLI (SIX,
                 DLI_FUNCISRT,
                 PCB_MASK,
                 IO_EMPPAYHS_RECORD,
                 EMP_QUALIFIED_SSA,
                 EMPPAY_QUALIFIED_SSA,
                 EMPPAYHS_UNQUALIFIED_SSA);

END P3000_INSERT_EMPPAYHS;

P9000_DISPLAY_ERROR: PROC;
```

```
                PUT SKIP LIST ('ERROR ENCOUNTERED - DETAIL FOLLOWS');
                PUT SKIP DATA (IO_EMPPAY_RECORD);
                PUT SKIP LIST ('DBD_NAME1:' ||  DBD_NAME);
                PUT SKIP LIST ('SEG_LEVEL1:' || SEG_LEVEL);
                PUT SKIP LIST ('STATUS_CODE:' || STATUS_CODE);
                PUT SKIP LIST ('PROC_OPT1 :' || PROC_OPT);
                PUT SKIP LIST ('SEG_NAME1 :' || SEG_NAME);
                PUT SKIP LIST ('KEY_FDBK1 :' || KEY_FDBK);
                PUT SKIP LIST ('NUM_SENSEG1:' || NUM_SENSEG);
                PUT SKIP LIST ('KEY_FDBK_AREA1:' || KEY_FDBK_AREA);

         END P9000_DISPLAY_ERROR;

         END PLIIMS8;
```

Now let's compile, link and run the program. Here is the output.

```
PLIIMS8: INSERT RECORDS
PROCESSING IN P100_INITIALIZATION
SUCCESSFUL READ OF EMPLOYEE 1111
PROCESSING IN P2000_GET_EMPPAY
SUCCESSFUL PAY READ : 20170101              SUCCESSFUL PAY READ :    87000.0
  6700.00              SUCCESSFUL PAY READ :    3625.00              SUCCESSF

PROCESSING IN P3000-INSERT-EMPPAYHS
SUCCESSFUL INSERT EMPPAYHS : 1111
SUCCESSFUL INSERT VALUES   :
IO_EMPPAYHS_RECORD.PAY_DATE='20170228'       IO_EMPPAYHS_RECORD.PAY_ANN_PAY=
IO_EMPPAYHS_RECORD.PAY_AMT=   3625.00
IO_EMPPAYHS_RECORD.FILLER65='
PROCESSING IN P1000_GET_NEXT_ROOT
SUCCESSFUL READ OF EMPLOYEE 1122
PROCESSING IN P2000_GET_EMPPAY
SUCCESSFUL PAY READ : 20170101              SUCCESSFUL PAY READ :    82000.0
  6000.00              SUCCESSFUL PAY READ :    3416.66              SUCCESSF

PROCESSING IN P3000-INSERT-EMPPAYHS
SUCCESSFUL INSERT EMPPAYHS : 1122
SUCCESSFUL INSERT VALUES   :
IO_EMPPAYHS_RECORD.PAY_DATE='20170228'       IO_EMPPAYHS_RECORD.PAY_ANN_PAY=
IO_EMPPAYHS_RECORD.PAY_AMT=   3416.66
IO_EMPPAYHS_RECORD.FILLER65='
PROCESSING IN P1000_GET_NEXT_ROOT
SUCCESSFUL READ OF EMPLOYEE 3217
PROCESSING IN P2000_GET_EMPPAY
SUCCESSFUL PAY READ : 20170101              SUCCESSFUL PAY READ :    65000.0
  5500.00              SUCCESSFUL PAY READ :    2708.33              SUCCESSF

PROCESSING IN P3000-INSERT-EMPPAYHS
SUCCESSFUL INSERT EMPPAYHS : 3217
SUCCESSFUL INSERT VALUES   :
IO_EMPPAYHS_RECORD.PAY_DATE='20170228'       IO_EMPPAYHS_RECORD.PAY_ANN_PAY=
IO_EMPPAYHS_RECORD.PAY_AMT=   2708.33
IO_EMPPAYHS_RECORD.FILLER65='
PROCESSING IN P1000_GET_NEXT_ROOT
SUCCESSFUL READ OF EMPLOYEE 4175
PROCESSING IN P2000_GET_EMPPAY
```

```
SUCCESSFUL PAY READ : 20170101                  SUCCESSFUL PAY READ :    55000.0
   1500.00             SUCCESSFUL PAY READ :    2291.66              SUCCESSF

PROCESSING IN P3000-INSERT-EMPPAYHS
SUCCESSFUL INSERT EMPPAYHS : 4175
SUCCESSFUL INSERT VALUES    :
IO_EMPPAYHS_RECORD.PAY_DATE='20170228'          IO_EMPPAYHS_RECORD.PAY_ANN_PAY=
IO_EMPPAYHS_RECORD.PAY_AMT=    2291.66
IO_EMPPAYHS_RECORD.FILLER65='
PROCESSING IN P1000_GET_NEXT_ROOT
SUCCESSFUL READ OF EMPLOYEE 4720
PROCESSING IN P2000_GET_EMPPAY
SUCCESSFUL PAY READ : 20170101                  SUCCESSFUL PAY READ :    80000.0
   2500.00             SUCCESSFUL PAY READ :    3333.33              SUCCESSF

PROCESSING IN P3000-INSERT-EMPPAYHS
SUCCESSFUL INSERT EMPPAYHS : 4720
SUCCESSFUL INSERT VALUES    :
IO_EMPPAYHS_RECORD.PAY_DATE='20170228'          IO_EMPPAYHS_RECORD.PAY_ANN_PAY=
IO_EMPPAYHS_RECORD.PAY_AMT=    3333.33
IO_EMPPAYHS_RECORD.FILLER65='
PROCESSING IN P1000_GET_NEXT_ROOT
SUCCESSFUL READ OF EMPLOYEE 4836
PROCESSING IN P2000_GET_EMPPAY
SUCCESSFUL PAY READ : 20170101                  SUCCESSFUL PAY READ :    62000.0
   2200.00             SUCCESSFUL PAY READ :    2583.33              SUCCESSF

PROCESSING IN P3000-INSERT-EMPPAYHS
SUCCESSFUL INSERT EMPPAYHS : 4836
SUCCESSFUL INSERT VALUES    :
IO_EMPPAYHS_RECORD.PAY_DATE='20170228'          IO_EMPPAYHS_RECORD.PAY_ANN_PAY=
IO_EMPPAYHS_RECORD.PAY_AMT=    2583.33
IO_EMPPAYHS_RECORD.FILLER65='
PROCESSING IN P1000_GET_NEXT_ROOT
SUCCESSFUL READ OF EMPLOYEE 6288
PROCESSING IN P2000_GET_EMPPAY
SUCCESSFUL PAY READ : 20170101                  SUCCESSFUL PAY READ :    70000.0
   2000.00             SUCCESSFUL PAY READ :    2916.66              SUCCESSF

PROCESSING IN P3000-INSERT-EMPPAYHS
SUCCESSFUL INSERT EMPPAYHS : 6288
SUCCESSFUL INSERT VALUES    :
IO_EMPPAYHS_RECORD.PAY_DATE='20170228'          IO_EMPPAYHS_RECORD.PAY_ANN_PAY=
IO_EMPPAYHS_RECORD.PAY_AMT=    2916.66
IO_EMPPAYHS_RECORD.FILLER65='
PROCESSING IN P1000_GET_NEXT_ROOT
SUCCESSFUL READ OF EMPLOYEE 7459
PROCESSING IN P2000_GET_EMPPAY
SUCCESSFUL PAY READ : 20170101                  SUCCESSFUL PAY READ :    85000.0
   4500.00             SUCCESSFUL PAY READ :    3541.66              SUCCESSF

PROCESSING IN P3000-INSERT-EMPPAYHS
SUCCESSFUL INSERT EMPPAYHS : 7459
SUCCESSFUL INSERT VALUES    :
IO_EMPPAYHS_RECORD.PAY_DATE='20170228'          IO_EMPPAYHS_RECORD.PAY_ANN_PAY=
IO_EMPPAYHS_RECORD.PAY_AMT=    3541.66
IO_EMPPAYHS_RECORD.FILLER65='
PROCESSING IN P1000_GET_NEXT_ROOT
** END OF DATABASE
FINISHED PROCESSING IN P200_MAINLINE
```

So that's how to insert a child segment under a higher level child. To make this more interesting, change the value of the pay date to January 31, 2017. Then compile and link and run again. Do this twice more with pay dates February 15, 2017 and February 28, 2017. Now we have four paychecks for each employee. We'll read all this data back in the next program.

Read Child Segments Down the Hierarchy (3 levels)

For PLIIMS9 you'll need to retrieve and display all the pay history segments for each employee. This should be fairly straightforward by now. Yes you'll need one more loop, and more navigation. But we need the practice to really drill the techniques in. Give this one a try, then take a long break and we'll compare code.

. . . .

Ok, I hope you are enjoying coding IMS in PLI! I'll bet you got your version of the program to work without any serious problems. Let me give you my code and see what you think. Note that I have switches both for end of database and for end of EMPPAYHS segments. The latter is needed for looping through the EMPPAYHS segments.

```
PLIIMS9: PROCEDURE (DB_PTR_PCB) OPTIONS(MAIN);
/************************************************************
* PROGRAM NAME :    PLIIMS9 -  READ EMPLOYEE HISTORY PAY RECORDS   *
*                   UNDER THEIR EMPPAY PARENTS. QUALIFIED SSA'S     *
*                   MUST BE PROVIDED FOR BOTH THE EMPLOYEE AND      *
*                   EMPPAY SEGMENTS.                                *
************************************************************/


/************************************************************
/*              W O R K I N G   S T O R A G E               *
************************************************************/

   DCL SW_END_OF_DB            STATIC BIT(01) INIT('0'B);
   DCL SW_END_OF_EMPPAYHS      STATIC BIT(01) INIT('0'B);
   DCL ONCODE                  BUILTIN;
   DCL DB_PTR_PCB              POINTER;

   DCL PLITDLI                 EXTERNAL ENTRY;

   DCL 01 DLI_FUNCTIONS,
          05 DLI_FUNCISRT      CHAR(04) INIT ('ISRT'),
          05 DLI_FUNCGU        CHAR(04) INIT ('GU  '),
          05 DLI_FUNCGN        CHAR(04) INIT ('GN  '),
          05 DLI_FUNCGHU       CHAR(04) INIT ('GHU '),
          05 DLI_FUNCGNP       CHAR(04) INIT ('GNP '),
          05 DLI_FUNCREPL      CHAR(04) INIT ('REPL'),
          05 DLI_FUNCDLET      CHAR(04) INIT ('DLET'),
```

185

```
        05  DLI_FUNCXRST          CHAR(04)  INIT ('XRST'),
        05  DLI_FUNCCHKP          CHAR(04)  INIT ('CHKP'),
        05  DLI_FUNCROLL          CHAR(04)  INIT ('ROLL');

DCL 01  IO_EMPLOYEE_RECORD,
        05  EMPL_ID               CHAR(04),
        05  FILLER1               CHAR(01),
        05  EMPL_LNAME            CHAR(30),
        05  FILLER2               CHAR(01),
        05  EMPL_FNAME            CHAR(20),
        05  FILLER3               CHAR(01),
        05  EMPL_YRS_SRV          CHAR(02),
        05  FILLER4               CHAR(01),
        05  EMPL_PRM_DTE          CHAR(10),
        05  FILLER5               CHAR(10);

DCL 01  IO_EMPPAY_RECORD,
        05  PAY_EFF_DATE          CHAR(8),
        05  PAY_REG_PAY           FIXED DEC (8,2),
        05  PAY_BON_PAY           FIXED DEC (8,2),
        05  SEMIMTH_PAY           FIXED DEC (8,2),
        05  FILLER55              CHAR(57);

DCL 01  IO_EMPPAYHS_RECORD,
        05  PAY_DATE              CHAR(8),
        05  PAY_ANN_PAY           FIXED DEC (8,2),
        05  PAY_AMT               FIXED DEC (8,2),
        05  FILLER65              CHAR(62);

DCL 01  PCB_MASK                  BASED(DB_PTR_PCB),
        05  DBD_NAME              CHAR(08),
        05  SEG_LEVEL             CHAR(02),
        05  STATUS_CODE           CHAR(02),
        05  PROC_OPT              CHAR(04),
        05  FILLER6               FIXED BIN (31),
        05  SEG_NAME              CHAR(08),
        05  KEY_FDBK              FIXED BIN (31),
        05  NUM_SENSEG            FIXED BIN (31),
        05  KEY_FDBK_AREA,
            10 EMPLOYEE_ID        CHAR(04),
            10 EMP_PAY_DATE       CHAR(08);

DCL 01  EMP_UNQUALIFIED_SSA,
        05  SEGNAME               CHAR(08)  INIT ('EMPLOYEE'),
        05  FILLER7               CHAR(01)  INIT (' ');

DCL 01  EMP_QUALIFIED_SSA,
        05  SEGNAME               CHAR(08)  INIT('EMPLOYEE'),
        05  FILLER8               CHAR(01)  INIT('('),
        05  FIELD                 CHAR(08)  INIT('EMPID'),
        05  OPER                  CHAR(02)  INIT(' ='),
        05  EMP_ID_VAL            CHAR(04)  INIT('    '),
        05  FILLER9               CHAR(01)  INIT(')');
```

```
      DCL 01 EMPPAY_UNQUALIFIED_SSA,
            05   SEGNAME             CHAR(08) INIT('EMPPAY  '),
            05   FILLER10            CHAR(01) INIT(' ');

      DCL 01 EMPPAY_QUALIFIED_SSA,
            05   SEGNAME             CHAR(08) INIT('EMPPAY  '),
            05   FILLER11            CHAR(01) INIT('('),
            05   FIELD               CHAR(08) INIT('EFFDATE '),
            05   OPER                CHAR(02) INIT(' ='),
            05   EFFDATE_VAL         CHAR(08) INIT('        '),
            05   FILLER12            CHAR(01) INIT(')');

      DCL 01 EMPPAYHS_UNQUALIFIED_SSA,
            05   SEGNAME             CHAR(08) INIT('EMPPAYHS'),
            05   FILLER13            CHAR(01) INIT(' ');

      DCL WS_PAY_DATE                CHAR(08) INIT ('20170215');

      DCL SEG_IO_AREA                CHAR(80) INIT (' ');

      DCL THREE                      FIXED BIN (31) INIT(3);
      DCL FOUR                       FIXED BIN (31) INIT(4);
      DCL FIVE                       FIXED BIN (31) INIT(5);
      DCL SIX                        FIXED BIN (31) INIT(6);

/*********************************************************************
/*              P R O G R A M   M A I N L I N E               *
*********************************************************************/

CALL P100_INITIALIZATION;
CALL P200_MAINLINE;
CALL P300_TERMINATION;

P100_INITIALIZATION: PROC;

    PUT SKIP LIST ('PLIIMS9: READ EMPPAYHS RECORDS');
    PUT SKIP LIST ('PROCESSING IN P100_INITIALIZATION');

    IO_EMPLOYEE_RECORD  = '';
    IO_EMPPAY_RECORD   = '';
    IO_EMPPAYHS_RECORD = '';
    PCB_MASK = '';

    /* DO INITIAL DB READ FOR FIRST EMPLOYEE RECORD */

    CALL PLITDLI (FOUR,
                  DLI_FUNCGN,
                  PCB_MASK,
                  IO_EMPLOYEE_RECORD,
                  EMP_UNQUALIFIED_SSA);

    IF STATUS_CODE = ' ' THEN;
```

```
            ELSE
                IF STATUS_CODE = 'GB' THEN
                    DO;
                        SW_END_OF_DB = '1'B;
                        PUT SKIP LIST ('** END OF DATABASE');
                    END;
                ELSE
                    DO;
                        CALL P9000_DISPLAY_ERROR;
                        RETURN;
                    END;

END P100_INITIALIZATION;

P200_MAINLINE: PROC;

    /*  MAIN LOOP - WALK THROUGH THE DATABASE GETTING EMPLOYEE
                   PAY HISTORY SEGMENTS.                      */

    IF SW_END_OF_DB THEN
        PUT SKIP LIST ('NO RECORDS TO PROCESS!!');
    ELSE
        DO WHILE (¬SW_END_OF_DB);

            PUT SKIP LIST ('SUCCESSFUL READ OF EMPLOYEE ' || EMPL_ID);

            /* ASSIGN KEY FOR EMPLOYEE LEVEL SSA AND GET EMPPAY SEG */

            EMP_ID_VAL = EMPL_ID;
            CALL P2000_GET_EMPPAY;
            IF STATUS_CODE ¬= ' ' THEN
                DO;
                    PUT SKIP LIST ('ERROR READING EMPPAY');
                    CALL P9000_DISPLAY_ERROR;
                    RETURN;
                END;
            ELSE
                DO;
                    PUT SKIP LIST ('SUCCESSFUL PAY READ : '
                        || IO_EMPPAY_RECORD);

                    /* ASSIGN KEY FOR EMPPAY LEVEL SSA FOR SEG */

                    EFFDATE_VAL = PAY_EFF_DATE;

                    SW_END_OF_EMPPAYHS = '0'B;
                    DO WHILE (¬SW_END_OF_EMPPAYHS);
                       CALL P3000_GET_NEXT_EMPPAYHS;
                    END; /* DO WHILE */

                    CALL P1000_GET_NEXT_ROOT;
                    IF STATUS_CODE = 'GB' THEN
                        DO;
```

188

```
                                SW_END_OF_DB = '1'B;
                                PUT SKIP LIST ('** END OF DATABASE');
                            END;
                        ELSE
                            IF STATUS_CODE = '  ' THEN;
                            ELSE
                                DO;
                                    CALL P9000_DISPLAY_ERROR;
                                    RETURN;
                                END;

                END; /* SUCCESSFULLY RETRIEVED PAY SEG */

        END; /* DO WHILE */

    PUT SKIP LIST ('FINISHED PROCESSING IN P200_MAINLINE');

END P200_MAINLINE;

P300_TERMINATION: PROC;

    PUT SKIP LIST ('PLIIMS9 - SUCCESSFULLY ENDED');

END P300_TERMINATION;

P1000_GET_NEXT_ROOT: PROC;

    PUT SKIP LIST ('PROCESSING IN P1000_GET_NEXT_ROOT');

    CALL PLITDLI (FOUR,
                  DLI_FUNCGN,
                  PCB_MASK,
                  IO_EMPLOYEE_RECORD,
                  EMP_UNQUALIFIED_SSA);

END P1000_GET_NEXT_ROOT;

P2000_GET_EMPPAY: PROC;

    PUT SKIP LIST ('PROCESSING IN P2000_GET_EMPPAY');

    CALL PLITDLI (FIVE,
                  DLI_FUNCGNP,
                  PCB_MASK,
                  IO_EMPPAY_RECORD,
                  EMP_QUALIFIED_SSA,
                  EMPPAY_UNQUALIFIED_SSA);

END P2000_GET_EMPPAY;

P3000_GET_NEXT_EMPPAYHS: PROC;

    PUT SKIP LIST ('PROCESSING IN P3000_GET_NEXT_EMPPAYHS');
```

```
        CALL PLITDLI (SIX,
                      DLI_FUNCGNP,
                      PCB_MASK,
                      IO_EMPPAYHS_RECORD,
                      EMP_QUALIFIED_SSA,
                      EMPPAY_QUALIFIED_SSA,
                      EMPPAYHS_UNQUALIFIED_SSA);

    SELECT (STATUS_CODE);
       WHEN (' ')
          DO;
             PUT SKIP LIST ('GOOD READ OF EMPPAYHS : '
                 || EMP_ID_VAL);
             PUT SKIP LIST ('PAY_DATE    : ' || PAY_DATE);
             PUT SKIP LIST ('PAY_ANN_PAY: ' || PAY_ANN_PAY);
             PUT SKIP LIST ('PAY_AMT     : ' || PAY_AMT);
          END;
       WHEN ('GE','GB')
          DO;
             SW_END_OF_EMPPAYHS = '1'B;
             PUT SKIP LIST ('NO MORE PAY HISTORY SEGMENTS');
          END;
       OTHERWISE
          DO;
             CALL P9000_DISPLAY_ERROR;
             SW_END_OF_EMPPAYHS = '1'B;
          END;

    END; /* SELECT */

END P3000_GET_NEXT_EMPPAYHS;

P9000_DISPLAY_ERROR: PROC;

    PUT SKIP LIST ('ERROR ENCOUNTERED - DETAIL FOLLOWS');
    PUT SKIP DATA (IO_EMPPAY_RECORD);
    PUT SKIP LIST ('DBD_NAME1:' ||  DBD_NAME);
    PUT SKIP LIST ('SEG_LEVEL1:' || SEG_LEVEL);
    PUT SKIP LIST ('STATUS_CODE:' || STATUS_CODE);
    PUT SKIP LIST ('PROC_OPT1 :' || PROC_OPT);
    PUT SKIP LIST ('SEG_NAME1 :' || SEG_NAME);
    PUT SKIP LIST ('KEY_FDBK1 :' || KEY_FDBK);
    PUT SKIP LIST ('NUM_SENSEG1:' || NUM_SENSEG);
    PUT SKIP LIST ('KEY_FDBK_AREA1:' || KEY_FDBK_AREA);

END P9000_DISPLAY_ERROR;

END PLIIMS9;
```

Compile, link, run. Here is the output.

```
PLIIMS9: READ EMPPAYHS RECORDS
```

190

```
PROCESSING IN P100_INITIALIZATION
SUCCESSFUL READ OF EMPLOYEE 1111
PROCESSING IN P2000_GET_EMPPAY
SUCCESSFUL PAY READ : 20170101                    SUCCESSFUL PAY READ :    87000.0
    6700.00             SUCCESSFUL PAY READ :    3625.00              SUCCESSF

PROCESSING IN P3000_GET_NEXT_EMPPAYHS
GOOD READ OF EMPPAYHS : 1111
PAY_DATE   : 20170228
PAY_ANN_PAY:   87000.00
PAY_AMT    :    3625.00
PROCESSING IN P3000_GET_NEXT_EMPPAYHS
NO MORE PAY HISTORY SEGMENTS
PROCESSING IN P1000_GET_NEXT_ROOT
SUCCESSFUL READ OF EMPLOYEE 1122
PROCESSING IN P2000_GET_EMPPAY
SUCCESSFUL PAY READ : 20170101                    SUCCESSFUL PAY READ :    82000.0
    6000.00             SUCCESSFUL PAY READ :    3416.66              SUCCESSF

PROCESSING IN P3000_GET_NEXT_EMPPAYHS
GOOD READ OF EMPPAYHS : 1122
PAY_DATE   : 20170228
PAY_ANN_PAY:   82000.00
PAY_AMT    :    3416.66
PROCESSING IN P3000_GET_NEXT_EMPPAYHS
NO MORE PAY HISTORY SEGMENTS
PROCESSING IN P1000_GET_NEXT_ROOT
SUCCESSFUL READ OF EMPLOYEE 3217
PROCESSING IN P2000_GET_EMPPAY
SUCCESSFUL PAY READ : 20170101                    SUCCESSFUL PAY READ :    65000.0
    5500.00             SUCCESSFUL PAY READ :    2708.33              SUCCESSF

PROCESSING IN P3000_GET_NEXT_EMPPAYHS
GOOD READ OF EMPPAYHS : 3217
PAY_DATE   : 20170228
PAY_ANN_PAY:   65000.00
PAY_AMT    :    2708.33
PROCESSING IN P3000_GET_NEXT_EMPPAYHS
NO MORE PAY HISTORY SEGMENTS
PROCESSING IN P1000_GET_NEXT_ROOT
SUCCESSFUL READ OF EMPLOYEE 4175
PROCESSING IN P2000_GET_EMPPAY
SUCCESSFUL PAY READ : 20170101                    SUCCESSFUL PAY READ :    55000.0
    1500.00             SUCCESSFUL PAY READ :    2291.66              SUCCESSF

PROCESSING IN P3000_GET_NEXT_EMPPAYHS
GOOD READ OF EMPPAYHS : 4175
PAY_DATE   : 20170228
PAY_ANN_PAY:   55000.00
PAY_AMT    :    2291.66
PROCESSING IN P3000_GET_NEXT_EMPPAYHS
NO MORE PAY HISTORY SEGMENTS
PROCESSING IN P1000_GET_NEXT_ROOT
SUCCESSFUL READ OF EMPLOYEE 4720
PROCESSING IN P2000_GET_EMPPAY
SUCCESSFUL PAY READ : 20170101                    SUCCESSFUL PAY READ :    80000.0
    2500.00             SUCCESSFUL PAY READ :    3333.33              SUCCESSF

PROCESSING IN P3000_GET_NEXT_EMPPAYHS
GOOD READ OF EMPPAYHS : 4720
```

```
PAY_DATE   : 20170228
PAY_ANN_PAY:   80000.00
PAY_AMT    :    3333.33
PROCESSING IN P3000_GET_NEXT_EMPPAYHS
NO MORE PAY HISTORY SEGMENTS
PROCESSING IN P1000_GET_NEXT_ROOT
SUCCESSFUL READ OF EMPLOYEE 4836
PROCESSING IN P2000_GET_EMPPAY
SUCCESSFUL PAY READ : 20170101                 SUCCESSFUL PAY READ :   62000.0
   2200.00            SUCCESSFUL PAY READ :   2583.33            SUCCESSF

PROCESSING IN P3000_GET_NEXT_EMPPAYHS
GOOD READ OF EMPPAYHS : 4836
PAY_DATE   : 20170228
PAY_ANN_PAY:   62000.00
PAY_AMT    :    2583.33
PROCESSING IN P3000_GET_NEXT_EMPPAYHS
NO MORE PAY HISTORY SEGMENTS
PROCESSING IN P1000_GET_NEXT_ROOT
SUCCESSFUL READ OF EMPLOYEE 6288
PROCESSING IN P2000_GET_EMPPAY
SUCCESSFUL PAY READ : 20170101                 SUCCESSFUL PAY READ :   70000.0
   2000.00            SUCCESSFUL PAY READ :   2916.66            SUCCESSF

PROCESSING IN P3000_GET_NEXT_EMPPAYHS
GOOD READ OF EMPPAYHS : 6288
PAY_DATE   : 20170228
PAY_ANN_PAY:   70000.00
PAY_AMT    :    2916.66
PROCESSING IN P3000_GET_NEXT_EMPPAYHS
NO MORE PAY HISTORY SEGMENTS
PROCESSING IN P1000_GET_NEXT_ROOT
SUCCESSFUL READ OF EMPLOYEE 7459
PROCESSING IN P2000_GET_EMPPAY
SUCCESSFUL PAY READ : 20170101                 SUCCESSFUL PAY READ :   85000.0
   4500.00            SUCCESSFUL PAY READ :   3541.66            SUCCESSF

PROCESSING IN P3000_GET_NEXT_EMPPAYHS
GOOD READ OF EMPPAYHS : 7459
PAY_DATE   : 20170228
PAY_ANN_PAY:   85000.00
PAY_AMT    :    3541.66
PROCESSING IN P3000_GET_NEXT_EMPPAYHS
NO MORE PAY HISTORY SEGMENTS
PROCESSING IN P1000_GET_NEXT_ROOT
** END OF DATABASE
FINISHED PROCESSING IN P200_MAINLINE
PLIIMS9 - SUCCESSFULLY ENDED
```

Ok I think we've covered the root-child relationships enough. You have some models to use for most anything you'd want to do in the hierarchy. Time to move on to other topics.

Additional IMS Programming Features

Retrieve Segments Using Searchable Fields

So far all the qualified SSA retrievals we've done have been based on a segment **key**. It is also possible to retrieve IMS segments by a searchable field that is not a key. For this example with program COBIMSA we will create a new field for our EMPLOYEE record layout, and then define this field in our DBD. Then we will write a program to search the database based on the employee social security number EMPL_SSN field.

Ok, where shall we put the field? We have a 9 byte social security number field, and we have 10 bytes of filler at the end of the record. Let's use the last 9 bytes of the record. Here is our new layout.

```
DCL 01 IO_EMPLOYEE_RECORD,
       05  EMPL_ID_IN          CHAR(04),
       05  FILLER1             CHAR(01),
       05  EMPL_LNAME          CHAR(30),
       05  FILLER2             CHAR(01),
       05  EMPL_FNAME          CHAR(20),
       05  FILLER3             CHAR(01),
       05  EMPL_YRS_SRV        CHAR(02),
       05  FILLER4             CHAR(01),
       05  EMPL_PRM_DTE        CHAR(10),
       05  FILLER5             CHAR(01),
       05  EMPL_SSN            CHAR(09);
```

Now let's assign EMPSSN values to the original flat file we used to load the database. Here it is:

```
BROWSE      USER01.EMPIFILE                              Line 00000000 Col 001 080
----+----1----+----2----+----3----+----4----+----5----+----6----+----7----+----8
 Command ===>                                              Scroll ===> CSR
****************************** Top of Data ********************************
1111 VEREEN                     CHARLES              12 2017-01-01 937253058
1122 JENKINS                    DEBORAH              05 2017-01-01 435092366
3217 JOHNSON                    EDWARD               04 2017-01-01 397342007
4175 TURNBULL                   FRED                 01 2016-12-01 542083017
4720 SCHULTZ                    TIM                  09 2017-01-01 650450254
4836 SMITH                      SANDRA               03 2017-01-01 028374669
6288 WILLARD                    JOE                  06 2016-01-01 209883920
7459 STEWART                    BETTY                07 2016-07-31 019572830
9134 FRANKLIN                   BRIANNA              00 2016-10-01 937293598
***************************** Bottom of Data *****************************
```

Now let's delete all existing records in the database using File Manager. Then we can run PLIIMS1 to reload from our flat file which now includes the EMPSSN values. Next we can browse the database and verify that the EMP_SSN field is populated (you will need

193

to scroll to the right to see the EMPSSN field).

```
Browse              USER01.IMS.EMPLOYEE.CLUSTER                Top of 9
Command ===>                                                   Scroll PAGE
                         Type KSDS      RBA                    Format CHAR
Key                                        Col 10
>----+----20---+----3----+----4----+----5----+----6---+----7---+----8----+---
**** Top of data ****
1 VEREEN                      CHARLES              12 2017-01-01 937253058..
2 JENKINS                     DEBORAH              05 2017-01-01 435092366..
7 JOHNSON                     EDWARD               04 2017-01-01 397342007..
5 TURNBULL                    FRED                 01 2016-12-01 542083017..
0 SCHULTZ                     TIM                  09 2017-01-01 650450254..
6 SMITH                       SANDRA               03 2017-01-01 028374669..
8 WILLARD                     JOE                  06 2016-01-01 209883920..
9 STEWART                     BETTY                07 2016-07-31 019572830..
4 FRANKLIN                    BRIANNA              00 2016-10-01 937293598..
```

Next step: To be able to search on a field in an IMS segment, the field must be identified in the DBD. Recall our original code for the DBD is as follows:

```
PRINT NOGEN
DBD NAME=EMPLOYEE,ACCESS=HISAM
DATASET DD1=EMPLOYEE,OVFLW=EMPLFLW
SEGM NAME=EMPLOYEE,PARENT=0,BYTES=80
FIELD NAME=(EMPID,SEQ,U),BYTES=04,START=1,TYPE=C
SEGM NAME=EMPPAY,PARENT=EMPLOYEE,BYTES=23
FIELD NAME=(EFFDATE,SEQ,U),START=1,BYTES=8,TYPE=C
SEGM  NAME=EMPPAYHS,PARENT=EMPPAY,BYTES=18
FIELD NAME=(PAYDATE,SEQ,U),START=1,BYTES=8,TYPE=C
DBDGEN
FINISH
END
```

The only searchable field right now on the EMPLOYEE segment is the primary key EMPID. To make the EMPSSN field searchable we must add it to the DBD. The appropriate code is bolded below. Note that our new field starts in position 72 of the record and is 9 bytes in length.

```
PRINT NOGEN
DBD NAME=EMPLOYEE,ACCESS=HISAM
DATASET DD1=EMPLOYEE,OVFLW=EMPLFLW
SEGM NAME-EMPLOYEE,PARENT=0,BYTES=80
FIELD NAME=(EMPID,SEQ,U),BYTES=04,START=1,TYPE=C
FIELD NAME=EMPSSN,START=72,BYTES=9,TYPE=C
SEGM NAME=EMPPAY,PARENT=EMPLOYEE,BYTES=23
FIELD NAME=(EFFDATE,SEQ,U),START=1,BYTES=8,TYPE=C
SEGM  NAME=EMPPAYHS,PARENT=EMPPAY,BYTES=18
FIELD NAME=(PAYDATE,SEQ,U),START=1,BYTES=8,TYPE=C
DBDGEN
FINISH
```

END

Now we can write a program to search on the EMPSSN field. We can clone the COBIMS2 program to make COBIMSA. One change we must make is to use a different qualified SSA than the one we started with. We need only change the field name in the SSA and create a value field with an appropriate specification (in this case a 9 position character field for the SSN key).

Here is our new structure:

```
DCL 01 EMP_QUALIFIED_SSA_EMPSSN,
        05  SEGNAME             CHAR(08) INIT('EMPLOYEE'),
        05  FILLER10            CHAR(01) INIT('('),
        05  FIELD               CHAR(08) INIT('EMPSSN'),
        05  OPER                CHAR(02) INIT(' ='),
        05  EMPSSN_VAL          CHAR(09) INIT('         '),
        05  FILLER11            CHAR(01) INIT(')');
```

Naturally you must load the EMPSSN_VAL variable with the social security value you are looking for. Let's use the social security number 937253058 for Charles Vereen who is employee number 1111. Here is our PLI program source.

```
PLIIMSA: PROCEDURE (DB_PTR_PCB) OPTIONS(MAIN);
/*******************************************************************
* PROGRAM NAME :   PLIIMSA - RETRIEVE A RECORD FROM EMPLOYEE DB   *
*                           USING SEARCH FIELD EMPSSN.            *
*******************************************************************/

/*******************************************************************
/*             W O R K I N G   S T O R A G E                      *
*******************************************************************/

   DCL ONCODE                  BUILTIN;
   DCL DB_PTR_PCB              POINTER;
   DCL PLITDLI                 EXTERNAL ENTRY;

   DCL 01 DLI_FUNCTIONS,
        05 DLI_FUNCISRT        CHAR(04) INIT ('ISRT'),
        05 DLI_FUNCGU          CHAR(04) INIT ('GU  '),
        05 DLI_FUNCGN          CHAR(04) INIT ('GN  '),
        05 DLI_FUNCGHU         CHAR(04) INIT ('GHU '),
        05 DLI_FUNCGNP         CHAR(04) INIT ('GNP '),
        05 DLI_FUNCREPL        CHAR(04) INIT ('REPL'),
        05 DLI_FUNCDLET        CHAR(04) INIT ('DLET'),
        05 DLI_FUNCXRST        CHAR(04) INIT ('XRST'),
        05 DLI_FUNCCHKP        CHAR(04) INIT ('CHKP'),
        05 DLI_FUNCROLL        CHAR(04) INIT ('ROLL');
```

195

```
DCL 01 IO_EMPLOYEE_RECORD,
        05  EMPL_ID_IN          CHAR(04),
        05  FILLER1             CHAR(01),
        05  EMPL_LNAME          CHAR(30),
        05  FILLER2             CHAR(01),
        05  EMPL_FNAME          CHAR(20),
        05  FILLER3             CHAR(01),
        05  EMPL_YRS_SRV        CHAR(02),
        05  FILLER4             CHAR(01),
        05  EMPL_PRM_DTE        CHAR(10),
        05  FILLER5             CHAR(01),
        05  EMPL_SSN            CHAR(09);

DCL 01 PCB_MASK                 BASED(DB_PTR_PCB),
        05 DBD_NAME             CHAR(08),
        05 SEG_LEVEL            CHAR(02),
        05 STATUS_CODE          CHAR(02),
        05 PROC_OPT             CHAR(04),
        05 FILLER6              FIXED BIN (31),
        05 SEG_NAME             CHAR(08),
        05 KEY_FDBK             FIXED BIN (31),
        05 NUM_SENSEG           FIXED BIN (31),
        05 KEY_FDBK_AREA,
           10 EMPLOYEE_ID       CHAR(04);

DCL 01 EMP_UNQUALIFIED_SSA,
        05  SEGNAME             CHAR(08) INIT ('EMPLOYEE'),
        05  FILLER7             CHAR(01) INIT (' ');

DCL 01 EMP_QUALIFIED_SSA,
        05  SEGNAME             CHAR(08) INIT('EMPLOYEE'),
        05  FILLER8             CHAR(01) INIT('('),
        05  FIELD               CHAR(08) INIT('EMPID'),
        05  OPER                CHAR(02) INIT(' ='),
        05  EMP_ID_VAL          CHAR(04) INIT('    '),
        05  FILLER9             CHAR(01) INIT(')');

DCL 01 EMP_QUALIFIED_SSA_EMPSSN,
        05  SEGNAME             CHAR(08) INIT('EMPLOYEE'),
        05  FILLER10            CHAR(01) INIT('('),
        05  FIELD               CHAR(08) INIT('EMPSSN'),
        05  OPER                CHAR(02) INIT(' ='),
        05  EMPSSN_VAL          CHAR(09) INIT('         '),
        05  FILLER11            CHAR(01) INIT(')');

DCL THREE                       FIXED BIN (31) INIT(3);
DCL FOUR                        FIXED BIN (31) INIT(4);
DCL FIVE                        FIXED BIN (31) INIT(5);
DCL SIX                         FIXED BIN (31) INIT(6);

/****************************************************************
/*              P R O G R A M   M A I N L I N E              *
****************************************************************/
```

```
CALL P100_INITIALIZATION;
CALL P200_MAINLINE;
CALL P300_TERMINATION;

P100_INITIALIZATION: PROC;

    PUT SKIP LIST ('PLIIMSA: GET RECORD FROM EMPLOYEE DB USING EMPSS');
    IO_EMPLOYEE_RECORD  = '';

END P100_INITIALIZATION;

P200_MAINLINE: PROC;

    /*  SET THE EMPLOYEE SEGMENT SEARCH ARGUMENT AND CALL PLITDLI */

    EMPSSN_VAL = '937253058';

    CALL PLITDLI (FOUR,
                  DLI_FUNCGU,
                  PCB_MASK,
                  IO_EMPLOYEE_RECORD,
                  EMP_QUALIFIED_SSA_EMPSSN);

    IF STATUS_CODE = '  ' THEN
       DO;
           PUT SKIP LIST ('SUCCESSFUL RETRIEVAL - SSN: ' || EMPL_SSN);
           PUT SKIP DATA(IO_EMPLOYEE_RECORD);
       END;
    ELSE
       CALL P400_DISPLAY_ERROR;

END P200_MAINLINE;

P300_TERMINATION: PROC;

    PUT SKIP LIST ('PLIIMSA - ENDED SUCCESSFULLY');

END P300_TERMINATION;

P400_DISPLAY_ERROR: PROC;

    PUT SKIP LIST ('ERROR ENCOUNTERED - DETAIL FOLLOWS');
    PUT SKIP LIST ('SEG_IO_AREA    :' || SEG_IO_AREA);
    PUT SKIP LIST ('DBD_NAME1:' ||  DBD_NAME);
    PUT SKIP LIST ('SEG_LEVEL1:' || SEG_LEVEL);
    PUT SKIP LIST ('STATUS_CODE:' || STATUS_CODE);
    PUT SKIP LIST ('PROC_OPT1 :' || PROC_OPT);
    PUT SKIP LIST ('SEG_NAME1 :' || SEG_NAME);
    PUT SKIP LIST ('KEY_FDBK1 :' || KEY_FDBK);
    PUT SKIP LIST ('NUM_SENSEG1:' || NUM_SENSEG);
    PUT SKIP LIST ('KEY_FDBK_AREA1:' || KEY_FDBK_AREA);
```

```
END P400_DISPLAY_ERROR;

END PLIIMSA;
```

Again we compile, link and execute. Here's the output:

```
PLIIMSA: GET RECORD FROM EMPLOYEE DB USING EMPSS
SUCCESSFUL RETRIEVAL - SSN: 937253058
IO_EMPLOYEE_RECORD.EMPL_ID_IN='1111'            IO_EMPLOYEE_RECORD.FILLER1=' '
IO_EMPLOYEE_RECORD.EMPL_LNAME='VEREEN                        '        IO_EMPLO
IO_EMPLOYEE_RECORD.EMPL_FNAME='CHARLES             '                  IO_EMPLO
IO_EMPLOYEE_RECORD.EMPL_YRS_SRV='12'             IO_EMPLOYEE_RECORD.FILLER4=' '
IO_EMPLOYEE_RECORD.EMPL_PRM_DTE='2017-01-01'     IO_EMPLOYEE_RECORD.FILLER5=' '
IO_EMPLOYEE_RECORD.EMPL_SSN='937253058';
PLIIMSA - ENDED SUCCESSFULLY
```

As you can see, we retrieved the desired record using the EMPSSN search field. So keep in mind that you can search on fields other than the key field as long as they are defined in the DBD. If you are going to be searching on a non-indexed field often, you'll want to check with your DBA about possibly defining a secondary index.

Retrieve Segments Using Boolean SSAs

The qualified SSA retrievals we've done so far have searched using a field value that is equal to a single searchable field. It is also possible to retrieve IMS segments using other Boolean operators such as greater than or less than. Additionally, you can specify more than one operator, such as > VALUE1 and < VALUE2.

For this example with program COBIMSB we will retrieve root segments for all employees whose EMPID is greater than 3000 and less than 7000. For that we simply need to create and use a new SSA. Here it is:

```
DCL 01 EMP_QUALIFIED_SSA_BOOL,
       05  SEGNAME             CHAR(08) INIT('EMPLOYEE'),
       05  FILLER10            CHAR(01) INIT('('),
       05  FIELD               CHAR(08) INIT('EMPID'),
       05  OPER                CHAR(02) INIT('>='),
       05  EMP_ID_VAL1         CHAR(04) INIT('    '),
       05  OPER2               CHAR(01) INIT('&'),
       05  FIELD2              CHAR(08) INIT('EMPID'),
       05  OPER3               CHAR(02) INIT('<='),
       05  EMP_ID_VAL2         CHAR(04) INIT('    '),
       05  FILLER11            CHAR(01) INIT(')');
```

For the above we must load our minimum value 3000 into EMP_ID_VAL1, and the ceiling value 7000 into EMP_ID_VAL2. Then we'll call the database using the

EMP_QUALIFIED_SSA_BOOL SSA. We'll do a loop through the database and our retrieval loop should only return those employee records that satisfy the Boolean SSA.

Here is our program source code. Not that we must check for both end of database (GB) and not found (GE) IMS status codes. The reason is that our boolean logic will likely result in a not found (no more segments meet the Boolean criteria) before it reaches the end of the database.

```
PLIIMSB: PROCEDURE (DB_PTR_PCB) OPTIONS(MAIN);
 /********************************************************************
 * PROGRAM NAME :   PLIIMSB - WALK THROUGH THE ROOT SEGMENTS OF     *
 *                            EMPLOYEE DB USING BOOLEAN SSA.        *
 ********************************************************************/

 /********************************************************************
 /*              W O R K I N G    S T O R A G E                     *
 ********************************************************************/

     DCL ONCODE                    BUILTIN;
     DCL DB_PTR_PCB                POINTER;
     DCL PLITDLI                   EXTERNAL ENTRY;
     DCL SW_END_OF_DB              STATIC BIT(01) INIT('0'B);

     DCL 01 DLI_FUNCTIONS,
            05 DLI_FUNCISRT        CHAR(04) INIT ('ISRT'),
            05 DLI_FUNCGU          CHAR(04) INIT ('GU  '),
            05 DLI_FUNCGN          CHAR(04) INIT ('GN  '),
            05 DLI_FUNCGHU         CHAR(04) INIT ('GHU '),
            05 DLI_FUNCGNP         CHAR(04) INIT ('GNP '),
            05 DLI_FUNCREPL        CHAR(04) INIT ('REPL'),
            05 DLI_FUNCDLET        CHAR(04) INIT ('DLET'),
            05 DLI_FUNCXRST        CHAR(04) INIT ('XRST'),
            05 DLI_FUNCCHKP        CHAR(04) INIT ('CHKP'),
            05 DLI_FUNCROLL        CHAR(04) INIT ('ROLL');

     DCL 01 IO_EMPLOYEE_RECORD,
            05  EMPL_ID_IN         CHAR(04),
            05  FILLER1            CHAR(01),
            05  EMPL_LNAME         CHAR(30),
            05  FILLER2            CHAR(01),
            05  EMPL_FNAME         CHAR(20),
            05  FILLER3            CHAR(01),
            05  EMPL_YRS_SRV       CHAR(02),
            05  FILLER4            CHAR(01),
            05  EMPL_PRM_DTE       CHAR(10),
            05  FILLER5            CHAR(01),
            05  EMPL_SSN           CHAR(09);

     DCL 01 PCB_MASK               BASED(DB_PTR_PCB),
            05 DBD_NAME            CHAR(08),
            05 SEG_LEVEL           CHAR(02),
```

199

```
             05 STATUS_CODE         CHAR(02),
             05 PROC_OPT            CHAR(04),
             05 FILLER6             FIXED BIN (31),
             05 SEG_NAME            CHAR(08),
             05 KEY_FDBK            FIXED BIN (31),
             05 NUM_SENSEG          FIXED BIN (31),
             05 KEY_FDBK_AREA,
                10 EMPLOYEE_ID      CHAR(04);

      DCL 01 EMP_UNQUALIFIED_SSA,
             05  SEGNAME            CHAR(08) INIT ('EMPLOYEE'),
             05  FILLER7            CHAR(01) INIT (' ');

      DCL 01 EMP_QUALIFIED_SSA,
             05  SEGNAME            CHAR(08) INIT('EMPLOYEE'),
             05  FILLER8            CHAR(01) INIT('('),
             05  FIELD              CHAR(08) INIT('EMPID'),
             05  OPER               CHAR(02) INIT(' ='),
             05  EMP_ID_VAL         CHAR(04) INIT('    '),
             05  FILLER9            CHAR(01) INIT(')');

      DCL 01 EMP_QUALIFIED_SSA_BOOL,
             05  SEGNAME            CHAR(08) INIT('EMPLOYEE'),
             05  FILLER10           CHAR(01) INIT('('),
             05  FIELD              CHAR(08) INIT('EMPID'),
             05  OPER               CHAR(02) INIT('>='),
             05  EMP_ID_VAL1        CHAR(04) INIT('    '),
             05  OPER2              CHAR(01) INIT('&'),
             05  FIELD2             CHAR(08) INIT('EMPID'),
             05  OPER3              CHAR(02) INIT('<='),
             05  EMP_ID_VAL2        CHAR(04) INIT('    '),
             05  FILLER11           CHAR(01) INIT(')');

      DCL THREE                     FIXED BIN (31) INIT(3);
      DCL FOUR                      FIXED BIN (31) INIT(4);
      DCL FIVE                      FIXED BIN (31) INIT(5);
      DCL SIX                       FIXED BIN (31) INIT(6);

/*****************************************************************
/*               P R O G R A M   M A I N L I N E              *
*****************************************************************/

CALL P100_INITIALIZATION;
CALL P200_MAINLINE;
CALL P300_TERMINATION;

P100_INITIALIZATION: PROC;

   PUT SKIP LIST ('PLIIMS3: TRAVERSE EMPLOYEE DATABASE ROOT SEGS');
   PCB_MASK = '';
   IO_EMPLOYEE_RECORD  = '';

  /*  SET THE EMPLOYEE SEGMENT SEARCH ARGUMENT */
```

200

```
        EMP_ID_VAL1 = '3000';
        EMP_ID_VAL2 = '7000';

    /* DO INITIAL DB READ FOR FIRST EMPLOYEE RECORD */

        CALL PLITDLI (FOUR,
                      DLI_FUNCGN,
                      PCB_MASK,
                      IO_EMPLOYEE_RECORD,
                      EMP_QUALIFIED_SSA_BOOL);

        IF STATUS_CODE = '  ' THEN;
        ELSE
            IF STATUS_CODE = 'GB' |
               STATUS_CODE = 'GB' THEN
               DO;
                   SW_END_OF_DB = '1'B;
                   PUT SKIP LIST ('** END OF DATABASE');
               END;
            ELSE
               DO;
                   CALL P400_DISPLAY_ERROR;
                   RETURN;
               END;

END P100_INITIALIZATION;

P200_MAINLINE: PROC;

    /*  MAIN LOOP - CYCLE THROUGH ALL ROOT SEGMENTS IN THE DB,
                    DISPLAYING THE DATA RETRIEVED              */

    IF SW_END_OF_DB THEN
        PUT SKIP LIST ('NO RECORDS TO PROCESS!!');
    ELSE
        DO WHILE (¬SW_END_OF_DB);
            PUT SKIP LIST ('SUCCESSFUL READ USING BOOLEAN SSA : ');
            PUT SKIP DATA (IO_EMPLOYEE_RECORD);

            CALL PLITDLI (FOUR,
                          DLI_FUNCGN,
                          PCB_MASK,
                          IO_EMPLOYEE_RECORD,
                          EMP_QUALIFIED_SSA_BOOL);

            IF STATUS_CODE = '  ' THEN;
            ELSE
                IF STATUS_CODE = 'GB' |
                   STATUS_CODE = 'GE' THEN
                   DO;
                       SW_END_OF_DB = '1'B;
                       PUT SKIP LIST ('** END OF DATABASE');
```

```
                END;
          ELSE
             DO;
                CALL P400_DISPLAY_ERROR;
                RETURN;
             END;

      END; /* DO WHILE */

    PUT SKIP LIST ('FINISHED PROCESSING IN P200_MAINLINE');

END P200_MAINLINE;

P300_TERMINATION: PROC;

    PUT SKIP LIST ('PLIIMSB - ENDED SUCCESSFULLY');

END P300_TERMINATION;

P400_DISPLAY_ERROR: PROC;

    PUT SKIP LIST ('ERROR ENCOUNTERED - DETAIL FOLLOWS');
    PUT SKIP LIST ('IO_EMPLOYEE_RECORD :'
       || IO_EMPLOYEE_RECORD);
    PUT SKIP LIST ('DBD_NAME1:' ||  DBD_NAME);
    PUT SKIP LIST ('SEG_LEVEL1:' || SEG_LEVEL);
    PUT SKIP LIST ('STATUS_CODE:' || STATUS_CODE);
    PUT SKIP LIST ('PROC_OPT1 :' || PROC_OPT);
    PUT SKIP LIST ('SEG_NAME1 :' || SEG_NAME);
    PUT SKIP LIST ('KEY_FDBK1 :' || KEY_FDBK);
    PUT SKIP LIST ('NUM_SENSEG1:' || NUM_SENSEG);
    PUT SKIP LIST ('KEY_FDBK_AREA1:' || KEY_FDBK_AREA);

 END P400_DISPLAY_ERROR;

END PLIIMSB;
```

After we compile, link and execute, here is the output. As you can see, the only employees retrieved are those whose ids fall between 3,000 and 7,000 inclusive.

```
PLIIMSB: TRAVERSE EMP DB USING BOOLEAN SSA
SUCCESSFUL READ USING BOOLEAN SSA :
IO_EMPLOYEE_RECORD.EMPL_ID='3217';
SUCCESSFUL READ USING BOOLEAN SSA :
IO_EMPLOYEE_RECORD.EMPL_ID='4175';
SUCCESSFUL READ USING BOOLEAN SSA :
IO_EMPLOYEE_RECORD.EMPL_ID='4720';
SUCCESSFUL READ USING BOOLEAN SSA :
IO_EMPLOYEE_RECORD.EMPL_ID='4836';
SUCCESSFUL READ USING BOOLEAN SSA :
IO_EMPLOYEE_RECORD.EMPL_ID='6288';
** END OF DATABASE
FINISHED PROCESSING IN P200_MAINLINE
```

202

Extended Boolean SSAs can be very handy when you need to ready a range of values, or for any retrieval that must satisfy multiple conditions.

Command Codes

IMS command codes change and/or extend the way an IMS call works. There are about 18 command codes that serve various purposes. See the table at the end of this topic for all the command codes and what they do.

We'll do an example of the C command code. The C command code allows you to issue a qualified SSA using the concatenated key for a child segment rather than using separate SSAs for the various parent/child segments. For example suppose we want to retrieve the paycheck record of employee 3217 for pay effective January 1, 2017, and for payday February 15, 2017. The concatenated key for that is as follows:

```
321720170101201702 15
```

This is the key for the root segment (3217) plus the key for the EMPPAY segment (20170101), plus the key for the EMPPAYHS segment (20170215).

To use the C command code, we must create a new SSA structure that uses both the C command code, and accommodates the concatenated key. It will look like this:

```
DCL 01 EMPPAYHS_CCODE_SSA,
       05   SEGNAME        CHAR(08) INIT('EMPPAYHS'),
       05   FILLER15       CHAR(02) INIT('*C'),
       05   FILLER16       CHAR(01) INIT('('),
       05   CONCATKEY      CHAR(20) INIT(' '),
       05   FILLER17       CHAR(01) INIT(')');
```

Like all SSAs, our new one includes the segment name. Position 9 of the SSA will contain an asterisk (or blank if a command code is not being used) Position 10 contains the command code if one is used. We put a C there to indicate we are using a concatenated key command code. We've named our concatenated key variable CONCATKEY (the name is arbitrary – you could use any name for this variable).

The CONCATKEY length is 20 bytes - 4 for the employee id, and 8 each for the salary effective date and the pay date. We could have initialized the concatenated key to the value we are looking for when we declared the variable. Instead we'll load it later using a MOVE statement.

Ok here is the complete code for PLIIMSC. It should look very familiar except for the SSA. For comparison, we will first use the regular three SSA method to call the 2/15 pay record. Then we will use a second call with the C command code method and a concatenated key. The results should be identical.

```
PLIIMSC: PROCEDURE (DB_PTR_PCB) OPTIONS(MAIN);
/*****************************************************************
* PROGRAM NAME :   PLIIMSC - RETRIEVE A RECORD FROM EMPLOYEE DB  *
*                            USING C COMMAND CODE TO PROVIDE A    *
*                            CONCATENATED KEY SSA.                *
*****************************************************************/


/*****************************************************************
/*                    W O R K I N G   S T O R A G E              *
*****************************************************************/

    DCL ONCODE                    BUILTIN;
    DCL DB_PTR_PCB                POINTER;
    DCL PLITDLI                   EXTERNAL ENTRY;

    DCL 01 DLI_FUNCTIONS,
           05 DLI_FUNCISRT        CHAR(04) INIT ('ISRT'),
           05 DLI_FUNCGU          CHAR(04) INIT ('GU  '),
           05 DLI_FUNCGN          CHAR(04) INIT ('GN  '),
           05 DLI_FUNCGHU         CHAR(04) INIT ('GHU '),
           05 DLI_FUNCGNP         CHAR(04) INIT ('GNP '),
           05 DLI_FUNCREPL        CHAR(04) INIT ('REPL'),
           05 DLI_FUNCDLET        CHAR(04) INIT ('DLET'),
           05 DLI_FUNCXRST        CHAR(04) INIT ('XRST'),
           05 DLI_FUNCCHKP        CHAR(04) INIT ('CHKP'),
           05 DLI_FUNCROLL        CHAR(04) INIT ('ROLL');

    DCL 01 IO_EMPLOYEE_RECORD,
           05  EMPL_ID_IN         CHAR(04),
           05  FILLER1            CHAR(01),
           05  EMPL_LNAME         CHAR(30),
           05  FILLER2            CHAR(01),
           05  EMPL_FNAME         CHAR(20), .
           05  FILLER3            CHAR(01),
           05  EMPL_YRS_SRV       CHAR(02),
           05  FILLER4            CHAR(01),
           05  EMPL_PRM_DTE       CHAR(10),
           05  FILLER5            CHAR(01),
           05  EMPL_SSN           CHAR(09);

    DCL 01 IO_EMPPAY_RECORD,
           05  PAY_EFF_DATE       CHAR(8),
           05  PAY_REG_PAY        FIXED DEC (8,2),
           05  PAY_BON_PAY        FIXED DEC (8,2),
           05  SEMIMTH_PAY        FIXED DEC (8,2),
           05  FILLER6            CHAR(57);
```

204

```
DCL 01 IO_EMPPAYHS_RECORD,
        05  PAY_DATE          CHAR(8),
        05  PAY_ANN_PAY       FIXED DEC (8,2),
        05  PAY_AMT           FIXED DEC (8,2),
        05  FILLER65          CHAR(62);

DCL 01 PCB_MASK               BASED(DB_PTR_PCB),
        05 DBD_NAME           CHAR(08),
        05 SEG_LEVEL          CHAR(02),
        05 STATUS_CODE        CHAR(02),
        05 PROC_OPT           CHAR(04),
        05 FILLER99           FIXED BIN (31),
        05 SEG_NAME           CHAR(08),
        05 KEY_FDBK           FIXED BIN (31),
        05 NUM_SENSEG         FIXED BIN (31),
        05 KEY_FDBK_AREA,
          10 EMPLOYEE_ID      CHAR(04);

DCL 01 EMP_UNQUALIFIED_SSA,
        05  SEGNAME           CHAR(08) INIT ('EMPLOYEE'),
        05  FILLER7           CHAR(01) INIT (' ');

DCL 01 EMP_QUALIFIED_SSA,
        05  SEGNAME           CHAR(08) INIT('EMPLOYEE'),
        05  FILLER8           CHAR(01) INIT('('),
        05  FIELD             CHAR(08) INIT('EMPID'),
        05  OPER              CHAR(02) INIT(' ='),
        05  EMP_ID_VAL        CHAR(04) INIT('    '),
        05  FILLER9           CHAR(01) INIT(')');

DCL 01 EMPPAY_UNQUALIFIED_SSA,
        05  SEGNAME           CHAR(08) INIT('EMPPAY  '),
        05  FILLER10          CHAR(01) INIT(' ');

DCL 01 EMPPAY_QUALIFIED_SSA,
        05  SEGNAME           CHAR(08) INIT('EMPPAY  '),
        05  FILLER11          CHAR(01) INIT('('),
        05  FIELD             CHAR(08) INIT('EFFDATE '),
        05  OPER              CHAR(02) INIT(' ='),
        05  EFFDATE_VAL       CHAR(08) INIT('        '),
        05  FILLER12          CHAR(01) INIT(')');

DCL 01 EMP_QUALIFIED_SSA_EMPSSN,
        05  SEGNAME           CHAR(08) INIT('EMPLOYEE'),
        05  FILLER10          CHAR(01) INIT('('),
        05  FIELD             CHAR(08) INIT('EMPSSN'),
        05  OPER              CHAR(02) INIT(' ='),
        05  EMPSSN_VAL        CHAR(09) INIT('         '),
        05  FILLER11          CHAR(01) INIT(')');

DCL 01 EMPPAYHS_UNQUALIFIED_SSA,
        05  SEGNAME           CHAR(08) INIT('EMPPAYHS'),
        05  FILLER12          CHAR(01) INIT(' ');
```

```
   DCL 01 EMPPAYHS_QUALIFIED_SSA,
          05  SEGNAME              CHAR(08) INIT('EMPPAYHS'),
          05  FILLER13             CHAR(01) INIT('('),
          05  FIELD                CHAR(08) INIT('PAYDATE '),
          05  OPER                 CHAR(02) INIT(' ='),
          05  PAYDATE_VAL          CHAR(08) INIT('        '),
          05  FILLER14             CHAR(01) INIT(')');

   DCL 01 EMPPAYHS_CCODE_SSA,
          05  SEGNAME              CHAR(08) INIT('EMPPAYHS'),
          05  FILLER15             CHAR(02) INIT('*C'),
          05  FILLER16             CHAR(01) INIT('('),
          05  CONCATKEY            CHAR(20) INIT(' '),
          05  FILLER17             CHAR(01) INIT(')');

   DCL THREE                       FIXED BIN (31) INIT(3);
   DCL FOUR                        FIXED BIN (31) INIT(4);
   DCL FIVE                        FIXED BIN (31) INIT(5);
   DCL SIX                         FIXED BIN (31) INIT(6);

/*******************************************************************
/*                P R O G R A M   M A I N L I N E               *
********************************************************************/

CALL P100_INITIALIZATION;
CALL P200_MAINLINE;
CALL P300_TERMINATION;

P100_INITIALIZATION: PROC;

   PUT SKIP LIST ('PLIIMSC: GET EMPPAYHS REC FROM DB USING CMD CODE');
   PUT SKIP LIST ('PROCESSING IN P100_INITIALIZATION');
   IO_EMPLOYEE_RECORD  = '';
   IO_EMPPAY_RECORD    = '';
   IO_EMPPAYHS_RECORD  = '';

END P100_INITIALIZATION;

P200_MAINLINE: PROC;

   /*  SET THE EMPLOYEE SEGMENT SEARCH ARGUMENT AND CALL PLITDLI */

   EMP_ID_VAL  = '3217';
   EFFDATE_VAL = '20170101';
   PAYDATE_VAL = '20170215';

   PUT SKIP LIST ('1ST CALL THE 2/15/2017 PAY REC WITH 3 SSA METHOD');

   CALL PLITDLI (SIX,
                 DLI_FUNCGU,
                 PCB_MASK,
                 IO_EMPPAYHS_RECORD,
```

206

```
                     EMP_QUALIFIED_SSA,
                     EMPPAY_QUALIFIED_SSA,
                     EMPPAYHS_QUALIFIED_SSA);

    SELECT (STATUS_CODE);
       WHEN (' ')
          DO;
             PUT SKIP LIST ('GOOD READ OF EMPPAYHS : ' || EMP_ID_VAL);
             PUT SKIP DATA (IO_EMPPAYHS_RECORD);
          END;
       WHEN ('GE','GB')
          PUT SKIP LIST ('PAY HIST SEG NOT FOUND FOR ' || EMP_ID_VAL);
       OTHERWISE
          DO;
             CALL P400_DISPLAY_ERROR;
             RETURN;
          END;

     END; /* SELECT */


    PUT SKIP LIST ('2ND CALL THE 2/15/2017 PAY REC WITH CMD CODE C');

    CONCATKEY = '32172017010120170215';

    CALL PLITDLI (FOUR,
                  DLI_FUNCGU,
                  PCB_MASK,
                  IO_EMPPAYHS_RECORD,
                  EMPPAYHS_CCODE_SSA);

    SELECT (STATUS_CODE);
       WHEN (' ')
          DO;
             PUT SKIP LIST ('GOOD READ OF EMPPAYHS : ' || EMP_ID_VAL);
             PUT SKIP DATA (IO_EMPPAYHS_RECORD);
          END;
       WHEN ('GE','GB')
          PUT SKIP LIST ('PAY HIST SEG NOT FOUND FOR ' || EMP_ID_VAL);
       OTHERWISE
          DO;
             CALL P400_DISPLAY_ERROR;
             RETURN;
          END;

     END; /* SELECT */

END P200_MAINLINE;

P300_TERMINATION: PROC;

    PUT SKIP LIST ('PLIIMSC - ENDED SUCCESSFULLY');

END P300_TERMINATION;
```

```
P400_DISPLAY_ERROR: PROC;

    PUT SKIP LIST ('ERROR ENCOUNTERED - DETAIL FOLLOWS');
    PUT SKIP LIST ('IO_EMPPAYHS_RECORD: ' || IO_EMPLOYEE_RECORD);
    PUT SKIP LIST ('DBD_NAME1:' ||  DBD_NAME);
    PUT SKIP LIST ('SEG_LEVEL1:' || SEG_LEVEL);
    PUT SKIP LIST ('STATUS_CODE:' || STATUS_CODE);
    PUT SKIP LIST ('PROC_OPT1 :' || PROC_OPT);
    PUT SKIP LIST ('SEG_NAME1 :' || SEG_NAME);
    PUT SKIP LIST ('KEY_FDBK1 :' || KEY_FDBK);
    PUT SKIP LIST ('NUM_SENSEG1:' || NUM_SENSEG);
    PUT SKIP LIST ('KEY_FDBK_AREA1:' || KEY_FDBK_AREA);

END P400_DISPLAY_ERROR;

END PLIIMSC;
```

Ok, once again we compile, link and execute. Here is our output.

```
PLIIMSC: GET EMPPAYHS REC FROM DB USING CMD CODE
PROCESSING IN P100_INITIALIZATION
1ST CALL THE 2/15/2017 PAY REC WITH 3 SSA METHOD
GOOD READ OF EMPPAYHS : 3217
IO_EMPPAYHS_RECORD.PAY_DATE='20170215'
IO_EMPPAYHS_RECORD.PAY_ANN_PAY=
IO_EMPPAYHS_RECORD.PAY_AMT=    2708.33
IO_EMPPAYHS_RECORD.FILLER65='
2ND CALL THE 2/15/2017 PAY REC WITH CMD CODE C
GOOD READ OF EMPPAYHS : 3217
IO_EMPPAYHS_RECORD.PAY_DATE='20170215'
IO_EMPPAYHS_RECORD.PAY_ANN_PAY=
IO_EMPPAYHS_RECORD.PAY_AMT=    2708.33
IO_EMPPAYHS_RECORD.FILLER65='
PLIIMSC - ENDED SUCCESSFULLY
```

Command codes can be very useful when you need the features they offer. Check out
the following table of the command codes and how they are used.[6]

6

https://www.ibm.com/support/knowledgecenter/en/SSEPH2_13.1.0/com.ibm.ims13.doc.apr/ims_cmdcodref.htm

Summary of Command Codes

Command Code	Description
A	Clear positioning and start the call at the beginning of the database.
C	Use the concatenated key of a segment to identify the segment.
D	Retrieve or insert a sequence of segments in a hierarchic path using only one call, instead of using a separate (path) call for each segment.
F	Back up to the first occurrence of a segment under its parent when searching for a particular segment occurrence. Disregarded for a root segment.
G	Prevent randomization or the calling of the HALDB Partition Selection exit routine and search the database sequentially.
L	Retrieve the last occurrence of a segment under its parent.
M	Move a subset pointer to the next segment occurrence after your current position. (Used with DEDBs only.)
N	Designate segments that you do not want replaced when replacing segments after a Get Hold call. Typically used when replacing a path of segments.
O	Either field names or both segment position and lengths can be contained in the SSA qualification for combine field position.
P	Set parentage at a higher level than what it usually is (the lowest-level SSA of the call).
Q	Reserve a segment so that other programs cannot update it until you have finished processing and updating it.
R	Retrieve the first segment occurrence in a subset. (Used with DEDBs only.)
S	Unconditionally set a subset pointer to the current position. (Used with DEDBs only.)
U	Limit the search for a segment to the dependents of the segment occurrence on which position is established.
V	Use the hierarchic level at the current position and higher as qualification for the segment.
W	Set a subset pointer to your current position, if the subset pointer is not already set. (Used

Command Code	Description
	with DEDBs only.)
Z	Set a subset pointer to 0, so it can be reused. (Used with DEDBs only.)
-	NULL. Use an SSA in command code format without specifying the command code. Can be replaced during execution with the command codes that you want.

Committing and Rolling Back Changes

Let's look at how we commit updated data to the database. This is not difficult to do using checkpoint calls. Using checkpoint **restart** is somewhat more involved, especially for running in DLI mode where you must use a log file. We'll provide examples of both checkpointing and checkpoint restarting. It will be better if we take it in two chunks with two programs, so that's what we'll do.

For COBIMSD our objective is to delete all the records in the database. We use the same walkthrough-the-database code we used in COBIMS3 except we will use GHN to do the walking, and we will add a DLET call after each GHN to delete the root segment. Note: all child segments are automatically deleted when a root segment is deleted.

We will also set up checkpointing to show it's usage. We will need to do four things before checkpointing can work.

1. Change the PSB to include an IO-PCB

2. Add an XRST call before any data related IMS calls are done

3. Add CHKP calls at specified intervals

4. Add code to reset database position after a checkpoint

Modifying the PSB to Add An IOPCB

We have to back up a bit to make a fundamental change to our PSB. In order to issue IMS service commands like CHKP (as opposed to database retrieval or update commands) you must use a special PCB called the IOPCB. Programs that run in BMP mode are always defined to use an IOPCB, but those that run in DLI mode by default do not have to use an IO-PCB (unless they are doing IMS service calls).

Since we have only been running in DLI mode and not issuing IMS service calls, we didn't define our PSB to include an IOPCB. Since we must now use an IOPCB to use CHKP calls, let's modify our PSB accordingly. The change is very simple and involves adding a **CMPAT=Y** clause after the PSBNAME= clause. Let's create a separate PSB named EMPPSBZ. It will be a clone of the EMPPSB except for the CMPAT=Y. Here is the code:

```
PRINT NOGEN
PCB    TYPE=DB,NAME=EMPLOYEE,KEYLEN=20,PROCOPT=AP
SENSEG NAME=EMPLOYEE,PARENT=0
SENSEG NAME=EMPPAY,PARENT=EMPLOYEE
SENSEG NAME=EMPPAYHS,PARENT=EMPPAY
SENSEG NAME=EMPDEP,PARENT=EMPLOYEE
PSBGEN LANG=PLI,PSBNAME=EMPLOYEE,CMPAT=YES
END
```

Let's save this as member EMPPSBZ in our library and run the PSBGEN process.

So what practical effect does this have if we use the EMPPSBZ PSB to run a program? It **implicitly** includes an IOPCB, meaning you don't see an IOPCB in the PSB, but it will be the first PCB pointer in the linkage between your program and IMS. Since we defined the PSB this way, you **must** handle the IOPCB in your program by:

- Including a structure for the IO_PCB, as well as a pointer variable for it.

- Including the IO_PCB pointer name in the parameter list included in the program declaration.

Here is our new IO_PCB structure, along with the corresponding pointer variable:

```
DCL 01 IO_PCB              BASED(IO_PTR_PCB),
       05 FILLER97         CHAR(10)  INIT(' '),
       05 IO_STATUS_CODE   CHAR(02)  INIT (' ');

DCL IO_PTR_PCB             POINTER;
```

And here is the change to the parameter list on the program definition.

```
PLIIMSD: PROCEDURE (IO_PTR_PCB,DB_PTR_PCB) OPTIONS(MAIN);
```

You MUST put the IO_PCB first in the parameter list before any database PCBs. The database PCBs that follow should be in the same order that they are defined in the PSB. Now we can move on to doing the restart call.

Adding an XRST Call to Initialization Routine

Now we need to include an XRST (extended restart facility) call to check for restart. Don't worry that we won't be restarting with this program yet (the reason is because we aren't logging our changes yet – be patient, we'll get there in the next program). The

XRST call is part of the procedure that we need to do symbolic checkpoints and eventually perform IMS restarts, so we include it here.

Note: In this text we will only deal with symbolic checkpoints. IMS also offers basic checkpoints, but these do not work with the extended restart facility (the XRST call and automated repositions, etc), so with basic checkpoints your program must do 100% of the code to perform a restart. Consequently basic checkpoints are of limited value and I don't deal with them in this text.

First, add some structures and variables to your working storage section. We'll talk about these in detail when we get to the executable code.

```
DCL 01 XRST_IOAREA,
       05 XRST_ID       CHAR(08) INIT('        '),
       05 FILLER10      CHAR(04) INIT('    ');

DCL XRST_IO_AREALEN    FIXED BIN(31) INIT (12);
DCL IO_AREALEN         FIXED BIN(31) INIT (08);
DCL CHKP_ID            CHAR(08) INIT( 'IMSD-   ');
DCL CHKP_NBR           FIXED DEC (3)  INIT(0);
DCL CHKP_COUNT         FIXED BIN (31) INIT(0);
       05 FILLER                PIC X(24) VALUE
           'COBIMSD  CHECK POINT NO:'.
DCL 01 CHKP_MESSAGE,
       05 FILLER11             CHAR(24)    INIT(
           'COBIMSD  CHECK POINT NO:'),
       05 CHKP_MESS_NBR    PIC '999',
       05 FILLER12             CHAR(15)    INIT( ',AT INPUT REC#:'),
       05 CHKP_MESS_REC    PIC 'ZZZZZ9',
       05 FILLER13             CHAR(10)    INIT(',AT EMP#:'),
       05 CHKP_MESS_EMP    CHAR(08)    INIT(' ');

DCL IMS_CHKP_AREA_LTH    FIXED BIN (31) INIT(07);

DCL 01 IMS_CHKP_AREA,
       05 CHKP_EMP_ID       CHAR(04)    INIT('0000'),
       05 CHKP_NBR_LAST     CHAR(03)    INIT('000');
```

Second, add this code at the beginning of your Initialization paragraph.

```
CALL PLITDLI (SIX,
              DLI_FUNCXRST,
              IO_PCB,
              XRST_IO_AREALEN,
              XRST_IOAREA,
              IMS_CHKP_AREA_LTH,
              IMS_CHKP_AREA);
```

```
IF IO_STATUS_CODE ¬= ' ' THEN
   DO;
      CALL P9000_DISPLAY_ERROR;
      RETURN;
   END;

IF XRST_ID ¬= ' ' THEN
   DO;
      CHKP_NBR = CHKP_NBR_LAST;
      PUT SKIP LIST ('*** COBIMSD IMS RESTART ***');
      PUT SKIP LIST ('*  LAST CHECK POINT :' || XRST_ID);
      PUT SKIP LIST ('*  EMPLOYEE NUMBER  :' || CHKP_EMP_ID);
   END;
ELSE
   DO;
      PUT SKIP LIST ('****** COBIMSD IMS NORMAL START ***');
      CALL P8000_TAKE_CHECKPOINT;
   END;
```

This code checks to see if our execution is being run as a restart. If it is, then we announce that it is a restart. If it is not, we announce a normal start. That's all we need to do with XRST right now. Later we will add code that handles the restart actions, and we'll explain the parameters at that time.

Adding the CHKP Call

Now let's add code for taking a checkpoint. We'll do this by coding a separate procedure. The required parameters for the call are the CHKP function, the IO_PCB structure, the length of an IO area that contains the checkpoint id, the IO area that contains the checkpoint id, the length of the checkpoint area, and the checkpoint area structure. The latter is where you save anything you want to save for restart, such as the last processed EMP_ID, record counters and anything else you want to save for a restart. Here is the code.

```
P8000_TAKE_CHECKPOINT: PROC;

   PUT SKIP LIST ('PROCESSING IN P8000_TAKE_CHECKPOINT');

   CHKP_NBR               = CHKP_NBR + 1;
   CHKP_NBR_LAST          = CHKP_NBR;
   SUBSTR(CHKP_ID,6,3)    = CHKP_NBR_LAST;
   CHKP_EMP_ID            = EMPL_ID;

   PUT SKIP LIST ('IO_AREALEN ' || IO_AREALEN);
   PUT SKIP LIST ('IMS_CHKP_AREA_LTH ' || IMS_CHKP_AREA_LTH);

   PUT SKIP LIST ('CHKP_ID = ' || CHKP_ID);
   PUT SKIP LIST (' ');
```

```
        CALL PLITDLI (SIX,
                      DLI_FUNCCHKP,
                      IO_PCB,
                      IO_AREALEN,
                      CHKP_ID,
                      IMS_CHKP_AREA_LTH,
                      IMS_CHKP_AREA);

    IF IO_STATUS_CODE ¬= '  ' THEN
        DO;
            PUT SKIP LIST ('TOOK AN ERROR DOING THE CHECKPOINT');
            PUT SKIP LIST ('IO_STATUS_CODE ' || IO_STATUS_CODE);
            CALL P9000_DISPLAY_ERROR;
            RETURN;
        END;
    ELSE
        DO;
            CHKP_COUNT = 0;
            CHKP_MESS_NBR = CHKP_NBR;
            CHKP_MESS_EMP = CHKP_EMP_ID;
            PUT SKIP LIST (CHKP_MESSAGE);
        END;

END P8000_TAKE_CHECKPOINT;
```

One final note: the third parameter in the CHKP call (the IO area length) is not actually used by IMS, but it must still be included for backward compatibility. You need only define a variable for it in the program.

Adding Code to Reposition in the Database After Checkpoint

Finally, we must create code to reposition the database after taking a checkpoint. The reason is that the checkpoint call causes the database position to be lost. If you continue GHN calls at this point without reestablishing your database position, you'll get an error.

So what we'll do is to ensure we have the next record to process and we'll include that in the checkpoint IO area that we are going to save. So our code will:

DLET a record

Read the next record and capture the employee id

If it is time to take a checkpoint then

Take a check point using the captured employee id that was just read

Reposition in the database using the captured employee id

214

The reposition code is as follows. Notice it is using a qualified SSA to get the exact record that is needed to reposition. Of course we must use a qualified SSA, and the EMP-ID that was retrieved in the GHN call before we took the checkpoint.

```
P1000_RESET_POSITION: PROC;

    PUT SKIP LIST ('PROCESSING IN P1000_RESET_POSITION');

    CALL PLITDLI (FOUR,
                  DLI_FUNCGHU,
                  PCB_MASK,
                  IO_EMPLOYEE_RECORD,
                  EMP_QUALIFIED_SSA);

    IF STATUS_CODE ¬= '  ' THEN
       DO;
          CALL P9000_DISPLAY_ERROR;
          RETURN;
       END;
    ELSE
       PUT SKIP LIST ('SUCCESSFUL REPOSITION AT EMP ID ' ||
          EMPL_ID);

END P1000_RESET_POSITION;
```

Ok, now we've performed all four items that will enable us to commit data updates by taking checkpoints at some interval. Let's make our record interval 5. So we have eight records in the database, and we'll take a checkpoints as follows:

- At the beginning of the program.

- After each 5 records have been processed.

- At the end of the program.

Here is our program code for PLIIMSD. As mentioned earlier, we haven't completed the code yet for a restart. But we now have the functionality to commit our data changes with the checkpoint call.

```
PLIIMSD: PROCEDURE (IO_PTR_PCB,DB_PTR_PCB) OPTIONS(MAIN);
/*****************************************************************
* PROGRAM NAME: PLIIMSD - WALK THROUGH THE EMPLOYEE (ROOT)      *
*                         SEGMENTS OF THE EMPLOYEE IMS DATABASE, *
*                         AND DELETE EACH ONE.                  *
*****************************************************************/
```

```
/*********************************************************************
*                   W O R K I N G   S T O R A G E                    *
*********************************************************************/

    DCL SW_END_OF_DB            STATIC BIT(01) INIT('0'B);
    DCL ONCODE                  BUILTIN;
    DCL DB_PTR_PCB              POINTER;
    DCL IO_PTR_PCB              POINTER;

    DCL PLITDLI                 EXTERNAL ENTRY;

    DCL 01 DLI_FUNCTIONS,
           05 DLI_FUNCISRT      CHAR(04) INIT ('ISRT'),
           05 DLI_FUNCGU        CHAR(04) INIT ('GU  '),
           05 DLI_FUNCGN        CHAR(04) INIT ('GN  '),
           05 DLI_FUNCGHU       CHAR(04) INIT ('GHU '),
           05 DLI_FUNCGNP       CHAR(04) INIT ('GNP '),
           05 DLI_FUNCREPL      CHAR(04) INIT ('REPL'),
           05 DLI_FUNCDLET      CHAR(04) INIT ('DLET'),
           05 DLI_FUNCXRST      CHAR(04) INIT ('XRST'),
           05 DLI_FUNCCHKP      CHAR(04) INIT ('CHKP'),
           05 DLI_FUNCROLL      CHAR(04) INIT ('ROLL');

    DCL 01 IO_EMPLOYEE_RECORD,
           05  EMPL_ID          CHAR(04),
           05  FILLER1          CHAR(01),
           05  EMPL_LNAME       CHAR(30),
           05  FILLER2          CHAR(01),
           05  EMPL_FNAME       CHAR(20),
           05  FILLER3          CHAR(01),
           05  EMPL_YRS_SRV     CHAR(02),
           05  FILLER4          CHAR(01),
           05  EMPL_PRM_DTE     CHAR(10),
           05  FILLER5          CHAR(10);

    DCL 01 EMP_UNQUALIFIED_SSA,
           05  SEGNAME          CHAR(08) INIT ('EMPLOYEE'),
           05  FILLER7          CHAR(01) INIT (' ');

    DCL 01 EMP_QUALIFIED_SSA,
           05  SEGNAME          CHAR(08) INIT('EMPLOYEE'),
           05  FILLER8          CHAR(01) INIT('('),
           05  FIELD            CHAR(08) INIT('EMPID'),
           05  OPER             CHAR(02) INIT(' ='),
           05  EMP_ID_VAL       CHAR(04) INIT('    '),
           05  FILLER9          CHAR(01) INIT(')');

    DCL THREE                   FIXED BIN (31) INIT(3);
    DCL FOUR                    FIXED BIN (31) INIT(4);
    DCL FIVE                    FIXED BIN (31) INIT(5);
    DCL SIX                     FIXED BIN (31) INIT(6);

    DCL 01 XRST_IOAREA,
```

```
        05 XRST_ID       CHAR(08) INIT('        '),
        05 FILLER10      CHAR(04) INIT('    ');

   DCL XRST_IO_AREALEN   FIXED BIN(31) INIT (12);
   DCL IO_AREALEN        FIXED BIN(31) INIT (08);
   DCL CHKP_ID           CHAR(08) INIT( 'IMSD-   ');
   DCL CHKP_NBR          FIXED DEC (3)  INIT(0);
   DCL CHKP_COUNT        FIXED BIN (31) INIT(0);

   DCL DB_PTR_PCB               POINTER;
   DCL IO_PTR_PCB               POINTER;


   DCL 01 CHKP_MESSAGE,
        05 FILLER11          CHAR(24)    INIT(
           'COBIMSD  CHECK POINT NO:'),
        05 CHKP_MESS_NBR    PIC '999',
        05 FILLER12          CHAR(15)    INIT( ',AT INPUT REC#:'),
        05 CHKP_MESS_REC    PIC 'ZZZZZ9',
        05 FILLER13          CHAR(10)    INIT(',AT EMP#:'),
        05 CHKP_MESS_EMP    CHAR(08)    INIT(' ');

   DCL IMS_CHKP_AREA_LTH    FIXED BIN (31) INIT(07);

   DCL 01 IMS_CHKP_AREA,
        05 CHKP_EMP_ID      CHAR(04)    INIT('0000'),
        05 CHKP_NBR_LAST    CHAR(03)    INIT('000');

   DCL 01 IO_PCB                BASED(IO_PTR_PCB),
        05 FILLER97             CHAR(10)  INIT(' '),
        05 IO_STATUS_CODE       CHAR(02)  INIT (' ');

   DCL 01 PCB_MASK              BASED(DB_PTR_PCB),
        05 DBD_NAME             CHAR(08),
        05 SEG_LEVEL            CHAR(02),
        05 STATUS_CODE          CHAR(02),
        05 PROC_OPT             CHAR(04),
        05 FILLER99             FIXED BIN (31),
        05 SEG_NAME             CHAR(08),
        05 KEY_FDBK             FIXED BIN (31),
        05 NUM_SENSEG           FIXED BIN (31),
        05 KEY_FDBK_AREA,
           10 KFB_EMPLOYEE_ID CHAR(04);

/*******************************************************************
/*              P R O G R A M   M A I N L I N E              *
*******************************************************************/

CALL P100_INITIALIZATION;
CALL P200_MAINLINE;
CALL P300_TERMINATION;

P100_INITIALIZATION: PROC;
```

217

```
PUT SKIP LIST ('PLIIMSD: TRAVERSE EMPLOYEE DATABASE ROOT SEGS');
PUT SKIP LIST ('PROCESSING IN P100_INITIALIZATION');
IO_PCB   = '';
PCB_MASK = '';
IO_EMPLOYEE_RECORD  = '';

/* CHECK FOR RESTART */

CALL PLITDLI (SIX,
              DLI_FUNCXRST,
              IO_PCB,
              XRST_IO_AREALEN,
              XRST_IOAREA,
              IMS_CHKP_AREA_LTH,
              IMS_CHKP_AREA);

IF IO_STATUS_CODE ¬= '  ' THEN
   DO;
       CALL P9000_DISPLAY_ERROR;
       RETURN;
   END;

IF XRST_ID ¬= ' ' THEN
   DO;
       CHKP_NBR = CHKP_NBR_LAST;
       PUT SKIP LIST ('*** COBIMSD IMS RESTART ***');
       PUT SKIP LIST ('*  LAST CHECK POINT :' || XRST_ID);
       PUT SKIP LIST ('*  EMPLOYEE NUMBER  :' || CHKP_EMP_ID);
   END;
ELSE
   DO;
       PUT SKIP LIST ('****** COBIMSD IMS NORMAL START ***');
       CALL P8000_TAKE_CHECKPOINT;
   END;

/* DO INITIAL DB READ FOR FIRST EMPLOYEE RECORD */

CALL PLITDLI (FOUR,
              DLI_FUNCGHN,
              PCB_MASK,
              IO_EMPLOYEE_RECORD,
              EMP_UNQUALIFIED_SSA);

IF STATUS_CODE = '  ' THEN;
ELSE
   IF STATUS_CODE = 'GB' THEN
      DO;
          SW_END_OF_DB = '1'B;
          PUT SKIP LIST ('** END OF DATABASE');
      END;
   ELSE
      DO;
```

218

```
                CALL P9000_DISPLAY_ERROR;
                RETURN;
            END;

END P100_INITIALIZATION;

P200_MAINLINE: PROC;

    /*  MAIN LOOP - CYCLE THROUGH ALL ROOT SEGMENTS IN THE DB,
                    DISPLAYING THE DATA RETRIEVED              */

    IF SW_END_OF_DB THEN
        PUT SKIP LIST ('NO RECORDS TO PROCESS!!');
    ELSE
        DO WHILE (¬SW_END_OF_DB);
            PUT SKIP LIST ('SUCCESSFUL GET-HOLD :'
                || EMPL_ID);

            /* DELETE THE SWGMENT */

            CALL PLITDLI (THREE,
                          DLI_FUNCDLET,
                          PCB_MASK,
                          IO_EMPLOYEE_RECORD);

            IF STATUS_CODE ¬= '  ' THEN
                DO;
                    CALL P9000_DISPLAY_ERROR;
                    RETURN;
                END;
            ELSE
                PUT SKIP LIST ('SUCCESSFUL DELETE OF EMP ' || EMPL_ID);

            /* NOW GET THE NEXT ROOT TO DELETE */

            CALL PLITDLI (FOUR,
                          DLI_FUNCGN,
                          PCB_MASK,
                          IO_EMPLOYEE_RECORD,
                          EMP_UNQUALIFIED_SSA);

            IF STATUS_CODE = '  ' THEN
                DO;
                    PUT SKIP LIST ('SUCCESSFUL GET HOLD: ' || EMPL_ID);
                    EMP_ID_VAL = EMPL_ID;
                    CHKP_COUNT = CHKP_COUNT + 1;
                    IF CHKP_COUNT >= 5 THEN
                        DO;
                            CALL P8000_TAKE_CHECKPOINT;
                            CALL P1000_RESET_POSITION;
                        END;
                END;
            ELSE
```

219

```
                    IF STATUS_CODE = 'GB' THEN
                        DO;
                            SW_END_OF_DB = '1'B;
                            PUT SKIP LIST ('** END OF DATABASE');
                        END;
                    ELSE
                        DO;
                            CALL P9000_DISPLAY_ERROR;
                            RETURN;
                        END;

         END; /* DO WHILE */

    PUT SKIP LIST ('FINISHED PROCESSING IN P200_MAINLINE');

END P200_MAINLINE;

P300_TERMINATION: PROC;

    PUT SKIP LIST ('PROCESSING IN P300_TERMINATION');

    CHKP_COUNT = CHKP_COUNT + 1;
    CALL P8000_TAKE_CHECKPOINT;

    PUT SKIP LIST ('PLIIMSD - SUCCESSFULLY ENDED');

END P300_TERMINATION;

P1000_RESET_POSITION: PROC;

    PUT SKIP LIST ('PROCESSING IN P1000_RESET_POSITION');

    CALL PLITDLI (FOUR,
                  DLI_FUNCGHU,
                  PCB_MASK,
                  IO_EMPLOYEE_RECORD,
                  EMP_QUALIFIED_SSA);

    IF STATUS_CODE ¬= '  ' THEN
        DO;
            CALL P9000_DISPLAY_ERROR;
            RETURN;
        END;
    ELSE
        PUT SKIP LIST ('SUCCESSFUL REPOSITION AT EMP ID ' || EMPL_ID);

END P1000_RESET_POSITION;

P8000_TAKE_CHECKPOINT: PROC;

    PUT SKIP LIST ('PROCESSING IN P8000_TAKE_CHECKPOINT');

    CHKP_NBR             = CHKP_NBR + 1;
```

```
       CHKP_NBR_LAST         = CHKP_NBR;
       SUBSTR(CHKP_ID,6,3) = CHKP_NBR_LAST;
       CHKP_EMP_ID           = EMPL_ID;

       PUT SKIP LIST ('IO_AREALEN ' || IO_AREALEN);
       PUT SKIP LIST ('IMS_CHKP_AREA_LTH ' || IMS_CHKP_AREA_LTH);

       PUT SKIP LIST ('CHKP_ID = ' || CHKP_ID);
       PUT SKIP LIST (' ');

       CALL PLITDLI (SIX,
                     DLI_FUNCCHKP,
                     IO_PCB,
                     IO_AREALEN,
                     CHKP_ID,
                     IMS_CHKP_AREA_LTH,
                     IMS_CHKP_AREA);

    IF IO_STATUS_CODE ¬= '  ' THEN
       DO;
          PUT SKIP LIST ('TOOK AN ERROR DOING THE CHECKPOINT');
          PUT SKIP LIST ('IO_STATUS_CODE ' || IO_STATUS_CODE);
          CALL P9000_DISPLAY_ERROR;
          RETURN;
       END;
    ELSE
       DO;
          CHKP_COUNT = 0;
          CHKP_MESS_NBR = CHKP_NBR;
          CHKP_MESS_EMP = CHKP_EMP_ID;
          PUT SKIP LIST (CHKP_MESSAGE);
       END;

END P8000_TAKE_CHECKPOINT;

P9000_DISPLAY_ERROR: PROC;

    PUT SKIP LIST ('ERROR ENCOUNTERED - DETAIL FOLLOWS');
    PUT SKIP LIST ('SEG_IO_AREA      :' || SEG_IO_AREA);
    PUT SKIP LIST ('DBD_NAME1:' ||  DBD_NAME);
    PUT SKIP LIST ('SEG_LEVEL1:' || SEG_LEVEL);
    PUT SKIP LIST ('STATUS_CODE:' || STATUS_CODE);
    PUT SKIP LIST ('PROC_OPT1 :' || PROC_OPT);
    PUT SKIP LIST ('SEG_NAME1 :' || SEG_NAME);
    PUT SKIP LIST ('KEY_FDBK1 :' || KEY_FDBK);
    PUT SKIP LIST ('NUM_SENSEG1:' || NUM_SENSEG);
    PUT SKIP LIST ('KEY_FDBK_AREA1:' || KEY_FDBK_AREA);

END P9000_DISPLAY_ERROR;

END PLIIMSD;
```

At this point, we can compile and link, and then run the program. Make sure your JCL specifies the EMPPSBZ PSB or you'll get an error.

```
PLIIMSD: DELETE EMPLOYEE DATABASE ROOT SEGS
PROCESSING IN P100_INITIALIZATION
****** PLIIMSD IMS NORMAL START ***
PROCESSING IN P8000_TAKE_CHECKPOINT

PLIIMSD   CHECK POINT NO:001,AT INPUT REC#:        ,AT EMP#:
PROCESSING IN P200_MAINLINE
SUCCESSFUL DELETE OF EMPLOYEE 1111
SUCCESSFUL GET HOLD :1122 JENKINS                    DEBORAH            05
SUCCESSFUL DELETE OF EMPLOYEE 1122
SUCCESSFUL GET HOLD :3217 JOHNSON                    EDWARD            04
SUCCESSFUL DELETE OF EMPLOYEE 3217
SUCCESSFUL GET HOLD :4175 TURNBULL                   FRED              01
SUCCESSFUL DELETE OF EMPLOYEE 4175
SUCCESSFUL GET HOLD :4720 SCHULTZ                    TIM               09
SUCCESSFUL DELETE OF EMPLOYEE 4720
SUCCESSFUL GET HOLD :4836 SMITH                      SANDRA            03
PROCESSING IN P8000_TAKE_CHECKPOINT
COBIMSD   CHECK POINT NO:002,AT INPUT REC#:        ,AT EMP#: 4836
PROCESSING IN P1000_RESET_POSITION
SUCCESSFUL REPOSITION AT EMP ID 4836
SUCCESSFUL DELETE OF EMPLOYEE 4836
SUCCESSFUL GET HOLD :6288 WILLARD                    JOE               06
SUCCESSFUL DELETE OF EMPLOYEE 6288
SUCCESSFUL GET HOLD :7459 STEWART                    BETTY             07
SUCCESSFUL DELETE OF EMPLOYEE 7459
END OF DATABASE
FINISHED PROCESSING IN P200_MAINLINE
PROCESSING IN P300_TERMINATION
PROCESSING IN P8000_TAKE_CHECKPOINT
PLIIMSD   CHECK POINT NO:003,AT INPUT REC#:        ,AT EMP#: 7459
** PLIIMSD - SUCCESSFULLY ENDED **
```

We now have an empty database. You can verify this by looking in your File Manager IMS if you have it, or you can try browsing the DATA file of the KSDS. Since it is empty, you'll get an error.

```
VSAM POINT RC X"08", Error Code X"20"
VSAM GET RC X"08", Error Code X"58"
Function terminated
***
```

We have shown we can commit updates to the database at some interval. In a real production environment we would not checkpoint every 5 records. More likely we would checkpoint at 500 records or 1,000 records or 2,000 records. You don't want to lock your data for too long, so find a record interval that commits at about once a minute, or whatever your DBA recommends.

Performing Checkpoint Restart

At this point, we've successfully committed data using checkpoints. This enables us to run efficiently and to not lock data for too long. However, we have not yet demonstrated how to perform a restart using the extended restart facility (XRST). To do that, we need to introduce IMS logging.

Using the IMS Log

To allow for IMS restartability, you must log all the transactions and checkpoints you take. When you stop the program (or when IMS stops it for an abend), your data modifications (ISRT, REPL, DLET) are automatically backed out to the last checkpoint. So typically, you will want to fix whatever the problem was, and then restart your program at the last checkpoint.

In your execution JCL for running IMS programs, there should be two DD statements that are probably dummied out.[7] The IEFRDER DD should definitely be there, and the IMSLOGR may be there (it is only referenced on restart so it might not be).

```
//IMSLOGR  DD DUMMY
//IEFRDER  DD DUMMY
```

Here's what these are used for when they are not dummied out (when actual file names are specified):

- IMSLOGR – the previous (existing) generation of IMS log file created for your DLI execution.

- IEFRDER – the new generation of the IMS log file created for your DLI execution to log any updates to the database performed by your program.

You'll want to create a generation data group for your IMS log file, and then define these DDs to use the 0 and +1 generation of this data set. I created USER01.IMSLOG with 5 generations, and I created an empty first generation. Next, I have un-dummied the IMSLOGR and IEFRDER DD's by coding the new log file as follows:

```
//IMSLOGR  DD DSN=USER01.IMSLOG(+0),
//           DISP=SHR
//IEFRDER  DD DSN=USER01.IMSLOG(+1),
//           DISP=(NEW,CATLG,CATLG),
```

---

[7] This discussion pertains to running a program in DLI mode. If you are running a program in BMP mode, the JCL does not contain these DDs because the program runs in the IMS online space which has its own transaction log.

```
//            UNIT=SYSDA,
//            SPACE=(TRK,(1,1),RLSE),
//            DCB=(RECFM=VB,BLKSIZE=4096,
//            LRECL=4092,BUFNO=2)
```

Now if you specify a checkpoint value when you restart your program, IMS will scan the IMS log to pick up the information from the last checkpoint. In our case, this information includes the last employee id that we read before issuing the checkpoint. You can then use that employee id key to reposition in the database for a restart.

Specifying a Checkpoint ID on Restart

You can specify the checkpoint id in the PARM value of the execute statement for your program. This is a positional parameter, so it must be placed correctly in the PARM sequence. Here is the JCL and I'm putting a sample checkpoint id at the right place in the PARM.

```
//GO     EXEC PGM=DFSRRC00,REGION=4M,
//     PARM=(DLI,&MBR,&PSB,7,0000,,0,'CHKP0003',N,0,0,,,N,N,,N,)
```

Restart Example

We need to reload the database now before we can do a restart example (remember we deleted all the records in the database earlier). You can run your COBIMS1 to do this. Although the database is empty, it is not being loaded for the first time. So you can use PSB EMPPSB instead of EMPPSBL. In fact you'll get an error (AI status code) if you use the EMPPSBL, so make sure you use EMPPSB.

When finished, verify that we have nine records in the database.

```
Browse            USER01.IMS.EMPLOYEE.DATA                    Top of 9
Command ===>                                                 Scroll PAGE
                        Type DATA      RBA                    Format CHAR
                                           Col 1
----+----10---+----2----+----3----+----4----+----5----+----6---+----7----+----
**** Top of data   ****
......1111 VEREEN              CHARLES          12 2017-01-01 93
......1122 JENKINS             DEBORAH          05 2017-01-01 43
......3217 JOHNSON             EDWARD           04 2017-01-01 39
......4175 TURNBULL            FRED             01 2016-12-01 54
......4720 SCHULTZ             TIM              09 2017-01-01 65
......4836 SMITH               SANDRA           03 2017-01-01 02
......6288 WILLARD             JOE              06 2016-01-01 20
......7459 STEWART             BETTY            07 2016-07-31 01
......9134 FRANKLIN            BRIANNA          00 2016-10-01 93
**** End of data   ****
```

For our example, we will create a new program COBIMSE and it will delete all the records in the database as we did with COBIMSD. We will checkpoint at 5 record intervals. You can start by copying COBIMSD to create COBIMSE. There will be two differences between COBIMSD and COBIMSE. One is that COBIMSE will intentionally cause a rollback when we encounter employee 7459. This will back out any data change to the previously taken checkpoint.

The other difference is that we will code restart logic in COBIMSE to reposition to the appropriate employee id in the data to continue processing on a restart. In between run 1 and run 2 of COBIMSE, the only change we will make to the program is to not do the rollback when it gets to employee id 7459.

If you are copying PLIIMSD to create PLIIMSE, you only need to make a few changes. First, let's create some new procedures. One procedure will get the first root in the database. We've been doing that in P100_INITIALIZATION, but now on a restart we need to call the reset position procedure instead. Separating these functions into separate procedures makes the code easier to read. Let's do this:

```
P1000-GET-FIRST-ROOT.

            CALL 'CBLTDLI' USING FOUR,
                  DLI-FUNCGHN,
                  PCB-MASK,
                  IO-EMPLOYEE-RECORD,
                  EMP-UNQUALIFIED-SSA

        IF STATUS-CODE = '   ' THEN
           NEXT SENTENCE
        ELSE
           IF STATUS-CODE = 'GB' THEN
              SET SW-END-OF-DB TO TRUE
              DISPLAY 'END OF DATABASE :'
           ELSE
              PERFORM P9000-DISPLAY-ERROR
              GOBACK
           END-IF.
```

Next let's rename P1000_RESET_POSITION to P2000_RESET_POSITION. That will keep the code more orderly. Finally, let's add the procedure to perform the rollback.

```
P3000_ROLLBACK: PROC;

        PUT SKIP LIST ('PROCESSING IN P3000_ROLLBACK');

        CALL PLITDLI (ONE,
```

```
                      DLI_FUNCROLL);

        IF IO_STATUS_CODE ¬= ' ' THEN
           DO;
               CALL P9000_DISPLAY_ERROR;
               RETURN;
           END;
        ELSE
           PUT SKIP LIST ('SUCCESSFUL ROLLBACK TO CHKPID ' || CHKP_ID);

    END P3000_ROLLBACK;
```

Now let's modify the initialization logic to handle either a normal start or a restart. On a normal start we'll get the first root in the database. On a restart we'll reposition at the EMP_ID saved in the checkpoint that we are using to do the restart.

```
            /* CHECK FOR RESTART */

            CALL PLITDLI (SIX,
                           DLI_FUNCXRST,
                           IO_PCB,
                           XRST_IO_AREALEN,
                           XRST_IOAREA,
                           IMS_CHKP_AREA_LTH,
                           IMS_CHKP_AREA);

        IF IO_STATUS_CODE ¬= ' ' THEN
           DO;
               CALL P9000_DISPLAY_ERROR;
               RETURN;
           END;

        IF XRST_ID ¬= ' ' THEN
           DO;
               SW_IMS_RESTART = '1'B;
               CHKP_NBR = CHKP_NBR_LAST;
               PUT SKIP LIST ('*** COBIMSE IMS RESTART ***');
               PUT SKIP LIST ('*  LAST CHECK POINT :' || XRST_ID);
               PUT SKIP LIST ('*  EMPLOYEE NUMBER  :' || CHKP_EMP_ID);
           END;
        ELSE
           DO;
               PUT SKIP LIST ('****** COBIMSE IMS NORMAL START ***');
               CALL P8000_TAKE_CHECKPOINT;
           END;

        IF SW_IMS_RESTART THEN
           DO;
               EMP_ID_VAL = CHKP_EMP_ID;
               CALL P2000_RESET_POSITION;
           END;
```

```
    ELSE
        CALL P1000_GET_FIRST_ROOT;
```

The value of XRST_ID will be non-blank if we are doing a restart. In that case we will turn on the SW_IMS_RESTART switch. Otherwise we will take the initial checkpoint. Now if the SW_IMS_RESTART is true, it means this is a restart so we load the employee id from the checkpoint area into the qualified EMPLOYEE qualified SSA value, and then we call the procedure to reset database position to where it was at that checkpoint.

If the value of XRST_ID is blank, then we are **not** doing a restart. In this case, we call the procedure to get the first root.

Finally, let's add a temporary statement to the execution loop. After a successful GET HOLD, check for employee id 7459, and call the rollback procedure. We will only do this on the first run of the program so as to force a rollback.

```
IF STATUS_CODE = '  ' THEN
    DO;
        PUT SKIP LIST ('SUCCESSFUL GET HOLD: ' || EMPL_ID);
        EMP_ID_VAL = EMPL_ID;
        CHKP_COUNT = CHKP_COUNT + 1;
        IF CHKP_COUNT >= 5 THEN
            DO;
                CALL P8000_TAKE_CHECKPOINT;
                CALL P2000_RESET_POSITION;
            END;
        IF EMPL_ID = '7459' THEN
            CALL P3000_ROLLBACK;
    END;
```

So here is our complete code listing. Make sure to review it carefully to be sure you understand what is happening.

```
PLIIMSE: PROCEDURE (IO_PTR_PCB,DB_PTR_PCB) OPTIONS(MAIN);
/***********************************************************
* PROGRAM NAME: PLIIMSE - WALK THROUGH THE EMPLOYEE (ROOT)    *
*                         SEGMENTS OF THE EMPLOYEE IMS DATABASE,  *
*                         AND DELETE EACH ONE. ROLL BACK CHANGES  *
*                         WHEN A PARTICULAR EMP ID IS ENCOUNTERED. *
***********************************************************/

/***********************************************************
/*            W O R K I N G   S T O R A G E               *
***********************************************************/

   DCL SW_END_OF_DB              STATIC BIT(01) INIT('0'B);
```

```
DCL SW_IMS_RESTART          STATIC BIT(01) INIT('0'B);
DCL ONCODE                  BUILTIN;
DCL DB_PTR_PCB              POINTER;
DCL IO_PTR_PCB              POINTER;

DCL PLITDLI                 EXTERNAL ENTRY;

DCL 01 DLI_FUNCTIONS,
       05 DLI_FUNCISRT      CHAR(04) INIT ('ISRT'),
       05 DLI_FUNCGU        CHAR(04) INIT ('GU  '),
       05 DLI_FUNCGN        CHAR(04) INIT ('GN  '),
       05 DLI_FUNCGHU       CHAR(04) INIT ('GHU '),
       05 DLI_FUNCGNP       CHAR(04) INIT ('GNP '),
       05 DLI_FUNCREPL      CHAR(04) INIT ('REPL'),
       05 DLI_FUNCDLET      CHAR(04) INIT ('DLET'),
       05 DLI_FUNCXRST      CHAR(04) INIT ('XRST'),
       05 DLI_FUNCCHKP      CHAR(04) INIT ('CHKP'),
       05 DLI_FUNCROLL      CHAR(04) INIT ('ROLL');

DCL 01 IO_EMPLOYEE_RECORD,
       05  EMPL_ID          CHAR(04),
       05  FILLER1          CHAR(01),
       05  EMPL_LNAME       CHAR(30),
       05  FILLER2          CHAR(01),
       05  EMPL_FNAME       CHAR(20),
       05  FILLER3          CHAR(01),
       05  EMPL_YRS_SRV     CHAR(02),
       05  FILLER4          CHAR(01),
       05  EMPL_PRM_DTE     CHAR(10),
       05  FILLER5          CHAR(10);

DCL 01 EMP_UNQUALIFIED_SSA,
       05  SEGNAME          CHAR(08) INIT ('EMPLOYEE'),
       05  FILLER7          CHAR(01) INIT (' ');

DCL 01 EMP_QUALIFIED_SSA,
       05  SEGNAME          CHAR(08) INIT('EMPLOYEE'),
       05  FILLER8          CHAR(01) INIT('('),
       05  FIELD            CHAR(08) INIT('EMPID'),
       05  OPER             CHAR(02) INIT(' ='),
       05  EMP_ID_VAL       CHAR(04) INIT('    '),
       05  FILLER9          CHAR(01) INIT(')');

DCL ONE                     FIXED BIN (31) INIT(1);
DCL TWO                     FIXED BIN (31) INIT(2);
DCL THREE                   FIXED BIN (31) INIT(3);
DCL FOUR                    FIXED BIN (31) INIT(4);
DCL FIVE                    FIXED BIN (31) INIT(5);
DCL SIX                     FIXED BIN (31) INIT(6);

DCL 01 XRST_IOAREA,
       05 XRST_ID   CHAR(08) INIT('        '),
       05 FILLER10  CHAR(04) INIT('    ');
```

```
      DCL XRST_IO_AREALEN      FIXED BIN(31) INIT (12);
      DCL IO_AREALEN           FIXED BIN(31) INIT (08);
      DCL CHKP_ID              CHAR(08) INIT( 'IMSE-   ');
      DCL CHKP_NBR             PIC '999' INIT('000');
      DCL CHKP_COUNT           FIXED BIN (31) INIT(0);

      DCL 01 CHKP_MESSAGE,
             05 FILLER11           CHAR(24)    INIT(
                 'COBIMSE   CHECK POINT NO:'),
             05 CHKP_MESS_NBR   PIC '999',
             05 FILLER12           CHAR(15)    INIT( ',AT INPUT REC#:'),
             05 CHKP_MESS_REC   PIC 'ZZZZZ9',
             05 FILLER13           CHAR(10)    INIT(',AT EMP#:'),
             05 CHKP_MESS_EMP   CHAR(08)    INIT(' ');

      DCL IMS_CHKP_AREA_LTH    FIXED BIN (31) INIT(07);

      DCL 01 IMS_CHKP_AREA,
             05 CHKP_EMP_ID    CHAR(04)    INIT('0000'),
             05 CHKP_NBR_LAST  CHAR(03)    INIT('000');

      DCL 01 IO_PCB                   BASED(IO_PTR_PCB),
             05 FILLER97           CHAR(10)   INIT(' '),
             05 IO_STATUS_CODE    CHAR(02)  INIT (' ');

      DCL 01 PCB_MASK                 BASED(DB_PTR_PCB),
             05 DBD_NAME           CHAR(08),
             05 SEG_LEVEL          CHAR(02),
             05 STATUS_CODE        CHAR(02),
             05 PROC_OPT           CHAR(04),
             05 FILLER99           FIXED BIN (31),
             05 SEG_NAME           CHAR(08),
             05 KEY_FDBK           FIXED BIN (31),
             05 NUM_SENSEG         FIXED BIN (31),
             05 KEY_FDBK_AREA,
                10 KFB_EMPLOYEE_ID CHAR(04);

/***********************************************************************
/*                  P R O G R A M   M A I N L I N E               *
 ***********************************************************************/

CALL P100_INITIALIZATION;
CALL P200_MAINLINE;
CALL P300_TERMINATION;

P100_INITIALIZATION: PROC;

    PUT SKIP LIST ('PLIIMSE: TRAVERSE EMPLOYEE DATABASE ROOT SEGS');
    PUT SKIP LIST ('PROCESSING IN P100_INITIALIZATION');
    IO_PCB   = '';
    PCB_MASK = '';
    IO_EMPLOYEE_RECORD  = '';
```

229

```
    /* CHECK FOR RESTART */

    CALL PLITDLI (SIX,
                  DLI_FUNCXRST,
                  IO_PCB,
                  XRST_IO_AREALEN,
                  XRST_IOAREA,
                  IMS_CHKP_AREA_LTH,
                  IMS_CHKP_AREA);

    IF IO_STATUS_CODE ¬= '  ' THEN
        DO;
            CALL P9000_DISPLAY_ERROR;
            RETURN;
        END;

    IF XRST_ID ¬= ' ' THEN
        DO;
            SW_IMS_RESTART = '1'B;
            CHKP_NBR = CHKP_NBR_LAST;
            PUT SKIP LIST ('*** COBIMSE IMS RESTART ***');
            PUT SKIP LIST ('*  LAST CHECK POINT :' || XRST_ID);
            PUT SKIP LIST ('*  EMPLOYEE NUMBER  :' || CHKP_EMP_ID);
        END;
    ELSE
        DO;
            PUT SKIP LIST ('****** COBIMSE IMS NORMAL START ***');
            CALL P8000_TAKE_CHECKPOINT;
        END;

    IF SW_IMS_RESTART THEN
        DO;
            EMP_ID_VAL = CHKP_EMP_ID;
            CALL P2000_RESET_POSITION;
        END;
    ELSE
        CALL P1000_GET_FIRST_ROOT;

END P100_INITIALIZATION;

P200_MAINLINE: PROC;

    /*  MAIN LOOP - CYCLE THROUGH ALL ROOT SEGMENTS IN THE DB,
                    DISPLAYING THE DATA RETRIEVED              */

    IF SW_END_OF_DB THEN
        PUT SKIP LIST ('NO RECORDS TO PROCESS!!');
    ELSE
        DO WHILE (¬SW_END_OF_DB);
            PUT SKIP LIST ('SUCCESSFUL GET-HOLD :'
                || EMPL_ID);
```

```
           /* DELETE THE SWGMENT */

           CALL PLITDLI (THREE,
                         DLI_FUNCDLET,
                         PCB_MASK,
                         IO_EMPLOYEE_RECORD);

       IF STATUS_CODE ¬= '  ' THEN
          DO;
             CALL P9000_DISPLAY_ERROR;
             RETURN;
          END;
       ELSE
          PUT SKIP LIST ('SUCCESSFUL DELETE OF EMP ' || EMPL_ID);

       /* NOW GET THE NEXT ROOT TO DELETE */

           CALL PLITDLI (FOUR,
                         DLI_FUNCGN,
                         PCB_MASK,
                         IO_EMPLOYEE_RECORD,
                         EMP_UNQUALIFIED_SSA);

       IF STATUS_CODE = '  ' THEN
          DO;
             PUT SKIP LIST ('SUCCESSFUL GET HOLD: ' || EMPL_ID);
             EMP_ID_VAL = EMPL_ID;
             CHKP_COUNT = CHKP_COUNT + 1;
             IF CHKP_COUNT >= 5 THEN
                DO;
                   CALL P8000_TAKE_CHECKPOINT;
                   CALL P2000_RESET_POSITION;
                END;
             IF EMPL_ID = '7459' THEN
                CALL P3000_ROLLBACK;
          END;
       ELSE
          IF STATUS_CODE = 'GB' THEN
             DO;
                SW_END_OF_DB = '1'B;
                PUT SKIP LIST ('** END OF DATABASE');
             END;
          ELSE
             DO;
                CALL P9000_DISPLAY_ERROR;
                RETURN;
             END;

   END; /* DO WHILE */

   PUT SKIP LIST ('FINISHED PROCESSING IN P200_MAINLINE');

END P200_MAINLINE;
```

```
P300_TERMINATION: PROC;

    PUT SKIP LIST ('PROCESSING IN P300_TERMINATION');

    CHKP_COUNT = CHKP_COUNT + 1;
    CALL P8000_TAKE_CHECKPOINT;

    PUT SKIP LIST ('PLIIMSE - SUCCESSFULLY ENDED');

END P300_TERMINATION;

P1000_GET_FIRST_ROOT: PROC;

    PUT SKIP LIST ('PROCESSING IN P1000_GET_FIRST_ROOT');

 /* DO INITIAL DB READ FOR FIRST EMPLOYEE RECORD */

    CALL PLITDLI (FOUR,
                  DLI_FUNCGHN,
                  PCB_MASK,
                  IO_EMPLOYEE_RECORD,
                  EMP_UNQUALIFIED_SSA);

    IF STATUS_CODE = '  ' THEN;
    ELSE
        IF STATUS_CODE = 'GB' THEN
            DO;
                SW_END_OF_DB = '1'B;
                PUT SKIP LIST ('** END OF DATABASE');
            END;
        ELSE
            DO;
                CALL P9000_DISPLAY_ERROR;
                RETURN;
            END;

END P1000_GET_FIRST_ROOT;

P2000_RESET_POSITION: PROC;

    PUT SKIP LIST ('PROCESSING IN P2000_RESET_POSITION');

    CALL PLITDLI (FOUR,
                  DLI_FUNCGHU,
                  PCB_MASK,
                  IO_EMPLOYEE_RECORD,
                  EMP_QUALIFIED_SSA);

    IF STATUS_CODE ¬= '  ' THEN
        DO;
            CALL P9000_DISPLAY_ERROR;
            RETURN;
```

232

```
          END;
      ELSE
          PUT SKIP LIST ('SUCCESSFUL REPOSITION AT EMP ID ' || EMPL_ID);

END P2000_RESET_POSITION;

P3000_ROLLBACK: PROC;

    PUT SKIP LIST ('PROCESSING IN P3000_ROLLBACK');

    CALL PLITDLI (ONE,
          DLI_FUNCROLL);

    IF IO_STATUS_CODE ¬= '  ' THEN
        DO;
            CALL P9000_DISPLAY_ERROR;
            RETURN;
        END;
    ELSE
        PUT SKIP LIST ('SUCCESSFUL ROLLBACK TO CHKPID ' || CHKP_ID);

END P3000_ROLLBACK;

P8000_TAKE_CHECKPOINT: PROC;

    PUT SKIP LIST ('PROCESSING IN P8000_TAKE_CHECKPOINT');

    CHKP_NBR               = CHKP_NBR + 1;
    CHKP_NBR_LAST          = CHKP_NBR;
    SUBSTR(CHKP_ID,6,3)    = CHKP_NBR_LAST;
    CHKP_EMP_ID            = EMPL_ID;

    PUT SKIP LIST ('IO_AREALEN ' || IO_AREALEN);
    PUT SKIP LIST ('IMS_CHKP_AREA_LTH ' || IMS_CHKP_AREA_LTH);

    PUT SKIP LIST ('CHKP_ID = ' || CHKP_ID);
    PUT SKIP LIST (' ');

    CALL PLITDLI (SIX,
                  DLI_FUNCCHKP,
                  IO_PCB,
                  IO_AREALEN,
                  CHKP_ID,
                  IMS_CHKP_AREA_LTH,
                  IMS_CHKP_AREA);

    IF IO_STATUS_CODE ¬= '  ' THEN
        DO;
            PUT SKIP LIST ('TOOK AN ERROR DOING THE CHECKPOINT');
            PUT SKIP LIST ('IO_STATUS_CODE ' || IO_STATUS_CODE);
            CALL P9000_DISPLAY_ERROR;
            RETURN;
        END;
```

233

```
        ELSE
           DO;
              CHKP_COUNT = 0;
              CHKP_MESS_NBR = CHKP_NBR;
              CHKP_MESS_EMP = CHKP_EMP_ID;
              PUT SKIP LIST (CHKP_MESSAGE);
           END;

   END P8000_TAKE_CHECKPOINT;

   P9000_DISPLAY_ERROR: PROC;

       PUT SKIP LIST ('ERROR ENCOUNTERED - DETAIL FOLLOWS');
       PUT SKIP LIST ('SEG_IO_AREA     :' || SEG_IO_AREA);
       PUT SKIP LIST ('DBD_NAME1:' || DBD_NAME);
       PUT SKIP LIST ('SEG_LEVEL1:' || SEG_LEVEL);
       PUT SKIP LIST ('STATUS_CODE:' || STATUS_CODE);
       PUT SKIP LIST ('PROC_OPT1 :' || PROC_OPT);
       PUT SKIP LIST ('SEG_NAME1 :' || SEG_NAME);
       PUT SKIP LIST ('KEY_FDBK1 :' || KEY_FDBK);
       PUT SKIP LIST ('NUM_SENSEG1:' || NUM_SENSEG);
       PUT SKIP LIST ('KEY_FDBK_AREA1:' || KEY_FDBK_AREA);

   END P9000_DISPLAY_ERROR;

   END PLIIMSE;
```

Compile and link, then run the program. The program will abend with IMS user code
U0778 because of the ROLL call. Here is the output:

```
** PROGRAM PLIIMSE START **
PROCESSING IN P100_INITIALIZATION
****** PLIIMSE IMS NORMAL START ***
PROCESSING IN P8000_TAKE_CHECKPOINT
CHECKPOINT ID IS IMSE-001
PLIIMSE  CHECK POINT NO:001    ,AT REC#:  ,AT EMP#:
PROCESSING IN P200_MAINLINE
SUCCESSFUL DELETE OF EMPLOYEE 1111
SUCCESSFUL GET HOLD :1122 JENKINS                 DEBORAH        05
SUCCESSFUL DELETE OF EMPLOYEE 1122
SUCCESSFUL GET HOLD :3217 JOHNSON                 EDWARD         04
SUCCESSFUL DELETE OF EMPLOYEE 3217
SUCCESSFUL GET HOLD :4175 TURNBULL                FRED           01
SUCCESSFUL DELETE OF EMPLOYEE 4175
SUCCESSFUL GET HOLD :4720 SCHULTZ                 TIM            09
SUCCESSFUL DELETE OF EMPLOYEE 4720
SUCCESSFUL GET HOLD :4836 SMITH                   SANDRA         03
PROCESSING IN P8000_TAKE_CHECKPOINT
CHECKPOINT ID IS IMSE-002
PLIIMSE  CHECK POINT NO:002    ,AT REC#:  ,AT EMP#:4836
PROCESSING IN P2000-RESET-POSITION
SUCCESSFUL REPOSITION AT EMP ID 4836
SUCCESSFUL DELETE OF EMPLOYEE 4836
SUCCESSFUL GET HOLD :6288 WILLARD                 JOE            06
```

```
SUCCESSFUL DELETE OF EMPLOYEE 6288
SUCCESSFUL GET HOLD :7459 STEWART                    BETTY              07
PROCESSING IN P3000_ROLLBACK
```

Note: If you prefer not to take a hard abend, then instead of issuing the ROLL IMS call you can issue ROLB. ROLB backs out changes the same as ROLL, but ROLB returns control to the application program instead of abending.

At this point, we can verify that the first 5 records got deleted, and also that the next deleted records were backed out.

```
Browse            USER01.IMS.EMPLOYEE.DATA                   Top of 4
Command ===>                                                 Scroll PAGE
                         Type DATA      RBA                  Format CHAR
                                        Col 1
----+----10---+----2----+----3----+----4----+----5----+----6----+----7----+----
****   Top of data  ****
......4836 SMITH                 SANDRA              03 2017-01-01 02
......6288 WILLARD               JOE                 06 2016-01-01 20
......7459 STEWART               BETTY               07 2016-07-31 01
......9134 FRANKLIN              BRIANNA             00 2016-10-01 93
****   End of data  ****
```

So, the next step is to remove the code in COBIMSE that forced the rollback, then restart the program. Go ahead and remove or comment out the code, recompile and then we'll set up our restart JCL.

The PARM should look like this. Note that the IMSE-002 is the last successful checkpoint in the prior run. You can verify this by looking at the output from the previous run. Here is our restart parm override:

```
//GO        EXEC PGM=DFSRRC00,REGION=4M,
//          PARM=(DLI,&MBR,&PSB,7,0000,,0,'IMSE-002',N,0,0,,,N,N,,N,)
```

Now run the program, and here is the output.

```
** PROGRAM PLIIMSE START **
PROCESSING IN P100_INITIALIZATION
*** PLIIMSE IMS RESTART ***
*   LAST CHECK POINT :IMSE-002
*   EMPLOYEE NUMBER  :4836
PROCESSING IN P2000_RESET_POSITION
SUCCESSFUL REPOSITION AT EMP ID 4836
PROCESSING IN P200_MAINLINE
SUCCESSFUL DELETE OF EMPLOYEE 4836
SUCCESSFUL GET HOLD :6288 WILLARD                    JOE                06
SUCCESSFUL DELETE OF EMPLOYEE 6288
SUCCESSFUL GET HOLD :7459 STEWART                    BETTY              07
```

```
SUCCESSFUL DELETE OF EMPLOYEE 7459
SUCCESSFUL GET HOLD :9134 FRANKLIN              BRIANNA          00
SUCCESSFUL DELETE OF EMPLOYEE 9134
END OF DATABASE
FINISHED PROCESSING IN P200_MAINLINE
PROCESSING IN P300_TERMINATION
PROCESSING IN P8000_TAKE_CHECKPOINT
CHECKPOINT ID IS IMSE-003
PLIIMSE  CHECK POINT NO:003     ,AT REC#:  ,AT EMP#:9134
** PLIIMSE - SUCCESSFULLY ENDED **
```

So we correctly restarted at employee id 4836, and then processed in GHN mode from there on. This is what should have happened. Now the database is empty, which we can confirm by trying to browse it.

```
VSAM POINT RC X"08", Error Code X"20"
VSAM GET RC X"08", Error Code X"58"
Function terminated
***
```

You now have a basic model for doing checkpoint restart. Frankly, checkpoint restart this is done somewhat differently in each of the major environments I've worked in. Often they use third party products (such as BMC) to keep track of checkpoints and to facilitate recovery. So you may need to learn the third party products. The symbolic checkpoint examples I've provided here, although plain vanilla, work just fine.

That pretty well wraps up basic IMS programming. There are plenty of other features you can use, but that will depend on your work environment. Every shop and application is different. Good luck with it, and enjoy!

IMS Programming Guidelines

Consider the PLI code examples in this text to be my own guidelines for coding IMS programs. There are more formal guidelines provided by IBM on their web site. [8]

---

[8] https://www.ibm.com/support/knowledgecenter/SSEPH2_12.1.0/com.ibm.ims12.doc.apg/ims_programguidelines.htm

Chapter Three Review Questions

1. What is the name of the interface program you call from a PLI program to perform IMS operations?

2. Here are some IMS return codes and . Explain briefly what each of them means: blank, GE, GB, II

3. What is an SSA?

4. Briefly explain these entities: DBD, PSB, PCB?

5. What is the use of CMPAT parameter in PSB ?

6. In IMS, what is the difference between a key field and a search field?

7. What does PROCOPT mean in a PCB?

8. What are the four basic parameters of a DLI retrieval call?

9. What are Qualified SSA and Unqualified SSA?

10. Which PSB parameter in a PSBGEN specifies the language in which the application program is written?

11. What does SENSEG stand for and how is it used in a PCB?

12. What storage mechanism/format is used for IMS index databases?

13. What are the DL/I commands to add, change and remove a segment?

14. What return code will you receive from IMS if the DL/I call was successful?

15. If you want to retrieve the last occurrence of a child segment under its parent, what command code could you use?

16. When would you use a GU call?

17. When would you use a GHU call?

18. What is the difference between running an IMS program as DLI and BMP ?

19. When would you use a GNP call?

20. Which IMS call is used to restart an abended program?

21. How do you establish parentage on a segment occurrence?

22. What is a checkpoint?

23. How do you update the primary key of an IMS segment?

24. Do you need to use a qualified SSA with REPL/DLET calls?

25. What is a root segment?

26. What are command codes?

Chapter Four : PLI Programming with DB2

Database 2 (DB2) is IBM's flagship relational database management system (DBMS). It was introduced for IBM mainframe computers in 1983. If you are working on a mainframe it is most likely you will be using DB2 for data management. Consequently we devote a lot of this text book to DB2 application development.

Basic z/OS Tools for DB2

Before we get into DB2 development activities, I want to introduce you to the environment we'll be working in. If you've used DB2 on the mainframe, you're almost certainly familiar with these tools and this will be a quick review. But if you have little or no exposure to DB2 on z/OS, we need to make sure you are familiar with how to access it and use the basic tools available.

DB2 Interactive

You'll do much of your DB2 work in DB2 Interactive which is now typically is titled **DB2 Primary Option Menu.** Regardless of which shop you work in, there should be a menu option on the ISPF main menu to get to DB2. It may be called DB2 or some other name with DB2 in it. On my system, the option is called DB2 and the description is DB2 Primary Menu. Select whichever option is on your main menu for DB2.

```
   Menu  Utilities  Compilers  Options  Status  Help
─────────────────────────────────────────────────────────────
                        ISPF Primary Option Menu
 Option ===>

 0   Settings      Terminal and user parameters       User ID . : USER01
 1   View          Display source data or listings    Time. . . : 21:19
 2   Edit          Create or change source data       Terminal. : 3278
 3   Utilities     Perform utility functions          Screen. . : 1
 4   Foreground    Interactive language processing    Language. : ENGLISH
 5   Batch         Submit job for language processing Appl ID . : ISR
 6   Command       Enter TSO or Workstation commands  TSO logon : MATPROC
 7   Dialog Test   Perform dialog testing             TSO prefix: HRUSER
 10  SCLM          SW Configuration Library Manager   System ID : MATE
 11  Workplace     ISPF Object/Action Workplace       MVS acct. : MT529
 12  DITTO         DITTO/ESA for MVS                  Release . : ISPF 6.0
 13  FMN           File Manager
 15  DB2           DB2 Primary Menu
 17  QMF           DB2 Query Management Facility
 S   SDSF          Spool Search and Display Facility

       Enter X to Terminate using log/list defaults
```

This is the DB2 main menu. Select the first option, which is SPUFI. SPUFI is an acronym for **SQL Processing Using File Input**.

Select option 1.

```
                              DB2I PRIMARY OPTION MENU          SSID: DB2X
     COMMAND ===>

     Select one of the following DB2 functions and press ENTER.

        1  SPUFI                 (Process SQL statements)
        2  DCLGEN                (Generate SQL and source language declarations)
        3  PROGRAM PREPARATION   (Prepare a DB2 application program to run)
        4  PRECOMPILE            (Invoke DB2 precompiler)
        5  BIND/REBIND/FREE      (BIND, REBIND, or FREE plans or packages)
        6  RUN                   (RUN an SQL program)
        7  DB2 COMMANDS          (Issue DB2 commands)
        8  UTILITIES             (Invoke DB2 utilities)
        D  DB2I DEFAULTS         (Set global parameters)
        Q  QMF                   (Query Management Facility
        X  EXIT                  (Leave DB2I)



     PRESS:                   END to exit      HELP for more information
```

You'll see the following screen.

```
                              SPUFI                            SSID: DB2X
     ===>

     Enter the input data set name:        (Can be sequential or partitioned)
        1  DATA SET NAME ... ===> 'HRUSER.SPUFI.CNTL(EXECSQL)'
        2  VOLUME SERIAL ... ===>           (Enter if not cataloged)
        3  DATA SET PASSWORD ===>           (Enter if password protected)

     Enter the output data set name:       (Must be a sequential data set)
        4  DATA SET NAME ... ===> 'HRUSER.SPUFI.OUT'

     Specify processing options:
        5  CHANGE DEFAULTS   ===> NO        (Y/N - Display SPUFI defaults panel?)
        6  EDIT INPUT ...... ===> YES       (Y/N - Enter SQL statements?)
        7  EXECUTE ......... ===> YES       (Y/N - Execute SQL statements?)
        8  AUTOCOMMIT ...... ===> YES       (Y/N - Commit after successful run?)
        9  BROWSE OUTPUT ... ===> YES       (Y/N - Browse output data set?)

     For remote SQL processing:
       10  CONNECT LOCATION  ===>



      PRESS:  ENTER to process    END to exit          HELP for more
     information
```

This is the place you can specify an input file which will contain the SQL, DDL, DML or DCL statements you wish to execute. We'll explain DDL, DML and DCL in future chapters. For now just think of it as the place you can run SQL.

I also recommend that you specify these processing options: NO for CHANGE DEFAULTS, and YES for EDIT INPUT, EXECUTE, AUTOMCOMMIT and BROWSE OUTPUT. You must also specify an output file to capture the results from your statements. If these files do not already exist you must allocate them.

When you press ENTER your input dataset will open and you can type the statements that you want to execute. In the example below, I've coded a SELECT statement to retrieve all records from a sample table named EMPLOYEE.

```
File   Edit   Edit_Settings   Menu   Utilities   Compilers   Test   Help


EDIT       USER01.SPUFI.CNTL(EXECSQL) - 01.00           Columns 00001 00072
Command ===>                                              Scroll ===> PAGE
***** ***************************** Top of Data *****************************
000001 SELECT * FROM EMPLOYEE;
***** ************************** Bottom of Data ***************************
```

When you press PF3, and then press ENTER again, the output dataset is shown with the results from the query.

```
   Menu   Utilities   Compilers   Help
ssssssssssssssssssssssssssssssssssssssssssssssssssssssssssssssssssssssssssss
BROWSE     USER01.SPUFI.OUT                        Line 00000000 Col 001 080
Command ===>                                              Scroll ===> PAGE
***************************** Top of Data ********************************
---------+---------+---------+---------+---------+---------+---------+---------+
SELECT * FROM EMPLOYEE;
---------+---------+---------+---------+---------+---------+---------+---------+
     EMPNO   NAME
---------+---------+---------+---------+---------+---------+---------+---------+
       100   SMITH
       200   JONES
DSNE610I NUMBER OF ROWS DISPLAYED IS 2
DSNE616I STATEMENT EXECUTION WAS SUCCESSFUL, SQLCODE IS 100
---------+---------+---------+---------+---------+---------+---------+---------+
---------+---------+---------+---------+---------+---------+---------+---------+
DSNE617I COMMIT PERFORMED, SQLCODE IS 0
DSNE616I STATEMENT EXECUTION WAS SUCCESSFUL, SQLCODE IS 0
---------+---------+---------+---------+---------+---------+---------+---------+
DSNE601I SQL STATEMENTS ASSUMED TO BE BETWEEN COLUMNS 1 AND 72
DSNE620I NUMBER OF SQL STATEMENTS PROCESSED IS 1
DSNE621I NUMBER OF INPUT RECORDS READ IS 2
DSNE622I NUMBER OF OUTPUT RECORDS WRITTEN IS 18
***************************** Bottom of Data ****************************
```

You will use SPUFI very frequently unless your shop has adopted another tool such as Data Studio.

DB2I Defaults

Your shop should have standard settings for DB2I defaults. If you are studying on your own, I recommend setting some defaults. First select option D from the DB2 Primary Option menu:

```
                         DB2I PRIMARY OPTION MENU            SSID: DB2X

COMMAND ===>

Select one of the following DB2 functions and press ENTER.

    1   SPUFI                    (Process SQL statements)
    2   DCLGEN                   (Generate SQL and source language declarations)
    3   PROGRAM PREPARATION      (Prepare a DB2 application program to run)
    4   PRECOMPILE               (Invoke DB2 precompiler)
    5   BIND/REBIND/FREE         (BIND, REBIND, or FREE plans or packages)
    6   RUN                      (RUN an SQL program)
    7   DB2 COMMANDS             (Issue DB2 commands)
    8   UTILITIES                (Invoke DB2 utilities)
    D   DB2I DEFAULTS            (Set global parameters)
    Q   QMF                      (Query Management Facility
    X   EXIT                     (Leave DB2I)




PRESS:                        END to exit     HELP for more information
```

Select the following options, specifying your correct DB2 subsystem identifier as the DB2 Name (ask your system admin if you are not sure – I have used DB2X as mine and that represents the subsystem identifier on my system).

Specify PLI as the application language. Our programming examples will be in PLI.

```
                              DB2I DEFAULTS PANEL 1
COMMAND ===>

Change defaults as desired:

   1  DB2 NAME ............. ===> DB2X      (Subsystem identifier)
   2  DB2 CONNECTION RETRIES ===> 0         (How many retries for DB2 connection)
   3  APPLICATION LANGUAGE   ===> PLI       (ASM, C, CPP, IBMCOB, FORTRAN, PLI)
   4  LINES/PAGE OF LISTING  ===> 60        (A number from 5 to 999)
   5  MESSAGE LEVEL ........ ===> I         (Information, Warning, Error, Severe)
   6  SQL STRING DELIMITER   ===> DEFAULT   (DEFAULT, ' or ")
   7  DECIMAL POINT ........ ===> .         (. or ,)
   8  STOP IF RETURN CODE >= ===> 8         (Lowest terminating return code)
   9  NUMBER OF ROWS ....... ===> 20        (For ISPF Tables)
  10  AS USER                ===>           (Userid to associate with the trusted
                                             connection)



PRESS:   ENTER to process    END to cancel         HELP for more information
```

DCLGEN

DCLGEN is an IBM utility that generates SQL data structures (table definition and host variables) for a table or view. DCLGEN stores the structure in a PDS member and then the PDS member can be included in a PLI or COBOL program by issuing an EXEC SQL INCLUDE statement. Put another way, DCLGEN generates table declarations (hence the name DCLGEN). Don't worry if this doesn't make sense yet. We'll generate and use these DCLGEN structures when we start writing programs.

Here's an example of running a DCLGEN for a table. You won't be able to execute it yet because we haven't created the table yet – we'll do this later in the chapter – this is just an example.

From the DB2 Primary Option menu, select option 2 for DCLGEN.

```
                          DB2I PRIMARY OPTION MENU            SSID: DB2X
COMMAND ===>
Select one of the following DB2 functions and press ENTER.

   1   SPUFI                 (Process SQL statements)
   2   DCLGEN                (Generate SQL and source language declarations)
   3   PROGRAM PREPARATION   (Prepare a DB2 application program to run)
   4   PRECOMPILE            (Invoke DB2 precompiler)
   5   BIND/REBIND/FREE      (BIND, REBIND, or FREE plans or packages)
   6   RUN                   (RUN an SQL program)
   7   DB2 COMMANDS          (Issue DB2 commands)
   8   UTILITIES             (Invoke DB2 utilities)
   D   DB2I DEFAULTS         (Set global parameters)
   Q   QMF                   (Query Management Facility
   X   EXIT                  (Leave DB2I)




PRESS:                      END to exit     HELP for more information
```

Now enter the DB2 table name, owner and the partitioned data set and member name to place the DCLGEN output into. In the example below we have a table named EMP_PAY_CHECK owned by HRSCHEMA. We want the output of the DCLGEN to be placed in member EMPPAYCK of partitioned dataset HRUSER.DCLGEN.PLI.

Once you've entered the required information, press ENTER.

```
                        DCLGEN                        SSID: DB2X
===>

Enter table name for which declarations are required:
 1   SOURCE TABLE NAME ===> EMP_PAY_CHECK

 2   TABLE OWNER ..... ===> HRSCHEMA

 3   AT LOCATION ..... ===>                                    (Optional)
Enter destination data set:         (Can be sequential or partitioned)
 4   DATA SET NAME ... ===> 'HRUSER.DCLGEN.PLI(EMPPAYCK)'
 5   DATA SET PASSWORD ===>          (If password protected)
Enter options as desired:
 6   ACTION .......... ===> ADD      (ADD new or REPLACE old declaration)
 7   COLUMN LABEL .... ===> NO       (Enter YES for column label)
 8   STRUCTURE NAME .. ===>                                    (Optional)
 9   FIELD NAME PREFIX ===>                                    (Optional)
10   DELIMIT DBCS .... ===> YES      (Enter YES to delimit DBCS identifiers)
11   COLUMN SUFFIX ... ===> NO       (Enter YES to append column name)
12   INDICATOR VARS .. ===> NO       (Enter YES for indicator variables)
13   ADDITIONAL OPTIONS===> NO       (Enter YES to change additional options

PRESS: ENTER to process    END to exit      HELP for more information
```

Next, you will receive a message indicating the DCLGEN has succeeded.☐

DSNE905I EXECUTION COMPLETE, MEMBER EMPPAYCK ADDED
***

Now you can browse the PDS member EMPPAYCK to see the resulting structures. The
first structure will declare the DB2 table definition, and the other structure will declare
PLI host variables that correspond to the table definition.

```
/**********************************************************************/
/* DCLGEN TABLE(HRSCHEMA.EMP_PAY_CHECK)                             */
/*        LIBRARY(USER01.DCLGEN.PLI(EMPPAYCK))                      */
/*        ACTION(REPLACE)                                           */
/*        LANGUAGE(PLI)                                             */
/*        APOST                                                     */
/* ... IS THE DCLGEN COMMAND THAT MADE THE FOLLOWING STATEMENTS    */
/**********************************************************************/
EXEC SQL DECLARE HRSCHEMARW.EMP_PAY_CHECK TABLE
        ( EMP_ID                       INTEGER NOT NULL,
          EMP_REGULAR_PAY              DECIMAL(8,2) NOT NULL,
          EMP_SEMIMTH_PAY              DECIMAL(8,2) NOT NULL
        ) ;
/**********************************************************************/
```

```
/* PLI DECLARATION FOR TABLE HRSCHEMA.EMP_PAY_CHECK              */
/*******************************************************************/
DCL 1 DCLEMP_PAY_CHECK,
      5 EMP_ID    BIN FIXED(31),
      5 EMP_REGULAR_PAY  DEC FIXED(8,2),
      5 EMP_SEMIMTH_PAY  DEC FIXED(8,2);
/*******************************************************************/
/* THE NUMBER OF COLUMNS DESCRIBED BY THIS DECLARATION IS 3       */
/*******************************************************************/
```

Again, the above structure can be included in your application program by simply issuing:

```
EXEC SQL
    INCLUDE EMPPAYCK;
```

Once you've included the DCLGEN structure in your application program, you have host variables declared for every column in the table, so you don't need to code these variables yourself.

Data Manipulation Language

Overview

In this chapter we will explore DML (Data Manipulation Language) which includes both SQL and several related topics.

Data Manipulation Language (DML) is used to add, change and delete data in a DB2 table. DML is one of the most basic and essential skills you must have as a DB2 professional. In this section we'll look at the five major DML statements: INSERT, UPDATE, DELETE, MERGE and SELECT.

XML data access and processing is another skill that you need to be familiar with. DB2 includes an XML data type and various functions for accessing and processing XML data. I'll assume you have a basic understanding of XML, but we'll do a quick review anyway. Then we'll look at some examples of creating an XML column, populating it, modifying it and manipulating it using XML functions such as XQuery.

Special registers allow you to access detailed information about the DB2 instance settings as well as certain session information. CURRENT DATE is an example of a special register. You can access special registers in SPUFI or in an application program and then use the information as needed.

Built-in functions can be used in SQL statements to return a result based on an argument. Think of these as productivity tools in that they can be used to replace custom coded functionality in an application program and thereby simplify development and maintenance. Whether your role is application developer, DBA or business services professional, the DB2 built-in functions can save you time if you know what they are and how to use them.

Database, Tablespace and Schema Conventions

Throughout this book we will be using a database called DBHR which is a database for a fictitious human relations department in a company. The main tablespace we will us is HRTS. Finally, our default schema will be HRSCHEMA. In some cases we will explicitly specify the schema in our DDL or SQL. If we don't explicitly specify a schema, it means we have defined the HRSCHEMA schema as the CURRENT SCHEMA so we don't need to specify it.

If you are following along and creating examples on your own system, you may of course use whatever database and schema is available to you on your system. If you want the basic DDL to create the objects named above, it is as follows:

```
CREATE DATABASE DBHR
STOGROUP SGHR
BUFFERPOOL BPHR
INDEXBP IBPHR
CCSID UNICODE;


CREATE TABLESPACE TSHR
      IN DBHR
      USING STOGROUP SGHR
        PRIQTY 50
        SECQTY 20
      LOCKSIZE PAGE
      BUFFERPOOL BPHR2;


CREATE SCHEMA HRSCHEMA
AUTHORIZATION DBA001;
```
← This should be your DB2 id, whatever it is.

DML SQL Statements

Data Manipulation Language (DML) is at the core of working with relational databases. You need to be very comfortable with DML statements: INSERT, UPDATE, DELETE, MERGE and SELECT. We'll cover the syntax and use of each of these. For purposes of this section, let's plan and create a very simple table. Here are the columns and data types for our table which we will name EMPLOYEE.

Field Name	Type	Attributes
EMP_ID	INTEGER	NOT NULL, PRIMARY KEY
EMP_LAST_NAME	VARCHAR(30)	NOT NULL
EMP_FIRST_NAME	VARCHAR(20)	NOT NULL
EMP_SERVICE_YEARS	INTEGER	NOT NULL, DEFAULT IS ZERO
EMP_PROMOTION_DATE	DATE	

The table can be created with the following DDL:

```
CREATE TABLE HRSCHEMA.EMPLOYEE(
EMP_ID INT NOT NULL,
EMP_LAST_NAME VARCHAR(30) NOT NULL,
EMP_FIRST_NAME VARCHAR(20) NOT NULL,
EMP_SERVICE_YEARS INT NOT NULL WITH DEFAULT 0,
EMP_PROMOTION_DATE DATE,
PRIMARY KEY(EMP_ID)) ;
```

We also need to create a unique index to support the primary key:

250

```
CREATE UNIQUE INDEX NDX_EMPLOYEE
     ON EMPLOYEE (EMP_ID);
```

INSERT Statement

The INSERT statement adds one or more rows to a table. There are three forms of the INSERT statement and you need to know the syntax of each of these.

1. Insert via Values

2. Insert via Select

3. Insert via FOR N ROWS

Insert Via Values

There are actually two sub-forms of the insert by values. One form explicitly names the target columns and the other does not. Generally when inserting a record you explicitly specify the target fields, followed by a VALUES clause that includes the actual values to apply to the new record. Let's use our EMPLOYEE table for this example:

```
INSERT INTO EMPLOYEE
(EMP_ID,
 EMP_LAST_NAME,
 EMP_FIRST_NAME,
 EMP_SERVICE_YEARS,
 EMP_PROMOTION_DATE)

VALUES (3217,
 'JOHNSON',
 'EDWARD',
 4,
 '01/01/2017')
```

Note that the values must be ordered in the same sequence that the columns are named in the INSERT query.

A second sub-form of the INSERT statement via values is to omit the target fields and simply provide the VALUES clause. You can do this only if your values clause includes values for ALL the columns in the correct positional order as defined in the table.

Here's an example of this second sub-form of insert via values:

```
INSERT INTO EMPLOYEE
VALUES (7459,
```

```
'STEWART',
'BETTY',
7,
'07/31/2016')
```

Note that EMP_ID is defined as a primary key on the table. If you try inserting a row for which the primary key already exists, you will receive a -803 error SQL code (more on this later when we discuss table objects in detail).

Here's an example of specifying the DEFAULT value for the EMP_SERVICE_YEARS column, and the NULL value for the EMP_PROMOTION_DATE.

```
INSERT INTO EMPLOYEE
(EMP_ID,
EMP_LAST_NAME,
EMP_FIRST_NAME,
EMP_SERVICE_YEARS,
EMP_PROMOTION_DATE)

VALUES (9134,
'FRANKLIN',
'ROSEMARY',
DEFAULT,
NULL);
```

When you define a column using WITH DEFAULT, you do not necessarily have to specify the actual default value in your DDL. DB2 provides implicit default values for most data types and if you just specify WITH DEFAULT and no specific value, the implicit default value will be used.

In the EMPLOYEE table we specified WITH DEFAULT 0 for the employee's service years. However, the implicit default value here is also zero because the column is defined as INTEGER. So we could have simply specified WITH DEFAULT and it would have the same result as specifying WITH DEFAULT 0.

The following table denotes the default values for the various data types.

Default Values for DB2 Data Types
This table appeared earlier in the book, but I include it again here because we are talking specifically about using defaults.

For columns of	Type	Default
Numbers	SMALLINT, INTEGER, BIGINT, DECIMAL, NUMERIC, REAL, DOUBLE, DECFLOAT, or FLOAT	0
Fixed-length strings	CHAR or GRAPHIC BINARY	Blanks Hexadecimal zeros
Varying-length strings	VARCHAR, CLOB, VARGRAPHIC, DBCLOB, VARBINARY, or BLOB	Empty string
Dates	DATE	CURRENT DATE
Times	TIME	CURRENT TIME
Timestamps	TIMESTAMP	CURRENT TIMESTAMP
ROWIDs	ROWID	DB2-generated

Before moving on to the Insert via Select option, let's take a look at the data we have in the table so far.

```
SELECT
EMP_ID,
EMP_LAST_NAME,
EMP_FIRST_NAME,
EMP_SERVICE_YEARS,
EMP_PROMOTION_DATE
FROM HRSCHEMA.EMPLOYEE
ORDER BY EMP_ID;
-------+---------+---------+---------+---------+---------+-------------
  EMP_ID  EMP_LAST_NAME   EMP_FIRST_NAME   EMP_SERVICE_YEARS  EMP_PROMOTION_DATE
-------+---------+---------+---------+---------+---------+-------------
    3217  JOHNSON         EDWARD                          4  2017-01-01
    7459  STEWART         BETTY                           7  2016-01-01
    9134  FRANKLIN        ROSEMARY                        0  ----------

DSNE610I NUMBER OF ROWS DISPLAYED IS 3
```

Insert via Select

You can use a SELECT query to extract data from one table and load it to another. You can even include literals or built in functions in the SELECT query in lieu of column names (if you need them). Let's do an example.

Suppose you work in HR and you have an employee recognition request table named EMPRECOG. This table is used to generate/store recognition requests for employees who have been promoted during a certain time frame. Once the request is fulfilled, the date completed will be populated by HR in a separate process. The table specification is as follows:

Field Name	Type	Attributes
EMP_ID	INTEGER	NOT NULL
EMP_PROMOTION_DATE	DATE	NOT NULL
EMP_RECOG_RQST_DATE	DATE	NOT NULL WITH DEFAULT
EMP_RECOG_COMP_DATE	DATE	

The DDL to create the table is as follows:

```
CREATE TABLE EMPRECOG(
EMP_ID INT NOT NULL,
EMP_PROMOTION_DATE DATE NOT NULL,
EMP_RECOG_RQST_DATE DATE
NOT NULL WITH DEFAULT,
EMP_RECOG_COMP_DATE DATE)
IN TSHR;
```

Your objective is to load this table with data from the EMPLOYEE table for any employee whose promotion date occurs during the current month. The selection criteria could be expressed as:

```
SELECT
EMP_ID,
EMP_PROMOTION_DATE
FROM HRSCHEMA.EMPLOYEE
WHERE MONTH(EMP_PROMOTION_DATE)
 = MONTH(CURRENT DATE)
```

To use this SQL in an INSERT statement on the EMPRECOG table, you would need to add another column for the request date (EMP_RECOG_RQST_DATE). Let's use the CURRENT DATE function to insert today's date. Now our select statement looks like this:

```
SELECT
EMP_ID,
EMP_PROMOTION_DATE,
CURRENT DATE AS RQST_DATE
FROM HRSCHEMA.EMPLOYEE
WHERE MONTH(EMP_PROMOTION_DATE)
     = MONTH(CURRENT DATE)
```

Assuming we are running the SQL on January 10, 2017 we should get the following results:

```
---------+---------+---------+---------+---------+
```

```
      EMP_ID  EMP_PROMOTION_DATE  RQST_DATE
---------+---------+---------+---------+---------+
      3217  2017-01-01          2017-01-10
DSNE610I NUMBER OF ROWS DISPLAYED IS 1
```

Finally, let's create the INSERT statement for the EMPRECOG table. Since our query does not include the EMP_RQST_COMP_DATE (assume that the **request complete** column will be populated by another HR process when the request is complete), we must specify the target column names we are populating. Otherwise we will get a mismatch between the number of columns we are loading and the number in the table.

Professional Note: In circumstances where you have values for all the table's columns, you don't have to include the column names. You could just use the INSERT INTO and SELECT statement. But it is handy to include the target column names, even when you don't have to. It makes the DML more self-documenting and helpful for the next developer. This is a good habit to develop – thinking of the next person that will maintain your code.

Here is our SQL:

```
INSERT INTO HRSCHEMA.EMPRECOG
(EMP_ID,
 EMP_PROMOTION_DATE,
 EMP_RECOG_RQST_DATE)
 SELECT
 EMP_ID,
 EMP_PROMOTION_DATE,
 CURRENT DATE AS RQST_DATE
 FROM EMPLOYEE
 WHERE MONTH(EMP_PROMOTION_DATE)
  = MONTH(CURRENT DATE)
```

If you are following along and running the examples, you may notice it doesn't work if the real date is not a January 2017 date. You can make this one work by specifying the comparison date as 1/1/2017. So your query would be:

```
INSERT INTO EMPRECOG
(EMP_ID,
 EMP_PROMOTION_DATE,
 EMP_RECOG_RQST_DATE)
 SELECT
 EMP_ID,
 EMP_PROMOTION_DATE,
 CURRENT DATE AS RQST_DATE
 FROM EMPLOYEE
 WHERE MONTH(EMP_PROMOTION_DATE)
  = MONTH('01/01/2017')
```

After you run the SQL, query the EMPRECOG table, and you can see the result:

```
SELECT * FROM HRSCHEMA.EMPRECOG;
---------+---------+---------+---------+---------+---------+---------+---
   EMP_ID EMP_PROMOTION_DATE  EMP_RECOG_RQST_DATE  EMP_RECOG_COMP_DATE
---------+---------+---------+---------+---------+---------+---------+---
     3217 2017-01-01          2017-01-10           -------------------
DSNE610I NUMBER OF ROWS DISPLAYED IS 1
```

The above is what we expect. Only one of the employees has a promotion date in January, 2017. This employee has been added to the EMPRECOG table with request date of January 10 and a NULL recognition completed date.

Insert via **FOR N ROWS**

The third form of the INSERT statement is used to insert multiple rows with a single statement. You can do this with an internal program table and host variables. We haven't talked yet about embedded SQL but we'll do a sample program now in PLI.

We'll use our EMPLOYEE table and insert two new rows using the INSERT via FOR N ROWS. Note that we define our host variables as arrays holding two elements.

```
DCL 01  HV_ID(2)             FIXED BIN(31);
DCL 01  HV_LAST_NAME(2)      CHAR(30);
DCL 01  HV_FIRST_NAME(2)     CHAR(20);
DCL 01  HV_SERVICE_YEARS(2)  FIXED BIN(31);
DCL 01  HV_PROMOTION_DATE(2) CHAR(10);
```

We load the arrays with data before doing the INSERT statement. Also notice the **FOR 2 ROWS** clause at the end of the SQL statement. You could also have an array with more than two rows. And the number of rows you insert using FOR X ROWS can be less than the actual array size.

```
PLIEMP1: PROCEDURE OPTIONS(MAIN) REORDER;
/***************************************************************
* PROGRAM NAME :  PLIEMP1 - PERFORM MULTI ROW INSERT TO DB2 TABLE *
***************************************************************/

/***************************************************************
/*              W O R K I N G   S T O R A G E              *
***************************************************************/

DCL 01  HV_ID(2)             FIXED BIN(31);
DCL 01  HV_LAST_NAME(2)      CHAR(30);
DCL 01  HV_FIRST_NAME(2)     CHAR(20);
DCL 01  HV_SERVICE_YEARS(2)  FIXED BIN(31);
```

```
    DCL 01  HV_PROMOTION_DATE(2) CHAR(10);

    DCL RET_SQL_CODE              FIXED BIN(31) INIT(0);
    DCL RET_SQL_CODE_PIC          PIC 'S999999999' INIT (0);

    EXEC SQL
      INCLUDE SQLCA;

    EXEC SQL
      INCLUDE EMPLOYEE;

/********************************************************************
 /*              P R O G R A M   M A I N L I N E            *
 ********************************************************************/

    PUT SKIP LIST ('SAMPLE PLI PROGRAM: MULTIPLE ROW INSERT');

    /* LOAD THE EMPLOYEE ARRAY */

        HV_ID(1)            = +4720;
        HV_LAST_NAME(1)     = 'SCHULTZ';
        HV_FIRST_NAME(1)    = 'TIM';
        HV_SERVICE_YEARS(1) = +9;
        HV_PROMOTION_DATE(1) = '01/01/2017';

        HV_ID(2)            = +6288;
        HV_LAST_NAME(2)     = 'WILLARD';
        HV_FIRST_NAME(2)    = 'JOE';
        HV_SERVICE_YEARS(2) = +6;
        HV_PROMOTION_DATE(2) = '01/01/2016';


        EXEC SQL
           INSERT INTO USER01.EMPLOYEE
           (EMP_ID,
            EMP_LAST_NAME,
            EMP_FIRST_NAME,
            EMP_SERVICE_YEARS,
            EMP_PROMOTION_DATE)

           VALUES
           (:HV_ID,
            :HV_LAST_NAME,
            :HV_FIRST_NAME,
            :HV_SERVICE_YEARS,
            :HV_PROMOTION_DATE)

           FOR 2 ROWS
           NOT ATOMIC CONTINUE ON SQLEXCEPTION;

        IF SQLCODE = 0 THEN;
        ELSE
           DO;
```

```
        EXEC SQL
            GET DIAGNOSTICS CONDITION 1
            :RET_SQL_CODE  = DB2_RETURNED_SQLCODE;

        RET_SQL_CODE_PIC  = RET_SQL_CODE;
        PUT SKIP LIST (RET_SQL_CODE_PIC);
     END;

END PLIEMP1;
```

An additional option for the multiple row INSERT is to specify ATOMIC or NOT ATOMIC. Specifying ATOMIC means that if any of the row operations fails, any successful row operations are rolled back. It's all or nothing. This may be what you want, but that will depend on your program design and how you plan to handle any failed rows.

```
        EXEC SQL
        INSERT INTO HRSCHEMA.EMPLOYEE
        (EMP_ID,
         EMP_LAST_NAME,
         EMP_FIRST_NAME,
         EMP_SERVICE_YEARS,
         EMP_PROMOTION_DATE)

        VALUES
        (:HV_ID,
         :HV_LAST-NAME,
         :HV_FIRST-NAME,
         :HV_SERVICE-YEARS,
         :HV_PROMOTION-DATE)
        FOR 2 ROWS
        ATOMIC;
```

Before you can run this program, it must be pre-compiled, compiled, link-edited and bound. How you do this depends on the shop. Typically you will either submit a JCL from your own library, or you will use a set of online panels to run the steps automatically. Check with a fellow programmer or system admin in your environment for the details of how to do this.

If you are renting a mainframe id with Mathru Technologies, they will provide you with the JCL to compile, bind and run your program.

After you've pre-compiled, compiled, link-edited and bound your program, run it. Now let's check out table contents:

```
SELECT
EMP_ID,
EMP_LAST_NAME,
EMP_FIRST_NAME,
EMP_SERVICE_YEARS,
```

```
EMP_PROMOTION_DATE
FROM EMPLOYEE
WHERE EMP_ID IN (3217, 4720, 6288, 7459, 9134)
ORDER BY EMP_ID;
---------+---------+---------+---------+---------+---------+---------+-------
   EMP_ID  EMP_LAST_NAME   EMP_FIRST_NAME   EMP_SERVICE_YEARS  EMP_PROMOTION_DATE
---------+---------+---------+---------+---------+---------+---------+-------
     3217  JOHNSON         EDWARD                          4  2017-01-01
     4720  SCHULTZ         TIM                             9  2017-01-01
     6288  WILLARD         JOE                             6  2016-01-01
     7459  STEWART         BETTY                           7  2016-01-01
     9134  FRANKLIN        ROSEMARY                        0  ---------
DSNE610I NUMBER OF ROWS DISPLAYED IS 5
```

On the ATOMIC option, you can specify NOT ATOMIC CONTINUE ON SQLEXCEPTION. In this case any successful row operations are still applied to the table, and any unsuccessful ones are not. The unsuccessfully inserted rows are discarded. The key point here is that NOT ATOMIC means the unsuccessful inserts do not cause the entire query to fail. Make sure to remember this point!

Note: You can also INSERT to an underlying table via a view. The syntax is exactly the same as for inserting to a table. This topic will be considered in a later chapter.

UPDATE Statement

The UPDATE statement is pretty straightforward. It changes one or more records based on specified conditions. There are two forms of the UPDATE statement:

1. The Searched Update

2. The Positioned Update

Searched Update

The searched update is performed on records that meet a certain search criteria using a WHERE clause. The basic form and syntax you need to know for the searched update is:

```
UPDATE <TABLENAME>
SET FIELDNAME = <VALUE>
WHERE <CONDITION>
```

For example, recall that we left the promotion date for employee 9134 with a NULL value. Now let's say we want to update the promotion date to October 1, 2016. We could use this SQL to do that:

```
UPDATE EMPLOYEE
SET EMP_PROMOTION_DATE = '10/01/2016'
WHERE EMP_ID = 9134;
```

If you have more than one column to update, you must use a comma to separate the column names. For example, let's update both the promotion date and the first name of the employee. We'll make the first name Brianna and the promotion date 10/1/2016.

```
UPDATE EMPLOYEE
SET EMP_PROMOTION_DATE = '10/01/2016',
    EMP_FIRST_NAME = 'BRIANNA'
WHERE EMP_ID = 9134;
```

Another sub-form of the UPDATE statement to be aware of is UPDATE without a WHERE clause. For example, to set the **EMP_RECOG_COMP_DATE** field to January 31, 2017 for every row in the EMPRECOG table, you could use this statement:

```
UPDATE EMPRECOG
SET EMP_RECOG_COMP_DATE = '01/31/2017';
```

Obviously you should be very careful using this form of UPDATE, as it will set the column value(s) you specify for every row in the table. This is normally not what you want, but it could be useful in cases where you need to initialize one or more fields for all rows of a relatively small table.

Positioned Update

The positioned update is an update based on a cursor in an application program. Let's continue with our EMPLOYEE table examples by creating an update DB2 program that will generate a result set based on a cursor and then update a set of records.

We need to specially set up test data for our example, so if you are following along, execute the following query:

```
UPDATE EMPLOYEE
SET EMP_LAST_NAME = LOWER(EMP_LAST_NAME)
WHERE
EMP_LAST_NAME IN ('JOHNSON', 'STEWART', 'FRANKLIN');
```

Now here is the current content of our EMPLOYEE table:

```
SELECT EMP_ID, EMP_LAST_NAME, EMP_FIRST_NAME
FROM EMPLOYEE
ORDER BY EMP_ID;


---------+---------+---------+---------+---------+---------+---
      EMP_ID  EMP_LAST_NAME                EMP_FIRST_NAME
---------+---------+---------+---------+---------+---------+---
      3217  johnson                        EDWARD
```

```
4720   SCHULTZ                 TIM
6288   WILLARD                 JOE
7459   stewart                 BETTY
9134   franklin                BRIANNA
```

As you can see we have some last names that are in lower case. Further, assume that we have decided we want to store all names in upper case. So we have to correct the lowercase data. We want to check all records in the EMPLOYEE table and if the last name is in lower case, we want to change it to upper case. We also want to report the name (both before and after correction) of the corrected records.

To accomplish our objective we'll define and open a cursor on the EMPLOYEE table. We can specify a WHERE clause that limits the result set to only those records where the EMP_LAST_NAME contains lower case characters. After we find them, we will change the case and replace the records.

To code a solution, first we need to identify the rows that include lower case letters in EMP_LAST_NAME. We can do this using the DB2 UPPER function. We'll compare the current contents of EMP_LAST_NAME to the value of UPPER(EMP_LAST_NAME) and if the results are not identical, we know that the row in question has lower case characters and needs to be changed. Our result set should include all rows where these two values are not identical. So our SQL would be:

```
SELECT EMP_ID, EMP_LAST_NAME
FROM HRSCHEMA.EMPLOYEE
WHERE EMP_LAST_NAME <> UPPER(EMP_LAST_NAME);
```

Once our FETCH statement has loaded the last name value into the host variable EMP_LAST_NAME, we can use the PLI UPPERCASE function to convert it from lower to uppercase.

```
EMP_LAST_NAME = UPPERCASE(EMP_LAST_NAME);
```

With this approach in mind, we are now ready to write the complete COBOL program. We will define and open the cursor, cycle through the result set using FETCH, modify the data and then do the UPDATE action specifying the current record of the cursor. That is what is meant by a positioned update – the cursor is positioned on the record to be changed, hence you do not need to specify a more elaborate WHERE clause in the UPDATE. Only the **WHERE CURRENT OF <cursor name>** clause need be specified.

Also we will include the FOR UPDATE clause in our cursor definition to tell DB2 that our intent is to update the data we retrieve. Here is the PLI code.

```
PLIEMP2: PROCEDURE OPTIONS(MAIN) REORDER;

/********************************************************************
* PROGRAM NAME :   PLIEMP2 - USE CURSOR TO UPDATE DB2 ROWS        *
********************************************************************/

/********************************************************************
/*                W O R K I N G   S T O R A G E                    *
********************************************************************/

   DCL RET_SQL_CODE              FIXED BIN(31) INIT(0);
   DCL RET_SQL_CODE_PIC          PIC 'S999999999' INIT (0);


   EXEC SQL
     INCLUDE SQLCA;

   EXEC SQL
     INCLUDE EMPLOYEE;

   EXEC SQL
     DECLARE EMP_CURSOR CURSOR FOR
     SELECT EMP_ID, EMP_LAST_NAME
     FROM USER01.EMPLOYEE
     WHERE EMP_LAST_NAME <> UPPER(EMP_LAST_NAME)
     FOR UPDATE OF EMP_LAST_NAME;

/********************************************************************
/*               P R O G R A M   M A I N L I N E                   *
********************************************************************/

   PUT SKIP LIST ('SAMPLE PLI PROGRAM: CURSOR TO UPDATE ROWS');

   EXEC SQL OPEN EMP_CURSOR;

   PUT SKIP LIST ('OPEN CURSOR SQLCODE: ' || SQLCODE);

   IF SQLCODE = 0 THEN
      DO UNTIL (SQLCODE ¬= 0);
         CALL P0100_FETCH_CURSOR;
      END;

   EXEC SQL CLOSE EMP_CURSOR;

   PUT SKIP LIST ('CLOSE CURSOR SQLCODE: ' || SQLCODE);

   IF SQLCODE ¬= 0 THEN
      DO;
         EXEC SQL
            GET DIAGNOSTICS CONDITION 1
            :RET_SQL_CODE  = DB2_RETURNED_SQLCODE;
```

```
              RET_SQL_CODE_PIC  = RET_SQL_CODE;
              PUT SKIP LIST (RET_SQL_CODE_PIC);
          END;

   P0100_FETCH_CURSOR: PROC;

      EXEC SQL
          FETCH EMP_CURSOR INTO :EMP_ID, :EMP_LAST_NAME;

      IF SQLCODE = 0 THEN
          DO;
              PUT SKIP LIST ('BEFORE CHANGE  ' || EMP_LAST_NAME);
              EMP_LAST_NAME = UPPERCASE(EMP_LAST_NAME);
              EXEC SQL
                 UPDATE HRSCHEMA.EMPLOYEE
                 SET EMP_LAST_NAME = :EMP_LAST_NAME
                 WHERE CURRENT OF EMP_CURSOR;
              IF SQLCODE = 0 THEN
                 PUT SKIP LIST ('AFTER CHANGE  ' || EMP_LAST_NAME);
          END;

   END P0100_FETCH_CURSOR;

   END PLIEMP2;
```

To avoid redundancy, from this point I will assume that you will pre-compile, compile, link-edit and bind your programs using whatever procedures are used in your shop. I won't mention those steps again. I will just assume that you perform them before you run the program.

Here is the output from running our PLI program:

```
      SAMPLE PLI PROGRAM: CURSOR TO UPDATE ROWS
      OPEN CURSOR SQLCODE:                 0
      BEFORE CHANGE  johnson
      AFTER CHANGE   JOHNSON
      BEFORE CHANGE  stewart
      AFTER CHANGE   STEWART
      BEFORE CHANGE  franklin
      AFTER CHANGE   FRANKLIN
      CLOSE CURSOR SQLCODE:                0
```

And here is the modified table:

```
      SELECT * FROM EMPLOYEE
      ORDER BY EMP_ID;
      --------+---------+---------+---------+---------+---------+---
          EMP_ID  EMP_LAST_NAME                 EMP_FIRST_NAME
      --------+---------+---------+---------+---------+---------+---
          3217  JOHNSON                       EDWARD
```

```
4720  SCHULTZ              TIM
6288  WILLARD              JOE
7459  STEWART              BETTY
9134  FRANKLIN             BRIANNA
```

This method of using a positioned cursor update is something you will use often, particularly when you do not know your result set beforehand, and anytime you need to examine the content of the record before you perform the update.

DELETE Statement

The DELETE statement is also pretty straightforward. It removes one or more records from the table based on specified conditions. As with the UPDATE statement, there are two forms of the DELETE statement:

1. The Searched Delete
2. The Positioned Delete

Searched DELETE

The searched delete is performed on records that meet a certain criteria, i.e., based on a WHERE clause. The basic form and syntax you need to remember for the searched DELETE is:

```
DELETE FROM <TABLENAME>
WHERE <CONDITION>
```

For example, we might want to remove the record for the employee with id 9134. We could use this SQL to do that:

```
DELETE FROM HRSCHEMA.EMPLOYEE WHERE EMP_ID = 9134;
```

Another sub-form of the DELETE statement to be aware of is the DELETE without a WHERE clause. For example, to remove all records from the EMPRECOG table, use this statement:

```
DELETE FROM HRSCHEMA.EMPRECOG;
```

Be very careful using this form of DELETE, as it will remove every record from the target table. This is normally not what you want, but it could be useful in cases where you need to initialize a relatively small table to empty.

Positioned Delete

The positioned DELETE is similar to the positioned UPDATE. It is a DELETE based on a cursor position in an application program. Let's create a DB2 program that will delete records based on a cursor. We'll have it delete any record where the employee has not received a promotion – don't feel bad for them, remember we're just using the example to illustrate a coding point!

Before we can proceed, we need to add a record to the EMPLOYEE table because currently we have no records that lack a promotion date. So we will add one.

```
INSERT INTO HRSCHEMA.EMPLOYEE
VALUES (1122, 'JENKINS', 'DEBORAH', 5, NULL);
```

At this time, we have a single record in the table for which the promotion data is NULL, which is employee 1122, Deborah Jenkins:

```
SELECT
EMP_ID,
EMP_LAST_NAME,
EMP_FIRST_NAME,
EMP_PROMOTION_DATE
FROM EMPLOYEE
ORDER BY EMP_ID;
---------+---------+---------+---------+---------+---------+---------+-
    EMP_ID  EMP_LAST_NAME      EMP_FIRST_NAME      EMP_PROMOTION_DATE
---------+---------+---------+---------+---------+---------+---------+-
      1122  JENKINS            DEBORAH             ----------
      3217  JOHNSON            EDWARD              2017-01-01
      4720  SCHULTZ            TIM                 2017-01-01
      6288  WILLARD            JOE                 2016-01-01
      7459  STEWART            BETTY               2016-07-31
DSNE610I NUMBER OF ROWS DISPLAYED IS 5
```

The SQL for our cursor should look like this:

```
SELECT EMP_ID,
FROM EMPLOYEE
WHERE EMP_PROMOTION_DATE IS NULL
FOR UPDATE
```

We'll include the FOR UPDATE clause with our cursor to ensure DB2 knows our intention is to use the cursor to delete the records we retrieve. In case you are wondering, there is no FOR DELETE clause. The FOR UPDATE clause covers both updates and deletes.

Our program code will look like this:

```pli
PLIEMP3: PROCEDURE OPTIONS(MAIN) REORDER;

/*******************************************************************
* PROGRAM NAME :   PLIEMP3 - USE CURSOR TO DELETE DB2 ROWS        *
*******************************************************************/

/*******************************************************************
/*                W O R K I N G   S T O R A G E                   *
*******************************************************************/

   DCL RET_SQL_CODE              FIXED BIN(31) INIT(0);
   DCL RET_SQL_CODE_PIC          PIC 'S999999999' INIT (0);


   EXEC SQL
     INCLUDE SQLCA;

   EXEC SQL
     INCLUDE EMPLOYEE;

   EXEC SQL
     DECLARE EMP_CURSOR CURSOR FOR
     SELECT EMP_ID
     FROM USER01.EMPLOYEE
     WHERE EMP_PROMOTION_DATE IS NULL
     FOR UPDATE;

/*******************************************************************
/*                P R O G R A M   M A I N L I N E                 *
*******************************************************************/

   PUT SKIP LIST ('SAMPLE PLI PROGRAM: CURSOR TO DELETE ROWS');

   EXEC SQL OPEN EMP_CURSOR;

   PUT SKIP LIST ('OPEN CURSOR SQLCODE: ' || SQLCODE);

   IF SQLCODE = 0 THEN
      DO UNTIL (SQLCODE ¬= 0);
         CALL P0100_FETCH_CURSOR;
      END;

   EXEC SQL CLOSE EMP_CURSOR;

   PUT SKIP LIST ('CLOSE CURSOR SQLCODE: ' || SQLCODE);

   IF SQLCODE ¬= 0 THEN
      DO;
         EXEC SQL
            GET DIAGNOSTICS CONDITION 1
            :RET_SQL_CODE  = DB2_RETURNED_SQLCODE;

         RET_SQL_CODE_PIC  = RET_SQL_CODE;
```

266

```
            PUT SKIP LIST (RET_SQL_CODE_PIC);
         END;

   P0100_FETCH_CURSOR: PROC;

      DCLEMPLOYEE = '';

      EXEC SQL
         FETCH EMP_CURSOR INTO :EMP_ID;

      IF SQLCODE = 0 THEN
         DO;
            EXEC SQL
               DELETE USER01.EMPLOYEE
               WHERE CURRENT OF EMP_CURSOR;
            IF SQLCODE = 0 THEN
               PUT SKIP LIST ('DELETED EMPLOYEE ' || EMP_ID);
         END;


   END P0100_FETCH_CURSOR;

   END PLIEMP3;
```

The output from the program looks like this:

```
      SAMPLE PLI PROGRAM: CURSOR TO DELETE ROWS
      OPEN CURSOR SQLCODE:               0
      DELETED EMPLOYEE          1122
      CLOSE CURSOR SQLCODE:              0
```

A single row was deleted from the table, as we can confirm by querying EMPLOYEE:

```
      SELECT EMP_ID,
      EMP_PROMOTION_DATE
      FROM HRSCHEMA.EMPLOYEE
      ORDER BY EMP_ID

      ---------+---------+---------+---------+---
          EMP_ID  EMP_PROMOTION_DATE
      ---------+---------+---------+---------+---
            3217  2017-01-01
            4720  2017-01-01
            6288  2016-01-01
            7459  2016-07-31
      DSNE610I NUMBER OF ROWS DISPLAYED IS 4
```

As with the positioned update statement, the positioned delete is something you will use when you do not know your result set beforehand, or when you have to first examine the content of the record and then decide whether or not to delete it.

MERGE Statement

The MERGE statement updates a target table or view using specified input data. Rows that already exist in the target table are updated as specified by the input source, and rows that do not exist in the target are inserted using data from that same input source.

So what problem does the merge solve? It adds/updates records for a table from a data source when you don't know whether the row already exists in the table or not. An example could be if you are updating data in your table based on a flat file you receive from another system, department or even another company. Assuming the other system does not send you an action code (add, change or delete), you won't know whether to use the INSERT or UPDATE statement.

One way of handling this situation is to first try doing an INSERT and if you get a -803 SQL error code, then you know the record already exists. In that case you would then need to do an UPDATE instead. Or you could first try doing an UPDATE and then if you received an SQLCODE +100, you would know the record does not exist and you would need to do an INSERT. This solution works, but it inevitably wastes some DB2 calls and could potentially slow down performance.

A more elegant solution is the MERGE statement. We'll look at an example of this below. You'll notice the example is a pretty long SQL statement, but don't be put off by that. The SQL is only slightly longer than the combined INSERT and UPDATE statements you would have needed to use otherwise.

Single Row Merge Using Values

Let's go back to our EMPLOYEE table for this example. Let's say we have employee information for Deborah Jenkins whom we previously deleted, and now we want to apply her information back to the table. This information is being fed to us from another system which also supplied an EMP_ID, but we don't know whether that EMP_ID already exists in our EMPLOYEE table or not. So let's use the MERGE statement:

```
MERGE INTO EMPLOYEE AS T
USING
(VALUES (1122,
'JENKINS',
'DEBORAH',
5,
NULL))
AS S
(EMP_ID,
 EMP_LAST_NAME,
 EMP_FIRST_NAME,
```

```
            EMP_SERVICE_YEARS,
            EMP_PROMOTION_DATE)
         ON S.EMP_ID = T.EMP_ID


      WHEN MATCHED
         THEN UPDATE
            SET T.EMP_LAST_NAME      = S.EMP_LAST_NAME,
                T.EMP_FIRST_NAME     = S.EMP_FIRST_NAME,
                T.EMP_SERVICE_YEARS  = S.EMP_SERVICE_YEARS,
                T.EMP_PROMOTION_DATE = S.EMP_PROMOTION_DATE


      WHEN NOT MATCHED
         THEN INSERT
            VALUES (S.EMP_ID,
            S.EMP_LAST_NAME,
            S.EMP_FIRST_NAME,
            S.EMP_SERVICE_YEARS,
            S.EMP_PROMOTION_DATE);
```

Note that the existing EMPLOYEE table is given with a T qualifier and the new information is given with S as the qualifier (these qualifiers are arbitrary – you can use anything you want). We are matching the new information to the table based on employee id. When the specified employee id is matched to an employee id on the table, an update is performed using the S values, i.e., the new information. If it is not matched to an existing record, then an insert is performed – again based on the S values.

To see that our MERGE action was successful, let's take another look at our EMPLOYEE table.

```
SELECT EMP_ID,
EMP_LAST_NAME,
EMP_FIRST_NAME,
EMP_PROMOTION_DATE
FROM EMPLOYEE
ORDER BY EMP_ID;

---------+---------+---------+---------+---------+---------+---------+--------
    EMP_ID  EMP_LAST_NAME         EMP_FIRST_NAME       EMP_PROMOTION_DATE
---------+---------+---------+---------+---------+---------+---------+--------
      1122  JENKINS               DEBORAH              ----------
      3217  JOHNSON               EDWARD               2017-01-01
      4720  SCHULTZ               TIM                  2017-01-01
      6288  WILLARD               JOE                  2016-01-01
      7459  STEWART               BETTY                2016-07-31
DSNE610I NUMBER OF ROWS DISPLAYED IS 5
```

Merge Using HOST Variables

You can also do a merge in an application program using host variables. For this example, let's create a new table and a new program. The table will be EMP_PAY and it will include the base and bonus pay for each employee identified by employee id. Here are the columns we need to define.

Field Name	Type	Attributes
EMP_ID	INTEGER	NOT NULL
EMP_REGULAR_PAY	DECIMAL	NOT NULL
EMP_BONUS	DECIMAL	

The DDL would look like this:

```
CREATE TABLE EMP_PAY(
EMP_ID INT NOT NULL,
EMP_REGULAR_PAY DECIMAL (8,2) NOT NULL,
EMP_BONUS_PAY DECIMAL   (8,2));
```

Next, let's add a few records:

```
INSERT INTO HRSCHEMA.EMP_PAY
VALUES (3217, 80000.00, 4000);

INSERT INTO HRSCHEMA.EMP_PAY
VALUES (7459, 80000.00, 4000);

INSERT INTO HRSCHEMA.EMP_PAY
VALUES (9134, 70000.00, NULL);
```

Now the current data in the table is as follows:

```
SELECT * FROM EMP_PAY;
---------+---------+---------+---------+----
    EMP_ID  EMP_REGULAR_PAY  EMP_BONUS_PAY
---------+---------+---------+---------+----
      3217         80000.00         4000.00
      7459         80000.00         4000.00
      9134         70000.00    -------------
```

Let's create an update file for the employees where some of the data is for brand new employees and some is for updating existing employees. We'll have the program read the file and use the input data with a MERGE statement to update the table. Here's the content of the file with the three fields, EMP_ID, EMP_REGULAR_PAY and EMP_BONUS_PAY:

```
----+----1----+----2----+----3---
```

270

```
        3217       65000.00   5500.00
        7459       85000.00   4500.00
        9134       75000.00   2500.00
        4720       80000.00   2500.00
        6288       70000.00   2000.00
```

Looking at these records we know we will need to update three records that are already on the table, and we need to add two that don't currently exist on the table.

Here is sample code for a MERGE program that is based on reading the above input file and applying the data to the EMP_PAY table. It differs from the single row insert example only in that we are using host variables for the update data rather than using hard coded values. The power of the MERGE statement should be getting clearer to you now.

```
PLIEMP4: PROCEDURE OPTIONS(MAIN) REORDER;
/********************************************************************
* PROGRAM NAME :   PLIEMP4 - USE DB2 MERGE WITH HOST VARIABLES.   *
********************************************************************/

/********************************************************************
*                  F I L E S                                       *
********************************************************************/
  DCL EMPFILE   FILE RECORD SEQL INPUT;

/********************************************************************
/*                W O R K I N G   S T O R A G E                   *
********************************************************************/

  DCL SW_END_OF_FILE            STATIC BIT(01) INIT('0'B);

  DCL 01 IN_EMPLOYEE_RECORD,
         05  EMPLOYEE_ID    CHAR(04),
         05  FILLER1        CHAR(05),
         05  REGULAR_PAY    PIC '99999V.99',
         05  FILLER2        CHAR(02),
         05  BONUS_PAY      PIC '9999V.99',
         05  FILLER3        CHAR(54);

  DCL EMP_REGULAR_PAY_FD  FIXED DEC (8,2);
  DCL EMP_BONUS_PAY_FD    FIXED DEC (8,2);


  DCL RET_SQL_CODE              FIXED BIN(31) INIT(0);
  DCL RET_SQL_CODE_PIC          PIC 'SZZZZZ9999' INIT (0);

  EXEC SQL
    INCLUDE SQLCA;

  EXEC SQL
    INCLUDE EMPPAY;
```

271

```
/********************************************************************
/*                O N   C O N D I T I O N S                        *
********************************************************************/

   ON ENDFILE (EMPFILE) SW_END_OF_FILE =  '1'B;

/********************************************************************
/*              P R O G R A M   M A I N L I N E                    *
********************************************************************/

    PUT SKIP LIST ('SAMPLE PLI PROGRAM: UPDATE USING MERGE');

          OPEN FILE (EMPFILE);

          READ FILE (EMPFILE) INTO (IN_EMPLOYEE_RECORD);

     /* MAIN LOOP - READ THE INPUT FILE, LOAD HOST VARIABLES   */
     /*             AND CALL THE MERGE ROUTINE.                */

          DO WHILE (¬SW_END_OF_FILE);

              EMP_ID              = EMPLOYEE_ID;
              EMP_REGULAR_PAY_FD = REGULAR_PAY;
              EMP_BONUS_PAY_FD   = BONUS_PAY;
              EMP_REGULAR_PAY     = EMP_REGULAR_PAY_FD;
              EMP_BONUS_PAY       = EMP_BONUS_PAY_FD;
              CALL A1000_MERGE_RECORD;
              READ FILE (EMPFILE) INTO (IN_EMPLOYEE_RECORD);

          END; /* DO WHILE */

          CLOSE FILE (EMPFILE);

     A1000_MERGE_RECORD: PROC;

          EXEC SQL

             MERGE INTO EMP_PAY AS TARGET
             USING (VALUES(:EMP_ID,
             :EMP_REGULAR_PAY,
             :EMP_BONUS_PAY))
             AS SOURCE(EMP_ID,
             EMP_REGULAR_PAY,
             EMP_BONUS_PAY)
             ON TARGET.EMP_ID = SOURCE.EMP_ID

             WHEN MATCHED THEN UPDATE
                SET TARGET.EMP_REGULAR_PAY
                       = SOURCE.EMP_REGULAR_PAY,
                    TARGET.EMP_BONUS_PAY
                       = SOURCE.EMP_BONUS_PAY
```

272

```
        WHEN NOT MATCHED THEN INSERT

            (EMP_ID,
             EMP_REGULAR_PAY,
             EMP_BONUS_PAY)
             VALUES
             (SOURCE.EMP_ID,
              SOURCE.EMP_REGULAR_PAY,
              SOURCE.EMP_BONUS_PAY);


     IF SQLCODE = 0 THEN
        PUT SKIP LIST ('RECORD MERGED SUCCESSFULLY ' || EMP_ID);
     ELSE
        DO;
           PUT SKIP LIST ('*** SQL ERROR ***');
           EXEC SQL
              GET DIAGNOSTICS CONDITION 1
                :RET_SQL_CODE  = DB2_RETURNED_SQLCODE;

           RET_SQL_CODE_PIC   = RET_SQL_CODE;
           PUT SKIP LIST (RET_SQL_CODE_PIC);
        END;

  END A1000_MERGE_RECORD;

 END PLIEMP4;
```

Here are the results from the program.

```
SAMPLE PLI PROGRAM: UPDATE USING MERGE
RECORD MERGED SUCCESSFULLY           3217
RECORD MERGED SUCCESSFULLY           4720
RECORD MERGED SUCCESSFULLY           6288
RECORD MERGED SUCCESSFULLY           7459
RECORD MERGED SUCCESSFULLY           9134
```

And now we can verify that the results were actually applied to the table.

```
     SELECT *
     from EMP_PAY

     ---------+---------+---------+---------+-------
       EMP_ID  EMP_REGULAR_PAY  EMP_BONUS_PAY
     ---------+---------+---------+---------+-------
         3217          65000.00          5500.00
         7459          85000.00          4500.00
         9134          75000.00          2500.00
         4720          80000.00          2500.00
         6288          70000.00          2000.00
```

```
DSNE610I NUMBER OF ROWS DISPLAYED IS 5
```

Again the power of the MERGE statement is that you do not need to know whether a record already exists when you apply the data to the table. The program logic is simplified – there is no trial and error to determine whether or not the record exists.

SELECT Statement

SELECT is the main statement you will use to retrieve data from a table or view. The basic syntax for the select statement is:

```
SELECT          <column names>
FROM            <table or view name>
WHERE           <condition>
ORDER BY <column name or number to sort by>
```

Let's return to our EMPLOYEE table for an example:

```
SELECT EMP_ID, EMP_LAST_NAME, EMP_FIRST_NAME
FROM HRSCHEMA.EMPLOYEE
WHERE EMP_ID = 3217;


---------+---------+---------+---------+---------+-----
    EMP_ID  EMP_LAST_NAME        EMP_FIRST_NAME
---------+---------+---------+---------+---------+-----
    3217  JOHNSON              EDWARD
DSNE610I NUMBER OF ROWS DISPLAYED IS 1
```

You can also change the column heading on the result set by specifying <column name> AS <literal>. For example:

```
SELECT EMP_ID AS "EMPLOYEE NUMBER",
EMP_LAST_NAME AS "EMPLOYEE LAST NAME",
EMP_FIRST_NAME AS "EMPLOYEE FIRST NAME"
FROM HRSCHEMA.EMPLOYEE
WHERE EMP_ID = 3217 ;
---------+---------+---------+---------+---------+---------+---
EMPLOYEE NUMBER  EMPLOYEE LAST NAME    EMPLOYEE FIRST NAME
---------+---------+---------+---------+---------+---------+---
    3217  JOHNSON              EDWARD
DSNE610I NUMBER OF ROWS DISPLAYED IS 1
```

Now let's look at some clauses that will further qualify the rows that are returned.

WHERE CONDITION

There are quite a lot of options for the WHERE condition. In fact, you can use multiple where conditions by specifying AND and OR clauses. Be aware of the equality operators which are:

=	Equal to
<>	Not equal to
>	Greater than
>=	Greater than or equal to
<	Less than
<=	Less than or equal to

Let's look at some various examples of WHERE conditions.

OR

```
SELECT EMP_ID, EMP_LAST_NAME, EMP_FIRST_NAME
FROM HRSCHEMA.EMPLOYEE
WHERE EMP_ID = 3217 OR EMP_ID = 9134;
---------+---------+---------+---------+---------+---------
    EMP_ID  EMP_LAST_NAME           EMP_FIRST_NAME
---------+---------+---------+---------+---------+---------
    3217   JOHNSON                 EDWARD
    9134   FRANKLIN                BRIANNA
DSNE610I NUMBER OF ROWS DISPLAYED IS 2
```

AND

```
SELECT EMP_ID,
EMP_LAST_NAME,
EMP_FIRST_NAME,
EMP_PROMOTION_DATE
FROM HRSCHEMA.EMPLOYEE
WHERE (EMP_SERVICE_YEARS > 1)
   AND (EMP_PROMOTION_DATE > '12/31/2016')

---------+---------+---------+---------+---------+---------+---------
    EMP_ID  EMP_LAST_NAME         EMP_FIRST_NAME      EMP_PROMOTION_DATE
---------+---------+---------+---------+---------+---------+---------
    3217   JOHNSON               EDWARD              2017-01-01
    4720   SCHULTZ               TIM                 2017-01-01
DSNE610I NUMBER OF ROWS DISPLAYED IS 2
```

IN

You can specify that the column value must be present in a specified collection of values, either those you code in the SQL explicitly or a collection that is a result of a query. Let's look at an example of specifying specific EMP_IDs.

```
SELECT EMP_ID,
EMP_LAST_NAME,
EMP_FIRST_NAME
FROM HRSCHEMA.EMPLOYEE
WHERE EMP_ID IN (3217, 9134);
---------+---------+---------+---------+---------+
    EMP_ID  EMP_LAST_NAME         EMP_FIRST_NAME
---------+---------+---------+---------+---------+
      3217  JOHNSON               EDWARD
      9134  FRANKLIN              BRIANNA
DSNE610I NUMBER OF ROWS DISPLAYED IS 2
```

Now let's provide a listing of employees who are in the EMPLOYEE table but are NOT in the EMP_PAY table yet. This example shows us two new techniques, use of the NOT keyword and use of a sub-select to create a collection result set. First, let's add a couple of records to the EMPLOYEE table:

```
INSERT INTO EMPLOYEE
(EMP_ID,
EMP_LAST_NAME,
EMP_FIRST_NAME,
EMP_SERVICE_YEARS,
EMP_PROMOTION_DATE)

VALUES (3333,
'FORD',
'JAMES',
7,
'10/01/2015');

INSERT INTO EMPLOYEE
(EMP_ID,
EMP_LAST_NAME,
EMP_FIRST_NAME,
EMP_SERVICE_YEARS,
EMP_PROMOTION_DATE)

VALUES (7777,
'HARRIS',
'ELISA',
2,
NULL);
```

Now let's run our mismatch query:

```
SELECT EMP_ID,
EMP_LAST_NAME,
EMP_FIRST_NAME
FROM EMPLOYEE
WHERE EMP_ID
NOT IN (SELECT EMP_ID FROM EMP_PAY);
---------+---------+---------+---------+---------+---------+-
   EMP_ID  EMP_LAST_NAME        EMP_FIRST_NAME
---------+---------+---------+---------+---------+---------+-
     3333  FORD                 JAMES
     7777  HARRIS               ELISA
DSNE610I NUMBER OF ROWS DISPLAYED IS 2
```

By the way you can also use the **EXCEPT** clause to identify rows in one table that have no counterpart in the other. For example, suppose we want the employee ids of any employee who has not received a paycheck. You could quickly identify them with this SQL:

```
SELECT EMP_ID
FROM EMPLOYEE
EXCEPT (SELECT EMP_ID FROM EMP_PAY);
---------+---------+---------+---------+---------+---
   EMP_ID
---------+---------+---------+---------+---------+---
     3333
     7777
DSNE610I NUMBER OF ROWS DISPLAYED IS 2
```

One limitation of the EXCEPT clause is that the two queries have to match exactly, so you could not bring back a column from EMPLOYEE that does not also exist in the EMP_PAY table. Still the EXCEPT is useful in some cases, especially where you need to identify discrepancies between tables using a single column.

BETWEEN

The BETWEEN clause allows you to specify a range of values inclusive of the start and end value you provide. Here's an example where we want to retrieve the employee id and pay rate for all employees whose pay rate is between 60,000 and 85,000 annually.

```
SELECT EMP_ID,
EMP_REGULAR_PAY
FROM EMP_PAY
WHERE EMP_REGULAR_PAY
BETWEEN 60000 AND 85000;
---------+---------+---------+---------+----
   EMP_ID  EMP_REGULAR_PAY
---------+---------+---------+---------+----
     3217          65000.00
```

```
        7459            85000.00
        9134            75000.00
        4720            80000.00
        6288            70000.00
DSNE610I NUMBER OF ROWS DISPLAYED IS 5
```

LIKE

You can use the LIKE predicate to select values that match a pattern. For example, let's choose all rows for which the last name begins with the letter B. The % character is used as a wild card for any string value or character. So in this case we are retrieving every record for which the EMP_FIRST_NAME starts with the letter B.

```
SELECT EMP_ID,
EMP_LAST_NAME,
EMP_FIRST_NAME
FROM HRSCHEMA.EMPLOYEE
WHERE EMP_FIRST_NAME LIKE 'B%'
```

```
---------+---------+---------+---------+---------+---------
    EMP_ID   EMP_LAST_NAME        EMP_FIRST_NAME
---------+---------+---------+---------+---------+---------
      7459   STEWART              BETTY
      9134   FRANKLIN             BRIANNA
DSNE610I NUMBER OF ROWS DISPLAYED IS 2
```

DISTINCT

Use the DISTINCT operator when you want to eliminate duplicate values. To illustrate this, let's create a couple of new tables. The first is called EMP_PAY_CHECK and we will use to store a calculated bi-monthly pay amount for each employee based on their annual salary. The DDL to create EMP_PAY_CHECK is a s follows:

```
CREATE TABLE EMP_PAY_CHECK(
EMP_ID INT NOT NULL,
EMP_REGULAR_PAY  DECIMAL (8,2) NOT NULL,
EMP_SEMIMTH_PAY DECIMAL (8,2) NOT NULL)
IN HRTS;
```

Now let's insert some data into the EMP_PAY_CHECK table by calculating a twice monthly pay check:

```
INSERT INTO EMP_PAY_CHECK
(SELECT EMP_ID,
EMP_REGULAR_PAY,
EMP_REGULAR_PAY / 24 FROM EMP_PAY);
```

278

Let's look at the results:

```
SELECT *
FROM HRSCHEMA.EMP_PAY_CHECK;
---------+---------+---------+---------+---------+--
   EMP_ID  EMP_REGULAR_PAY  EMP_SEMIMTH_PAY
---------+---------+---------+---------+---------+--
      3217           65000.00           2708.33
      7459           85000.00           3541.66
      9134           75000.00           3125.00
      4720           80000.00           3333.33
      6288           70000.00           2916.66
DSNE610I NUMBER OF ROWS DISPLAYED IS 5
```

We now know how much each employee should make in their pay check. The next step is to create a history table of each pay check the employee receives. First we'll create the table and then we'll load it with data.

```
CREATE TABLE EMP_PAY_HIST(
EMP_ID INT NOT NULL,
EMP_PAY_DATE  DATE NOT NULL,
EMP_PAY_AMT   DECIMAL (8,2) NOT NULL)
IN HRTS;
```

We can load the history table by creating pay checks for the first four pay periods of the year like this:

```
INSERT INTO EMP_PAY_HIST
SELECT EMP_ID,
 '01/15/2017',
 EMP_SEMIMTH_PAY
 FROM EMP_PAY_CHECK;

INSERT INTO EMP_PAY_HIST
SELECT EMP_ID,
 '01/31/2017',
 EMP_SEMIMTH_PAY
 FROM EMP_PAY_CHECK;

INSERT INTO EMP_PAY_HIST
SELECT EMP_ID,
 '02/15/2017',
 EMP_SEMIMTH_PAY
 FROM EMP_PAY_CHECK;

INSERT INTO EMP_PAY_HIST
SELECT EMP_ID,
 '02/28/2017',
```

```
        EMP_SEMIMTH_PAY
        FROM EMP_PAY_CHECK;
```

Now we can look at the history table content which is as follows:

```
        SELECT * from HRSCHEMA.EMP_PAY_HIST;
        ---------+---------+---------+---------+------
            EMP_ID  EMP_PAY_DATE  EMP_PAY_AMT
        ---------+---------+---------+---------+------
            3217  2017-01-15         2708.33
            7459  2017-01-15         3541.66
            9134  2017-01-15         3125.00
            4720  2017-01-15         3333.33
            6288  2017-01-15         2916.66
            3217  2017-01-31         2708.33
            7459  2017-01-31         3541.66
            9134  2017-01-31         3125.00
            4720  2017-01-31         3333.33
            6288  2017-01-31         2916.66
            3217  2017-02-15         2708.33
            7459  2017-02-15         3541.66
            9134  2017-02-15         3125.00
            4720  2017-02-15         3333.33
            6288  2017-02-15         2916.66
            3217  2017-02-28         2708.33
            7459  2017-02-28         3541.66
            9134  2017-02-28         3125.00
            4720  2017-02-28         3333.33
            6288  2017-02-28         2916.66
        DSNE610I NUMBER OF ROWS DISPLAYED IS 20
```

If you want a list of all employees who got a paycheck during the month of February, you would need to eliminate the duplicate entries because there are two for each employee. You could accomplish that with this SQL:

```
        SELECT DISTINCT EMP_ID
        FROM HRSCHEMA.EMP_PAY_HIST
        WHERE MONTH(EMP_PAY_DATE) = '02'

        ---------+---------+---------+---------+-----
            EMP_ID
        ---------+---------+---------+---------+-----
            3217
            4720
            6288
            7459
            9134
        DSNE610I NUMBER OF ROWS DISPLAYED IS 5
```

The DISTINCT operator ensures that only unique records are selected based on the columns you are returning. This is important because if you included additional columns in the results, any value that makes the record unique will also make it **NOT** a duplicate.

Let's add the payment date to our query and see the results:

```
SELECT DISTINCT EMP_ID, EMP_PAY_DATE
FROM HRSCHEMA.EMP_PAY_HIST
WHERE MONTH(EMP_PAY_DATE) = '02'

---------+---------+---------+---------+----
    EMP_ID  EMP_PAY_DATE
---------+---------+---------+---------+----
      3217  2017-02-15
      3217  2017-02-28
      4720  2017-02-15
      4720  2017-02-28
      6288  2017-02-15
      6288  2017-02-28
      7459  2017-02-15
      7459  2017-02-28
      9134  2017-02-15
      9134  2017-02-28
DSNE610I NUMBER OF ROWS DISPLAYED IS 10
```

Since the combination of the employee id and payment date makes each record unique, you'll get multiple rows for each employee. So you must be careful in using DISTINCT to ensure that the structure of your query is really what you want.

FETCH FIRST X ROWS ONLY

You can limit your result set by using the FETCH FIRST X ROWS ONLY clause. For example, suppose you just want the employee id and names of the first four records from the employee table. You can code it as follows:

```
SELECT EMP_ID,
EMP_LAST_NAME,
EMP_FIRST_NAME
FROM HRSCHEMA.EMPLOYEE
FETCH FIRST 4 ROWS ONLY
---------+---------+---------+---------+---------+-
    EMP_ID  EMP_LAST_NAME      EMP_FIRST_NAME
---------+---------+---------+---------+---------+-
      3217  JOHNSON            EDWARD
      7459  STEWART            BETTY
      9134  FRANKLIN           BRIANNA
      4720  SCHULTZ            TIM
DSNE610I NUMBER OF ROWS DISPLAYED IS 4
```

Keep in mind that when you order the results you may get different records. For example if you order by last name, you would get this result:

```
SELECT EMP_ID,
EMP_LAST_NAME,
EMP_FIRST_NAME
FROM HRSCHEMA.EMPLOYEE
ORDER BY EMP_LAST_NAME
FETCH FIRST 4 ROWS ONLY

---------+---------+---------+---------+---------+-
    EMP_ID   EMP_LAST_NAME        EMP_FIRST_NAME
---------+---------+---------+---------+---------+-
      3333   FORD                 JAMES
      9134   FRANKLIN             BRIANNA
      7777   HARRIS               ELISA
      3217   JOHNSON              EDWARD
DSNE610I NUMBER OF ROWS DISPLAYED IS 4
```

SUBQUERY

A subquery is essentially a query within a query. Suppose for example we want to list the employee or employees who make the largest salary in the company. You can use a subquery to determine the maximum salary, and then use that value in the WHERE clause.

```
SELECT EMP_ID, EMP_REGULAR_PAY
FROM EMP_PAY
WHERE EMP_REGULAR_PAY
    = (SELECT MAX(EMP_REGULAR_PAY)
          FROM EMP_PAY);
---------+---------+---------+---------+----
    EMP_ID   EMP_REGULAR_PAY
---------+---------+---------+---------+----
      7459          85000.00
DSNE610I NUMBER OF ROWS DISPLAYED IS 1
```

What if there is more than one employee who makes the highest salary? Let's bump two people up to 85000 (and 4500 bonus) and see.

```
UPDATE EMP_PAY
SET EMP_REGULAR_PAY = 85000.00,
    EMP_BONUS_PAY = 4500
WHERE EMP_ID IN (4720,9134);
```

Here are the results:

```
        SELECT * FROM EMP_PAY;
---------+---------+---------+---------+----
    EMP_ID  EMP_REGULAR_PAY  EMP_BONUS_PAY
---------+---------+---------+---------+----
      3217          65000.00         5500.00
      7459          85000.00         4500.00
      9134          85000.00         4500.00
      4720          85000.00         4500.00
      6288          70000.00         2000.00
DSNE610I NUMBER OF ROWS DISPLAYED IS 5
```

Now let's see if our subquery still works:

```
        SELECT EMP_ID, EMP_REGULAR_PAY
        FROM EMP_PAY
        WHERE EMP_REGULAR_PAY
           = (SELECT MAX(EMP_REGULAR_PAY)
                 FROM EMP_PAY);
---------+---------+---------+---------+----
    EMP_ID  EMP_REGULAR_PAY
---------+---------+---------+---------+----
      7459          85000.00
      9134          85000.00
      4720          85000.00
DSNE610I NUMBER OF ROWS DISPLAYED IS 3
```

The query pulls all three of the highest paid employees. Subqueries are very powerful in that any value you can produce via a subquery can be substituted into a main query as selection or exclusion criteria.

GROUP BY

You can summarize data using the GROUP BY clause. For example, let's determine how many distinct employee salary rates there are and how many employees are paid those amounts.

```
        SELECT EMP_REGULAR_PAY,
          COUNT(*) AS "HOW MANY"
          FROM EMP_PAY
          GROUP BY EMP_REGULAR_PAY

---------+---------+---------+---------+-
EMP_REGULAR_PAY      HOW MANY
---------+---------+---------+---------+-
      65000.00            1
      70000.00            1
      85000.00            3
DSNE610I NUMBER OF ROWS DISPLAYED IS 3
```

283

ORDER BY

You can sort the display into ascending or descending sequence using the ORDER BY clause. To take the query we were just using for the group-by, let's present the data in descending sequence:

```
SELECT EMP_REGULAR_PAY,
   COUNT(*) AS "HOW MANY"
   FROM EMP_PAY
   GROUP BY EMP_REGULAR_PAY
   ORDER BY EMP_REGULAR_PAY DESC


---------+---------+---------+---------+-----
EMP_REGULAR_PAY      HOW MANY
---------+---------+---------+---------+-----
      85000.00              3
      70000.00              1
      65000.00              1
DSNE610I NUMBER OF ROWS DISPLAYED IS 3
```

HAVING

You could also use the GROUP BY with a HAVING clause that limits the results to only those groups that meet another condition. Let's specify that the group must have more than one employee in it to be included in the results.

```
SELECT EMP_REGULAR_PAY,
   COUNT(*) AS "HOW MANY"
   FROM EMP_PAY
   GROUP BY EMP_REGULAR_PAY
   HAVING COUNT(*) > 1
   ORDER BY EMP_REGULAR_PAY DESC


---------+---------+---------+---------+-
EMP_REGULAR_PAY      HOW MANY
---------+---------+---------+---------+-
      85000.00              3
DSNE610I NUMBER OF ROWS DISPLAYED IS 1
```

Or if you want pay rates that have only one employee you could specify the count 1.

```
SELECT EMP_REGULAR_PAY,
   COUNT(*) AS "HOW MANY"
   FROM EMP_PAY
   GROUP BY EMP_REGULAR_PAY
   HAVING COUNT(*) = 1
   ORDER BY EMP_REGULAR_PAY DESC
```

284

```
---------+---------+---------+---------+------
EMP_REGULAR_PAY     HOW MANY
---------+---------+---------+---------+------
        70000.00            1
        65000.00            1
DSNE610I NUMBER OF ROWS DISPLAYED IS 2
```

Before we move on, let's reset our two employees to whom we gave a temporary raise. Otherwise our EMP_PAY and EMP_PAY_CHECK tables will not be in sync.

```
UPDATE EMP_PAY
SET EMP_REGULAR_PAY = 80000.00,
    EMP_BONUS_PAY = 2500
WHERE EMP_ID = 4720;

UPDATE EMP_PAY
SET EMP_REGULAR_PAY = 75000.00,
    EMP_BONUS_PAY = 2500
WHERE EMP_ID = 9134;
```

Now our EMP_PAY table is restored:

```
    SELECT * FROM EMP_PAY;
---------+---------+---------+---------+--------
    EMP_ID  EMP_REGULAR_PAY  EMP_BONUS_PAY
---------+---------+---------+---------+--------
      3217         65000.00        5500.00
      7459         85000.00        4500.00
      9134         75000.00        2500.00
      4720         80000.00        2500.00
      6288         70000.00        2000.00
DSNE610I NUMBER OF ROWS DISPLAYED IS 5
```

CASE Expressions

In some situations you may need to code more complex conditional logic into your queries. Assume we have a requirement to report all employees according to seniority. We've invented the classifications ENTRY, ADVANCED and SENIOR. We want to report those who have less than a year service as ENTRY, employees who have a year or more service but less than 5 years as ADVANCED, and all employees with 5 years or more service as SENIOR. Here is a sample query that performs this using a CASE expression:

```
SELECT EMP_ID,
EMP_LAST_NAME,
EMP_FIRST_NAME,
CASE
   WHEN EMP_SERVICE_YEARS  < 1 THEN 'ENTRY'
   WHEN EMP_SERVICE_YEARS  < 5 THEN 'ADVANCED'
```

285

```
      ELSE 'SENIOR'
    END CASE
    FROM HRSCHEMA.EMPLOYEE;
---------+---------+---------+---------+---------+---------+------
    EMP_ID   EMP_LAST_NAME        EMP_FIRST_NAME        CASE
---------+---------+---------+---------+---------+---------+------
      3217   JOHNSON              EDWARD                SENIOR
      7459   STEWART              BETTY                 SENIOR
      9134   FRANKLIN             BRIANNA               ENTRY
      4720   SCHULTZ              TIM                   SENIOR
      6288   WILLARD              JOE                   SENIOR
      3333   FORD                 JAMEs                 SENIOR
      7777   HARRIS               ELISA                 ADVANCED
DSNE610I NUMBER OF ROWS DISPLAYED IS 7
```

You'll notice that the column heading for the case result is CASE. If you want to use a more meaningful column heading, then instead of closing the CASE statement with END CASE, close it with END AS <some literal>. So if we want to call the result of the CASE expression an employee's "LEVEL", code it this way:

```
    SELECT EMP_ID,
    EMP_LAST_NAME,
    EMP_FIRST_NAME,
    CASE
       WHEN EMP_SERVICE_YEARS  < 1 THEN 'ENTRY'
       WHEN EMP_SERVICE_YEARS  < 5 THEN 'ADVANCED'
       ELSE 'SENIOR'
    END AS LEVEL
    FROM HRSCHEMA.EMPLOYEE ;


---------+---------+---------+---------+---------+---------+-------
    EMP_ID   EMP_LAST_NAME        EMP_FIRST_NAME        LEVEL
---------+---------+---------+---------+---------+---------+-------
      3217   JOHNSON              EDWARD                SENIOR
      7459   STEWART              BETTY                 SENIOR
      9134   FRANKLIN             BRIANNA               ENTRY
      4720   SCHULTZ              TIM                   SENIOR
      6288   WILLARD              JOE                   SENIOR
      3333   FORD                 JAMEs                 SENIOR
      7777   HARRIS               ELISA                 ADVANCED
DSNE610I NUMBER OF ROWS DISPLAYED IS 7
```

JOINS

Now let's look at some cases where we need to pull data from more than one table. To do this we can use a join. Before we start running queries I want to add one row to the EMP_PAY_CHECK table. This is needed to make some of the joins work later, so bear with me.

```
INSERT INTO EMP_PAY_CHECK
VALUES
(7033,
77000.00,
77000 / 24);
```

Now our EMP_PAY_CHECK has these rows.

```
    SELECT * FROM EMP_PAY_CHECK;
---------+---------+---------+---------+------
    EMP_ID  EMP_REGULAR_PAY  EMP_SEMIMTH_PAY
---------+---------+---------+---------+------
      3217         65000.00          2708.33
      7459         85000.00          3541.66
      9134         75000.00          3125.00
      4720         80000.00          3333.33
      6288         70000.00          2916.66
      7033         77000.00          3208.00
DSNE610I NUMBER OF ROWS DISPLAYED IS 6
```

Inner joins

An inner join combines each row of one table with matching rows of the other table, keeping only the rows in which the join condition is true. You can join more than two tables but keep in mind that the more tables you join, the more record I/O is required and this could be a performance consideration. When I say a "performance consideration" I do not mean it is necessarily a problem. I mean it is one factor of many to keep in mind when designing an application process.

Let's do an example of a join. Assume we want a report that includes employee id, first and last names and pay rate for each employee. To accomplish this we need data from both the EMPLOYEE and the EMP_PAY tables. We can match the tables on EMP_ID which is the column they have in common.

We can perform our join either implicitly or with the JOIN verb (explicitly). In the first example will do the join implicitly by specifying we want to include rows for which the EMP_ID in the EMPLOYEE table matches the EMP_ID in the EMP_PAY table. The join is specified by the equality in the WHERE condition: WHERE A.EMP_ID = B.EMP_ID.

```
    SELECT A.EMP_ID,
    A.EMP_LAST_NAME,
    A.EMP_FIRST_NAME,
    B.EMP_REGULAR_PAY
    FROM HRSCHEMA.EMPLOYEE A, HRSCHEMA.EMP_PAY B
    WHERE A.EMP_ID = B.EMP_ID
    ORDER BY EMP_ID
```

287

```
---------+---------+---------+---------+---------+---------+---------+---
        EMP_ID  EMP_LAST_NAME      EMP_FIRST_NAME           EMP_REGULAR_PAY
---------+---------+---------+---------+---------+---------+---------+---
          3217  JOHNSON            EDWARD                         65000.00
          4720  SCHULTZ            TIM                            80000.00
          6288  WILLARD            JOE                            70000.00
          7459  STEWART            BETTY                          85000.00
          9134  FRANKLIN           BRIANNA                        75000.00
DSNE610I NUMBER OF ROWS DISPLAYED IS 5
```

Notice that in the SQL the column names are prefixed with a tag that is associated with the table being referenced. This is needed in all cases where the column being referenced exists in both tables (using the same column name). In this case, if you do not specify the qualifying tag, you will get an error that your column name reference is ambiguous, i.e., DB2 does not know which column from which table you are referencing.

Moving on, you can use an explicit join by specifying the JOIN or INNER JOIN verbs. This is actually a best practice because it helps keep the query clearer for those developers who follow you, especially as your queries get more complex.

```
SELECT A.EMP_ID,
A.EMP_LAST_NAME,
A.EMP_FIRST_NAME,
B.EMP_REGULAR_PAY
FROM HRSCHEMA.EMPLOYEE A
INNER JOIN
HRSCHEMA.EMP_PAY B
ON A.EMP_ID = B.EMP_ID
ORDER BY EMP_ID
---------+---------+---------+---------+---------+---------+---------+---
        EMP_ID  EMP_LAST_NAME      EMP_FIRST_NAME           EMP_REGULAR_PAY
---------+---------+---------+---------+---------+---------+---------+---
          3217  JOHNSON            EDWARD                         65000.00
          4720  SCHULTZ            TIM                            80000.00
          6288  WILLARD            JOE                            70000.00
          7459  STEWART            BETTY                          85000.00
          9134  FRANKLIN           BRIANNA                        75000.00
DSNE610I NUMBER OF ROWS DISPLAYED IS 5
```

Finally let's do a join with three tables just to extend the concepts. We'll join the EMPLOYEE, EMP_PAY and EMP_PAY_HIST tables for pay date February 15 as follows:

```
SELECT A.EMP_ID,
A.EMP_LAST_NAME,
B.EMP_REGULAR_PAY,
C.EMP_PAY_AMT
FROM HRSCHEMA.EMPLOYEE A
   INNER JOIN
      HRSCHEMA.EMP_PAY  B ON A.EMP_ID = B.EMP_ID
```

288

```
          INNER JOIN
             HRSCHEMA.EMP_PAY_HIST C ON B.EMP_ID = C.EMP_ID
          WHERE C.EMP_PAY_DATE = '2/15/2017'
       ---------+---------+---------+---------+---------+---------+-----
          EMP_ID  EMP_LAST_NAME        EMP_REGULAR_PAY  EMP_PAY_AMT
       ---------+---------+---------+---------+---------+---------+-----
            3217  JOHNSON                    65000.00      2708.33
            7459  STEWART                    85000.00      3541.66
            9134  FRANKLIN                   75000.00      3125.00
            4720  SCHULTZ                    80000.00      3333.33
            6288  WILLARD                    70000.00      2916.66
       DSNE610I NUMBER OF ROWS DISPLAYED IS 5
```

Now let's move on to outer joins. There are three types of outer joins. A **left outer join** includes matching rows from both tables plus any rows from the first table (the LEFT table) that were missing from the other table but that otherwise satisfied the WHERE condition. A **right outer join** includes matching rows from both tables plus any rows from the second (the RIGHT) table that were missing from the join but that otherwise satisfied the WHERE condition. A **full outer join** includes matching rows from both tables, plus those in either table that were not matched but which otherwise satisfied the WHERE condition. We'll look at examples of all three types of outer joins.

Left Outer Join

Let's try a left outer join to include matching rows from the EMPLOYEE and EMP_PAY tables, plus any rows in the EMPLOYEE table that might not be in the EMP_PAY table. In this case we are not using a WHERE clause because the table is very small and we want to see all the results. But keep in mind that we could use a WHERE clause.

```
          SELECT A.EMP_ID,
          A.EMP_LAST_NAME,
          A.EMP_FIRST_NAME,
          B.EMP_REGULAR_PAY
          FROM HRSCHEMA.EMPLOYEE A
          LEFT OUTER JOIN
          HRSCHEMA.EMP_PAY B
          ON A.EMP_ID = B.EMP_ID
          ORDER BY EMP_ID


       ---------+---------+---------+---------+---------+---------+---------+---
          EMP_ID  EMP_LAST_NAME       EMP_FIRST_NAME      EMP_REGULAR_PAY
       ---------+---------+---------+---------+---------+---------+---------+---
            3217  JOHNSON             EDWARD                    65000.00
            3333  FORD                JAMES               ---------------
            4720  SCHULTZ             TIM                       80000.00
            6288  WILLARD             JOE                       70000.00
            7459  STEWART             BETTY                     85000.00
            7777  HARRIS              ELISA               ---------------
            9134  FRANKLIN            BRIANNA                   75000.00
       DSNE610I NUMBER OF ROWS DISPLAYED IS 7
```

289

As you can see, we've included two employees who have not been assigned an annual salary yet. James Ford and Elisa Harris have NULL as their regular pay. The LEFT JOIN says we want all records in the first (left) table that satisfy the query even if there is no matching record in the right table. That's why the query results included the two unmatched records.

Let's do another left join, and this time we'll join the EMPLOYEE table with the EMP_PAY_CHECK table. Like before, we want all records from the EMPLOYEE and EMP_PAY_CHECK tables that match on EMP_ID, plus any EMPLOYEE records that could not be matched to EMP_PAY_CHECK.

```
SELECT A.EMP_ID,
A.EMP_LAST_NAME,
A.EMP_FIRST_NAME,
B.EMP_SEMIMTH_PAY
FROM HRSCHEMA.EMPLOYEE A
LEFT OUTER JOIN
HRSCHEMA.EMP_PAY_CHECK B
ON A.EMP_ID = B.EMP_ID
ORDER BY EMP_ID
```

EMP_ID	EMP_LAST_NAME	EMP_FIRST_NAME	EMP_SEMIMTH_PAY
3217	JOHNSON	EDWARD	2708.33
3333	FORD	JAMEs	---------------
4720	SCHULTZ	TIM	3333.33
6288	WILLARD	JOE	2916.66
7459	STEWART	BETTY	3541.66
7777	HARRIS	ELISA	---------------
9134	FRANKLIN	BRIANNA	3125.00

```
DSNE610I NUMBER OF ROWS DISPLAYED IS 7
```

Again we find two records in the EMPLOYEE table with no matching EMP_PAY_CHECK records. From a business standpoint that could be a problem unless the two are new hires who have not received their first pay check.

Right Outer Join

Meanwhile, now let us turn it around and do a right join. In this case we want all matching records in the EMPLOYEE and EMP_PAY_CHECK records plus any unmatched records in the EMP_PAY_CHECK table (the right hand table). We could also add a WHERE condition such that the EMP_SEMIMTH_PAY column has to be populated (cannot be NULL). Let's do that.

```
SELECT B.EMP_ID,
A.EMP_LAST_NAME,
A.EMP_FIRST_NAME,
B.EMP_SEMIMTH_PAY
FROM HRSCHEMA.EMPLOYEE A
   RIGHT OUTER JOIN
      HRSCHEMA.EMP_PAY_CHECK B
         ON A.EMP_ID = B.EMP_ID
WHERE EMP_SEMIMTH_PAY IS NOT NULL;
```

```
---------+---------+---------+---------+---------+---------+---------+---
    EMP_ID  EMP_LAST_NAME           EMP_FIRST_NAME          EMP_SEMIMTH_PAY
---------+---------+---------+---------+---------+---------+---------+---
      3217  JOHNSON                 EDWARD                          2708.33
      4720  SCHULTZ                 TIM                             3333.33
      6288  WILLARD                 JOE                             2916.66
      7033  --------------------    --------------------            3208.00
      7459  STEWART                 BETTY                           3541.66
      9134  FRANKLIN                BRIANNA                         3125.00
DSNE610I NUMBER OF ROWS DISPLAYED IS 6
```

Now we have a case where there is a record in the EMP_PAY_CHECK table for employee 7033, but that same employee number is NOT in the EMPLOYEE table. That is absolutely something to research! It is important to find out why this condition exists (of course we know it exists because we intentionally added an unmatched record to set up the example).

But let's pause for a moment. You may be thinking that this is not a realistic example because any employee getting a paycheck would also *have* to be in the EMPLOYEE table, so this mismatch condition would never happen. I chose this example for a few reasons. One reason is to point out the importance of referential data integrity. The reason the above exception is even *possible* is because we haven't defined a referential integrity relationship between these two tables. For now just know that these things can and do happen when a system has not been designed with tight referential integrity in place.

A second reason I chose this example is to highlight outer joins as a useful tool in tracking down data discrepancies between tables (subqueries are another useful tool). Keep this example in mind when you are called on by your boss or your client to troubleshoot a data integrity problem in a high pressure, time sensitive situation. You need all the tools you can get.

The third reason for choosing this example is that it very clearly demonstrates what a right join is – it includes all records from both tables that can be matched and that satisfy the WHERE condition, plus any unmatched records in the "right" table that otherwise meet the WHERE condition (in this case that the EMP_SEMIMTH_PAY is populated).

Full Outer Join

Finally, let's do a full outer join to include both matched and unmatched records from both tables that meet the where condition. This will expose all the discrepancies we already uncovered, but now we'll do it with a single query.

```
SELECT A.EMP_ID,
  A.EMP_LAST_NAME,
  B.EMP_SEMIMTH_PAY
  FROM EMPLOYEE A
     FULL OUTER JOIN
```

```
          EMP_PAY_CHECK B
              ON A.EMP_ID = B.EMP_ID;
---------+---------+---------+---------+---------+--
     EMP_ID  EMP_LAST_NAME         EMP_SEMIMTH_PAY
---------+---------+---------+---------+---------+--
       3217  JOHNSON                      2708.33
       3333  FORD                  ---------------
       4720  SCHULTZ                      3333.33
       6288  WILLARD                      2916.66
    ---------  --------------------        3208.00
       7459  STEWART                      3541.66
       7777  HARRIS                ---------------
       9134  FRANKLIN                     3125.00
DSNE610I NUMBER OF ROWS DISPLAYED IS 8
```

So with the FULL OUTER join we have identified the missing EMPLOYEE record, as well as the two EMP_PAY_CHECK records that may be missing. Again these examples are intended both to explain the difference between the join types, and also to lend support to troubleshooting efforts where data integrity is involved.

One final comment. The outer join examples we've given so far point to potential issues with the data, and these joins are in fact helpful in diagnosing such problems. But there are many cases where an entry in one table does not necessarily imply an entry in another. For example, suppose we have an EMP_SPOUSE table that exists to administer company benefits. A person who is single has no spouse, so they would not have an entry in the EMP_SPOUSE table. When querying for all persons covered by company benefits, an inner join between EMPLOYEE and EMP_SPOUSE would incorrectly exclude any employee who doesn't have a spouse. So you'd need a LEFT JOIN using EMPLOYEE and EMP_SPOUSE to return all insured employees plus their spouses. Your data model will govern what type of joins are needed, so be familiar with it.

UNION and INTERSECT

Another way to combine the results from two or more tables (or in some complex cases, to combine different result sets from a single table) is to use the UNION and INTERSECT statements. In some cases this can be preferable to doing a join.

Union

The UNION predicate combines the result sets from sub-SELECT queries. To understand how this might be useful, let's look at three examples. First, let's say we have two companies that have merged to form a third company. We have two tables EMP_COMPA and EMP_COMPB that we have structured with an EMP_ID, EMP_LAST_NAME and EMP_FIRST_NAME. We are going to structure a third table which will create all new employee ids by generation using an identity column. The DDL for the new table looks like this:

292

```
CREATE TABLE HRSCHEMA.EMPLOYEE_NEW(
EMP_ID INT GENERATED ALWAYS AS IDENTITY,
EMP_OLD_ID INTEGER,
EMP_LAST_NAME VARCHAR(30) NOT NULL,
EMP_FIRST_NAME VARCHAR(20) NOT NULL)
IN TSHR;
```

Now we can load the table using a UNION as follows:

```
INSERT INTO
HRSCHEMA.EMPLOYEE_NEW

SELECT EMP_ID,
EMP_LAST_NAME,
EMP_FIRST_NAME
FROM HRSCHEMA.EMP_COMPA

UNION

SELECT EMP_ID,
EMP_LAST_NAME,
EMP_FIRST_NAME
FROM HRSCHEMA.EMP_COMPB;
```

This will load the new table with data from both the old tables, and the new employee numbers will be auto-generated. Notice that by design we keep the old employee numbers for cross reference if needed.

When using a UNION, the column list must be identical in terms of the number of columns and data types, but the column names need not be the same. The UNION operation looks at the columns by position in the subqueries, not by name.

Let's look at two other examples of UNION queries. First, recall that earlier we used a full outer join to return all employee ids, including those that exist in one table but not the other.

```
SELECT A.EMP_ID,
B.EMP_ID,
A.EMP_LAST_NAME,
B.EMP_SEMIMTH_PAY
FROM HRSCHEMA.EMPLOYEE A
   FULL OUTER JOIN
      HRSCHEMA.EMP_PAY_CHECK B
         ON A.EMP_ID = B.EMP_ID;
```

If we just needed a unique list of employee id numbers from the EMPLOYEE and EMP_PAY_CHECK tables, we could instead use this UNION SQL:

```
SELECT EMP_ID
FROM HRSCHEMA.EMPLOYEE
UNION
SELECT EMP_ID
FROM HRSCHEMA.EMP_PAY_CHECK

---------+---------+---------+---------+-
     EMP_ID
---------+---------+---------+---------+-
     3217
     3333
     4720
     6288
     7033
     7459
     7777
     9134
DSNE610I NUMBER OF ROWS DISPLAYED IS 8
```

If you are wondering why we didn't get duplicate employee numbers in our list, it is because the UNION statement automatically eliminates duplicates. If for some reason you need to retain the duplicates, you would need to specify UNION ALL.

One final example will show how handy the UNION predicate is. Suppose that you want to query the EMPLOYEE table to get a list of all employee names for an upcoming company party. But you also have a contractor who (by business rules) cannot be in the EMPLOYEE table. You still want to include the contractor's name in the result set for whom to invite to the party. Let's say you want to identify the contractor with a pseudo-employee-id of 9999, and the contractor's name is Janet Ko.

You could code the query as follows:

```
SELECT EMP_ID,
EMP_LAST_NAME,
EMP_FIRST_NAME
FROM HRSCHEMA.EMPLOYEE
UNION
SELECT 9999,
'KO',
'JANET'
FROM SYSIBM.SYSDUMMY1;

---------+---------+---------+---------+-----

---------+---------+---------+---------+-----
```

```
3217   JOHNSON            EDWARD
3333   FORD               JAMES
4720   SCHULTZ            TIM
6288   WILLARD            JOE
7459   STEWART            BETTY
7777   HARRIS             ELISA
9134   FRANKLIN           BRIANNA
9999   KO                 JANET
DSNE610I NUMBER OF ROWS DISPLAYED IS 8
```

Now you have listed all the employees plus your contractor friend Janet on your query results. This is a useful technique when you have a "mostly" table driven system that also has some exceptions to the business rules. Sometimes a system has one-off situations that simply don't justify full blown changes to the system design. UNION can help in these cases.

Intersect

The INTERSECT predicate returns a combined result set that consists of all of the matching rows (existing in **both** result sets). In one of the earlier UNION examples, we wanted all employee ids as long as they existed in either the EMPLOYEE table or the EMP_PAY_CHECK table.

```
SELECT EMP_ID
FROM HRSCHEMA.EMPLOYEE
UNION
SELECT EMP_ID
FROM HRSCHEMA.EMP_PAY_CHECK

---------+---------+---------
    EMP_ID
---------+---------+---------
      3217
      4720
      6288
      7033
      7459
      9134
```

Now let's say we only want a list of employee ids that appear in both tables. The INTERSECT will accomplish that for us and we only need to change that one word in the query:

```
SELECT EMP_ID
FROM HRSCHEMA.EMPLOYEE
INTERSECT
SELECT EMP_ID
FROM HRSCHEMA.EMP_PAY_CHECK
```

295

```
---------+---------+---------+---------+--------
     EMP_ID
---------+---------+---------+---------+--------
       3217
       4720
       6288
       7459
       9134
DSNE610I NUMBER OF ROWS DISPLAYED IS 5
```

Common Table Expression

A common table expression is a result set that you can create and then reference in a query as though it were a table. It sometimes makes coding easier. Take this as an example. Suppose we need to work with an aggregated year-to-date total pay for each employee. Recall that our table named EMPL_PAY_HIST includes these fields:

```
(EMP_ID INTEGER NOT NULL,
EMP_PAY_DATE DATE NOT NULL,
EMP_PAY_AMT DECIMAL (8,2) NOT NULL);
```

Assume further that we have created the following SQL that includes aggregated totals for the employees' pay:

```
WITH EMP_PAY_SUM (EMP_ID, EMP_PAY_TOTAL) AS
(SELECT EMP_ID,
SUM(EMP_PAY_AMT)
AS EMP_PAY_TOTAL
FROM EMP_PAY_HIST
GROUP BY EMP_ID)

SELECT B.EMP_ID,
A.EMP_LAST_NAME,
A.EMP_FIRST_NAME,
B.EMP_PAY_TOTAL
FROM EMPLOYEE A
INNER JOIN
EMP_PAY_SUM B
ON A.EMP_ID = B.EMP_ID;
```

What we've done is to create a temporary result set named EMP_PAY_SUM that can be queried by SQL as if it were a table. This helps break down the data requirement into two pieces, one of which summarizes the pay data and the other of which adds columns from other tables.

This example may not seem like much because you could have as easily combined the two SQLs into one. But as your data stores get more numerous, and your queries and joins grow more complex, you may find that common table expressions can simplify queries both for you and for the developer that follows you.

Here's the result of our common table expression and the query against it.

```
WITH EMP_PAY_SUM (EMP_ID, EMP_PAY_TOTAL) AS
(SELECT EMP_ID,
SUM(EMP_PAY_AMT)
AS EMP_PAY_TOTAL
FROM EMP_PAY_HIST
GROUP BY EMP_ID)

SELECT B.EMP_ID,
A.EMP_LAST_NAME,
A.EMP_FIRST_NAME,
B.EMP_PAY_TOTAL
FROM EMPLOYEE A
INNER JOIN
EMP_PAY_SUM B
ON A.EMP_ID = B.EMP_ID;
```

```
---------+---------+---------+---------+---------+---------+---------+-------
    EMP_ID  EMP_LAST_NAME      EMP_FIRST_NAME            EMP_PAY_TOTAL
---------+---------+---------+---------+---------+---------+---------+-------
      3217  JOHNSON            EDWARD                        10833.32
      4720  SCHULTZ            TIM                           13333.32
      6288  WILLARD            JOE                           11666.64
      7459  STEWART            BETTY                         14166.64
      9134  FRANKLIN           BRIANNA                       12500.00
DSNE610I NUMBER OF ROWS DISPLAYED IS 5
```

XML

XML is a highly used standard for exchanging self-describing data files or documents. Even if you work in a shop that does not use the DB2 XML data type or XML functions, it is good to know how to use these. A complete tutorial on XML is well beyond the scope of this book. We'll review some XML basics, but if you have little or no experience with XML, I strongly suggest that you purchase some books to acquire this knowledge. The following are a few that can help fill in the basics:

XML in a Nutshell, Third Edition 3rd Edition by Elliotte Rusty Harold
(ISBN 978-0596007645)

XSLT 2.0 and XPath 2.0 Programmer's Reference by Michael Kay
(ISBN: 978-0470192740)

XQuery: Search Across a Variety of XML Data by Priscilla Walmsley
(ISBN: ISBN-13: 978-1491915103)

Basic XML Concepts

You may know that XML stands for Extensible Markup Language. XML technology is cross-platform and independent of machine and software. It provides a structure that consists of both data and data element tags, and so it describes the data in both human readable and machine readable format. The tag names for the elements are defined by the developer/user of the data.

XML Structure

XML has a tree type structure that is required to begin with a root element and then it expands to the branches. To continue our discussion of the EMPLOYEE domain, let's take a simple XML example with an employee profile as the root. We'll include the employee id, the address and birth date. The XML document might look like this:

```
<?xml version="1.0" encoding="UTF-8"?>
<EMP_PROFILE>
  <EMP_ID>4175</EMP_ID>
  <EMP_ADDRESS>
<STREET>6161 MARGARET LANE</STREET>
<CITY>ERINDALE</CITY>
<STATE>AR</STATE>
<ZIP_CODE>72653</ZIP_CODE>
</EMP_ADDRESS>
<BIRTH_DATE>07/14/1991</BIRTH_DATE>
</EMP_PROFILE>
```

XML documents frequently begin with a declaration which includes the XML version and the encoding scheme of the document. In our example, we are using XML version 1.0 which is still very common. This declaration is optional but it's a best practice to include it.

Notice after the version specification that we continue with the tag name EMP_PROFILE enclosed by the <> symbols. The employee profile element ends with /EMP_PROFILE enclosed by the <> symbols. Similarly each sub-element is tagged and enclosed and the value (if any) appears between the opening and closing of the element.

XML documents must have a single root element, i.e., one element that is the root of all other elements. If you want more than one EMP_PROFILE in a document, then you would need a higher level element to contain the profiles. For example you could have a DEPARTMENT element that contains employee profiles, and a COMPANY element that contains DEPARTMENTS.

All elements must have a closing tag. Elements that are not populated can be represented by an opening and closing with nothing in between. For example, if an employee's birthday is not known, it can be represented by `<BIRTH_DATE></BIRTH_DATE>` or you can use the short hand form `<BIRTH_DATE/>`.

The example document includes elements such as the employee id, address and birth date. The address is broken down into a street name, city, state and zip code. Comments can be included in an XML document by following the following format:

```
<!-- This is a sample comment -->
```

By default, white space is preserved in XML documents.

Ok, so we've given you a drive-thru version of XML. We have almost enough information to move on to how to manipulate XML data in DB2. Before we get to that, let's briefly look at two XML-related technologies that we will need.

XML Related Technologies

XPath

The extensible path language (XPath) is used to locate and extract information from an XML document using "path" expressions through the XML nodes. For example, in the case of the employee XML document we created earlier, you could locate and return a zip code value by specifying the path.

Recall this structure:

```
<EMP_PROFILE>
    <EMP_ID>4175</EMP_ID>
    <EMP_ADDRESS>
        <STREET>6161 MARGARET LANE</STREET>
        <CITY>ERINDALE</CITY>
        <STATE>AR</STATE>
        <ZIP_CODE>72653</ZIP_CODE>
    </EMP_ADDRESS>
    <BIRTH_DATE>07/14/1991</BIRTH_DATE>
</EMP_PROFILE>
```

In this example, the employee profile nodes with zip code 72653 can be identified using the following path:

```
/EMP_PROFILE/ADDRESS[ZIP_CODE=72653]
```

The XPath expression for all employees who live in Texas as follows:

```
/EMP_PROFILE/ADDRESS[STATE="TX"]
```

XQuery

XQuery enables us to query XML data using XPath expressions. It is similar to how we query relational data using SQL, but of course the syntax is different. Here's an example of pulling the employee id of every employee who lives at a zip code greater than 90000 from an XML document named **employees.xml**.

```
for $x in doc("employees.xml")employee/profile/address/zipcode
where $x/zipcode>90000
order by $x/zipcode
return $x/empid
```

In DB2 you run an XQuery using the built-in function **XMLQUERY**. We'll show you some examples using XMLQUERY shortly.

DB2 Support for XML

The **pureXML** technology provides support for XML under DB2 for z/OS. DB2 includes an XML data type and many built-in DB2 functions to validate, traverse and manipulate XML data. The DB2 XML data type can store well-formed XML documents in their hierarchical form and retrieve entire documents or portions of documents.

You can execute DML operations such as inserting, updating and deleting XML documents. You can index and create triggers on XML columns. Finally, you can extract data items from an XML document and then store those values in columns of relational tables using the SQL XMLTABLE built-in function.

XML Examples
XML for the EMPLOYEE table

Suppose that we need to implement a new interface with our employee benefits providers who use XML as the data exchange format. This could give us a reason to store our detailed employee information in an XML structure within the EMPLOYEE table. For our purposes, we will add a column named EMP_PROFILE to the EMPLOYEE table and make it an XML column. Here's the DDL:

```
ALTER TABLE HRSCHEMA.EMPLOYEE
ADD COLUMN EMP_PROFILE XML;
```

We could also establish an XML schema to validate our data structure, but for the moment we'll just deal with the basic SQL operations. As long as the XML is well formed, DB2 will accept it without a schema to validate against.

Let's assume we are going to add a record to the EMPLOYEE table for employee Fred Turnbull who has employee id 4175, has 1 year if service and was promoted on 12/1/2016. Here's a sample XML document structure we want for storing the employee profile:

```
<EMP_PROFILE>
   <EMP_ID>4175</EMP_ID>
   <EMP_ADDRESS>
       <STREET>6161 MARGARET LANE</STREET>
       <CITY>ERINDALE</CITY>
       <STATE>AR</STATE>
       <ZIP_CODE>72653</ZIP_CODE>
   </EMP_ADDRESS>
   <BIRTH_DATE>07/14/1991</BIRTH_DATE>
</EMP_PROFILE>
```

INSERT With XML

Now we can insert the new record as follows:

```
INSERT INTO HRSCHEMA.EMPLOYEE
(EMP_ID,
 EMP_LAST_NAME,
 EMP_FIRST_NAME,
 EMP_SERVICE_YEARS,
 EMP_PROMOTION_DATE,
 EMP_PROFILE)
VALUES (4175,
'TURNBULL',
'FRED',
1,
'12/01/2016',
'
<EMP_PROFILE>
  <EMP_ID>4175</EMP_ID>
  <EMP_ADDRESS>
<STREET>6161 MARGARET LANE</STREET>
<CITY>ERINDALE</CITY>
<STATE>AR</STATE>
<ZIP_CODE>72653</ZIP_CODE>
</EMP_ADDRESS>
<BIRTH_DATE>07/14/1991</BIRTH_DATE>
</EMP_PROFILE>
');
```

SELECT With XML

You can do a SELECT on an XML column and depending on what query tool you are using, you can display the content of the record in fairly readable form. Since the XML data is stored as one long string, it may be difficult to read in its entirety without reformatting. We'll look at some options for that later. Let's select the column we just added using SPUFI.

```
SELECT EMP_ID, EMP_PROFILE FROM HRSCHEMA.EMPLOYEE
WHERE EMP_ID = 4175;
-------+---------+---------+---------+---------+---------+---------+-----
    EMP_ID  EMP_PROFILE
-------+---------+---------+---------+---------+---------+---------+-----
    4175  <?xml version="1.0" encoding="IBM037"?><EMP_PROFILE><EMP_ID>41
```

In SPUFI, you would need to scroll to the right to see the rest of the column contents.

UPDATE With XML

To update an XML column you can use standard SQL if you want to update the entire content of the column. Suppose we want to change the address. This SQL will do it:

```
UPDATE HRSCHEMA.EMPLOYEE
SET EMP_PROFILE
 = '<EMP_PROFILE>
        <EMP_ID>3217</EMP_ID>
        <EMP_ADDRESS>
            <STREET>2913 PATE DR</STREET>
            <CITY>FORT WORTH</CITY>
            <STATE>TX</STATE>
            <ZIP_CODE>76105</ZIP_CODE>
        </EMP_ADDRESS>
        <BIRTH_DATE>03/15/1952</BIRTH_DATE>
    </EMP_PROFILE>
  '
WHERE EMP_ID = 3217;
```

DELETE With XML

If you wish to delete the entire EMP_PROFILE, you can set it to NULL as follows:

```
UPDATE HRSCHEMA.EMPLOYEE
SET EMP_PROFILE = NULL
WHERE EMP_ID = 3217;

SELECT EMP_ID, EMP_PROFILE FROM HRSCHEMA.EMPLOYEE
WHERE EMP_ID = 3217;
-------+---------+---------+---------+---------+---------+---------+-----
    EMP_ID  EMP_PROFILE
```

302

```
-------+---------+---------+---------+---------+---------+---------+-----
    3217 -------------------------------------------------------------
```

As you can see, the EMP_PROFILE column has been set to NULL. At this point, only one row in the EMPLOYEE table has the EMP_PROFILE populated.

```
SELECT EMP_ID, EMP_PROFILE FROM HRSCHEMA.EMPLOYEE;

-------+---------+---------+---------+---------+---------+---------+--------
   EMP_ID  EMP_PROFILE
-------+---------+---------+---------+---------+---------+---------+--------
    3217 -------------------------------------------------------------
    7459 -------------------------------------------------------------
    9134 -------------------------------------------------------------
    4175 <?xml version="1.0" encoding="IBM037"?><EMP_PROFILE><EMP_ID>4175<
```

Let's go ahead and add the XML data back to this record so we can use it later for other XML queries.

```
UPDATE HRSCHEMA.EMPLOYEE
SET EMP_PROFILE
 = '<EMP_PROFILE>
          <EMP_ID>3217</EMP_ID>
          <EMP_ADDRESS>
                 <STREET>2913 PATE DR</STREET>
                 <CITY>FORT WORTH</CITY>
                 <STATE>TX</STATE>
                 <ZIP_CODE>76105</ZIP_CODE>
          </EMP_ADDRESS>
          <BIRTH_DATE>03/15/1952</BIRTH_DATE>
     </EMP_PROFILE>
   '
WHERE EMP_ID = 3217;
```

Also, let's update one more record so we have a bit more data to work with.

```
UPDATE EMPLOYEE
SET EMP_PROFILE
 = '<EMP_PROFILE>
   <EMP_ID>7459</EMP_ID>
   <EMP_ADDRESS>
      <STREET>6742 OAK ST</STREET>
      <CITY>DALLAS</CITY>
      <STATE>TX</STATE>
      <ZIP_CODE>75277</ZIP_CODE>
     </EMP_ADDRESS>
     <BIRTH_DATE>09/22/1963</BIRTH_DATE>
    </EMP_PROFILE>
   '
WHERE EMP_ID = 7459;
```

XML BUILTIN FUNCTIONS

XMLQUERY

XMLQUERY is the DB2 builtin function that enables you to run XQuery. Here is an example of using XMLQUERY with the XQuery **xmlcolumn** function to retrieve an XML element from the EMP_PROFILE element. In this case we will select the zip code for employee 4175.

```
SELECT XMLQUERY
('for $info
in db2-fn:xmlcolumn("HRSCHEMA.EMPLOYEE.EMP_PROFILE")/EMP_PROFILE
return $info/EMP_ADDRESS/ZIP_CODE') AS ZIPCODE
from HRSCHEMA.EMPLOYEE
where EMP_ID = 4175

ZIPCODE
--------------------------
<ZIP_CODE>72653</ZIP_CODE>
```

Notice that the data is returned in XML format. If you don't want the data returned with its XML structure, simply add the XQuery text() function at the end of the return string, as below:

```
SELECT XMLQUERY
('for $info
in db2-fn:xmlcolumn("HRSCHEMA.EMPLOYEE.EMP_PROFILE")/EMP_PROFILE
return $info/EMP_ADDRESS/ZIP_CODE/text()') AS ZIPCODE
FROM HRSCHEMA.EMPLOYEE
WHERE EMP_ID = 4175;
```

The result of this query will not include the XML format.

```
ZIPCODE
-------
  72653
```

XMLEXISTS

The XMLEXISTS predicate specifies an XQuery expression. If the XQuery expression returns an empty sequence, the value of the XMLEXISTS predicate is false. Otherwise, XMLEXISTS returns true and those rows matching the XMLEXISTS value of true are returned.

XMLEXISTS enables us to specify rows based on the XML content which is often what you want to do. Suppose you want to return the first and last names of all employees who live in the state of Texas? This query with XMLEXISTS would accomplish it:

```
SELECT EMP_LAST_NAME, EMP_FIRST_NAME
FROM HRSCHEMA.EMPLOYEE
WHERE
XMLEXISTS('$info/EMP_PROFILE[EMP_ADDRESS/STATE/text()="TX"]'
PASSING EMP_PROFILE AS "info");


---------+---------+---------+---------+---------+---------+---
EMP_LAST_NAME                       EMP_FIRST_NAME
---------+---------+---------+---------+---------+---------+---
JOHNSON                             EDWARD
STEWART                             BETTY
```

You can also use XMLEXISTS with update and delete functions.

XMLSERIALIZE

The XMLSERIALIZE function returns a serialized XML value of the specified data type that is generated from the first argument. You can use this function to generate an XML structure from relational data. Here's an example.

```
SELECT E.EMP_ID,
XMLSERIALIZE(XMLELEMENT ( NAME "EMP_FULL_NAME",
    E.EMP_FIRST_NAME || ' ' || E.EMP_LAST_NAME)
              AS CLOB(100)) AS "RESULT"
    FROM HRSCHEMA.EMPLOYEE E;
---------+---------+---------+---------+---------+---------+-
    EMP_ID  RESULT
---------+---------+---------+---------+---------+---------+-
      3217  <EMP_FULL_NAME>EDWARD JOHNSON</EMP_FULL_NAME>
      7459  <EMP_FULL_NAME>BETTY STEWART</EMP_FULL_NAME>
      9134  <EMP_FULL_NAME>BRIANNA FRANKLIN</EMP_FULL_NAME>
      4175  <EMP_FULL_NAME>FRED TURNBULL</EMP_FULL_NAME>
      4720  <EMP_FULL_NAME>TIM SCHULTZ</EMP_FULL_NAME>
      6288  <EMP_FULL_NAME>JOE WILLARD</EMP_FULL_NAME>
      3333  <EMP_FULL_NAME>JAMEs FORD</EMP_FULL_NAME>
      7777  <EMP_FULL_NAME>ELISA HARRIS</EMP_FULL_NAME>
DSNE610I NUMBER OF ROWS DISPLAYED IS 8
```

XMLTABLE

The XMLTABLE function can be used to convert XML data to relational data. You can then use it for traditional SQL such as in joins. To use XMLTABLE you must specify the relational column names you want to use. Then you point these column names to the XML content using path expressions. For this example we'll pull address information from the profile:

305

```
SELECT X.*
FROM HRSCHEMA.EMPLOYEE,
XMLTABLE ('$x/EMP_PROFILE'
          PASSING EMP_PROFILE as "x"

    COLUMNS
      STREET  VARCHAR(20) PATH 'EMP_ADDRESS/STREET',
      CITY    VARCHAR(20) PATH 'EMP_ADDRESS/CITY',
      STATE   VARCHAR(02) PATH 'EMP_ADDRESS/STATE',
      ZIP     VARCHAR(10) PATH 'EMP_ADDRESS/ZIP_CODE') ;
      AS X
---------+---------+---------+---------+---------+---------+-
STREET                     CITY                STATE  ZIP
---------+---------+---------+---------+---------+---------+-
2913 PATE DR               FORT WORTH          TX     76105
6742 OAK ST                DALLAS              TX     75277
6161 MARGARET LANE         ERINDALE            AR     72653
DSNE610I NUMBER OF ROWS DISPLAYED IS 3
```

XMLMODIFY

XMLMODIFY allows you to make changes within the XML document. There are three expressions available for XMLMODIFY: insert, delete and replace. Here is a sample of using the replace expression to change the ZIP_CODE element of the EMP_ADDRESS for employee 4175:

```
UPDATE HRSCHEMA.EMPLOYEE
SET EMP_PROFILE
= XMLMODIFY('replace value of node
HRSCHEMA.EMPLOYEE/EMP_PROFILE/EMP_ADDRESS/ZIP_CODE
with "72652" ')
WHERE EMP_ID = 4175;
```

Now let's verify that the statement worked successfully by finding the zip code on EMP_ID 4175.

```
SELECT XMLQUERY
('for $info
in db2-fn:xmlcolumn("HRSCHEMA.EMPLOYEE.EMP_PROFILE")/EMP_PROFILE
return $info/EMP_ADDRESS/ZIP_CODE/text()') AS ZIPCODE
from HRSCHEMA.EMPLOYEE
where EMP_ID = 4175;

-------------------------------------------
ZIPCODE
-------------------------------------------
  72652
```

Important: to use XMLMODIFY, you must have created the table in a universal table space (UTS). Otherwise you will receive this SQLCODE error when you try to use the XMLMODIFY function:

```
DSNT408I SQLCODE = -4730, ERROR:  INVALID SPECIFICATION OF XML COLUMN
          EMPLOYEE.EMP_PROFILE IS NOT DEFINED IN THE XML VERSIONING
          FORMAT,REASON 1
```

SPECIAL REGISTERS

Special registers allow you to access detailed information about the DB2 instance settings as well as certain session information. CURRENT DATE is an example of a special register that is often used in programming (see example below).

The following are SQL examples of some commonly used special registers. I suggest that you focus on these.

CURRENT CLIENT_USERID

CURRENT CLIENT_USERID contains the value of the client user ID from the client information that is specified for the connection. In the following example, the TSO logon id of the user is HRSCHEMA.

```
SELECT CURRENT CLIENT_USERID
FROM SYSIBM.SYSDUMMY1;
---------+---------+---------

---------+---------+---------
HRSCHEMA
```

CURRENT DATE

CURRENT DATE specifies a date that is based on a reading of the time-of-day clock when the SQL statement is executed at the current server. This is often used in application programs to establish the processing date.

```
SELECT CURRENT DATE
FROM SYSIBM.SYSDUMMY1;
---------+---------+--

---------+---------+--
2017-01-13
```

CURRENT DEGREE

CURRENT DEGREE specifies the degree of parallelism for the execution of queries that are dynamically prepared by the application process. A value of "ANY" enables parallel processing. A value of 1 prohibits parallel processing. You can query for the value of the CURRENT DEGREE as follows:

```
SELECT CURRENT DEGREE
FROM SYSIBM.SYSDUMMY1;
---------+---------+-----

---------+---------+-----
1
```

CURRENT MEMBER

CURRENT MEMBER specifies the member name of a current DB2 data sharing member on which a statement is executing. The value of CURRENT MEMBER is a character string. More information on data sharing is provided later.

CURRENT OPTIMIZATION HINT

CURRENT OPTIMIZATION HINT specifies the user-defined optimization hint that DB2 should use to generate the access path for dynamic statements.

CURRENT RULES

CURRENT RULES specifies whether certain SQL statements are executed in accordance with DB2 rules or the rules of the SQL standard.

```
SELECT CURRENT RULES
FROM SYSIBM.SYSDUMMY1;
--------+---------+----

--------+---------+----
DB2
```

CURRENT SCHEMA

CURRENT SCHEMA specifies the schema name used to qualify unqualified database object references in dynamically prepared SQL statements.

```
SELECT CURRENT SCHEMA
FROM SYSIBM.SYSDUMMY1;
--------+---------+---

--------+---------+---
HRSCHEMA
```

CURRENT SERVER

CURRENT SERVER specifies the location name of the current server.

```
SELECT CURRENT SERVER
FROM SYSIBM.SYSDUMMY1;
---------+---------+--------

---------+---------+--------
LOCRGNA
```

CURRENT SQLID

CURRENT SQLID specifies the SQL authorization ID of the process.

```
SELECT CURRENT SQLID
FROM SYSIBM.SYSDUMMY1;
---------+---------+----

HRSCHEMA
```

CURRENT TEMPORAL BUSINESS_TIME

CURRENT TEMPORAL BUSINESS_TIME specifies a TIMESTAMP(12) value that is used in the default BUSINESS_TIME period specification for references to application-period temporal tables.

CURRENT TEMPORAL SYSTEM_TIME

CURRENT TEMPORAL SYSTEM_TIME specifies a TIMESTAMP(12) value that is used in the default SYSTEM_TIME period specification for references to system-period temporal tables.

CURRENT TIME

The CURRENT TIME special register specifies a time that is based on a reading of the time-of-day clock when the SQL statement is executed at the current server.

```
SELECT CURRENT TIME
FROM SYSIBM.SYSDUMMY1;
---------+---------+----

10.12.12
```

CURRENT TIMESTAMP

The CURRENT TIMESTAMP special register specifies a timestamp based on the time-of-day clock at the current server.

```
SELECT CURRENT TIMESTAMP
FROM SYSIBM.SYSDUMMY1;
```

```
---------+---------+--------

---------+---------+--------
2017-01-13-10.12.51.778225
```

SESSION_USER

SESSION_USER specifies the primary authorization ID of the process.

```
SELECT SESSION_USER
FROM SYSIBM.SYSDUMMY1;
---------+---------+-----

---------+---------+-----
HRSCHEMA
```

NOTE: You can use all special registers in a user-defined function or a stored procedure.
However, you can modify only some of the special registers. The following are the special registers that can be modified:

- CURRENT APPLICATION COMPATIBILITY
- CURRENT APPLICATION ENCODING SCHEME
- CURRENT DEBUG MODE
- CURRENT DECFLOAT ROUNDING MODE
- CURRENT DEGREE
- CURRENT EXPLAIN MODE
- CURRENT GET_ACCEL_ARCHIVE
- CURRENT LOCALE LC_CTYPE
- CURRENT MAINTAINED TABLE TYPES FOR OPTIMIZATION
- CURRENT OPTIMIZATION HINT
- CURRENT PACKAGE PATH
- CURRENT PACKAGESET
- CURRENT PATH
- CURRENT PRECISION
- CURRENT QUERY ACCELERATION
- CURRENT REFRESH AGE
- CURRENT ROUTINE VERSION
- CURRENT RULES
- CURRENT SCHEMA
- CURRENT SQLID1
- CURRENT TEMPORAL BUSINESS_TIME

- CURRENT TEMPORAL SYSTEM_TIME
- ENCRYPTION PASSWORD
- SESSION TIME ZONE

BUILT-IN FUNCTIONS

Built-in functions can be used in SQL statements to return a result based on an argument. These functions are great productivity tools because they can replace custom coded functionality in an application program. Whether your role is application developer, DBA or business services professional, the DB2 built-in functions can save you a great deal of time and effort if you know what they are and how to use them.

There are three types of builtin functions:

1. Aggregate

2. Scalar

3. Table

We'll look at examples of each of these types.

AGGREGATE Functions

An aggregate function receives a set of values for each argument (such as the values of a column) and returns a single-value result for the set of input values. These are especially useful in data analytics. Here are some examples of commonly used aggregate functions.

AVERAGE

The AVERAGE function returns the average of a set of numbers. Using our EMP_PAY table, you could get the average EMP_REGULAR_PAY for your employees like this:

```
SELECT AVG(EMP_REGULAR_PAY) FROM EMP_PAY;
---------+---------+---------+---------+--
    75000.00000000000000000000
DSNE610I NUMBER OF ROWS DISPLAYED IS 1
```

COUNT

The COUNT function returns the number of rows or values in a set of rows or values. Suppose you want to know how many employees you have. You could use this SQL to find out:

```
SELECT COUNT(*)
FROM EMPLOYEE;
---------+---------+---------+---------+-----
```

```
---------+---------+---------+---------+-----
          8
DSNE610I NUMBER OF ROWS DISPLAYED IS 1
```

MAX

The MAX function returns the maximum value in a set of values.

MIN

The MIN function returns the minimum value in a set of values.

In the next two examples, we use the MAX and MIN functions to determine the highest and lowest paid employees:

```
SELECT MAX(EMP_REGULAR_PAY)
FROM EMP_PAY;
---------+---------+--------

---------+---------+--------
   85000.00
```

Now if we want know which both the maximum salary and the employee who earns it, it is a bit more complex, but not much:

```
SELECT EMP_ID, EMP_REGULAR_PAY
FROM EMP_PAY
WHERE EMP_REGULAR_PAY =
(SELECT MAX(EMP_REGULAR_PAY) FROM EMP_PAY)
;
---------+---------+---------+---------+------
     EMP_ID  EMP_REGULAR_PAY
---------+---------+---------+---------+------
       7459          85000.00
```

Similarly, we can find the minimum using the MIN function.

```
SELECT MIN(EMP REGULAR_PAY)
FROM EMP_PAY;

---------+---------+---------+-
   65000.00


SELECT EMP_ID, EMP_REGULAR_PAY
FROM EMP_PAY
WHERE EMP_REGULAR_PAY =
(SELECT MIN(EMP_REGULAR_PAY) FROM EMP_PAY);
```

```
---------+---------+---------+---------+---
    EMP_ID  EMP_REGULAR_PAY
---------+---------+---------+---------+---
      3217          65000.00
```

SUM

The SUM function returns the sum of a set of numbers. Suppose you need to know what your base payroll will be for the year. You could find out with this SQL:

```
SELECT SUM(EMP_REGULAR_PAY)
FROM EMP_PAY;
---------+---------+---------+---------

---------+---------+---------+---------
        375000.00
DSNE610I NUMBER OF ROWS DISPLAYED IS 1
```

SCALAR Functions

A scalar function can be used wherever an expression can be used. It is often used to calculate a value or to influence the result of a query. Again we'll provide some examples, and then a complete list of the scalar functions and what they do.

COALESCE

The COALESCE function returns the value of the first nonnull expression. It is normally used to assign some alternate value when a NULL value is encountered that would otherwise cause an entire record to be excluded from the results. For example, consider the EMP_PAY table with data as follows:

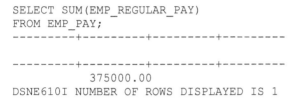

```
    SELECT *
    FROM EMP_PAY;
---------+---------+---------+---------+---------
    EMP_ID  EMP_REGULAR_PAY  EMP_BONUS_PAY
---------+---------+---------+---------+---------
      3217          65000.00          5500.00
      7459          85000.00          4500.00
      9134          75000.00          2500.00
      4720          80000.00          2500.00
      6288          70000.00          2000.00
DSNE610I NUMBER OF ROWS DISPLAYED IS 5
```

To demonstrate how COALESCE works, let's change the bonus pay amount for employee 9134 to NULL.

```
UPDATE EMP_PAY
SET EMP_BONUS_PAY = NULL
WHERE EMP_ID = 9134;
```

Now our data looks like this:

```
SELECT *
FROM EMP_PAY;
---------+---------+---------+---------+------
    EMP_ID   EMP_REGULAR_PAY   EMP_BONUS_PAY
---------+---------+---------+---------+------
      3217          65000.00         5500.00
      7459          85000.00         4500.00
      9134          75000.00      -------------
      4720          80000.00         2500.00
      6288          70000.00         2000.00
DSNE610I NUMBER OF ROWS DISPLAYED IS 5
```

Ok, here's the example. Let's find the average bonus pay in the EMP_PAY table.

```
SELECT AVG(EMP_BONUS_PAY)
AS AVERAGE_BONUS
FROM EMP_PAY;
---------+---------+---------+---------
                  AVERAGE_BONUS
---------+---------+---------+---------
    3625.0000000000000000000000
```

There is a potential problem here! The problem is that the average bonus is not 3625, it is 2900 (total 14,500 divided by five employees). The problem here is that one of the employee records has NULL in the EMP_BONUS_PAY column. Consequently this record was excluded from the calculated average because NULL is not a numeric value and therefore cannot be included in a computation.

Assuming that you do want to include this record in your results to get the correct average, you will need to convert the NULL to numeric value zero. You can do this using the COALESCE function.

```
SELECT AVG(COALESCE(EMP_BONUS_PAY,0))
AS AVERAGE_BONUS
FROM EMP_PAY;
---------+---------+---------+---------+-----
                  AVERAGE_BONUS
---------+---------+---------+---------+-----
       2900.00000000000000000
DSNE610I NUMBER OF ROWS DISPLAYED IS 1
```

314

The above says calculate the average EMP_BONUS_PAY using the first non-null value of EMP_BONUS_PAY or zero. Since employee 9134 has a NULL value in the EMP_BONUS_PAY field, DB2 substitutes a zero instead of the NULL. Zero is a numeric value, so this record can now be included in the computation of the average. This gives the correct average which is 2900.

Before we move on let's reset the bonus pay on our employee 9134 so that it can be used correctly for other queries later in the study guide.

```
UPDATE HRSCHEMA.EMP_PAY
SET EMP_BONUS_PAY = 2500.00
WHERE EMP_ID = 9134;
```

You can use COALESCE anytime you need to include a record that would otherwise be excluded due to a NULL value. Converting the NULL to a value will ensure the record can be included in the results.

CONCAT

The CONCAT function combines two or more strings. Suppose for example you want to list each employee's first and last names from the EMPLOYEE table. You could so it with this SQL:

```
SELECT
CONCAT(CONCAT(EMP_FIRST_NAME,' '),EMP_LAST_NAME)
AS EMP_FULL_NAME
FROM HRSCHEMA.EMPLOYEE;
---------+---------+---------+---------+---------+---
EMP_FULL_NAME
---------+---------+---------+---------+---------+---
EDWARD JOHNSON
BETTY STEWART
BRIANNA FRANKLIN
FRED TURNBULL
TIM SCHULTZ
JOE WILLARD
JAMEs FORD
ELISA HARRIS
DSNE610I NUMBER OF ROWS DISPLAYED IS 8
```

LCASE

The LCASE function returns a string in which all the characters are converted to lowercase characters. I can't think of many good applications for this, but here is an example of formatting the last name of each employee to lower case. Note: this function does not change any value on the table, it is only formatting the value for presentation.

```
SELECT EMP_ID, LCASE(EMP_LAST_NAME)
FROM HRSCHEMA.EMPLOYEE;
---------+---------+---------+---------+---
    EMP_ID
---------+---------+---------+---------+---
    3217  johnson
    7459  stewart
    9134  franklin
    4175  turnbull
    4720  schultz
    6288  willard
    3333  ford
    7777  harris
DSNE610I NUMBER OF ROWS DISPLAYED IS 8
```

LEFT

The LCASE function returns a string that consists of the specified number of leftmost bytes of the specified string units. Suppose you have an application that needs the first four letters of the last name (my pharmacy does this as part of the automated prescription filling process). You could accomplish that with this SQL:

```
SELECT EMP_ID, LEFT(EMP_LAST_NAME,4)
FROM HRSCHEMA.EMPLOYEE;
---------+---------+---------+---------+-----
    EMP_ID
---------+---------+---------+---------+-----
    3217  JOHN
    7459  STEW
    9134  FRAN
    4175  TURN
    4720  SCHU
    6288  WILL
    3333  FORD
    7777  HARR
DSNE610I NUMBER OF ROWS DISPLAYED IS 8
```

MAX

The MAX function returns the maximum value in a set of values. For example if we wanted to know the largest base pay for our EMP_PAY table, we could use this SQL:

```
SELECT MAX(EMP_REGULAR_PAY)
AS HIGHEST_PAY
FROM HRSCHEMA.EMP_PAY;
---------+---------+-------
HIGHEST_PAY
---------+---------+-------
    85000.00
```

MIN

The MIN scalar function returns the minimum value in a set of values. For example if we wanted to know the largest base pay for our EMP_PAY table, we could use this SQL:

```
SELECT MIN(EMP_REGULAR_PAY)
AS LOWEST_PAY
FROM HRSCHEMA.EMP_PAY

---------+---------+-------
LOWEST_PAY
---------+---------+-------
  65000.00
```

MONTH

The MONTH function returns the month part of a date value. We used this one earlier to compare the month of the employee's promotion to the current month.

```
SELECT
EMP_ID,
EMP_PROMOTION_DATE,
CURRENT DATE AS RQST_DATE
FROM HRSCHEMA.EMPLOYEE
WHERE MONTH(EMP_PROMOTION_DATE)
 = MONTH(CURRENT DATE);

---------+---------+---------+---------+---------+----
    EMP_ID  EMP_PROMOTION_DATE  RQST_DATE
---------+---------+---------+---------+---------+----
      3217  2017-01-01          2017-01-19
      7459  2016-01-01          2017-01-19
      4720  2017-01-01          2017-01-19
      6288  2016-01-01          2017-01-19
DSNE610I NUMBER OF ROWS DISPLAYED IS 4
```

REPEAT

The REPEAT function returns a character string that is composed of an argument that is repeated a specified number of times. Suppose for example that you wanted to display 10 asterisks as a literal field on a report. You could specify it this way:

```
SELECT
EMP_ID,
REPEAT('*',10) AS "FILLER LITERAL",
EMP_SERVICE_YEARS
FROM HRSCHEMA.EMPLOYEE;
---------+---------+---------+---------+---------+-
    EMP_ID  FILLER LITERAL  EMP_SERVICE_YEARS
---------+---------+---------+---------+---------+-
      3217  **********                      6
      7459  **********                      7
      9134  **********                      0
```

```
      4175  *********                        1
      4720  *********                        9
      6288  *********                        6
      3333  *********                        7
      7777  *********                        2
DSNE610I NUMBER OF ROWS DISPLAYED IS 8
```

SPACE

The SPACE function returns a character string that consists of the number of blanks that the argument specifies. You could use this in place of the quotation literals (especially when you want a lot of spaces). The example I'll give uses the SPACE function instead of having to concatenate an empty string using quotation marks.

```
SELECT
  CONCAT(CONCAT(EMP_FIRST_NAME,SPACE(1)),
  EMP_LAST_NAME)
  AS EMP_FULL_NAME
  FROM HRSCHEMA.EMPLOYEE;

---------+---------+---------+---------+----
EMP_FULL_NAME
---------+---------+---------+---------+----
EDWARD JOHNSON
BETTY STEWART
BRIANNA FRANKLIN
FRED TURNBULL
TIM SCHULTZ
JOE WILLARD
JAMEs FORD
ELISA HARRIS
DSNE610I NUMBER OF ROWS DISPLAYED IS 8
```

SUBSTR

The SUBSTR function returns a substring of a string. Let's use the earlier example of retrieving the first four letters of the last name via the LEFT function. You could also accomplish that with this SQL:

```
SELECT EMP_ID, SUBSTR(EMP_LAST_NAME,1,4)
  FROM HRSCHEMA.EMPLOYEE;
---------+---------+---------+---------+---
    EMP_ID
---------+---------+---------+---------+---
      3217  JOHN
      7459  STEW
      9134  FRAN
      4175  TURN
      4720  SCHU
      6288  WILL
```

```
           3333  FORD
           7777  HARR
     DSNE610I NUMBER OF ROWS DISPLAYED IS 8
```

The 1,4 means starting in position one for a length of four. Of course, you could use a different starting position. An example that might make more sense is reformatting the current date. For example:

```
SELECT CURRENT DATE,
SUBSTR(CHAR(CURRENT DATE),6,2)
|| '/'
||SUBSTR(CHAR(CURRENT DATE),9,2)
|| '/'
|| SUBSTR(CHAR(CURRENT DATE),1,4)
AS REFORMED_DATE
FROM SYSIBM.SYSDUMMY1;
---------+---------+---------+---
            REFORMED_DATE
---------+---------+---------+---
2017-01-12  01/12/2017
```

UCASE

The UCASE function returns a string in which all the characters are converted to uppercase characters. Here is an example of changing the last name of each employee to upper case. First we will have to covert the uppercase EMP_LAST_NAME values to lowercase. We can do that using the LOWER function. Let's do this for a single row:

```
UPDATE HRSCHEMA.EMPLOYEE
SET EMP_LAST_NAME
= LOWER(EMP_LAST_NAME)
WHERE EMP_ID = 3217;
```

We can verify that the data did in fact get changed to lower case.

```
   SELECT EMP_LAST_NAME
   FROM HRSCHEMA.EMPLOYEE
   WHERE EMP_ID = 3217;
---------+---------+---------+---------
EMP_LAST_NAME
---------+---------+---------+---------
johnson
DSNE610I NUMBER OF ROWS DISPLAYED IS 1
```

Now let's use the UCASE function to have the EMP_LAST_NAME display as upper case.

```
   SELECT EMP_ID, UCASE(EMP_LAST_NAME)
   FROM HRSCHEMA.EMPLOYEE
```

```
      WHERE EMP_ID = 3217;
---------+---------+---------+---------+---------
      EMP_ID
---------+---------+---------+---------+---------
      3217   JOHNSON
DSNE610I NUMBER OF ROWS DISPLAYED IS 1
```

Note that the SELECT query did not change any data on the table. We have simply reformatted the data for presentation. Now let's actually convert the data on the record back to upper case:

```
UPDATE HRSCHEMA.EMPLOYEE
SET EMP_LAST_NAME = UPPER(EMP_LAST_NAME)
WHERE EMP_ID = 3217;
```

And we'll verify that it reverted back to uppercase:

```
   SELECT EMP_LAST_NAME
   FROM HRSCHEMA.EMPLOYEE
   WHERE EMP_ID = 3217;
---------+---------+---------+---------+---
EMP_LAST_NAME
---------+---------+---------+---------+---
JOHNSON
DSNE610I NUMBER OF ROWS DISPLAYED IS 1
```

YEAR

The YEAR function returns the year part of a value that is a character or graphic string. The value must be a valid string representation of a date or timestamp.

```
   SELECT CURRENT DATE AS TODAYS_DATE,
   YEAR(CURRENT DATE) AS CURRENT_YEAR
   FROM SYSIBM.SYSDUMMY1;

   ---------+---------+---------+---------
   TODAYS_DATE   CURRENT_YEAR
   ---------+---------+---------+---------
   2017-01-12          2017
```

TABLE Functions

These functions are primarily used by system administrators and/or DBAs. It is good to know what they do, but it is unlikely that you would be using them for programming tasks.

ADMIN_TASK_LIST

The ADMIN_TASK_LIST function returns a table with one row for each of the tasks that are defined in the administrative task scheduler task list.

ADMIN_TASK_OUTPUT

For an execution of a stored procedure, the ADMIN_TASK_OUTPUT function returns the output parameter values and result sets, if available. If the task that was executed is not a stored procedure or the requested execution status is not available, the function returns an empty table.

ADMIN_TASK_STATUS

The ADMIN_TASK_STATUS function returns a table with one row for each task that is defined in the administrative task scheduler task list. Each row indicates the status of the task for the last time it was run.

MQREADALL

The MQREADALL function returns a table that contains the messages and message metadata from a specified MQSeries® location without removing the messages from the queue.

MQREADALLCLOB

The MQREADALLCLOB function returns a table that contains the messages and message metadata from a specified MQSeries location without removing the messages from the queue.

MQRECEIVEALL

The MQRECEIVEALL function returns a table that contains the messages and message metadata from a specified MQSeries location and removes the messages from the queue.

MQRECEIVEALLCLOB

The MQRECEIVEALLCLOB function returns a table that contains the messages and message metadata from a specified MQSeries location and removes the messages from the queue.

XMLTABLE

The XMLTABLE function returns a result table from the evaluation of XQuery expressions, possibly by using specified input arguments as XQuery variables. Each item in the result sequence of the row XQuery expression represents one row of the result table.

ROW functions

UNPACK

The UNPACK function returns a row of values that are derived from unpacking the input binary string. It is used to unpack a string that was encoded according to the PACK function.

Application Programming with DB2

CURSORS

A cursor is a pointer to a record in a result set returned in an application program or stored procedure. If you do programming in DB2 with result sets, you will need to understand cursors. First let's talk about the types of cursors and the rules governing them. That will give you a good idea of what type of cursor to select for your processing. Then we'll provide a programming example of using a cursor.

Types of Cursors

Cursors are scrollable or nonscrollable, sensitive or insensitive, static or dynamic. A non-scrollable cursor moves sequentially through a result set. A scrollable cursor can move where you want it to move within the result set. Scrollable cursors can be sensitive or insensitive. A sensitive cursor can be static or dynamic.

To declare a cursor as scrollable, you use the SCROLL keyword. In addition, a scrollable cursor is either sensitive or insensitive, and you specify this with the SENSITIVE and INSENSITIVE keywords. Finally to specify a sensitive cursors as static or dynamic, use the STATIC or DYNAMIC keyword.

INSENSITIVE SCROLL

If you declare a cursor as INSENSITIVE SCROLL, it means that the result set is static. Neither the size nor the ordering of the rows can be changed. Also you cannot change any data values of the rows. Finally, if any rows change in the underlying table or view after you open the cursor, those changes will not be visible to the cursor (and the changes will not be reflected in the result set).

SENSITIVE STATIC SCROLL

If you declare a cursor as SENSITIVE STATIC SCROLL, it means that the result set is static. Neither the size nor the ordering of the rows can be changed. If any rows change in the underlying table or view after you open the cursor, those changes will not be visible to the cursor (and the changes will not be reflected in the result set). An exception to this is if you specify SENSITIVE on the FETCH statement

You **can** change the rows in the rowset and the changes will be reflected in the result set. Also, if you change a row such that it no longer satisfies the query upon which the cursor is based, that row disappears from the result set. Additionally, if a row in a result set is deleted from the underlying table, the row will disappear from the result set.

SENSITIVE DYNAMIC SCROLL

If you declare a cursor as SENSITIVE DYNAMIC SCROLL, it means that the size of the result set and the ordering can change each time you do a fetch. The rowset would change if there are any changes to the underlying table after the cursor is opened.

Any rows in the rowset can be changed and deleted, and the changes will be reflected in the result set. If you change a row such that it no longer satisfies the query upon which the cursor is based, that row disappears from the result set. Additionally, if a row in a result set is deleted from the underlying table, the row will disappear from the result set.

Additional Cursor Options

A cursor can specify WITHOUT HOLD or WITH HOLD, the main difference being whether or not the cursor is closed on a COMMIT. Specifying WITHOUT HOLD allows a cursor to be closed when a COMMIT operation occurs. Specifying WITH HOLD prevents the cursor from being closed when a COMMIT takes place.

A cursor can specify WITHOUT RETURN or WITH RETURN, the difference being whether the result set is intended to be returned to a calling program or procedure. Specifying WITH RETURN means that the result set is meant to be returned from the procedure it is generated in. Specifying WITHOUT RETURN means that the cursor's result set is not intended to be returned from the procedure it is generated in.

A cursor can also specify WITH ROWSET POSITIONING or WITHOUT ROWSET POSITIONING. If you specify WITH ROWSET POSITIONING, then your cursor can return either a single row or rowset (multiple rows) with a single FETCH statement. If WITHOUT ROWSET POSITIONING is specified, it means the cursor can only return a single row with a FETCH statement.

Sample Program

To use cursors in a program, you must:

1. Declare the cursor

2. Open the Cursor

3. Fetch the cursor (one or more times)

4. Close the cursor

Here is a basic program that uses a cursor to retrieve and update records. We showed this program earlier in the DML chapter to demonstrate the positioned UPDATE

324

operation. If you haven't used cursors much, I suggest getting very familiar with the structure of this program.

Let's say that we want to check all records in the EMPLOYEE table and if the first or last name is in lower case, we want to change it to upper case and display the employee number of the corrected record. Let's first set up some test data:

```
UPDATE HRSCHEMA.EMPLOYEE
SET EMP_LAST_NAME = LOWER(EMP_LAST_NAME)
WHERE
EMP_LAST_NAME IN ('JOHNSON', 'STEWART', 'FRANKLIN');
```

After you execute this SQL, here's the current content of the EMPLOYEE table:

```
SELECT EMP_ID, EMP_LAST_NAME, EMP_FIRST_NAME
FROM HRSCHEMA.EMPLOYEE;
---------+---------+---------+---------+---------+-----
    EMP_ID  EMP_LAST_NAME        EMP_FIRST_NAME
---------+---------+---------+---------+---------+-----
      3217  johnson              EDWARD
      7459  stewart              BETTY
      9134  franklin             BRIANNA
      4720  SCHULTZ              TIM
      6288  WILLARD              JOE
      1122  JENKINS              DEBBIE
      4175  TURNBULL             FREDERICK
      1001  HENDERSON            JOHN
DSNE610I NUMBER OF ROWS DISPLAYED IS 8
```

To accomplish our objective we'll define and open a cursor on the EMPLOYEE table. We can specify a WHERE clause that limits the result set to only those records that contain lower case characters. After we find them, we will change the case to upper and replace the records.

First we need to identify the rows that include lower case letters in column EMP_LAST_NAME. We can do this using the UPPER function. We'll compare the current contents of the EMP_LAST_NAME to the value of UPPER(EMP_LAST_NAME) and if the results are not identical, the row in question has lower case and needs to be changed. Our result set should include all rows where these two values are not identical. So our SQL would be:

```
SELECT EMP_ID, EMP_LAST_NAME
FROM EMPLOYEE
WHERE EMP_LAST_NAME <> UPPER(EMP_LAST_NAME)
```

325

Once we've placed the last name value in the host variable EMP-LAST-NAME, we can use the PLI UPPERCASE function to convert lowercase to uppercase.

```
EMP_LAST_NAME = UPPERCASE(EMP_LAST_NAME);
```

Now we are ready to write the program. So we define and open the cursor, cycle through the result set using FETCH, modify the data and then do the UPDATE action specifying the current record of the cursor. This is what is meant by a positioned update – the cursor is positioned on the record to be changed, hence you do not need to specify a more elaborate WHERE clause in the UPDATE. Only the **WHERE CURRENT OF <cursor name>** clause need be specified.

Also notice we will include the **FOR UPDATE** clause in our cursor definition to ensure DB2 knows our intent is to update the data we retrieve.

The program code follows:

```
PLIEMP2: PROCEDURE OPTIONS(MAIN) REORDER;

/******************************************************************
* PROGRAM NAME :   PLIEMP2 - USE CURSOR TO UPDATE DB2 ROWS        *
******************************************************************/

/******************************************************************
/*              W O R K I N G    S T O R A G E                    *
******************************************************************/

   DCL RET_SQL_CODE            FIXED BIN(31) INIT(0);
   DCL RET_SQL_CODE_PIC        PIC 'S999999999' INIT (0);


   EXEC SQL
     INCLUDE SQLCA;

   EXEC SQL
     INCLUDE EMPLOYEE;

   EXEC SQL
     DECLARE EMP_CURSOR CURSOR FOR
     SELECT EMP_ID, EMP_LAST_NAME
     FROM HRSCHEMA.EMPLOYEE
     WHERE EMP_LAST_NAME <> UPPER(EMP_LAST_NAME)
     FOR UPDATE OF EMP_LAST_NAME;


/******************************************************************
/*              P R O G R A M    M A I N L I N E                  *
******************************************************************/
```

```pli
      PUT SKIP LIST ('SAMPLE PLI PROGRAM: CURSOR TO UPDATE ROWS');

      EXEC SQL OPEN EMP_CURSOR;

      PUT SKIP LIST ('OPEN CURSOR SQLCODE: ' || SQLCODE);

      IF SQLCODE = 0 THEN
         DO UNTIL (SQLCODE ¬= 0);
            CALL P0100_FETCH_CURSOR;
         END;

      EXEC SQL CLOSE EMP_CURSOR;

      PUT SKIP LIST ('CLOSE CURSOR SQLCODE: ' || SQLCODE);

      IF SQLCODE ¬= 0 THEN
         DO;
            EXEC SQL
               GET DIAGNOSTICS CONDITION 1
               :RET_SQL_CODE  = DB2_RETURNED_SQLCODE;

            RET_SQL_CODE_PIC  = RET_SQL_CODE;
            PUT SKIP LIST (RET_SQL_CODE_PIC);
         END;


P0100_FETCH_CURSOR: PROC;

   EXEC SQL
       FETCH EMP_CURSOR INTO :EMP_ID, :EMP_LAST_NAME;

   IF SQLCODE = 0 THEN
      DO;
         PUT SKIP LIST ('BEFORE CHANGE  ' || EMP_LAST_NAME);
         EMP_LAST_NAME = UPPERCASE(EMP_LAST_NAME);
         EXEC SQL
            UPDATE HRSCHEMA.EMPLOYEE
            SET EMP_LAST_NAME = :EMP_LAST_NAME
            WHERE CURRENT OF EMP_CURSOR;
         IF SQLCODE = 0 THEN
            PUT SKIP LIST ('AFTER CHANGE  ' || EMP_LAST_NAME);
      END;


END P0100_FETCH_CURSOR;

END PLIEMP2;
```

Compile, link and run the program. And here is the modified table:

```
    SELECT EMP_ID,
```

```
    EMP_LAST_NAME,
    EMP_FIRST_NAME
    FROM HRSCHEMA.EMPLOYEE;
---------+---------+---------+---------+---------+-----
    EMP_ID  EMP_LAST_NAME        EMP_FIRST_NAME
---------+---------+---------+---------+---------+-----
     3217  JOHNSON              EDWARD
     7459  STEWART              BETTY
     9134  FRANKLIN             BRIANNA
     4720  SCHULTZ              TIM
     6288  WILLARD              JOE
     1122  JENKINS              DEBBIE
     4175  TURNBULL             FREDERICK
     1001  HENDERSON            JOHN
DSNE610I NUMBER OF ROWS DISPLAYED IS 8
```

This method of using a positioned cursor update is something you will use often, particularly when you do not know your result set beforehand, or anytime you need to examine the content of the record before you perform the update.

Error Handling

In over three decades of experience with DB2, I believe one of the most neglected areas in programmer training is problem resolution. I'm not sure why this is, but I'd like to provide some standards that may help save time and make programmers more effective. First, let's look at SQLCODE processing, and then we'll look at standardizing an error reporting routine.

SQLCODES

When using embedded SQL with DB2 you include a SQLCA structure which includes an SQLCODE variable. DB2 sets the SQLCODE after each SQL statement. The SQLCODE should be interrogated to determine the success or failure of the SQL statement.

The value of the SQLCODE can be interpreted generally as follows:

> If SQLCODE = 0, execution was successful.
> If SQLCODE > 0, execution was successful with a warning.
> If SQLCODE < 0, execution was not successful.
> SQLCODE = 100, "no data" was found.

Here's an example of an SQL error message when a query is executed via SPUFI. In this case, the last name column is incorrectly spelled (it should be EMP_LAST_NAME) so DB2 does not recognize it. The -206 is accompanied by an explanation. A more complete explanation and recommendations for action to take is available if you look up the SQLCODE on the IBM product documentation web site.

328

```
SELECT EMP_ID, EMP_LASTNAME
  FROM HRSCHEMA.EMPLOYEE;
---------+---------+---------+---------+---------+---------+---------+---
DSNT408I SQLCODE = -206, ERROR:  EMP_LASTNAME IS NOT VALID IN THE CONTEXT
         WHERE IT IS USED
DSNT418I SQLSTATE   = 42703 SQLSTATE RETURN CODE
DSNT415I SQLERRP    = DSNXORSO SQL PROCEDURE DETECTING ERROR
DSNT416I SQLERRD    = -100 0  0  -1  0  0 SQL DIAGNOSTIC INFORMATION
DSNT416I SQLERRD    = X'FFFFFF9C'  X'00000000'  X'00000000'  X'FFFFFFFF'
           X'00000000'  X'00000000' SQL DIAGNOSTIC INFORMATION
```

There are far too many SQL codes to memorize! I suggest concentrating on the codes listed below. Most developers have run into these at one time or another. They tend to be pretty common.

Common Error SQLCODES

-117   THE NUMBER OF VALUES ASSIGNED IS NOT THE SAME AS THE
        NUMBER OF SPECIFIED OR IMPLIED COLUMNS

-180   THE DATE, TIME, OR TIMESTAMP VALUE value IS INVALID

-181   THE STRING REPRESENTATION OF A DATETIME VALUE IS NOT A
        VALID DATETIME VALUE

-203   A REFERENCE TO COLUMN column-name IS AMBIGUOUS

-206   Object-name IS NOT VALID IN THE CONTEXT WHERE IT IS USED

-305   THE NULL VALUE CANNOT BE ASSIGNED TO OUTPUT HOST VARIABLE
        NUMBER position-number BECAUSE NO INDICATOR VARIABLE IS
        SPECIFIED

-501   THE CURSOR IDENTIFIED IN A FETCH OR CLOSE STATEMENT IS NOT
        OPEN

-502   THE CURSOR IDENTIFIED IN AN OPEN STATEMENT IS ALREADY OPEN

-803   AN INSERTED OR UPDATED VALUE IS INVALID BECAUSE THE INDEX
        IN INDEX SPACE indexspace-name CONSTRAINS COLUMNS OF THE
        TABLE SO NO TWO ROWS CAN CONTAIN DUPLICATE VALUES IN THOSE
        COLUMNS. RID OF EXISTING ROW IS X record-id

-805   DBRM OR PACKAGE NAME location-name.collection-id.dbrm-
        name.consistency-token NOT FOUND IN PLAN plan-name. REASON
        reason-code

-811   THE RESULT OF AN EMBEDDED SELECT STATEMENT OR A SUBSELECT
        IN THE SET CLAUSE OF AN UPDATE STATEMENT IS A TABLE OF
        MORE THAN ONE ROW, OR THE RESULT OF A SUBQUERY OF A BASIC
        PREDICATE IS MORE THAN ONE VALUE

-818   THE PRECOMPILER-GENERATED TIMESTAMP x IN THE LOAD MODULE
        IS DIFFERENT FROM THE BIND TIMESTAMP y BUILT FROM THE DBRM
        z

-904   UNSUCCESSFUL EXECUTION CAUSED BY AN UNAVAILABLE RESOURCE.
        REASON reason-code, TYPE OF RESOURCE resource-type, AND
        RESOURCE NAME resource-name.

-911   THE CURRENT UNIT OF WORK HAS BEEN ROLLED BACK DUE TO
        DEADLOCK OR TIMEOUT. REASON reason-code, TYPE OF RESOURCE
        resource-type, AND RESOURCE NAME resource-name

-913   UNSUCCESSFUL EXECUTION CAUSED BY DEADLOCK OR TIMEOUT.
        REASON CODE reason-code, TYPE OF RESOURCE resource-type,
        AND RESOURCE NAME resource-name.

-922   AUTHORIZATION FAILURE: error-type ERROR. REASON reason-
        code.

Standardizing an Error Routine:

For optimal use of the SQLCODEs returned from DB2, I suggest you create and use a standard error routine in all your embedded SQL programs. I'll provide a model you can use, but first let's create a simple program and force an error to demonstrate the kind of problem resolution information that would be useful.

In this case, let's select a value into a host variable using a fullselect query. But we will make sure the fullselect query encounters more than one row. That will cause a -811 SQLCODE error which we could trap and display. But it would be better if DB2 returned the full error description. We can do that if we call a utility program named DSNTIAR. So let's create a common DB2 error subroutine with DSNTIAR so that we can use it in all our DB2 programs.

First, create these working storage variables.

```
DCL 01 ERR_MSG AUTOMATIC,
       05 ERR_LGTH           FIXED BIN (31) INIT (864),
       05 ERR_TXT(10)        CHAR(72);

DCL ERR_TXT_LGTH             FIXED BIN (15) INIT (72);
DCL ERR_NDX                  FIXED BIN (31) INIT (0);
```

330

The message and text length variables as well as the SQLCA structure will be passed to DSNTIAR.

Then declare program DSNTIAR as an external entry.

```
DCL DSNTIAR ENTRY OPTIONS(ASM INTER RETCODE);
```

Next, create a subroutine as follows to call DSNTIAR and display the returned output from that utility.

```
P9999_SQL_ERROR: PROC;

   PUT SKIP LIST (ERR_REC);

   CALL DSNTIAR (SQLCA, ERR_MSG, ERR_TXT_LGTH);

   IF RETCODE = 0 THEN
      DO ERR_NDX = 1 TO 10;
         PUT SKIP DATA (ERR_TXT(ERR_NDX));
      END; /* DO */
   ELSE
      PUT SKIP LIST ('DSNTIAR ERROR CODE = ' || RETCODE);

END P9999_SQL_ERROR;
```

Finally we can modify our code to call the error routine anytime a bad SQL code is returned.

```
EXEC SQL
   SELECT EMP_ID
   INTO :HV_ID
   FROM HRSCHEMA.EMPLOYEE
   WHERE EMP_ID >= 3217;


IF SQLCODE ¬= 0 THEN
   DO;
      SQLCODE_VIEW = SQLCODE;
      ERR_TAB = 'EMPLOYEE';
      ERR_PARA = 'MAIN';
      ERR_EMPID = HV_ID;
      CALL P9999_SQL_ERROR;
   END;
```

Here is the complete program listing.

```
PLIEMP5: PROCEDURE OPTIONS(MAIN) REORDER;
/*******************************************************************
*                                                                 *
* PROGRAM NAME :   PLIEMP5 - PROGRAM USING DB2 SELECT WITH ERROR   *
*                            TO DEMONSTRATE COMMON ERROR ROUTINE.  *
*                                                                 *
*******************************************************************/

 /*******************************************************************
 *               E X T E R N A L   E N T R I E S                   *
 *******************************************************************/

    DCL DSNTIAR ENTRY OPTIONS(ASM INTER RETCODE);

 /*******************************************************************
 *               W O R K I N G   S T O R A G E                     *
 *******************************************************************/

    DCL HV_ID              FIXED BIN (31) INIT (0);
    DCL HV_LAST_NAME       CHAR(30) INIT (' ');
    DCL HV_FIRST_NAME      CHAR(20) INIT (' ');
    DCL HV_SERVICE_YEARS   FIXED BIN (31) INIT (0);
    DCL HV_PROMOTION_DATE  CHAR(10) INIT (' ');

    DCL 01 ERR_REC,
           05 FILLER1          CHAR(10) INIT ('SQLCODE = '),
           05 SQLCODE_VIEW     PIC '-999',
           05 ERR_EMPID        FIXED BIN (31) INIT (0),
           05 FILLER2          CHAR(01) INIT (' '),
           05 ERR_TAB          CHAR(08) INIT (' '),
           05 ERR_PARA         CHAR(15) INIT (' ');

    DCL 01 ERR_MSG AUTOMATIC,
           05 ERR_LGTH         FIXED BIN (31) INIT (864),
           05 ERR_TXT(10)      CHAR(72);

    DCL ERR_TXT_LGTH           FIXED BIN (15) INIT (72);
    DCL ERR_NDX                FIXED BIN (31) INIT (0);


    EXEC SQL
      INCLUDE SQLCA;

    EXEC SQL
      INCLUDE EMPLOYEE;

 /*******************************************************************
 /*              P R O G R A M   M A I N L I N E                    *
 *******************************************************************/

    PUT SKIP LIST ('SAMPLE PLI PROGRAM: COMMON ERROR ROUTINE');

           DCLEMPLOYEE = '';
```

332

```
        /* SELECT AN EMPLOYEE */

            EXEC SQL
                SELECT EMP_ID
                INTO :HV_ID
                FROM HRSCHEMA.EMPLOYEE
                WHERE EMP_ID >= 3217;

            IF SQLCODE ¬= 0 THEN
                DO;
                    SQLCODE_VIEW = SQLCODE;
                    ERR_TAB = 'EMPLOYEE';
                    ERR_PARA = 'MAIN';
                    ERR_EMPID = HV_ID;
                    CALL P9999_SQL_ERROR;
                END;


    P9999_SQL_ERROR: PROC;

        PUT SKIP LIST (ERR_REC);

        CALL DSNTIAR (SQLCA, ERR_MSG, ERR_TXT_LGTH);

        IF RETCODE = 0 THEN
            DO ERR_NDX = 1 TO 10;
                PUT SKIP DATA (ERR_TXT(ERR_NDX));
            END; /* DO */
        ELSE
            PUT SKIP LIST ('DSNTIAR ERROR CODE = ' || RETCODE);

    END P9999_SQL_ERROR;

END PLIEMP5;
```

Now when we recompile, bind and rerun the program, the outlook looks like this:

```
SAMPLE PLI PROGRAM: COMMON ERROR ROUTINE
SQLCODE =                -811                              4175
MAIN
SQLCODE = -811     EMPLOYEE        MAIN          000000000
 DSNT408I SQLCODE = -811, ERROR:  THE RESULT OF AN EMBEDDED SELECT
          STATEMENT OR A SUBSELECT IN THE SET CLAUSE OF AN UPDATE
          STATEMENT IS A TABLE OF MORE THAN ONE ROW, OR THE RESULT OF A
          SUBQUERY OF A BASIC PREDICATE IS MORE THAN ONE VALUE
 DSNT418I SQLSTATE   = 21000 SQLSTATE RETURN CODE
 DSNT415I SQLERRP    = DSNXREMS SQL PROCEDURE DETECTING ERROR
 DSNT416I SQLERRD    = -140  0  0  -1  0  0 SQL DIAGNOSTIC INFORMATION
 DSNT416I SQLERRD    = X'FFFFFF74'  X'00000000'  X'00000000'
          X'FFFFFFFF'  X'00000000'  X'00000000' SQL DIAGNOSTIC
          INFORMATION
```

The SQLCODE details, along with the other information we printed in the ERR-REC (such as the table name and paragraph name) are now displayed to SYSPRINT. This information is more helpful for debugging than just having the SQL code. Moreover, you can create these declarations and routines as copybooks and include them in all your DB2 programs. When used, they ensure standardization throughout your shop. They also will save a lot of time by making useful error-related information available on a consistent basis. I strongly recommend that you implement this standard in your shop!

Dynamic versus Static SQL

Static SQL
Static SQL statements are embedded within an application program that is written in a traditional programming language such as COBOL or PL/I. The statement is prepared before the program is executed, and the executable statement persists after the program ends. You can use static SQL when you know before run time what SQL statements your application needs to use.

As a practical matter, when you use static SQL you cannot change the form of SQL statements unless you make changes to the program and recompile and bind it. However, you can increase the flexibility of those statements by using host variables. So for example you could write an SQL that retrieves employee information for all employees with X years of service where the X becomes a host variable that you load at run time. Using static SQL and host variables is more secure than using dynamic SQL.

Dynamic SQL
Unlike static SQL which is prepared before the program runs, with dynamic SQL DB2 prepares and executes the SQL statements at run time as part of the program's execution. Dynamic SQL is a good choice when you do not know the format of an SQL statement before you write or run a program. An example might be a user interface that allows a web application to submit SQL statements to a background COBOL program for execution. In this case, you wouldn't know the structure of the statement the client submits until run time.

Applications that use dynamic SQL create an SQL statement in the form of a character string. A typical dynamic SQL application takes the following steps:

- Translates the input data into an SQL statement.

- Prepares the SQL statement to execute and acquires a description of the result table (if any).

334

- Obtains, for SELECT statements, enough main storage to contain retrieved data.

- Executes the statement or fetches the rows of data.

- Processes the returned information.

- Handles SQL return codes.

Performance Comparison of Static versus Dynamic SQL

Ordinarily static SQL is more efficient than dynamic because the former is prepared and optimized before the program executes. For static SQL statements DB2 typically determines the access path when you bind the plan or package - the exception being if you code REOPT(ALWAYS) in your bind statement. If you code REOPT(ALWAYS) on a package that has static SQL, DB2 will determine the access path when you bind the plan or package and again at run time using the values of host variables and parameter markers (if included).

For dynamic SQL statements, DB2 determines the access path at run time, when the statement is prepared. The cost of preparing a dynamic statement many times can lead to a performance that is worse than with static SQL. However you can consider these options to improve your performance with dynamic SQL:

1. You can improve performance by caching dynamic statements. To do this, set subsystem parameter CACHEDYN=YES.

2. With dynamic SQL you can also re-optimize your query by using the REOPT bind options. If you are not using the CACHEDYN=YES, you can use the REOPT(ALWAYS) bind option to ensure the best access path. But keep in mind this may slow performance for frequently used dynamic statements.

3. If you are using the CACHEDYN=YES subsystem parameter setting, you can use bind option REOPT(ONCE) and DB2 will only determine the optimal access path the first time the statement is executed. It saves that access path in the dynamic statement cache.

4. If you specify REOPT(AUTO), DB2 will look at any statements with parameter markers and determine whether a new access path might improve performance. If it determines that it would, DB2 will generate a new access path.

To conclude this section, you generally want to use static SQL when you know the structure of your SQL statement and when performance is a significant goal. Use dynamic SQL when you need the flexibility of not knowing the structure of your SQL until run time.

Program Preparation

Before a DB2 program can be run, it must be prepared. Depending on what type of application it is, the programs may need to be pre-compiled, compiled, link-edited and bound. Let's consider each of these steps.

Precompile

Embedded SQL programs (those for which the SQL is embedded in an application program such as COBOL or PL/I) must be precompiled using either the DB2 precompiler or the DB2 coprocessor. The reason is the language compilers such as COBOL do not recognize SQL statements. The precompiler does two things:

- It translates the SQL statements into something that can be compiled.

- It outputs a DBRM (database request module) which is a file that includes all the SQL statements and is used to communicate with DB2.

Compile, link-edit

The program must also be compiled and link-edited to produce an executable load module. DB2 keeps track of the timestamp on the executable module and the timestamp on the DBRM module and these must match or you will receive a -805 SQL error.

Bind

After the precompile, the DBRM must be bound to a package. A package is a compiled version of a DBRM and so it includes the executable versions of SQL statements. You can also specify a collection name when you bind a package. A collection is a group of related packages. Here is a sample BIND PACKAGE statement:

```
BIND PACKAGE(HRSCHEMA)  -
MEMBER(PLIEMP6)       -
OWNER(HRSCHEMA)         -
QUALIFIER(HRSCHEMA)     -
ACTION(REPLACE)       -
CURRENTDATA(NO)       -
EXPLAIN(NO)           -
ISOLATION(CS)         -
VALIDATE  (BIND)      -
RELEASE   (COMMIT)
```

Packages themselves are not executable without being added to a DB2 plan. Here is a sample BIND PLAN statement:

```
BIND   PLAN      (PLIEMP6) -
       PKLIST    (HRSCHEMA.PLIEMP6) -
       ACTION    (REP)       -
       ISOLATION (CS)        -
       EXPLAIN   (YES)       -
       VALIDATE  (BIND)      -
       RELEASE   (COMMIT)    -
       OWNER     (HRSCHEMA)    -
       QUALIFIER (HRSCHEMA)
```

Non-Embedded SQL Applications

Some application types do not require the precompile, compile/link-edit and bind steps.

- REXX procedures are interpreted and not compiled, so they do not need to be precompiled, compiled/link-edited and bound.

- ODBC applications use dynamic SQL only, so they do not require precompile.

- Java applications containing only JDBC do not need precompile or binding. However Java applications using the SQLJ interface are embedded SQL and they need precompile and bind steps.

Data Concurrency

Isolation Levels & Bind Release Options

Isolation level means the degree to which a DB2 application's activities are isolated from the operations of other DB2 applications. The isolation level for a package is specified when the package is bound, although you can override the package isolation level in an SQL statement. There are four isolation levels: Repeatable Read, Read Stability, Cursor Stability and Uncommitted Read.

ISOLATIONS LEVELS

Repeatable Read (RR)

Repeatable Read ensures that a query issued multiple times within the same unit of work will produce the exact same results. It does this by locking all rows that could affect the result. It does not permit any adds/changes/deletes to the table that could affect the result.

Read Stability (RS)

Read Stability locks for the duration of the transaction those rows that are returned by a query, but it allows additional rows to be added to the table.

Cursor Stability (CS)

Cursor Stability only locks the row that the cursor is placed on (and any rows it has updated during the unit of work). This is the default isolation level if no other is specified.

Uncommitted Read (UR)

Uncommitted Read permits reading of uncommitted changes which may never be applied to the database. It does not lock any rows at all unless the row(s) is updated during the unit of work.

An IBM recommended best practice prefers isolation levels in this order:

1. Cursor stability (CS)

2. Uncommitted read (UR)

3. Read stability (RS)

4. Repeatable read (RR)

Of course the chosen isolation level depends on the scenario. We'll look at specific scenarios now.

Isolation Levels for Specific Situations

When your environment is basically read-only (such as with data warehouse environments), use UR **(UNCOMMITTED READ)** because it incurs the least overhead.

If you want to maximize data concurrency without seeing uncommitted data, use the CS **(CURSOR STABILITY)** isolation level. CS only locks the row where the cursor is placed (and any other rows which have been changed since the last commit point), thus maximizing concurrency compared to RR or RS.

If you want no existing rows that were retrieved to be changed by other processes during your unit of work, but you don't mind if new rows are inserted, use RS **(READ STABILITY)**.

Finally if you must lock all rows that satisfy the query and also not permit any new rows to be added that could change the result of the query, use RR (**REPEATABLE READ**).

Based on the above, if we wanted to order the isolation levels from most to least impact on performance, the order would be:

1. REPEATABLE READ (RR)

2. READ STABILITY (RS)

3. CURSOR STABILITY (CS)

4. UNCOMMITTED READ (UR)

Finally, in DB2 11 there is a `SKIP LOCKED DATA` clause for the SELECT statement that allows it to bypass any rows that are current locked by other applications. For example:

```
SELECT *
FROM HRSCHEMA.EMP_PAY
SKIP LOCKED DATA;
```

To use `SKIP LOCKED DATA` the application must use either cursor stability (CS) or read stability (RS) isolation level. The `SKIP LOCKED DATA` clause is ignored if the isolation level is uncommitted read (UR) or repeatable read (RR).

How to Specify/Override Isolation Level
To specify an isolation level at bind time, use the ISOLATION keyword with the abbreviated form of the isolation level you want. For example:

```
ISOLATION(CS)
```

If you want to override an isolation level in a query, specify the override at the end of the query by using the WITH <isolation level abbreviation> clause. For example, to override the default isolation level of CS to use UR instead on a query, code the following and notice we've used `WITH UR` at the end of the query:

```
SELECT EMP_ID,
EMP_LAST_NAME,
EMP_FIRST_NAME
FROM EMPLOYEE
ORDER BY EMP_ID
WITH UR;
```

Bind Release Options

The RELEASE bind option determines when any acquired locks are released. The two options are DEALLOCATE and COMMIT. Specifying RELEASE(DEALLOCATE) means the acquired locks will be released when the application session ends. Specifying RELEASE(COMMIT) means locks are released at a commit point. Under TSO this means when a DB2 COMMIT statement is issued. Under IMS a commit occurs when a CHKP or SYNC IMS call is issued. Under CICS a commit occurs when a SYNCPOINT is issued.

As a practical matter, the best concurrency is achieved by using RELEASE(COMMIT) because locks are generally released sooner than the end of the application. However, assuming the program commits frequently, this will result in more processing time than if using RELEASE(DEALLOCATE). So you must weigh your objectives and decide accordingly.

The RELEASE option is only applicable to static SQL statements, i.e., those bound before your program runs. Dynamic SQL statements release the locks at the next commit point.

COMMIT, ROLLBACK, and SAVEPOINTS

Central to understanding transaction management is the concept of a unit of work. A unit of work begins when a program is initiated. Multiple adds, changes and deletes may then take place during the same unit of work. The changes are not made permanent until a commit point is reached. A unit of work ends in one of three ways:

1. When a commit is issued.

2. When a rollback is issued.

3. When the program ends.

Let's look at each of these.

COMMIT

The COMMIT statement ends a transaction and makes the changes permanent and visible to other processes. Also, when a program ends, there is an implicit COMMIT. This is important to know; however an IBM recommended best practice is to do an explicit COMMIT at the end of the program.

Here are some other points about COMMIT to know and remember:

- For an IMS/DB2 program, an IMS **CHKP** call causes a commit of both DB2 and IMS changes made during the unit of work. For CICS, an **EXEC CICS SYNCPOINT** call is made to commit DB2 data.

- The DB2 COMMIT statement does not work in an IMS/DB2 or CICS/DB2 program because in those cases transaction management is performed by the IMS and CICS transaction managers. You won't receive an error for issuing the COMMIT statement, it simply will not work.

- Autonomous procedures were introduced in DB2 11; these procedures run with their own units of work, separate from the calling program.

ROLLBACK

A ROLLBACK statement ends a transaction without making changes permanent – the changes are simply discarded. This is done either intentionally by the application when it determines there is a reason to ROLLBACK the changes and it issues a ROLLBACK explicitly, or because the system traps an error that requires it to do a ROLLBACK of changes. In both cases, the rolled back changes are those that have been made since the last COMMIT point. If no COMMITs have been issued, then all changes made in the session are rolled back.

You can also issue a ROLLBACK TO <savepoint> if you are using SAVEPOINTS. We'll take a look at that shortly.

Here are some other points about ROLLBACK to know and remember:

- The abend of a process causes an implicit ROLLBACK.

- Global variable contents are not affected by ROLLBACK.

SAVEPOINT

The SAVEPOINT statement creates a point within a unit of recovery to which you can roll back changes. This is similar to using ROLLBACK to backout changes since the last COMMIT point, except a SAVEPOINT gives you even more control because it allows a partial ROLLBACK **between** COMMIT points.

You might wonder what the point is of using a SAVEPOINT. Let's take an example. Suppose you have a program that does INSERT statements and you program logic to

COMMIT every 500 inserts. If you issue a ROLLBACK, then all updates since the last COMMIT will be backed out. That's pretty straightforward.

But suppose you are updating information for vendors from a file of updates that is sorted by vendor, and if there is an error you want to rollback to where you started updating records for that vendor. And you want all other updates since the last COMMIT point to be applied to the database. This is different than rolling back to the last COMMIT point, and you can do it by setting a new SAVEPOINT each time the vendor changes. Issuing a SAVEPOINT enables you to execute several SQL statements as a single executable block between COMMIT statements. You can then undo changes back out to that savepoint by issuing a ROLLBACK TO SAVEPOINT statement.

Example
Let's do a simple example. First, create a new table and then add some records to the table. We'll create a copy of EMP_PAY.

```
CREATE TABLE HRSCHEMA.EMP_PAY_X
LIKE HRSCHEMA.EMP_PAY
IN TSHR;
```

Now let's add some records. We'll add one record, then create a SAVEPOINT, add another record and then roll back to the SAVEPOINT. This should leave us with only the first record in the table.

```
INSERT INTO EMP_PAY_X
VALUES(1111,
45000.00,
1200.00);

SAVEPOINT A ON ROLLBACK RETAIN CURSORS;

INSERT INTO EMP_PAY_X
VALUES(2222,
55000.00,
1500.00);

ROLLBACK TO SAVEPOINT A;
```

We can verify that only the first record was added to the table:

```
SELECT * FROM HRSCHEMA.EMP_PAY_X;
---------+---------+---------+---------+---------+----
    EMP_ID   EMP_REGULAR_PAY   EMP_BONUS_PAY
---------+---------+---------+---------+---------+----
    1111          45000.00          1200.00
```

If you have multiple SAVEPOINT S and you ROLLBACK to one of them, then the ROLLBACK will include updates made after any later SAVEPOINT S. Let's illustrate this with an example. We'll set three SAVEPOINT s: A, B and C. We'll add a record, then issue savepoint and we'll do this three times. Then we'll ROLLBACK to the first SAVEPOINT which is A. What we're saying is that any updates made after A will be backed out, which includes the INSERTs made after SAVEPOINTs B and C. Let's try this:

```
INSERT INTO EMP_PAY_X
VALUES(2222,
55000.00,
1500.00);

SAVEPOINT A ON ROLLBACK RETAIN CURSORS;

INSERT INTO EMP_PAY_X
VALUES(3333,
65000.00,
2500.00);

SAVEPOINT B ON ROLLBACK RETAIN CURSORS;

INSERT INTO EMP_PAY_X
VALUES(4444,
75000.00,
2000.00);

SAVEPOINT C ON ROLLBACK RETAIN CURSORS;

ROLLBACK TO SAVEPOINT A;


  SELECT * FROM HRSCHEMA.EMP_PAY_X;
---------+---------+---------+---------+---------
    EMP_ID  EMP_REGULAR_PAY  EMP_BONUS_PAY
---------+---------+---------+---------+---------
      1111          45000.00         1200.00
      2222          55000.00         1500.00
DSNE610I NUMBER OF ROWS DISPLAYED IS 2
```

Now as you can see, only the first record (2222) was inserted because we specified ROLLBACK all the way to SAVEPOINT A. Note that the 1111 record was already in the table.

Things to Remember about SAVEPOINT

- If you specify UNIQUE in the SAVEPOINT declaration, you cannot reuse the SAVEPOINT name in the same unit of work.

- If you specify ON ROLLBACK RETAIN CURSORS it means cursors are not closed after a rollback to SAVEPOINT.

- If you specify ON ROLLBACK RETAIN LOCKS this means that any locks acquired after the SAVEPOINT are not released. This is also the default.

- If the SAVEPOINT name is not specified on a ROLLBACK, then all updates back to the last COMMIT point are backed out and all SAVEPOINTs are erased.

Units of Work

A unit of work is a set of database operations in an application that is ended by a commit, a rollback or the end of the application process. A commit or rollback operation applies only to the set of changes made within that unit of work. An application process can involve one or many units of work.

Once a commit action occurs, the database changes are permanent and visible to other application processes. Any locks obtained by the application process are held until the end of the unit of work. So if you update 10 records within one unit of work, the records are all locked until a commit point.

As explained elsewhere, in distributed environments where you update data stores on more than one system, a two-phase commit is performed. The two phase commit ensures that data is consistent between the two systems by either fully commiting or fully rolling back the unit of work. The two phase commit consists of a commit-request phase and an actual commit phase.

Autonomous Transactions

Autonomous Transactions Basics

Autonomous procedures were introduced in DB2 11, so some questions about these transactions are very likely to appear on the exam. Autonomous transactions are native SQL procedures which run with their own units of work, separate from the calling program. If a calling program issues a ROLLBACK to back out its changes, the committed changes of the autonomous procedure are not affected.

Autonomous procedures can be called by normal application programs, other stored procedures, user-defined functions or triggers. Autonomous procedures can also invoke triggers, perform SQL statements, and execute commit and rollback statements.

Restrictions

Be sure to be familiar with these restrictions and limitations on using autonomous procedures:

- Only native SQL procedures can be defined as autonomous.

- Parallelism is disabled for autonomous procedures.

- An autonomous procedure cannot call another autonomous procedure.

- Autonomous procedures cannot see uncommitted changes from the calling application.

- DYNAMIC RESULT SETS 0 must be specified when autonomous procedures are used.

- Stored procedure parameters must not be defined as a LOB data type, or any distinct data type that is based on a LOB or XML value.

- Autonomous procedures do not share locks with the calling application, meaning that the autonomous procedure might timeouts because of lock contention with the calling application.

Applications

Autonomous procedures are useful for logging information about error conditions encountered by an application program. Similarly they can be used for creating an audit trail of activity for transactions.

Checkpoint/Restart processing

This section concerns the commit, rollback and recovery of an application or application program. We already covered the use of COMMIT, ROLLBACK and SAVEPOINTs in prior subsections. Here we'll apply the COMMIT and ROLLBACK in a DB2 program.

DB2 Program

For the DB2 program, we use the COMMIT statement at appropriate intervals. Let's use our update PLI program and employ both the COMMIT and the ROLLBACK options.

Let's say that we'll commit every 5 records.[9] So we set up a commit counter called COMMIT_CTR and we'll increment it each time we update a record. Once the counter reaches 200 updates, we'll issue a COMMIT statement and reset our record counter to zero. If we perform an update that fails, we'll issue a ROLLBACK. Note that we also added our generic SQL error handling routine. This will simplify our problem determination in case we encounter an error.

Go ahead and run an SQL to flip all the surnames on the table to lower case:

```
UPDATE HRSCHEMA.EMPLOYEE
SET EMP_LAST_NAME = LOWER(EMP_LAST_NAME);
```

Here's the program code. Note that you must define the cursor WITH HOLD in order to keep it open when using COMMIT. Otherwise the COMMIT will close the cursor.

```
PLIEMPC: PROCEDURE OPTIONS(MAIN) REORDER;

/******************************************************************
* PROGRAM NAME :   PLIEMPC - PROGRAM DEMONSTRATING USE OF         *
*                            COMMIT AND ROLLBACK PROCESSING.      *
******************************************************************/

/******************************************************************
*              E X T E R N A L   E N T R I E S                    *
******************************************************************/

   DCL DSNTIAR ENTRY OPTIONS(ASM INTER RETCODE);

/******************************************************************
/*             W O R K I N G   S T O R A G E                      *
******************************************************************/

   DCL COMMIT_CTR              FIXED BIN(31) INIT(0);
   DCL RET_SQL_CODE            FIXED BIN(31) INIT(0);
   DCL RET_SQL_CODE_PIC        PIC 'S999999999' INIT (0);

   DCL 01 ERR_REC,
          05 FILLER1           CHAR(10) INIT ('SQLCODE = '),
          05 SQLCODE_VIEW       PIC '-999',
          05 ERR_EMPID          FIXED BIN (31) INIT (0),
          05 FILLER2            CHAR(01) INIT (' '),
          05 ERR_TAB            CHAR(08) INIT (' '),
          05 ERR_PARA           CHAR(15) INIT (' ');
```

---

[9] In production you would commit much less frequently, possibly every 1,000 or 2,000 records. We are just using 5 as our frequency because we have a small subset of records.

```
DCL 01 ERR_MSG AUTOMATIC,
      05 ERR_LGTH            FIXED BIN (31) INIT (864),
      05 ERR_TXT(10)         CHAR(72);

DCL ERR_TXT_LGTH            FIXED BIN (15) INIT (72);
DCL ERR_NDX                FIXED BIN (31) INIT (0);


EXEC SQL
  INCLUDE SQLCA;

EXEC SQL
  INCLUDE EMPLOYEE;

EXEC SQL
  DECLARE EMP_CURSOR CURSOR WITH HOLD FOR
  SELECT EMP_ID, EMP_LAST_NAME
  FROM HRSCHEMA.EMPLOYEE
  WHERE EMP_LAST_NAME <> UPPER(EMP_LAST_NAME)
  FOR UPDATE OF EMP_LAST_NAME;


/********************************************************************
/*              P R O G R A M   M A I N L I N E             *
********************************************************************/

   PUT SKIP LIST ('SAMPLE PLI PROGRAM: UPDATE USING CURSOR');

   EXEC SQL OPEN EMP_CURSOR;

   PUT SKIP LIST ('OPEN CURSOR SQLCODE: ' || SQLCODE);

   IF SQLCODE = 0 THEN
      DO UNTIL (SQLCODE ¬= 0);
         CALL P0100_FETCH_CURSOR;
      END;
   ELSE
      CALL P9999_SQL_ERROR;

   EXEC SQL CLOSE EMP_CURSOR;

   PUT SKIP LIST ('CLOSE CURSOR SQLCODE: ' || SQLCODE);

   IF SQLCODE ¬= 0 THEN
      DO;
         EXEC SQL
            GET DIAGNOSTICS CONDITION 1
            :RET_SQL_CODE  = DB2_RETURNED_SQLCODE;

         RET_SQL_CODE_PIC  = RET_SQL_CODE;
         PUT SKIP LIST (RET_SQL_CODE_PIC);
      END;
```

```
P0100_FETCH_CURSOR: PROC;

    DCLEMPLOYEE = '';

    EXEC SQL
        FETCH EMP_CURSOR INTO :EMP_ID, :EMP_LAST_NAME;

    IF SQLCODE = 0 THEN
        DO;
            PUT SKIP LIST ('BEFORE CHANGE  ' || EMP_LAST_NAME);
            EMP_LAST_NAME = UPPERCASE(EMP_LAST_NAME);
            EXEC SQL
                UPDATE HRSCHEMA.EMPLOYEE
                SET EMP_LAST_NAME = :EMP_LAST_NAME
                WHERE CURRENT OF EMP_CURSOR;

            IF SQLCODE = 0 THEN
                DO;
                    PUT SKIP LIST ('AFTER CHANGE  ' || EMP_LAST_NAME);
                    COMMIT_CTR = COMMIT_CTR + 1;
                    IF COMMIT_CTR >= 5 THEN
                            DO;
                        EXEC SQL COMMIT;
                        COMMIT_CTR = 0;
                    END;
                END;
            ELSE
                DO;
                    CALL P9999_SQL_ERROR;
                    EXEC SQL ROLLBACK;
                END;
        END;

    ELSE
        IF SQLCODE = +100 THEN
            PUT SKIP LIST ('*** NO MORE RECORDS TO PROCESS!!');
        ELSE
            CALL P9999_SQL_ERROR;

END P0100_FETCH_CURSOR;

P9999_SQL_ERROR: PROC;

    PUT SKIP LIST (ERR_REC);

    CALL DSNTIAR (SQLCA, ERR_MSG, ERR_TXT_LGTH);

    IF RETCODE = 0 THEN
        DO ERR_NDX = 1 TO 10;
            PUT SKIP DATA (ERR_TXT(ERR_NDX));
        END; /* DO */
    ELSE
        PUT SKIP LIST ('DSNTIAR ERROR CODE = ' || RETCODE);
```

```
END P9999_SQL_ERROR;

END PLIEMPC;
```

And here is the output:

```
SAMPLE PLI PROGRAM: UPDATE USING CURSOR
OPEN CURSOR SQLCODE:               0
BEFORE CHANGE  johnson
AFTER CHANGE   JOHNSON
BEFORE CHANGE  stewart
AFTER CHANGE   STEWART
BEFORE CHANGE  franklin
AFTER CHANGE   FRANKLIN
BEFORE CHANGE  schultz
AFTER CHANGE   SCHULTZ
BEFORE CHANGE  willard
AFTER CHANGE   WILLARD
EXECUTING COMMIT
BEFORE CHANGE  turnbull
AFTER CHANGE   TURNBULL
*** NO MORE RECORDS TO PROCESS!!
```

IMS Program

For the IMS program, you must issue the IMS CHKP call to commit both IMS and DB2 data. IMS programming is beyond the scope of this exam, but you do need to know a few things about use of the DB2 COMMIT statement in an IMS program:

1. In an IMS program, the DB2 COMMIT statement will not commit DB2 changes.

2. IMS/DB2 will not tell you that your DB2 COMMIT statement didn't work – it will not generate an error, the COMMIT statement will simply have no effect.

3. You must use the IMS CHKP statement to commit both IMS and DB2 data.

4. Similarly, if you want to back out uncommitted DB2 changes, the ROLLBACK statement will not work. You must use the IMS ROLL or ROLB statements.

5. ROLB means that any changes are backed out to the last checkpoint, and then control is returned to the calling program which can continue processing. ROLL means that any changes are backed out to the last checkpoint, and then the program is terminated with abend code U0778.

349

Stored Procedures

A stored procedure is a set of compiled statements that is stored on the DB2 server. The stored procedures typically include SQL statements to access data in a DB2 table. Stored procedures are similar to sub-programs in that they can be called by other programs. Specifically, stored procedures are invoked by the CALL statement as in:

```
CALL <stored procedure name><(parameters)>
```

Stored procedures can be called from an application program such as COBOL, from a Rexx exec, from QMF or from Data Studio. Stored procedures are created using the CREATE PROCEDURE statement. The details of the stored procedure depend on whether it is external or native. We'll look at examples of each.

Types of stored procedures

There are three types of stored procedures:

- Native SQL Procedure
- External stored procedure
- External SQL Procedure

Native SQL procedures

A native SQL procedure is a procedure that consists exclusively of SQL statements, and is created entirely within the CREATE PROCEDURE statement. Native SQL procedures are not associated with an external program.

External stored procedures

An external stored procedure is one written in a programming language such as COBOL or Java.

External SQL procedures

An external SQL procedure is a procedure that is composed of SQL statements, and is created and implemented like an external stored procedure (including having an external program).

External Stored Procedure Programming Languages.

When you want to create an external stored procedure, the the following programming languages can be used:

- Assembler
- C

350

- C++
- COBOL
- REXX
- PL/I

Examples of Stored Procedures

Native SQL Stored Procedure

Let's start with a procedure that will return the first and last names of an employee, given an employee number. We will pass employee number as an IN parameter and receive the employee's first and last names as OUT parameters. Since we are only using SQL statements, we will specify the SQL language in the definition, and specify our intent to read data.

```
CREATE PROCEDURE GETEMP (IN EMP_NO INT,
  OUT EMP_LNAME VARCHAR(30),
  OUT EMP_FNAME VARCHAR(20))

LANGUAGE SQL
READS SQL DATA

  BEGIN
     SELECT EMP_LAST_NAME,
            EMP_FIRST_NAME
     INTO EMP_LNAME,
          EMP_FNAME
     FROM HRSCHEMA.EMPLOYEE
     WHERE EMP_ID = EMP_NO;
  END
```

Now we need a program to call the stored procedure. Here is a PLI program to do that.

```
PLIEMP6: PROCEDURE OPTIONS(MAIN) REORDER;

/********************************************************************
*                                                                  *
* PROGRAM NAME :   PLIEMP6 - PROGRAM TO CALL A STORED PROCEDURE.    *
*                                                                  *
********************************************************************/

/********************************************************************
*                 E X T E R N A L   E N T R I E S                   *
********************************************************************/

   DCL DSNTIAR ENTRY OPTIONS(ASM INTER RETCODE);
```

```
/*********************************************************************
*                  W O R K I N G   S T O R A G E                    *
*********************************************************************/

   DCL HV_ID              FIXED BIN (31) INIT (0);
   DCL HV_LAST_NAME       CHAR(30) INIT (' ');
   DCL HV_FIRST_NAME      CHAR(20) INIT (' ');

   DCL 01 ERR_REC,
          05 FILLER1            CHAR(10) INIT ('SQLCODE = '),
          05 SQLCODE_VIEW       PIC '-999',
          05 ERR_EMPID          FIXED BIN (31) INIT (0),
          05 FILLER2            CHAR(01) INIT (' '),
          05 ERR_TAB            CHAR(08) INIT (' '),
          05 ERR_PARA           CHAR(15) INIT (' ');

   DCL 01 ERR_MSG AUTOMATIC,
          05 ERR_LGTH           FIXED BIN (31) INIT (864),
          05 ERR_TXT(10)        CHAR(72);

   DCL ERR_TXT_LGTH            FIXED BIN (15) INIT (72);
   DCL ERR_NDX                FIXED BIN (31) INIT (0);

   EXEC SQL
     INCLUDE SQLCA;

   EXEC SQL
     INCLUDE EMPLOYEE;

/*********************************************************************
/*                  P R O G R A M   M A I N L I N E                 *
*********************************************************************/

   PUT SKIP LIST ('SAMPLE PLI PROGRAM: CALL STORED PROCEDURE');

         DCLEMPLOYEE = '';

     /* SELECT AN EMPLOYEE */

         HV_ID = 3217;

         EXEC SQL
            CALL HRSCHEMA.GETEMP(:HV_ID,
                                 :HV_LAST_NAME,
                                 :HV_FIRST_NAME);

         IF SQLCODE ¬= 0 THEN
            DO;
                SQLCODE_VIEW = SQLCODE;
                ERR_TAB = 'EMPLOYEE';
                ERR_PARA = 'MAIN';
                ERR_EMPID = HV_ID;
                CALL P9999_SQL_ERROR;
```

352

```
            END;

        ELSE
          PUT SKIP LIST ('PROC CALL SUCCESSFUL '
                    || TRIM(HV_LAST_NAME)
                    || ' ' || TRIM(HV_FIRST_NAME)
                    || ' ' || HV_ID);


P9999_SQL_ERROR: PROC;

    PUT SKIP LIST (ERR_REC);

    CALL DSNTIAR (SQLCA, ERR_MSG, ERR_TXT_LGTH);

    IF RETCODE = 0 THEN
       DO ERR_NDX = 1 TO 10;
          PUT SKIP DATA (ERR_TXT(ERR_NDX));
       END; /* DO */
    ELSE
       PUT SKIP LIST ('DSNTIAR ERROR CODE = ' || RETCODE);

END P9999_SQL_ERROR;

END PLIEMP6;
```

And here is the result of the run:

```
        SAMPLE PLI PROGRAM: CALL STORED PROCEDURE
        PROC CALL SUCCESSFUL JOHNSON EDWARD          3217
```

External Stored Procedure

Now let's do the same procedure but we'll make it an external procedure and we'll implement it in PLI. First let's define the procedure and we'll call it GETEMP2. Note: it is important to specify the correct WLM environment for external procedures. You might need to check with your DBA or system admin for this information.

```
        CREATE PROCEDURE HRSCHEMA.GETEMP2P
        (IN EMP_NO INT,
         OUT EMP_LNAME VARCHAR(30),
         OUT EMP_FNAME VARCHAR(20))

        LANGUAGE PLI
        READS SQL DATA
        EXTERNAL NAME "PLIEMP7"
        COLLID HRSCHEMA
        ASUTIME NO LIMIT
        PARAMETER STYLE GENERAL
```

353

```
        STAY RESIDENT NO
        WLM ENVIRONMENT DB2XENV1
        PROGRAM TYPE MAIN
        SECURITY DB2
        RESULT SETS 0
        COMMIT ON RETURN NO
```

Now we need to write the PLI program. Here is one that will perform this task.

```
PLIEMP7: PROCEDURE (LK_EMP_VARIABLES);
/*******************************************************************
*                                                                 *
* PROGRAM NAME :   PLIEMP7 - PROGRAM USED AS A STORED PROCEDURE.   *
*                                                                 *
*******************************************************************/

/*******************************************************************
*                E X T E R N A L   E N T R I E S                   *
*******************************************************************/

   DCL DSNTIAR ENTRY OPTIONS(ASM INTER RETCODE);

/*******************************************************************
*                W O R K I N G   S T O R A G E                     *
*******************************************************************/

   DCL 01 LK_EMP_VARIABLES,
          05  HV_ID            FIXED BIN (31),
          05  HV_LAST_NAME     CHAR(30),
          05  HV_FIRST_NAME    CHAR(20);

   DCL 01 ERR_REC,
          05 FILLER1           CHAR(10) INIT ('SQLCODE = '),
          05 SQLCODE_VIEW       PIC '-999',
          05 ERR_EMPID          FIXED BIN (31) INIT (0),
          05 FILLER2            CHAR(01) INIT (' '),
          05 ERR_TAB            CHAR(08) INIT (' '),
          05 ERR_PARA           CHAR(15) INIT (' ');

   DCL 01 ERR_MSG AUTOMATIC,
          05 ERR_LGTH           FIXED BIN (31) INIT (864),
          05 ERR_TXT(10)        CHAR(72);

   DCL ERR_TXT_LGTH            FIXED BIN (15) INIT (72);
   DCL ERR_NDX                 FIXED BIN (31) INIT (0);


   EXEC SQL
     INCLUDE SQLCA;

   EXEC SQL
     INCLUDE EMPLOYEE;
```

354

```
/******************************************************************
/*                P R O G R A M   M A I N L I N E               *
/******************************************************************/

     PUT SKIP LIST ('SAMPLE PLI PROGRAM: CALLED STORED PROCEDURE');

          DCLEMPLOYEE = '';

       /* SELECT AN EMPLOYEE */

          EXEC SQL
             SELECT EMP_LAST_NAME,
                    EMP_FIRST_NAME
             INTO  :HV_LAST_NAME,
                   :HV_FIRST_NAME
             FROM HRSCHEMA.EMPLOYEE
             WHERE EMP_ID = :HV_ID;

          IF SQLCODE ¬= 0 THEN
             DO;
                SQLCODE_VIEW = SQLCODE;
                ERR_TAB = 'EMPLOYEE';
                ERR_PARA = 'MAIN';
                ERR_EMPID  = HV_ID;
                CALL P9999_SQL_ERROR;
             END;


     P9999_SQL_ERROR: PROC;

        PUT SKIP LIST (ERR_REC);

        CALL DSNTIAR (SQLCA, ERR_MSG, ERR_TXT_LGTH);

        IF RETCODE = 0 THEN
           DO ERR_NDX = 1 TO 10;
              PUT SKIP DATA (ERR_TXT(ERR_NDX));
           END; /* DO */
        ELSE
           PUT SKIP LIST ('DSNTIAR ERROR CODE = ' || RETCODE);

     END P9999_SQL_ERROR;

END PLIEMP7;
```

Now we need a program to call the external stored procedure. We can clone the one we used to call the native stored procedure. That was PLIEMP6 and all we need to do is change the name of the procedure we are calling. The new program name is PLIEMP8.

```
PLIEMP8: PROCEDURE OPTIONS(MAIN) REORDER;
/**********************************************************************
*                                                                    *
* PROGRAM NAME :   PLIEMP8 - PROGRAM TO CALL A STORED PROCEDURE.      *
*                                                                    *
**********************************************************************/

/**********************************************************************
*                E X T E R N A L   E N T R I E S                      *
**********************************************************************/

   DCL DSNTIAR ENTRY OPTIONS(ASM INTER RETCODE);

/**********************************************************************
*                W O R K I N G   S T O R A G E                        *
**********************************************************************/

   DCL HV_ID            FIXED BIN (31) INIT (0);
   DCL HV_LAST_NAME     CHAR(30) INIT (' ');
   DCL HV_FIRST_NAME    CHAR(20) INIT (' ');

   DCL 01 ERR_REC,
          05 FILLER1            CHAR(10) INIT ('SQLCODE = '),
          05 SQLCODE_VIEW       PIC '-999',
          05 ERR_EMPID          FIXED BIN (31) INIT (0),
          05 FILLER2            CHAR(01) INIT (' '),
          05 ERR_TAB            CHAR(08) INIT (' '),
          05 ERR_PARA           CHAR(15) INIT (' ');

   DCL 01 ERR_MSG AUTOMATIC,
          05 ERR_LGTH           FIXED BIN (31) INIT (864),
          05 ERR_TXT(10)        CHAR(72);

   DCL ERR_TXT_LGTH             FIXED BIN (15) INIT (72);
   DCL ERR_NDX                  FIXED BIN (31) INIT (0);

   EXEC SQL
     INCLUDE SQLCA;

   EXEC SQL
     INCLUDE EMPLOYEE;

/**********************************************************************
/*               P R O G R A M   M A I N L I N E                      *
**********************************************************************/

   PUT SKIP LIST ('SAMPLE PLI PROGRAM: CALL STORED PROCEDURE');

        DCLEMPLOYEE = '';

     /* SELECT AN EMPLOYEE */

        HV_ID = 3217;
```

```
        EXEC SQL
            CALL HRSCHEMA.GETEMP2P(:HV_ID,
                                    :HV_LAST_NAME,
                                    :HV_FIRST_NAME);

        IF SQLCODE ¬= 0 THEN
            DO;
                SQLCODE_VIEW = SQLCODE;
                ERR_TAB = 'EMPLOYEE';
                ERR_PARA = 'MAIN';
                ERR_EMPID = HV_ID;
                CALL P9999_SQL_ERROR;
            END;

        ELSE
            PUT SKIP LIST ('PROC CALL SUCCESSFUL '
                            || TRIM(HV_LAST_NAME)
                            || ' ' || TRIM(HV_FIRST_NAME)
                            || ' ' || HV_ID);


    P9999_SQL_ERROR: PROC;

        PUT SKIP LIST (ERR_REC);

        CALL DSNTIAR (SQLCA, ERR_MSG, ERR_TXT_LGTH);

        IF RETCODE = 0 THEN
            DO ERR_NDX = 1 TO 10;
                PUT SKIP DATA (ERR_TXT(ERR_NDX));
            END; /* DO */
        ELSE
            PUT SKIP LIST ('DSNTIAR ERROR CODE = ' || RETCODE);

    END P9999_SQL_ERROR;

END PLIEMP8;
```

Now when we run this program, it will call the stored procedure and display these results:

```
    SAMPLE PLI PROGRAM: CALL STORED PROCEDURE
    PROC CALL SUCCESSFUL JOHNSON EDWARD               3217
```

Stored Procedure Error Handling

So far the stored procedures we've created did not encounter error conditions. Let's refine our GETEMP stored procedure to handle unexpected SQL codes. One especially good thing about native SQL procedures is that when you call them the SQL code is reflected in the SQLCA of the calling program. So you need only interrogate the SQLCODE as you normally would to detect an error.

Let's try running our PLIEMP6 (which calls GETEMP) and specify a nonexistent employee id, for example 3218. If we run this, here is the output we'll receive:

```
SAMPLE PLI PROGRAM: CALL STORED PROCEDURE
SQLCODE = -305      GETEMP          MAIN            000003218
 DSNT408I SQLCODE = -305, ERROR:  THE NULL VALUE CANNOT BE ASSIGNED TO
          OUTPUT HOST VARIABLE NUMBER 2 BECAUSE NO INDICATOR VARIABLE IS
          SPECIFIED
 DSNT418I SQLSTATE    = 22002 SQLSTATE RETURN CODE
 DSNT415I SQLERRP     = DSNXROHB SQL PROCEDURE DETECTING ERROR
 DSNT416I SQLERRD     = -115  0   0   -1   0   0 SQL DIAGNOSTIC INFORMATION
 DSNT416I SQLERRD     = X'FFFFFF8D'  X'00000000'  X'00000000'
          X'FFFFFFFF'  X'00000000'  X'00000000' SQL DIAGNOSTIC
          INFORMATION
```

This result indicates that our query in the GETEMP procedure did not return a value. The problem is that we didn't define indicator variables in our COBOL program and use them in the call to the stored procedure. Indicator variables are used to identify a situation where a NULL value was encountered in a query. This is important since a DB2 NULL value cannot be loaded into the specified PLI host variable. PLI does not know what a DB2 NULL value is, so you must add indicator variables to your query to prevent the -305 SQL result.

Once a query completes you can check the indicator variable and if its value is -1, that means a NULL was encountered for that column and the value in the host variable is a default value (typically zero for numeric variables and space for character variables). The query does not fail and you can decide what to do with the default result value (if anything).

Let's define indicator variables in our PLIEMP6 program for the EMP_FIRST_NAME and EMP_LAST_NAME columns.

```
DCL 01 HV_INDICATOR_VARS,
       10  IND_HV_LAST_NAME  FIXED BIN (15) INIT(0),
       10  IND_HV_FIRST_NAME FIXED BIN (15) INIT(0);
```

Now these indicator variables must be used in the query. So our call to the GETEMP stored procedure becomes:

```
CALL HRSCHEMA.GETEMP2(:HV_ID,
                      :HV_LAST-NAME: IND_HV_LAST_NAME,
                      :HV-FIRST-NAME: IND_HV_FIRST_NAME)
```

358

Now when we call the stored procedure we will get a +100 SQLCODE which simply means the record for employee 3218 was not found.

```
SAMPLE PLI PROGRAM: CALL STORED PROCEDURE
SQLCODE =  100      GETEMP         MAIN           000003218
 DSNT404I SQLCODE = 100, NOT FOUND:   ROW NOT FOUND FOR FETCH, UPDATE, OR
DELETE, OR THE RESULT OF A QUERY IS AN EMPTY TABLE
 DSNT418I SQLSTATE   = 02000 SQLSTATE RETURN CODE
 DSNT415I SQLERRP    = DSNXRFF SQL PROCEDURE DETECTING ERROR
 DSNT416I SQLERRD    = -110  0  0  -1  0  0 SQL DIAGNOSTIC INFORMATION
 DSNT416I SQLERRD    = X'FFFFFF92'  X'00000000'  X'00000000'
           X'FFFFFFFF'  X'00000000'  X'00000000' SQL DIAGNOSTIC
           INFORMATION
```

Unlike native SQL procedures, when you call an external stored procedure you cannot use the calling program's SQLCODE value to determine the status of the procedure. However you can define additional OUT parameters to pass back information to the calling program. For example, in our PLIEMP7 program we have parameter named **LK_EMP_VARIABLES** being passed into the program. It is defined in the program as a structure as follows:

```
DCL 01 LK_EMP_VARIABLES,
       05  HV_ID          FIXED BIN (31),
       05  HV_LAST_NAME   CHAR(30),
       05  HV_FIRST_NAME  CHAR(20);
```

You can add some diagnostic variables to the stored procedure OUT parameter list, such as SQLCODE, SQLSTATE and message (the latter to send a customized message back to the calling program). Recall that program COBEMP7 is associated with stored procedure GETEMP2, so let's add the new variables to GETEMP2:

```
CREATE PROCEDURE HRSCHEMA.GETEMP2
(IN EMP_NO INT,
 OUT EMP_LNAME VARCHAR(30),
 OUT EMP_FNAME VARCHAR(20),
 OUT PRM_SQLCODE INT,
 OUT PRM_SQLSTATE CHAR(5),
 OUT PRM_MESSAGE  CHAR(80))
```

You would also need to add these variables to the program linkage variable list.

```
DCL 01 LK_EMP_VARIABLES,
       05  HV_ID          FIXED BIN (31),
       05  HV_LAST_NAME   CHAR(30),
       05  HV_FIRST_NAME  CHAR(20)
```

359

```
05  PRM_SQLCODE    CHAR(5),
05  PRM_SQLSTATE   CHAR(5),
05  PRM_MESSAGE    CHARX(80);
```

Now if an error is encountered you can assign the diagnostic values to your parameter variables:

```
PRM_SQLCODE  = SQLCODE;
PRM_SQLSTATE = SQLSTATE;
PRM_MESSAGE  = 'ERROR IN PROC GETEMP';
```

Since these variables are OUT parameters, they will be returned to the calling program and you can interrogate the values for diagnostic purposes.

More Stored Procedure Examples

Let's do a few more examples of stored procedures, and in this case we'll create some data access routines. Specifically we'll create stored procedures to retrieve information for an employee, to add or update an employee, and to delete an employee.

For retrieving employee data, we'll simply expand our GETEMP procedure to include all of the original fields we created the table with. We'll call the new procedure GET_EMP_INFO.

```
CREATE PROCEDURE HRSCHEMA.GET_EMP_INFO
(IN EMP_NO INT,
 OUT EMP_LNAME VARCHAR(30),
 OUT EMP_FNAME VARCHAR(20),
 OUT EMP_SRVC_YRS INT,
 OUT EMP_PROM_DATE DATE,
 OUT EMP_PROF XML,
 OUT EMP_SSN  CHAR(09))

LANGUAGE SQL
READS SQL DATA

BEGIN
   SELECT EMP_LAST_NAME,
          EMP_FIRST_NAME,
          EMP_SERVICE_YEARS,
          EMP_SERVICE_YEARS,
          EMP_PROMOTION_DATE,
          EMP_PROFILE,
          EMP_SSN
     INTO EMP_LNAME,
          EMP_FNAME,
          EMP_SRVC_YRS,
          EMP_PROM_DATE,
```

```
                    EMP_PROF,
                    EMP_SSN
            FROM HRSCHEMA.EMPLOYEE
            WHERE EMP_ID = EMP_NO;

        END #
```

Next, we'll create a procedure that merges the input data into the table, either adding it if it is a new record, or updating it if an old record.

```
CREATE PROCEDURE HRSCHEMA.MRG_EMP_INFO
(IN EMP_NO INT,
 IN EMP_LNAME VARCHAR(30),
 IN EMP_FNAME VARCHAR(20),
 IN EMP_SRVC_YRS INT,
 IN EMP_PROM_DATE DATE,
 IN EMP_PROF XML,
 IN EMP_SSN  CHAR(09))


LANGUAGE SQL
MODIFIES SQL DATA

BEGIN
    MERGE INTO HRSCHEMA.EMPLOYEE AS T
    USING
     (VALUES (EMP_NO,
     EMP_LNAME,
     EMP_FNAME,
     EMP_SRVC_YRS,
     EMP_PROM_DATE,
     EMP_PROF,
     EMP_SSN))
    AS S
    (EMP_ID,
     EMP_LAST_NAME,
     EMP_FIRST_NAME,
     EMP_SERVICE_YEARS,
     EMP_PROMOTION_DATE,
     EMP_PROFILE,
     EMP_SSN)
    ON S.EMP_ID = T.EMP_ID

    WHEN MATCHED
      THEN UPDATE
        SET EMP_ID              = S.EMP_ID,
            EMP_LAST_NAME       = S.EMP_LAST_NAME,
            EMP_FIRST_NAME      = S.EMP_FIRST_NAME,
            EMP_SERVICE_YEARS   = S.EMP_SERVICE_YEARS,
            EMP_PROMOTION_DATE  = S.EMP_PROMOTION_DATE,
            EMP_PROFILE         = S.EMP_PROFILE,
```

```
                    EMP_SSN                 = S.EMP_SSN

          WHEN NOT MATCHED
             THEN INSERT
                VALUES (S.EMP_ID,
                S.EMP_LAST_NAME,
                S.EMP_FIRST_NAME,
                S.EMP_SERVICE_YEARS,
                S.EMP_PROMOTION_DATE,
                S.EMP_PROFILE,
                S.EMP_SSN) ;

       END #
```

Finally, let's take care of the delete function. This one is easy.

```
     CREATE PROCEDURE HRSCHEMA.DLT_EMP_INFO
     (IN EMP_NO INT)

      LANGUAGE SQL
      MODIFIES SQL DATA

      BEGIN
         DELETE FROM HRSCHEMA.EMPLOYEE
         WHERE EMP_ID = EMP_NO;

      END #
```

Before we can use these procedures we must grant access to them. In our case we will grant to PUBLIC, but normally you will grant access only to your developer and user groups.

```
     GRANT EXECUTE ON PROCEDURE HRSCHEMA.GET_EMP_INFO TO PUBLIC;

     GRANT EXECUTE ON PROCEDURE HRSCHEMA.MRG_EMP_INFO TO PUBLIC;

     GRANT EXECUTE ON PROCEDURE HRSCHEMA.DLT_EMP_INFO TO PUBLIC;
```

Next we need a PLI program to test each of these stored procedures. Here is one that works:

```
PLIEMPH: PROCEDURE OPTIONS(MAIN) REORDER;

/******************************************************************
* PROGRAM NAME :   PLIEMPH - CALL SEVERAL STORED PROCEDURES      *
*                            FOR DATA ACCESS.                    *
******************************************************************/
```

```
/********************************************************************
*             E X T E R N A L    E N T R I E S                     *
********************************************************************/

   DCL DSNTIAR ENTRY OPTIONS(ASM INTER RETCODE);

/********************************************************************
/*              W O R K I N G    S T O R A G E                     *
********************************************************************/

   DCL COMMIT_CTR              FIXED BIN(31) INIT(0);
   DCL RET_SQL_CODE            FIXED BIN(31) INIT(0);
   DCL RET_SQL_CODE_PIC        PIC 'S999999999' INIT (0);

   DCL 01 ERR_REC,
         05 FILLER1            CHAR(10) INIT ('SQLCODE = '),
         05 SQLCODE_VIEW       PIC '-999',
         05 ERR_EMPID          FIXED BIN (31) INIT (0),
         05 FILLER2            CHAR(01) INIT (' '),
         05 ERR_TAB            CHAR(08) INIT (' '),
         05 ERR_PARA           CHAR(15) INIT (' ');

   DCL 01 ERR_MSG AUTOMATIC,
         05 ERR_LGTH           FIXED BIN (31) INIT (864),
         05 ERR_TXT(10)        CHAR(72);

   DCL ERR_TXT_LGTH            FIXED BIN (15) INIT (72);
   DCL ERR_NDX                 FIXED BIN (31) INIT (0);


   DCL 01 HV_INDICATOR_VARS,
      10  IND_HV_LAST_NAME  FIXED BIN (15) INIT(0),
      10  IND_HV_FIRST_NAME FIXED BIN (15) INIT(0),
      10  IND_HV_SRVC_YEARS FIXED BIN (15) INIT(0),
      10  IND_HV_PROM_DATE  FIXED BIN (15) INIT(0),
      10  IND_HV_PROFILE    FIXED BIN (15) INIT(0),
      10  IND_HV_SSN        FIXED BIN (15) INIT(0);

   EXEC SQL
     INCLUDE SQLCA;

   EXEC SQL
     INCLUDE EMPLOYEE;



/********************************************************************
/*              P R O G R A M    M A I N L I N E                   *
********************************************************************/

   PUT SKIP LIST ('SAMPLE PLI PROGRAM: CALL SOME STORED PROCEDURE');

   PUT SKIP LIST ('DISPLAY MERGE EMPLOYEE INFORMATION');
```

```
EMP_ID                = 7938;
EMP_LAST_NAME         = 'WINFIELD';
EMP_FIRST_NAME        = 'STANLEY';
EMP_SERVICE_YEARS     = +3;
EMP_PROMOTION_DATE    = ' ';
IND_HV_PROM_DATE      = -1;
EMP_PROFILE           = ' ';
IND_HV_PROFILE        = -1;
EMP_SSN               = '382734509';

EXEC SQL

    CALL HRSCHEMA.MRG_EMP_INFO
        (:EMP_ID,
         :EMP_LAST_NAME        :IND_HV_LAST_NAME,
         :EMP_FIRST_NAME       :IND_HV_FIRST_NAME,
         :EMP_SERVICE_YEARS    :IND_HV_SRVC_YEARS,
         :EMP_PROMOTION_DATE   :IND_HV_PROM_DATE,
         :EMP_PROFILE          :IND_HV_PROFILE,
         :EMP_SSN              :IND_HV_SSN);

    IF SQLCODE ¬= 0 THEN
        DO;
            PUT SKIP LIST ('MERGE CALL FAILED ' || EMP_ID);
            SQLCODE_VIEW     =  SQLCODE;
            ERR_TAB          = 'EMPLOYEE';
            ERR_PARA         = 'MAIN';
            ERR_DETAIL       = EMP_ID;
            CALL P9999_SQL_ERROR;
        END;

    ELSE
        DO;
            PUT SKIP LIST ('MERGE CALL SUCCESSFUL ' || EMP_ID);
            PUT SKIP LIST (EMP_LAST_NAME);
            PUT SKIP LIST (EMP_FIRST_NAME);
            PUT SKIP LIST (EMP_SERVICE_YEARS);
            PUT SKIP LIST (EMP_PROMOTION_DATE);
            PUT SKIP LIST (EMP_SSN);
        END;

PUT SKIP LIST ('DISPLAY EMPLOYEE INFORMATION');

EMP_ID = 7938;

EXEC SQL

    CALL HRSCHEMA.GET_EMP_INFO
        (:EMP_ID,
         :EMP_LAST_NAME        :IND_HV_LAST_NAME,
         :EMP_FIRST_NAME       :IND_HV_FIRST_NAME,
         :EMP_SERVICE_YEARS    :IND_HV_SRVC_YEARS,
         :EMP_PROMOTION_DATE   :IND_HV_PROM_DATE,
```

```
            :EMP_PROFILE           :IND_HV_PROFILE,
            :EMP_SSN               :IND_HV_SSN);

     IF SQLCODE ¬= 0 THEN
        DO;
           PUT SKIP LIST ('GET CALL FAILED ' || EMP_ID);
           SQLCODE_VIEW     =  SQLCODE;
           ERR_TAB          = 'EMPLOYEE';
           ERR_PARA         = 'MAIN';
           ERR_DETAIL       = EMP_ID;
           CALL P9999_SQL_ERROR;
        END;

     ELSE
        DO;
           PUT SKIP LIST ('GET CALL SUCCESSFUL ' || EMP_ID);
           PUT SKIP LIST (EMP_LAST_NAME);
           PUT SKIP LIST (EMP_FIRST_NAME);
           PUT SKIP LIST (EMP_SERVICE_YEARS);
           PUT SKIP LIST (EMP_PROMOTION_DATE);
           PUT SKIP LIST (EMP_SSN);
        END;


PUT SKIP LIST ('UPDATE EMPLOYEE INFORMATION');

EMP_ID              = 7938;
EMP_LAST_NAME       = 'WINFIELD';
EMP_FIRST_NAME      = 'SAMUEL';
EMP_SERVICE_YEARS   = +2;
EMP_PROMOTION_DATE  = ' ';
IND_HV_PROM_DATE    = -1;
EMP_PROFILE         = ' ';
IND_HV_PROFILE      = -1;
EMP_SSN             = '382734595';

EXEC SQL

   CALL HRSCHEMA.MRG_EMP_INFO
      (:EMP_ID,
       :EMP_LAST_NAME      :IND_HV_LAST_NAME,
       :EMP_FIRST_NAME     :IND_HV_FIRST_NAME,
       :EMP_SERVICE_YEARS  :IND_HV_SRVC_YEARS,
       :EMP_PROMOTION_DATE :IND_HV_PROM_DATE,
       :EMP_PROFILE        :IND_HV_PROFILE,
       :EMP_SSN            :IND_HV_SSN);

   IF SQLCODE ¬= 0 THEN
      DO;
         PUT SKIP LIST ('UPDATE MERGE CALL FAILED ' || EMP_ID);
         SQLCODE_VIEW     =  SQLCODE;
         ERR_TAB          = 'EMPLOYEE';
         ERR_PARA         = 'MAIN';
```

```
               ERR_DETAIL        = EMP_ID;
               CALL P9999_SQL_ERROR;
           END;

       ELSE
           DO;
               PUT SKIP LIST ('UPDATE MERGE CALL SUCCESSFUL ' || EMP_ID);
               PUT SKIP LIST (EMP_LAST_NAME);
               PUT SKIP LIST (EMP_FIRST_NAME);
               PUT SKIP LIST (EMP_SERVICE_YEARS);
               PUT SKIP LIST (EMP_PROMOTION_DATE);
               PUT SKIP LIST (EMP_SSN);
           END;


   PUT SKIP LIST ('DISPLAY UPDATED EMPLOYEE INFORMATION');

   EMP_ID = +7938;

   EXEC SQL

       CALL HRSCHEMA.GET_EMP_INFO
           (:EMP_ID,
            :EMP_LAST_NAME       :IND_HV_LAST_NAME,
            :EMP_FIRST_NAME      :IND_HV_FIRST_NAME,
            :EMP_SERVICE_YEARS   :IND_HV_SRVC_YEARS,
            :EMP_PROMOTION_DATE  :IND_HV_PROM_DATE,
            :EMP_PROFILE         :IND_HV_PROFILE,
            :EMP_SSN             :IND_HV_SSN);

       IF SQLCODE ¬= 0 THEN
           DO;
               PUT SKIP LIST ('GET CALL FAILED ' || EMP_ID);
               SQLCODE_VIEW    = SQLCODE;
               ERR_TAB         = 'EMPLOYEE';
               ERR_PARA        = 'MAIN';
               ERR_DETAIL      = EMP_ID;
               CALL P9999_SQL_ERROR;
           END;
       ELSE
           DO;
               PUT SKIP LIST ('GET CALL SUCCESSFUL ' || EMP_ID);
               PUT SKIP LIST (EMP_LAST_NAME);
               PUT SKIP LIST (EMP_FIRST_NAME);
               PUT SKIP LIST (EMP_SERVICE_YEARS);
               PUT SKIP LIST (EMP_PROMOTION_DATE);
               PUT SKIP LIST (EMP_SSN);
           END;

   PUT SKIP LIST ('DISPLAY DELETED EMPLOYEE INFORMATION');

   EMP_ID = 7938;
```

```
        EXEC SQL

          CALL HRSCHEMA.DLT_EMP_INFO
             (:EMP_ID);

          IF SQLCODE ¬= 0 THEN
             DO;
                PUT SKIP LIST ('DELETE CALL FAILED ' || EMP_ID);
                SQLCODE_VIEW    =  SQLCODE;
                ERR_TAB         = 'EMPLOYEE';
                ERR_PARA        = 'MAIN';
                ERR_DETAIL      = EMP_ID;
                CALL P9999_SQL_ERROR;
             END;

          ELSE
             DO;
                PUT SKIP LIST ('DELETE CALL SUCCESSFUL ' || EMP_ID);
                PUT SKIP LIST (EMP_LAST_NAME);
                PUT SKIP LIST (EMP_FIRST_NAME);
                PUT SKIP LIST (EMP_SERVICE_YEARS);
                PUT SKIP LIST (EMP_PROMOTION_DATE);
                PUT SKIP LIST (EMP_SSN);
             END;


P9999_SQL_ERROR: PROC;

   PUT SKIP LIST (ERR_REC);

   CALL DSNTIAR (SQLCA, ERR_MSG, ERR_TXT_LGTH);

   IF RETCODE = 0 THEN
      DO ERR_NDX = 1 TO 10;
         PUT SKIP DATA (ERR_TXT(ERR_NDX));
      END; /* DO */
   ELSE
      PUT SKIP LIST ('DSNTIAR ERROR CODE = ' || RETCODE);

END P9999_SQL_ERROR;

END PLIEMPH;
```

And here is the output:

```
        SAMPLE PLI PROGRAM: CALL SOME STORED PROCEDURE
        DISPLAY MERGE EMPLOYEE INFORMATION
        MERGE CALL SUCCESSFUL          7938
        WINFIELD
        STANLEY
                     3
```

```
382734509


DISPLAY EMPLOYEE INFORMATION
GET CALL SUCCESSFUL              7938
WINFIELD
STANLEY
              3


382734509


UPDATE EMPLOYEE INFORMATION
UPDATE MERGE CALL SUCCESSFUL              7938
WINFIELD
SAMUEL
              2


382734595


DISPLAY UPDATED EMPLOYEE INFORMATION
GET CALL SUCCESSFUL              7938
WINFIELD
SAMUEL
              2


382734595


DISPLAY DELETED EMPLOYEE INFORMATION
DELETE CALL SUCCESSFUL              7938
WINFIELD
SAMUEL
              2


382734595
```

This concludes our discussion of stored procedures. As you can tell, stored procedures are a very powerful technology that promotes reusability and can help minimize custom coding.

User Defined Functions

A user defined function (UDF) is one written by an application programmer or DBA, as opposed to those functions provided out of the box by DB2. UDFs extend DB2 functionality by allowing new functions to be created. As a function, a UDF always returns a value, and is called with the CALL statement.

```
CALL <UDF name><parameters>
```

Types of UDF

There are five varieties of UDFs as follows:

- SQL Scalar Function
- SQL Table Function
- External Scalar Function
- External Table Function
- Sourced Function

Examples of UDFs

SQL Scalar Function

An SQL scalar function will return a single value using only SQL statements. There is no external program. You may recall earlier we established a business rule that an employee's "level" was based on their years of service. We used an SQL with a CASE statement to return a value of JUNIOR, ADVANCED or SENIOR. Here's the SQL we used earlier:

```
SELECT EMP_ID,
EMP_LAST_NAME,
EMP_FIRST_NAME,
CASE
   WHEN EMP_SERVICE_YEARS  < 1 THEN 'ENTRY'
   WHEN EMP_SERVICE_YEARS  < 5 THEN 'ADVANCED'
   ELSE 'SENIOR'
END CASE
FROM HRSCHEMA.EMPLOYEE
---------+---------+---------+---------+---------+---------+-----
    EMP_ID  EMP_LAST_NAME    EMP_FIRST_NAME       CASE
---------+---------+---------+---------+---------+---------+-----
      3217  JOHNSON          EDWARD               ADVANCED
      7459  STEWART          BETTY                SENIOR
      9134  FRANKLIN         BRIANNA              ENTRY
      4175  TURNBULL         FRED                 ADVANCED
      4720  SCHULTZ          TIM                  SENIOR
      6288  WILLARD          JOE                  SENIOR
DSNE610I NUMBER OF ROWS DISPLAYED IS 6
```

Now let's say we have several programs that need to generate these values. We could copy the same SQL to each program, but what if the logic changes in the future? Either the cutoff years or the named literals could change. In that case it would be convenient to only have to make the change in one place. A UDF can accomplish that objective.

369

We'll create a UDF that accepts an integer which is the years of service, and then it will return the literal value that represents the employee's level of service in the company. First, we must define the UDF to DB2. We need to specify at least:

- The name of the function
- Input parameter type
- Return parameter type

Now let's code the UDF:

```
CREATE FUNCTION HRSCHEMA.EMP_LEVEL (YRS_SRVC INT)
    RETURNS VARCHAR(10)
    READS SQL DATA
    RETURN
    (SELECT
     CASE
        WHEN YRS_SRVC  < 1 THEN 'ENTRY      '
        WHEN YRS_SRVC  < 5 THEN 'ADVANCED   '
        ELSE 'SENIOR     '
     END CASE
     FROM SYSIBM.SYSDUMMY1)
```

Note that we specify SYSIBM.SYSDUMMY1 as our table. This is only to complete the SQL syntax which otherwise would fail because we don't have a source table. You can use SYSIBM.SYSDUMMY1 any time you are executing SQL that retrieves data from a built-in or user defined function.

Finally, we can run a query against the new UDF:

```
SELECT HRSCHEMA.EMP_LEVEL(7)
AS EMP_LVL
FROM SYSIBM.SYSDUMMY1;

---------+---------+---------+---------+----
   EMP_LVL
---------+---------+---------+---------+----
   SENIOR

DSNE610I NUMBER OF ROWS DISPLAYED IS 1
```

The above is a very simple example, and the SQL in this case does not actually access a table. Let's do one more that will access a table. How about a UDF that will return the full name of an employee given the employee's id number?

```
CREATE FUNCTION HRSCHEMA.EMP_FULLNAME (EMP_NO INT)
    RETURNS VARCHAR(40)
```

370

```
      READS SQL DATA
      RETURN
      SELECT
      EMP_FIRST_NAME || ' ' || EMP_LAST_NAME AS FULL_NAME
      FROM HRSCHEMA.EMPLOYEE
      WHERE EMP_ID  = EMP_NO;
```

Now let's run the query to use this UDF:

```
   SELECT HRSCHEMA.EMP_FULLNAME(3217) AS FULLNAME
   FROM SYSIBM.SYSDUMMY1;


      ---------+---------+---------+---------+----
          FULLNAME
      ---------+---------+---------+---------+----

          EDWARD JOHNSON

   DSNE610I NUMBER OF ROWS DISPLAYED IS 1
```

SQL Table Function

An SQL table function returns a table of values. Let's again replace the common table expression we used earlier. Remember it goes like this:

```
   WITH EMP_PAY_SUM (EMP_ID, EMP_PAY_TOTAL) AS
   (SELECT EMP_ID,
   SUM(EMP_PAY_AMT)
   AS EMP_PAY_TOTAL
   FROM EMP_PAY_HIST
   GROUP BY EMP_ID)

   SELECT EMP_ID,
   EMP_PAY_TOTAL
   FROM EMP_PAY_SUM
   ;

---------+---------+---------+---------+----
    EMP_ID        EMP_PAY_TOTAL
---------+---------+---------+---------+----
     3217              9166.64
     7459             13333.32
     9134             13333.32
DSNE610I NUMBER OF ROWS DISPLAYED IS 3
```

Now let's define the UDF:

```
   CREATE FUNCTION HRSCHEMA.EMP_PAY_SUM ()
      RETURNS TABLE (EMP_ID  INTEGER,
                     EMP_PAY_TOTAL DECIMAL (9,2))
      READS SQL DATA
      RETURN
```

```
SELECT EMP_ID,
SUM(EMP_PAY_AMT)
AS EMP_PAY_TOTAL
FROM EMP_PAY_HIST
GROUP BY EMP_ID
```

And then we'll call it using SPUFI. Notice that we invoke the **TABLE** function to return the values generated by the EMP_PAY_SUM UDF.

```
SELECT * FROM TABLE(HRSCHEMA.EMP_PAY_SUM()) AS EPS
---------+---------+---------+---------+---------+---
    EMP_ID  EMP_PAY_TOTAL
---------+---------+---------+---------+---------+---
      3217        9166.64
      7459       13333.32
      9134       13333.32
DSNE610I NUMBER OF ROWS DISPLAYED IS 3
```

External Scalar Function

An external scalar function is one that returns a single scalar value, usually based on some parameter value that is passed in. The function is implemented using a program, hence the designation as an "external" function.

You may recall earlier we created a UDF that returned a string value for an employee "level" based on the years of service. We could create a similar external UDF using a program. To create the PLI version of our function, we will create EMP_LEVEL2P.

```
CREATE FUNCTION HRSCHEMA.EMP_LEVEL2P (INT)
RETURNS VARCHAR(10)
EXTERNAL NAME 'EMPLEVEP'
LANGUAGE PLI
NOSQL
FENCED
PARAMETER STYLE SQL
---------+---------+---------+---------+---------+-------
DSNE616I STATEMENT EXECUTION WAS SUCCESSFUL, SQLCODE IS 0
```

Now we need to implement this procedure by way of an external program named EMPLEVEP (the name of the external program must match what we specified above in the EXTERNAL NAME clause). Although in this case we will use PLI, the external portion of a UDF can be written in any of these languages:

- ASSEMBLER
- C or C++

372

- COBOL
- JAVA
- PL/I

Here is the PLI program code.

```
EMPLEVEP: PROCEDURE (LK_EMP_VARIABLES);

/*****************************************************************
* PROGRAM NAME :    EMPLEVEP - PROGRAM USED AS A USER DEFINED    *
*                              FUNCTION.                         *
*****************************************************************/

/*****************************************************************
*               E X T E R N A L   E N T R I E S                 *
*****************************************************************/

   DCL DSNTIAR ENTRY OPTIONS(ASM INTER RETCODE);

/*****************************************************************
/*              W O R K I N G   S T O R A G E                   *
*****************************************************************/

   DCL 01 LK_EMP_VARIABLES,
          10  LK_YEARS          FIXED BIN(31),
          10  LK_EMP_LEVEL      CHAR(10);

/*****************************************************************
/*              P R O G R A M   M A I N L I N E                 *
*****************************************************************/

   PUT SKIP LIST ('SAMPLE PLI PROGRAM: USER DEFINED FUNCTION');

  /* DETERMINE EMPLOYEE SERVICE LEVEL BASED ON YEARS OF SERVICE */

     SELECT(LK_YEARS);

        WHEN (0)        LK_EMP_LEVEL = 'ENTRY';
        WHEN (1,2,3,4)  LK_EMP_LEVEL = 'ADVANCED';
        OTHERWISE       LK_EMP_LEVEL = 'SENIOR';

     END; /* SELECT */


END EMPLEVEP;
```

Now we can call this function from another program or even from SPUFI:

```
SELECT HRSCHEMA.EMP_LEVEL2P(0) AS EMP_LVL
FROM SYSIBM.SYSDUMMY1;
```

```
---------+---------+---------+---------+----
    EMP_LVL
---------+---------+---------+---------+----

    ENTRY


    SELECT HRSCHEMA.EMP_LEVEL2P(2) AS EMP_LVL
    FROM SYSIBM.SYSDUMMY1;

---------+---------+---------+---------+----
    EMP_LVL
---------+---------+---------+---------+----

    ADVANCED


    SELECT HRSCHEMA.EMP_LEVEL2P(7) AS EMP_LVL
    FROM SYSIBM.SYSDUMMY1;
---------+---------+---------+---------+----
    EMP_LVL
---------+---------+---------+---------+----

    SENIOR
```

External Table Function

An external table function returns a table of values. Here we could use such a function as a replacement for the common table expression we used earlier in this study guide. Let's first return to that.

```
    WITH EMP_PAY_SUM (EMP_ID, EMP_PAY_TOTAL) AS
    (SELECT EMP_ID,
    SUM(EMP_PAY_AMT)
    AS EMP_PAY_TOTAL
    FROM EMP_PAY_HIST
    GROUP BY EMP_ID)

    SELECT EMP_ID,
    EMP_PAY_TOTAL
    FROM EMP_PAY_SUM;


---------+---------+---------+---------+----
    EMP_ID         EMP_PAY_TOTAL
---------+---------+---------+---------+----
      3217              9166.64
      7459             13333.32
      9134             13333.32
DSNE610I NUMBER OF ROWS DISPLAYED IS 3
```

374

Normally common table expressions are used with complex SQL to simplify things. Ours is not very complex, but we could simplify even further by using a UDF instead of the common table expression. To do this, let's define the UDF:

```
CREATE FUNCTION HRSCHEMA.EMP_PAY_SUMP ()
RETURNS TABLE (EMP_ID    INTEGER,
              EMP_PAY_TOTAL DECIMAL (9,2) )
EXTERNAL NAME EMPPAYTP
LANGUAGE PLI
PARAMETER STYLE DB2SQL
READS SQL DATA
RESULTS SETS 1
FENCED
```

Now let's create our PLI program that implements the UDF. This can be done by defining a cursor to return a result set to the calling program.

```
EMPPAYTP: PROCEDURE (MAIN);
/*********************************************************************
* PROGRAM NAME :   EMPPAYTP - EXTERNAL TABLEFUNCTION FOR EMP_PAY.  *
*********************************************************************/

/*********************************************************************
*                 E X T E R N A L   E N T R I E S                    *
*********************************************************************/

   DCL DSNTIAR ENTRY OPTIONS(ASM INTER RETCODE);

/*********************************************************************
/*               W O R K I N G   S T O R A G E                      *
*********************************************************************/

   EXEC SQL
     INCLUDE SQLCA;

   EXEC SQL
     INCLUDE EMPPAYTL;

   EXEC SQL
     DECLARE EMP_PAY_CSR CURSOR WITH RETURN FOR
     SELECT EMP_ID,
     SUM(EMP_PAY_AMT)
     AS EMP_PAY_TOTAL
     FROM HRSCHEMA.EMP_PAY_HIST
     GROUP BY EMP_ID;

/*********************************************************************
/*               P R O G R A M   M A I N L I N E                    *
*********************************************************************/
```

```
       PUT SKIP LIST ('SAMPLE PLI PROGRAM: EXTERNAL TABLE FUNCTION');

       EXEC SQL OPEN EMP_PAY_CSR;

       PUT SKIP LIST ('OPEN CURSOR SQLCODE: ' || SQLCODE);

   END EMPPAYTP;
```

We could call the UDF either in SPUFI or with a program such as the following.

```
   PLIEMPA: PROCEDURE OPTIONS(MAIN);

   /*******************************************************************
    * PROGRAM NAME :   PLIEMPA - PROGRAM TO CALL EMP_PAY_SUM UDF.     *
    *******************************************************************/

   /*******************************************************************
    *                 E X T E R N A L   E N T R I E S                 *
    *******************************************************************/

       DCL DSNTIAR ENTRY OPTIONS(ASM INTER RETCODE);

   /*******************************************************************
   /*                W O R K I N G   S T O R A G E                    *
    *******************************************************************/

       DCL COMMIT_CTR              FIXED BIN(31) INIT(0);
       DCL RET_SQL_CODE            FIXED BIN(31) INIT(0);
       DCL RET_SQL_CODE_PIC        PIC 'S999999999' INIT (0);

       DCL 01 ERR_REC,
              05 FILLER1           CHAR(10) INIT ('SQLCODE = '),
              05 SQLCODE_VIEW      PIC '-999',
              05 ERR_EMPID         FIXED BIN (31) INIT (0),
              05 FILLER2           CHAR(01) INIT (' '),
              05 ERR_TAB           CHAR(08) INIT (' '),
              05 ERR_PARA          CHAR(15) INIT (' ');

       DCL 01 ERR_MSG AUTOMATIC,
              05 ERR_LGTH          FIXED BIN (31) INIT (864),
              05 ERR_TXT(10)       CHAR(72);

       DCL ERR_TXT_LGTH            FIXED BIN (15) INIT (72);
       DCL ERR_NDX                 FIXED BIN (31) INIT (0);

       DCL EMP_ID_PIC              PIC 'ZZZZ9999';
       DCL EMP_PAY_TTL             FIXED DEC (8,2);
       DCL EMP_PAY_TTL_PIC         PIC '999999.99';

       EXEC SQL
         INCLUDE SQLCA;
```

```
    EXEC SQL
        INCLUDE EMPPAYTL;

    EXEC SQL
        DECLARE CRSR_EMPPAYTL CURSOR FOR
        SELECT EMP_ID, EMP_PAY_TOTAL
        FROM TABLE(HRSCHEMA.EMP_PAY_SUMP()) AS EPS
        FOR READ ONLY;

/*********************************************************************
/*              P R O G R A M    M A I N L I N E                    *
*********************************************************************/

    PUT SKIP LIST ('SAMPLE PLI PROGRAM: CALL EXTERNAL TABLE
        FUNCTION');

    EXEC SQL OPEN CRSR_EMPPAYTL;

    IF SQLCODE = 0 THEN
        DO UNTIL (SQLCODE ¬= 0);
            CALL P0100_FETCH_CURSOR;
        END;
    ELSE
        PUT SKIP LIST ('BAD SQLCODE ON CURSOR OPEN = ' || SQLCODE);

    EXEC SQL CLOSE CRSR_EMPPAYTL;

    PUT SKIP LIST ('CLOSE CURSOR SQLCODE: ' || SQLCODE);

    IF SQLCODE ¬= 0 THEN
        PUT SKIP LIST ('BAD SQLCODE ON CLOSE CURSOR ' || SQLCODE);

P0100_FETCH_CURSOR: PROC;

    EXEC SQL
        FETCH CRSR_EMPPAYTL
        INTO
        :EMP_ID,
        :EMP_PAY_TTL;

    IF SQLCODE = 0 THEN
        DO;
            EMP_ID_PIC      = EMP_ID;
            EMP_PAY_TTL_PIC = EMP_PAY_TTL;
    *       PUT SKIP LIST (EMP_ID_PIC || ' ' || EMP_PAY_TTL_PIC);
        END;
    ELSE
        IF SQLCODE = +100 THEN
            PUT SKIP LIST ('*** NO MORE RECORDS TO PROCESS!!');
        ELSE
            PUT SKIP LIST ('BAD SQLCODE = ' || SQLCODE);

END P0100_FETCH_CURSOR;
```

377

```
END PLIEMPA;
```

And here are the results

```
SAMPLE PLI PROGRAM: CALL EXTERNAL TABLE FUNCTION
        3217   9166.64
        7459  13333.32
        9134  13333.32
*** NO MORE RECORDS TO PROCESS!!
CLOSE CURSOR SQLCODE:              0
```

Sourced Function

A sourced function redefines or extends an existing DB2 function. It is typically written to enable the processing of user defined data types in a function. For example, suppose you define a Canadian dollar type as follows:

```
CREATE DISTINCT TYPE HRSCHEMA.CANADIAN_DOLLAR AS DECIMAL (9,2);
```

Now create a table using this type:

```
CREATE TABLE HRSCHEMA.CAN_PAY_TBL
  (EMP_ID INT,
   PAY_DATE DATE,
   PAY_AMT CANADIAN_DOLLAR)
   IN DBMATE1.TSHRSCHEMA;
```

Now assume we've loaded 4 rows into the table, and we want to query a sum of the PAY_AMT rows. Here is our data.

```
    SELECT * FROM HRSCHEMA.CAN_PAY_TBL;

    ---------+---------+---------+---------
        EMP_ID  PAY_DATE       PAY_AMT
    ---------+---------+---------+---------
        3217  2017-01-01       5500.50
        3217  2017-02-01       5500.50
        3217  2017-03-01       5500.50
        3217  2017-04-01       5500.50
DSNE610I NUMBER OF ROWS DISPLAYED IS 4
```

And here is the summarization query:

```
    SELECT SUM(PAY_AMT) FROM HRSCHEMA.CAN_PAY_TBL;
---------+---------+---------+---------+---------+---------+--------
DSNT408I SQLCODE = -440, ERROR:  NO AUTHORIZED FUNCTION NAMED SUM HAVING
COMPATIBLE ARGUMENTS WAS FOUND
DSNT418I SQLSTATE    = 42884 SQLSTATE RETURN CODE
DSNT415I SQLERRP     = DSNXORFN SQL PROCEDURE DETECTING ERROR
DSNT416I SQLERRD     = -100 0  0  -1  0  0 SQL DIAGNOSTIC INFORMATION
DSNT416I SQLERRD     = X'FFFFFF9C' X'00000000' X'00000000' X'FFFFFFFF'
           X'00000000' X'00000000' SQL DIAGNOSTIC INFORMATION
```

We received an error because the SUM function in DB2 does not know about a CANADIAN_DOLLAR type of input parameter, so the value we passed is an "incompatible argument". To fix this we must extend the SUM function to work with CANADIAN_DOLLAR input type by creating a user defined function based on the SUM function but accepting a CANADIAN_DOLLAR argument. Try this one:

```
CREATE FUNCTION SUM(CANADIAN_DOLLAR)
RETURNS DECIMAL (9,2)
SOURCE SYSIBM.SUM(DECIMAL)
---------+---------+---------+---------+---------+---------+-----
DSNE616I STATEMENT EXECUTION WAS SUCCESSFUL, SQLCODE IS 0
```

Now you have a SUM function for which CANADIAN_DOLLAR is an input parameter. When DB2 processes the query it will use the new user defined version of the SUM function because that's the one that matches your query arguments. Your SUM query will work now.

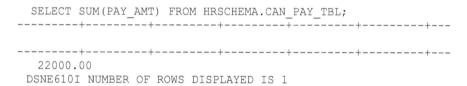

```
    SELECT SUM(PAY_AMT) FROM HRSCHEMA.CAN_PAY_TBL;
---------+---------+---------+---------+---------+---------+---------+---

---------+---------+---------+---------+---------+---------+---------+---
   22000.00
DSNE610I NUMBER OF ROWS DISPLAYED IS 1
```

This concludes the section on User Defined Functions.

Triggers

A trigger performs a set of actions when an INSERT, UPDATE or DELETE takes place. Triggers are stored in the database which is a significant advantage of using them instead of application logic.

The CREATE TRIGGER statement defines a trigger and builds a trigger package at the current server. Advantages of using a trigger include:

- Ability to write to other tables for audit trail.
- Ability to read other tables for validation.

- Ability to compare data before and after update operations.

Types of triggers

There are three types of triggers:

- INSERT
- UPDATE
- DELETE

A MERGE action also fires INSERT and UPDATE triggers (if they exist) depending on whether the MERGE causes an INSERT or UPDATE.

Timings of triggers

There are three timings of triggers as well:

- BEFORE
- AFTER
- INSTEAD OF

A BEFORE trigger performs its action before the SQL operation (INSERT, UPDATE or DELETE) that fired the trigger. An AFTER trigger performs its action after the SQL operation (INSERT, UPDATE or DELETE) that fired the trigger. An INSTEAD OF trigger is completely different that the other two timings – it enables ADD, UPDATE or DELETE operation through what would normally be a read-only view. We'll explain that more when we get to the INSTEAD OF example below.

The basic syntax of the CREATE TRIGGER statement is:

```
CREATE TRIGGER <trigger name>
<AFTER / BEFORE / INSTEAD OF>
ON <table name>
REFERENCING <see examples>
FOR EACH ROW
<action to take>
```

Examples of Triggers

Sample After Trigger

One common use of triggers is to automatically add records to a history table when there is a change to the records in a base table. In this case we will create a history table to store previous versions of pay rates in the EMP_PAY table. We can create the history table like this:

```
CREATE TABLE HRSCHEMA.EMP_PAY_HST LIKE HRSCHEMA.EMP_PAY;
```

And then we'll add an additional column to the history table to keep track of when the record was added:

```
ALTER TABLE HRSCHEMA.EMP_PAY_HST
ADD AUDIT_DATE TIMESTAMP DEFAULT CURRENT TIMESTAMP;
```

Now we will create a trigger so that when a change is made to an EMP_PAY record, we will write the old version of the record to the history table. The trigger knows about the old and new versions of the record we are modifying so we specify the OLD version of the record and the fields to be added to the history table.

```
CREATE TRIGGER HRSCHEMA.TRG_EMP_PAY
AFTER UPDATE ON HRSCHEMA.EMP_PAY_X
REFERENCING OLD AS oldcol NEW AS newcol
FOR EACH ROW MODE DB2SQL
    INSERT INTO HRSCHEMA.EMP_PAY_HST(
    EMP_ID,
    EMP_REGULAR_PAY,
    EMP_BONUS_PAY,
    AUDIT_DATE)
    VALUES
    (oldcol.EMP_ID,
    oldcol.EMP_REGULAR_PAY,
    oldcol.EMP_BONUS_PAY,
    CURRENT TIMESTAMP)
```

Now let's look at an EMP_PAY record, modify it, and then see if the old version get's added to the history table:

```
SELECT * FROM HRSCHEMA.EMP_PAY
WHERE EMP_ID = 3217;
-------+---------+---------+---------+------
    EMP_ID   EMP_REGULAR_PAY   EMP_BONUS_PAY
```

```
-------+---------+---------+---------+------
       3217          55000.00        5500.00
NE610I NUMBER OF ROWS DISPLAYED IS 1
```

Let's change the `EMP_REGULAR_PAY` to 57000.

```
UPDATE HRSCHEMA.EMP_PAY
SET EMP_REGULAR_PAY = 57000
WHERE EMP_ID = 3217;
```

Now if we select from the history table, we see the previous version of the record and it was added today:

```
SELECT * FROM HRSCHEMA.EMP_PAY_HST
  WHERE EMP_ID = 3217;
---------+---------+---------+---------+---------+---------+-----
    EMP_ID  EMP_REGULAR_PAY  EMP_BONUS_PAY  AUDIT_DATE
---------+---------+---------+---------+---------+---------+-----
      3217          55000.00         5500.00 2017-02-24-07.08.39.
DSNE610I NUMBER OF ROWS DISPLAYED IS 1
```

Note: the temporal tables introduced in DB2 10 provides more functionality for storing record history for system time enabled tables. Keep this in mind when designing your tables. But the trigger technique described above is still a very reliable way of automating the capture of record history.

Sample BEFORE Trigger

For this example, assume two tables:

- `DEPTMENT` which has department codes and descriptions.
- `EMP_DATA_X` which has an employee id, first and last names, and a department code.

Let's say we have a business rule that the department column in `EMP_DAT_X` can only have values that exist in the `DEPTMENT` table. Of course we could create a referential constraint with a foreign key, but let's say we prefer to implement this rule as a trigger instead. The trigger should prevent invalid updates and return an error message if a user tries to update a `EMP_DATA_X` record using a deprtment code that is not in the `DEPTMENT` table. This trigger would accomplish this job:

```
CREATE TRIGGER HRSCHEMA.BLOCK_DEPT_UPDATE
NO CASCADE BEFORE UPDATE OF
EMP_DEPT ON HRSCHEMA.EMP_DATA_X
REFERENCING NEW AS N
FOR EACH ROW MODE DB2SQL
```

```
WHEN (N.EMP_DEPT
    NOT IN (SELECT DEPT_CODE FROM DEPTMENT))
    BEGIN ATOMIC
       SIGNAL SQLSTATE '85101' ('Invalid department code');
    END
```

Currently the data in these tables looks like this:

```
     SELECT * FROM HRSCHEMA.DEPTMENT;
     ---------+---------+---------+---------+
     DEPT_CODE  DEPT_NAME
     ---------+---------+---------+---------+
     DPTA         DEPARTMENT A
     DPTB         DEPARTMENT B
     DSNE610I NUMBER OF ROWS DISPLAYED IS 2


     SELECT * FROM EMP_DATA_X

     ---------+---------+---------+---------+---------+---------+-----
        EMP_ID  EMP_LNAME          EMP_FNAME          EMP_DEPT
     ---------+---------+---------+---------+---------+---------+-----
          8888  JONES              WILLIAM            DPTA
     DSNE610I NUMBER OF ROWS DISPLAYED IS 1
```

If we try this SQL it will fail because department code "DPTC" does not exist in the DEPTMENT table. And the result is as we expected, plus the error text is what we defined in the trigger:

```
     UPDATE HRSCHEMA.EMP_DATA_X
     SET EMP_DEPT = 'DPTC'
     WHERE EMP_ID = 8888;
     ---------+---------+---------+---------+---------+---------+---------+--
     DSNT408I SQLCODE = -438, ERROR:  APPLICATION RAISED ERROR WITH DIAGNOSTIC TEXT:
     Invalid department code
     DSNT418I SQLSTATE   = 85101 SQLSTATE RETURN CODE
     DSNT415I SQLERRP    = DSNXRTYP SQL PROCEDURE DETECTING ERROR
     DSNT416I SQLERRD    = 1 0  0  -1  0  0 SQL DIAGNOSTIC INFORMATION
     DSNT416I SQLERRD    = X'00000001'  X'00000000'  X'00000000'  X'FFFFFFFF'
            X'00000000'  X'00000000' SQL DIAGNOSTIC INFORMATION
```

Sample INSTEAD OF Trigger

An INSTEAD OF trigger is different than all other types of triggers. The purpose of an INSTEAD OF trigger is to allow updates to take place from what is normally a read-only view. You may know that a view that includes more than one table is read only. Let's look at an example of creating ansd updating data using a view with an INSTEAD OF trigger.

383

We'll start with a query that joins certain columns in the EMPLOYEE table with the EMP_PAY table.

```
SELECT
 A.EMP_ID,
 A.EMP_LAST_NAME,
 B.EMP_REGULAR_PAY
 FROM HRSCHEMA.EMPLOYEE A, HRSCHEMA.EMP_PAY B
 WHERE A.EMP_ID = B.EMP_ID;
---------+---------+---------+---------+---------+--
    EMP_ID  EMP_LAST_NAME        EMP_REGULAR_PAY
---------+---------+---------+---------+---------+--
    3217   JOHNSON                   55000.00
    7459   STEWART                   80000.00
    9134   FRANKLIN                  80000.00
    4720   SCHULTZ                   80000.00
    6288   WILLARD                   70000.00
DSNE610I NUMBER OF ROWS DISPLAYED IS 5
```

Now let's create a view based on this query:

```
CREATE VIEW HRSCHEMA.EMP_PROFILE_PAY
AS
SELECT
A.EMP_ID,
A.EMP_LAST_NAME,
B.EMP_REGULAR_PAY
FROM HRSCHEMA.EMPLOYEE A, HRSCHEMA.EMP_PAY B
WHERE A.EMP_ID = B.EMP_ID;
---------+---------+---------+---------+---------+--------
DSNE616I STATEMENT EXECUTION WAS SUCCESSFUL, SQLCODE IS 0
---------+---------+---------+---------+---------+--------
```

And now we can query the data using the view:

```
SELECT * FROM HRSCHEMA.EMP_PROFILE_PAY
---------+---------+---------+---------+---------+-
    EMP_ID  EMP_LAST_NAME        EMP_REGULAR_PAY
---------+---------+---------+---------+---------+-
    3217   JOHNSON                   55000.00
    7459   STEWART                   80000.00
    9134   FRANKLIN                  80000.00
    4720   SCHULTZ                   80000.00
    6288   WILLARD                   70000.00
DSNE610I NUMBER OF ROWS DISPLAYED IS 5
```

Now suppose we want to use this view to update the EMP_REGULAR_PAY column. Let's try and see what happens:

384

```
UPDATE HRSCHEMA.EMP_PROFILE_PAY
SET EMP_REGULAR_PAY = 65000
WHERE EMP_ID = 3217;
```

```
---------+---------+---------+---------+---------+---------+---------+-------
DSNT408I SQLCODE = -151, ERROR:   THE UPDATE OPERATION IS INVALID BECAUSE THE
         CATALOG DESCRIPTION OF COLUMN HRSCHEMA.EMP_PROFILE_PAY.EMP_REGULAR_PAY
         INDICATES THAT IT CANNOT BE UPDATED
DSNT418I SQLSTATE    = 42808 SQLSTATE RETURN CODE
DSNT415I SQLERRP     = DSNXOST SQL PROCEDURE DETECTING ERROR
DSNT416I SQLERRD     = -400 0  0  -1  0  0 SQL DIAGNOSTIC INFORMATION
DSNT416I SQLERRD     = X'FFFFFE70'  X'00000000'  X'00000000'  X'FFFFFFFF'
         X'00000000'  X'00000000' SQL DIAGNOSTIC INFORMATION
```

As you can see, we are not allowed to perform updates using this view. However, we can perform the updates through this view if we create an INSTEAD OF trigger on the view. The DDL looks like this:

```
CREATE TRIGGER HRSCHEMA.EMP_PROF_PAY_UPDATE
INSTEAD OF UPDATE ON HRSCHEMA.EMP_PROFILE_PAY
   REFERENCING NEW AS NEWEMP OLD AS OLDEMP
      FOR EACH ROW
      MODE DB2SQL
        BEGIN ATOMIC
           UPDATE HRSCHEMA.EMP_PAY AS E
             SET (EMP_REGULAR_PAY)
                = (NEWEMP.EMP_REGULAR_PAY)
           WHERE NEWEMP.EMP_ID = E.EMP_ID ;
        END
```

The trigger is intercepting the UPDATE request from the EMP_PROFILE_PAY view and performing a direct update to the EMP_PAY table.

Now let's try our update:

```
UPDATE HRSCHEMA.EMP_PROFILE_PAY
SET EMP_REGULAR_PAY = 65000
WHERE EMP_ID = 3217;
```

Finally let's select the row we just changed using the view:

```
SELECT * FROM HRSCHEMA.EMP_PROFILE_PAY
WHERE EMP_ID = 3217;
```

```
EMP_ID      EMP_LAST_NAME       EMP_REGULAR_PAY
------      -------------       ----------------
  3217      JOHNSON                    65000.00
```

And as we can see, the EMP_REGULAR_PAY did get changed.

Of course when all is said and done, you could simply have updated the base table to begin with. However, views can give you more control over what users and/or programmers are allowed to see and change in a table. The point of the INSTEAD OF triggers is to allow you to use a view as the interface for all adds, changes and deletes.

Important to Remember Trigger Information

- A trigger is fired by an INSERT, UPDATE or DELETE of a record in a table.

- By default, the LOAD operation does not fire triggers. However, if the SHRLEVEL CHANGE option is included on the LOAD statement, triggers will be fired.

- You cannot use a FOR EACH STATEMENT with BEFORE or INSTEAD OF timing. FOR EACH STATEMENT means your trigger logic is to be applied only once after the triggering statement finishes processing the affected rows.

- If you do not specify a list of column names in the trigger, an update operation on any column of the subject table will fire the trigger.

- A trigger can call a local stored procedure.

- A trigger cascade occurs when the SQL statements executed by one trigger fires one or more other triggers (for example, a trigger action on one table might write a row to another table which in turn has an INSERT trigger on it that performs some other action).

- If a column is included on a table for which a trigger is defined, the column cannot be dropped from the table unless the trigger is first dropped.

- If you alter a column definition for a table in which a trigger is defined on that column, the trigger packages are invalidated.

- If you drop a table for which a trigger has been defined, the trigger is also dropped automatically.

Referential Integrity

Referential Constraints Overview

A referential constraint is the rule that the non-NULL values of a foreign key are valid only if they also appear as values of a parent key. The table that contains the parent key is called the parent table of the referential constraint, and the table that contains the foreign key is a dependent of that table. Referential integrity ensures data integrity by using primary and foreign key relationships between tables.

In DB2 you define a referential constraint by specifying in the child table a column which references a column in a parent table. For example, in a company you could have a DEPARTMENT with column DEPT_CODE, and an EMPLOYEE table that includes a column DEPT that represents the department code an employee is assigned to. The rule would be that you cannot have a value in the EMPLOYEE table DEPT column that does not have a corresponding DEPT_CODE value in the DEPARTMENT table. You can think of this as a parent and child relationship between the DEPARTMENT table and the EMPLOYEE table.

Adding a Foreign Key Relationship

You add a foreign key relationship by performing an ALTER on the child table.

```
ALTER TABLE EMPLOYEE
    FOREIGN KEY FK_DEPT_EMP (DEPT)
        REFERENCES DEPARTMENT(DEPT_CODE) ;

---------+---------+---------+---------+---------+---------+--------
DSNT404I SQLCODE = 162, WARNING:  TABLE SPACE DBHR.TSHR HAS BEEN PLACED IN
CHECK PENDING
```

The constraint was built, but before you can use it you must do a CHECK DATA on your tablespace which has been put into CHECK PENDING status. The DB2 command for this is CHECK DATA and our case the command will be:

```
CHECK DATA TABLESPACE DBHR.TSHR
```

Once the CHECK DATA finishes, your tablespace is taken out of CHECK PENDING and you can continue, provided there were no errors.

Now if you try to update an EMPLOYEE record with a DEPT value that does not have a DEPT_CODE with the same value as the DEPT value you are using, you'll get an SQL error -530 which means a violation of a foreign key.

```
UPDATE HRSCHEMA.EMP_DATA
SET DEPT = 'DPTB'

---------+---------+---------+---------+---------+---------+--------
DSNT408I SQLCODE = -530, ERROR:  THE INSERT OR UPDATE VALUE OF FOREIGN KEY
FK_DEPT_EMP IS INVALID
```

And this is the full explanation of the error.

```
-530
THE INSERT OR UPDATE VALUE OF FOREIGN KEY constraint-name IS INVALID
Explanation
An insert or update operation attempted to place a value in a
foreign key of the object table; however, this value was not equal
to some value of the parent key of the parent table.
When a row is inserted into a dependent table, the insert value of a
foreign key must be equal to the value of the parent key of some row
of the parent table in the associated relationship.

When the value of the foreign key is updated, the update value of a
foreign key must be equal to the value of the parent key of some row
of the parent table of the associated relationship.
```

We know now that the parent table DEPARTMENT does not have DEPT_CODE DPTB in it, and it must be added before the EMPLOYEE record can be updated.

Deleting a Record from the Parent Table

Now let's talk about what happens if you want to delete a record from the parent table. Assuming no EMPLOYEE records are linked to that DEPARTMENT record, deleting that record may be fine. But what if you are trying to delete a DEPARTMENT record whose DEPT_CODE is referenced by one or more records in the EMPLOYEE table?

Let's look at a record in the table:

```
SELECT EMP_ID, DEPT
 FROM HRSCHEMA.EMPLOYEE
WHERE EMP_ID = 1788;
--------+---------+------
   EMP_ID  DEPT
--------+---------+------
    1788  DPTA
```

Ok, we know that the DEPT_CODE in use is DPTA. Now let's try to delete DPTA from the DEPARTMENT table.

```
DELETE FROM DEPARTMENT
WHERE DEPT_CODE = 'DPTA';
---------+---------+---------+---------+---------+---------+--------
```

```
DSNT408I SQLCODE = -532, ERROR:  THE RELATIONSHIP FK_DEPT_EMP RESTRICTS THE
DELETION OF ROW WITH RID X'0000002201'
```

If we try to remove the DEPT_CODE from the DEPARTMENT table, we will get a -532 SQL error telling us our SQL is in violation of the referential constraint. That's probably what we want, but there are some other options for how to handle the situation.

You can specify the action that will take place upon deleting a parent record by including an ON DELETE clause in the foreign key definition. If no action is specified, or if RESTRICT is specified with the ON DELETE clause, then the parent record cannot be deleted unless all child records which reference that record are first deleted. RESTRICT is the most commonly used ON DELETE value (or just omitting the ON DELETE clause which has the same effect). This is the case above.

Here are the two other options:

If **ON DELETE CASCADE** is specified, then any rows in the child table that correspond to the parent record will also be deleted. Wow, that is probably not what we want, but there may be cases where this function is useful. Possibly if a certain product is discontinued you might want to delete all pending SHIPPING table entries for it. I can't think of many other needs for this, but be aware that this option is available.

If **ON DELETE SET NULL** is specified, then the foreign key field will be set to NULL for corresponding rows that reference the parent record that is being deleted.

Let's redefine our constraint to use this last:

```
ALTER TABLE HRSCHEMA.EMPLOYEE
DROP CONSTRAINT FK_DEPT_EMP;

 ALTER TABLE HRSCHEMA.EMPLOYEE
    FOREIGN KEY FK_DEPT_EMP (DEPT)
       REFERENCES HRSCHEMA.DEPARTMENT (DEPT_CODE)
          ON DELETE SET NULL;
---------+---------+---------+---------+---------+---------+--------
DSNT404I SQLCODE = 162, WARNING:  TABLE SPACE DBHR.TSHR HAS BEEN PLACED IN
CHECK PENDING
```

Go ahead and run the CHECK DATA to clear the CHECK PENDING condition.

Now try deleting the DPTA record from the DEPARTMENT table:

```
DELETE FROM DEPARTMENT
 WHERE DEPT_CODE = 'DPTA';
---------+---------+---------+--------
```

```
DSNE615I NUMBER OF ROWS AFFECTED IS 1
```

We see that the delete was successful. So now let's check and see if the DEPT value for the child record has been set to NULL.

```
SELECT EMP_ID, DEPT
FROM HRSCHEMA.EMP_DATA
WHERE EMP_ID = 1788;
---------+---------+---------+--------
     EMP_ID  DEPT
---------+---------+---------+--------
       1788  ----
DSNE610I NUMBER OF ROWS DISPLAYED IS 1
```

And in fact the DEPT column has been set to NULL.

This closes our discussion of referential integrity. For designing and maintaining your systems, make sure you understand what a referential constraint is, the syntax for creating a foreign key relationship, and the various options/outcomes for the ON DELETE clause.

Special Tables

Temporal and Archive Tables

Temporal Tables

Temporal tables were introduced to DB2 in version 10. Briefly, a temporal table is one that keeps track of "versions" of data over time and allows you to query data according to the time frame. It is important to understand what problems you can solve with the technologies, such as automatically preventing overlapping rows for business time. We'll get to that in the examples.

Some benefits of DB2's built in support for managing temporal data include:

- Reduces application logic
- Can automatically maintain a history of table changes
- Ensures consistent handling of time related events

Now let's look at the two varieties of time travel in DB2, which are business time (sometimes referred to as application time) and system time.

Business Time

An employee's pay typically changes over time. Besides wanting to know the current salary, there may be many scenarios under which an HR department or supervisor might need to know what pay rate was in effect for an employee at some time in the past. We might also need to allow for cases where the employee terminated for some period of time and then returned. Or maybe they took a non-paid leave of absence. This is the concept of business time and it can be fairly complex depending on the business rules required by the application. It basically means a period of time in which the data is accurate. You could think of it as a data value an effective date and discontinue date.

A table can only have one business time period. When a BUSINESS_TIME period is defined for a table, DB2 generates a check constraint in which the end column value must be greater than the begin column value. Once a table is version enabled, the following clauses allow you to pull data for a particular bsuiness time period:

```
FOR BUSINESS_TIME FROM ... TO ...
FOR BUSINESS_TIME BETWEEN... AND...
```

For example:

```
SELECT * FROM HRSCHEMA.EMP_PAY
FOR BUSINESS_TIME BEWTWEEN '2017-01-01' AND '2017-02-01'
ORDER BY EMP_ID;
```

System Time

System time simply means the time during which a piece of data is in the database, i.e., when the data was added, changed or deleted. Sometimes it is important to know this. For example a user might enter an employee's salary change on a certain date but the effective date of the salary change might be earlier or later than the date it was actually entered into the system. An audit trail table often has a timestamp that can be considered system time at which a transaction occurred.

Like with business time, once a table is version-enabled for system time, the following clauses allow you to pull data for a particular system period:

```
FOR SYSTEM_TIME FROM ... TO ...
FOR SYSTEM_TIME BETWEEN... AND...
```

For example, maybe we want to know see several series of EMPLOYEE table records that were changed over a period of a month. Assuming a system version enabled table, this would work:

```
SELECT * FROM HRSCHEMA.EMPLOYEE
FOR SYSTEM_TIME BEWTWEEN '2017-01-01' AND '2017-02-01'
ORDER BY EMP_ID;
```

Bitemporal Support

In some cases you may need to support both business and system time in the same table. DB2 supports this and it is called bitemporal support. Now let's move on to some examples of all three types of temporal tables!

Business Time Example

You create a temporal table by adding columns for the start and ending period for which the data is valid. Let's do an example. We could modify our existing EMP_PAY table and we'll do that, but first let's look at how we would have defined it if we originally made it a temporal table.

Our original DDL for creating EMP_PAY looks like this:

```
CREATE TABLE HRSCHEMA.EMP_PAY(
EMP_ID INT NOT NULL,
EMP_REGULAR_PAY DECIMAL (8,2) NOT NULL,
EMP_BONUS_PAY DECIMAL   (8,2))
PRIMARY KEY (EMP_ID))
IN TSHR;
```

To create this table as a temporal table, we could have used this DDL instead and our new table name is EMP_PAYX:

```
CREATE TABLE HRSCHEMA.EMP_PAYX(
EMP_ID INT NOT NULL,
EMP_REGULAR_PAY DECIMAL (8,2) NOT NULL,
EMP_BONUS_PAY DECIMAL   (8,2)),
BUS_START    DATE   NOT NULL,
BUS_END      DATE   NOT NULL,

PERIOD BUSINESS_TIME(BUS_START, BUS_END),

PRIMARY KEY (EMP_ID, BUSINESS_TIME WITHOUT OVERLAPS))
IN TSHR;
```

Now let's insert a few rows into the table. Keep in mind that we now have a start and end date for which the information is valid. That could pose a problem if our end date is really "until further notice". Some applications solve that problem by establishing a date in the distant future as the standard end date for current data. We'll use 12/31/2099 for this example. For convenience we can use the existing EMP_PAY table to load EMP_PAYX using a query:

```
INSERT INTO HRSCHEMA.EMP_PAYX
SELECT EMP_ID,
EMP_REGULAR_PAY,
EMP_BONUS_PAY,
'2017-01-01',
'2099-12-31'
FROM HRSCHEMA.EMP_PAY;
```

Here's our resulting data:

```
SELECT * FROM HRSCHEMA.EMP_PAYX;

EMP_ID   EMP_REGULAR_PAY   EMP_BONUS_PAY BUS_START    BUS_END
------   ---------------   ------------- ----------   ----------
  3217          55000.00         5500.00 2017-01-01   2099-12-31
  7481          80000.00         4500.00 2017-01-01   2099-12-31
  9134          80000.00         2500.00 2017-01-01   2099-12-31
```

Now let's suppose employee 3217 has been given a raise to 60K per year effective 2/1/2017. First we need to set the end business date on the existing record.

```
UPDATE HRSCHEMA.EMP_PAYX
SET BUS_END     = '2017-02-01'
WHERE EMP_ID = 3217;
```

IMPORTANT: both system and business time are inclusive of start date and exclusive of end date. That means when you set an end date, you'll usually want to add a day to the true end date and use that as the end date. For example, to set an employee salary effective January 1, 2017 and ending at midnight on January 31, 2017 you would use start date 2017-01-01. But you would use end date 2017-02-01. Otherwise January 31 will not be included when you do your query for business time through 1/31/2017.

If the above is a little confusing, it is because generally date related evaluations do not work this way (if you say BETWEEN two dates, it means inclusive at both ends), but this one does work this way. So be sure that you get this! For setting business and system time, the **start date is inclusive** but the **end date is exclusive**. Now let's add the new row:

```
INSERT INTO HRSCHEMA.EMP_PAYX
```

```
VALUES (3217,
60000.00,
5500.00,
'2017-02-01',
'2099-12-31')
```

Here's the result when you query all rows:

```
SELECT * FROM HRSCHEMA.EMP_PAYX ORDER BY EMP_ID;

EMP_ID EMP_REGULAR_PAY      EMP_BONUS_PAY  BUS_START    BUS_END
------ ----------------     -------------  ----------   ----------
  3217         55000.00          5500.00   2017-01-01   2017-02-01
  3217         60000.00          5500.00   2017-02-01   2099-12-31
  7459         80000.00          4500.00   2017-01-01   2099-12-31
  9134         80000.00          2500.00   2017-01-01   2099-12-31
```

Note that there are now two records for employee 3217. However, if you query this data as of 2/1/2017, you would get a different result than if you queried it for business time 1/15/2017. Recall that querying data in temporal tables is supported by specific temporal clauses, including:

```
AS OF
FROM
BETWEEN
```

```
SELECT * FROM HRSCHEMA.EMP_PAYX
FOR BUSINESS_TIME AS OF '2017-02-01'
ORDER BY EMP_ID;

EMP_ID     EMP_REGULAR_PAY      EMP_BONUS_PAY  BUS_START    BUS_END
------     ----------------     -------------  ----------   ----------
  3217            60000.00          5500.00    2017-02-01   2099-12-31
  7459            80000.00          4500.00    2017-01-01   2099-12-31
  9134            80000.00          2500.00    2017-01-01   2099-12-31
```

```
SELECT * FROM HRSCHEMA.EMP_PAYX
FOR BUSINESS_TIME AS OF '2017-01-15'
ORDER BY EMP_ID;

EMP_ID     EMP_REGULAR_PAY      EMP_BONUS_PAY  BUS_START    BUS_END
------     ----------------     -------------  ----------   ----------
  3217            55000.00          5500.00    2017-01-01   2017-02-01
  7459            80000.00          4500.00    2017-01-01   2099-12-31
  9134            80000.00          2500.00    2017-01-01   2099-12-31
```

Since you defined the primary key with non-overlapping business times, DB2 will not allow you to enter any overlapping start and end dates. That saves some coding and solves one of the most pervasive and time-consuming application design errors I've observed over the years.

System Time Example

When you want to capture actions taken on a table at a particular time, use system time. Suppose you want to keep a snapshot of every record BEFORE it is changed. DB2's temporal table functionality also includes automated copying of a "before" image of each record to a history table. This feature can be used in lieu of using triggers which are also often used to store a history of each version of a record.

Let's take the example of our EMPLOYEE table. For business audit purposes, we want to capture all changes made to it. To do this is pretty easy. Follow these steps:

- Add system time fields to the base table
- Create a history table
- Version-enable the base table

Adding system time to the table is as simple as adding the time fields needed to track system time.

```
ALTER TABLE HRSCHEMA.EMPLOYEE
ADD COLUMN SYS_START TIMESTAMP(12)
GENERATED ALWAYS AS ROW BEGIN NOT NULL;

ALTER TABLE HRSCHEMA.EMPLOYEE
ADD COLUMN SYS_END TIMESTAMP(12)
GENERATED ALWAYS AS ROW END NOT NULL;

ALTER TABLE HRSCHEMA.EMPLOYEE
ADD COLUMN TRANS_ID TIMESTAMP(12) NOT NULL GENERATED
ALWAYS AS TRANSACTION START ID;

ALTER TABLE HRSCHEMA.EMPLOYEE
ADD PERIOD SYSTEM_TIME (SYS_START, SYS_END);
```

Now let's explore one more temporal table feature – the history table. There may be cases in which you want to maintain a record of all changes made to table. You can do this automatically by defining a history table and enabling your base table for versioning. Let's create a history table EMPLOYEE_HISTORY and we'll make it identical to EMPLOYEE.

```
CREATE TABLE EMPLOYEE_HISTORY LIKE EMPLOYEE;
```

Now we can enable versioning in the EMPLOYEE table like this:

```
ALTER TABLE EMPLOYEE
ADD VERSIONING
USE HISTORY TABLE EMPLOYEE_HISTORY
```

At this point we can make a change to one of the EMPLOYEE records and we expect to see the old version of the record in the history table.

```
UPDATE HRSCHEMA.EMPLOYEE
SET EMP_FIRST_NAME = 'FREDERICK'
WHERE EMP_ID = 4175;
```

Assume that today is January 30, 2017 so that's when we changed our data. When you query with a specified system time, DB2 implicitly joins the base table and the history table. For example, let's pull data for employee 4175 as of 1/15/2017:

```
SELECT EMP_ID, EMP_FIRST_NAME, SYS_START, SYS_END
FROM HRSCHEMA.EMPLOYEE
FOR SYSTEM_TIME AS OF '2017-01-15'
WHERE EMP_ID = 4175;

EMP_ID  EMP_FIRST_NAME  SYS_START             SYS_END
------  --------------  --------------------  --------------------------
 4175   FRED            0001-01-01 00:00:00.0  2017-01-30 17:29:38.608073
```

Notice that the previous version of the record is pulled up (FRED instead of FREDERICK) because we specified system time 1/15/2017, so that means we want the record that was present in the table on 1/15/2017.

Now let's perform the same query for system time as of February 1, 2017.

```
SELECT EMP_ID, EMP_FIRST_NAME, SYS_START, SYS_END
FROM HRSCHEMA.EMPLOYEE
FOR SYSTEM_TIME AS OF '2017-02-01'
WHERE EMP_ID = 4175;

EMP_ID  EMP_FIRST_NAME  SYS_START                  SYS_END
------  --------------  -------------------------  --------------------
 4175   FREDERICK       2017-01-30 17:29:38.608073  9999-12-30 00:00:00.0
```

Now you've got the most current record with the modified name FREDERICK. That is pretty cool feature and most if it happens automatically once you set it up. It can really help save time when researching particular values that were in the table somctime in the past.

NOTE: You can only use a history table with a system time enabled table.

Bi-Temporal Example

Finally, let's do an example where you need both business time and system time enabled for the same table. Let's go back go our `EMP_PAY` table and create yet another version called `EMP_PAYY`:

```
CREATE TABLE HRSCHEMA.EMP_PAYY(
EMP_ID INT NOT NULL,
EMP_REGULAR_PAY DECIMAL (8,2) NOT NULL,
EMP_BONUS_PAY DECIMAL   (8,2)),
BUS_START   DATE  NOT NULL,
BUS_END     DATE  NOT NULL,
SYS_START   TIMESTAMP(12)
GENERATED ALWAYS AS ROW BEGIN NOT NULL,
SYS_END     TIMESTAMP(12)
GENERATED ALWAYS AS ROW END NOT NULL,
 TRANS_ID TIMESTAMP(12) NOT NULL GENERATED
                             ALWAYS AS TRANSACTION START ID;

PERIOD BUSINESS_TIME(BUS_START, BUS_END),
PERIOD SYSTEM_TIME (SYS_START, SYS_END);

PRIMARY KEY (EMP_ID, BUSINESS_TIME WITHOUT OVERLAPS))
IN TSHR;
```

You'll still need to create the history table and version enable `EMP_PAYY`.

```
CREATE TABLE EMP_PAYY_HISTORY LIKE EMP_PAYY;
```

Now we can enable versioning in the `EMP_PAYY` table like this:

```
ALTER TABLE EMP_PAYY
ADD VERSIONING
USE HISTORY TABLE EMP_PAYY_HISTORY;
```

This concludes our discussion of DB2's support for temporal tables and time travel queries. This is a very powerful technology and I encourage you to learn it not just to pass the exam, but to take advantage of it's features that improve your client's access to actionable business information. It can also ease the application development and production support efforts!

Archive Tables

Archive tables are similar to history tables, but are unrelated to temporal tables. An **archive table** is a table that stores data that was deleted from another table which is called an **archive-enabled table**. When a row is deleted from the archive-enabled table,

DB2 automatically adds the row to the archive table. When you query the archive-enabled table, you can specify whether or not to include archived records or not. We'll look at these features in an example.

Assume we want to delete some records from our EMPLOYEE table and we want to automatically archive the deleted records to a new table EMPLOYEE_ARCHIVE. Assume that the new table is already set up and defined correctly, i.e., with the same column definitions as EMPLOYEE.

To enable archiving of deleted records from table EMPLOYEE you would execute the following:

```
ALTER TABLE EMPLOYEE
ENABLE ARCHIVE
USE EMPLOYEE_ARCHIVE;
```

To automatically archive records, set the global variable SYSIBMADM.MOVE_TO_ARCHIVE to Y or E. MOVE_TO_ARCHIVE indicates whether deleting a record from an archive-enabled table should store a copy of the deleted record in the archive table. The values are:

- Y - store a copy of the deleted record, and also make any attempted insert/update operation against the archive table an error.
- E - store a copy of the deleted record.
- N- do not store a copy of the deleted record.

In the future when you query the EMPLOYEE you can choose to include or exclude the archived records in a given session. To do this, your package must first be bound with the ARCHIVESENSITIVE(YES) bind option. Then the package/program should set the GET_ARCHIVE global variable to Y (the default is N). At this point, any query against the archive-enabled table during this session will automatically include data from both the archive-enabled table and its corresponding archive table.

In our EMPLOYEE example, suppose we have a package EMP001 that is bound with ARCHIVESENSITIVE(YES). Suppose further that the program issues this SQL:

```
SET SYSIBMADM.GET_ARCHIVE = 'Y';
```

At this point any query we issue during this session against EMPLOYEE will automatically return any qualifying rows from both EMPLOYEE and EMPLOYEE_ARCHIVE. For example:

```
SELECT EMP_ID, EMP_LAST_NAME, EMPL_FIRST_NAME
FROM EMPLOYEE
ORDER BY EMP_ID;
```

If the package needs to revert to only picking up data from the EMPLOYEE table, it can simply issue the SQL:

```
SET SYSIBMADM.GET_ARCHIVE = 'N';
```

Some design advantages of an archive table are:

1. Your historical data is managed automatically. You don't need to manually move older data to a separate table.

2. The scope of your query is controlled using a global variable. Consequently you can modify your query results to include or exclude the archive table data and you don't have to change the SQL statement (only the global variable value).

3. Older rows that are less often retrieved can be stored in a separate table which could potentially be located on a cheaper device.

Materialized Query Tables

A materialized query table (MQT) basically stores the result set of a query. It is used to store aggregate results from one or more other tables. MQTs are often used to improve performance for certain aggregation queries by providing pre-computed results. Consequently, MQTs are most often used in analytic or data warehousing environments.

MQTs are either system-maintained or user maintained. For a system maintained table, the data can be updated using the REFRESH TABLE statement. A user-maintained MQT can be updated using the LOAD utility, and also the UPDATE, INSERT, and DELETE SQL statements.

Let's do an example of an MQT that summarizes monthly payroll. Assume we have a source table named EMP_PAY_HIST which will be a history of each employee's salary for each paycheck. The table is defined as follows:

Column Name	Definition
EMP_ID	Numeric
EMP_PAY_DATE	Date
EMP_PAY_AMT	Decimal(8,2)

The DDL for the table is as follows:

```
CREATE TABLE HRSCHEMA.EMP_PAY_HIST(
EMP_ID                INT NOT NULL,
EMP_PAY_DATE          DATE NOT NULL,
EMP_PAY_AMT           DECIMAL (8,2) NOT NULL)
IN TSHR;
```

Now let's assume the data in the table is the twice-monthly pay amount for each employee for the first two months of 2017. Perhaps you have a payroll program that loads the table each pay period, possibly using a query like this where the date changes with the payroll period:

```
INSERT INTO HRSCHEMA.EMP_PAY_HIST
SELECT EMP_ID,
'01/15/2017',
EMP_SEMIMTH_PAY
FROM HRSCHEMA.EMP_PAY_CHECK;
```

Assume that the data is as follows:

```
SELECT * FROM EMP_PAY_HIST ORDER BY EMP_PAY_DATE, EMP_ID;
---------+---------+---------+---------+---------+---------
    EMP_ID  EMP_PAY_DATE  EMP_PAY_AMT
---------+---------+---------+---------+---------+---------
      3217  2017-01-15       2291.66
      7459  2017-01-15       3333.33
      9134  2017-01-15       3333.33
      3217  2017-01-31       2291.66
      7459  2017-01-31       3333.33
      9134  2017-01-31       3333.33
      3217  2017-02-15       2291.66
      7459  2017-02-15       3333.33
      9134  2017-02-15       3333.33
      3217  2017-02-28       2291.66
      7459  2017-02-28       3333.33
      9134  2017-02-28       3333.33
DSNE610I NUMBER OF ROWS DISPLAYED IS 12
```

Finally, let's assume we regularly need an aggregated total of each employee's year to date pay. We could do this with a materialized query table. Let's build the query that will summarize the employee pay from the beginning of the year to current date:

```
SELECT EMP_ID, SUM(EMP_PAY_AMT) AS EMP_PAY_YTD
FROM HRSCHEMA.EMP_PAY_HIST
GROUP BY EMP_ID
ORDER BY EMP_ID;
---------+---------+---------+---------+---------
    EMP_ID              EMP_PAY_YTD
---------+---------+---------+--------_+---------
    3217                  9166.64
    7459                 13333.32
    9134                 13333.32
DSNE610I NUMBER OF ROWS DISPLAYED IS 3
```

Now let's create the MQT using this query and we'll make it a system managed table:

```
CREATE TABLE EMP_PAY_TOT (EMP_ID, EMP_PAY_YTD) AS
(SELECT EMP_ID, SUM(EMP_PAY_AMT) AS EMP_PAY_YTD
FROM HRSCHEMA.EMP_PAY_HIST
GROUP BY EMP_ID)
DATA INITIALLY DEFERRED
REFRESH DEFERRED
MAINTAINED BY SYSTEM
ENABLE QUERY OPTIMIZATION;
```

We can now populate the table by issuing the REFRESH TABLE statement as follows:

```
REFRESH TABLE HRSCHEMA.EMP_PAY_TOT;
```

Finally we can query the MQT as follows:

```
SELECT * FROM HRSCHEMA.EMP_PAY_TOT;

---------+---------+---------+---------+---------+--------
    EMP_ID              EMP_PAY_YTD
---------+---------+---------+---------+---------+--------
    3217                  9166.64
    7459                 13333.32
    9134                 13333.32
DSNE610I NUMBER OF ROWS DISPLAYED IS 3
```

Temporary Tables

Sometimes you may need to create a DB2 table for the duration of a session but no longer than that. For example you may have a programming situation where it is convenient to have a temporary table which you can load for these operations:

- To join the data in the temporary table with another table

401

- To store intermediate results that you can query later in the program
- To load data from a flat file into a relational format

Let's assume that you only need the temporary table for the duration of a session or iteration of a program because temporary tables are dropped automatically as soon as the session ends.

Temporary tables are created using either the CREATE statement or the DECLARE statement. The differences will be explored in the Application Design section of this book. For now we will just look at an example of creating a table called EMP_INFO using both methods:

```
CREATE GLOBAL TEMPORARY TABLE
EMP_INFO(
EMP_ID   INT,
EMP_LNAME  VARCHAR(30),
EMP_FNAME  VARCHAR(30));

DECLARE GLOBAL TEMPORARY TABLE
EMP_INFO(
EMP_ID   INT,
EMP_LNAME  VARCHAR(30),
EMP_FNAME  VARCHAR(30));
```

When using the LIKE clause to create a temporary table, the implicit table definition includes only the column name, data type and NULLability characteristic of each of the columns of the source table, and any column defaults. The temporary table does NOT have any unique constraints, foreign key constraints, triggers, indexes, table partitioning keys, or distribution keys.

CREATED Temporary Tables
Created temporary tables:

- Have an entry in the system catalog (SYSIBM.SYSTABLES)
- Cannot have indexes
- Their columns cannot use default values (except NULL)
- Cannot have constraints
- Cannot be used with DB2 utilities
- Cannot be used with the UPDATE statement
- If DELETE is used at all, it will delete all rows from the table
- Do not provide for locking or logging

DECLARED Temporary Tables

A declared temporary table offers some advantages over created temporary tables.

- Can have indexes and check constraints
- Can use the UPDATE statement
- Can do positioned deletes

So declared temporary tables offer more flexibility than created temporary tables. However, when a session ends, DB2 will automatically delete both the rows in the table and the table definition. So if you want a table definition that persists in the DB2 catalog for future use, you would need to use a created temporary table.

Things to remember about temporary tables:

- Use temporary tables when you need the data only for the duration of the session.

- Created temporary tables can provide excellent performance because they do not use locking or logging.

- Declared temporary tables can also be very efficient because you can choose not to log, and they only allow limited locking.

- The schema for a temporary table is always SESSION.

- If you create a temporary table and you wish to replace any existing temporary table that has the same name, use the WITH REPLACE clause.

- If you create a temporary table from another table using the LIKE clause, the temporary table will NOT have any unique constraints, foreign key constraints, triggers, indexes, table partitioning keys, or distribution keys from the original table.

Chapter Five Review Questions

1. Which of the following is NOT a valid data type for use as an identity column?

    a. INTEGER
    b. REAL
    c. DECIMAL
    d. SMALLINT

2. You need to store numeric integer values of up to 5,000,000,000. What data type is appropriate for this?

    a. INTEGER
    b. BIGINT
    c. LARGEINT
    d. DOUBLE

3. Which of the following is NOT a LOB (Large Object) data type?

    a. CLOB
    b. BLOB
    c. DBCLOB
    d. DBBLOB

4. If you want to add an XML column VAR1 to table TBL1, which of the following would accomplish that?

    a. ALTER TABLE TBL1 ADD VAR1 XML
    b. ALTER TABLE TBL1 ADD COLUMN VAR1 XML
    c. ALTER TABLE TBL1 ADD COLUMN VAR1 (XML)
    d. ALTER TABLE TBL1 ADD XML COLUMN VAR1

5. If you want rows that have similar key values to be stored physically close to each other, what keyword should you specify when you create an index?

   a. UNIQUE
   b. ASC
   c. INCLUDE
   d. CLUSTER

6. Assume a table where certain columns contain sensitive data and you don't want all users to see these columns. Some other columns in the table must be made accessible to all users. What type of object could you create to solve this problem?

   a. INDEX
   b. SEQUENCE
   c. VIEW
   d. TRIGGER

7. To grant a privilege to all users of the database, grant the privilege to whom?

   a. ALL
   b. PUBLIC
   c. ANY
   d. DOMAIN

8. Tara wants to grant CONTROL of table TBL1 to Bill, and also allow Bill to grant the same privilege to other users. What clause should Tara use on the GRANT statement?

   a. WITH CONTROL OPTION
   b. WITH GRANT OPTION
   c. WITH USE OPTION
   d. WITH REVOKE OPTION

9. Which of the following will generate DB2 SQL data structures for a table or view that can be used in a PLI or COBOL program?

   a. DECLARE
   b. INCLUDE
   c. DCLGEN
   d. None of the above.

10. Assuming you are using a DB2 precompiler, which of the following orders the DB2 program preparation steps correctly?

    a. Precompile SQL, Bind Package, Bind Plan.
    b. Precompile SQL, Bind Plan, Bind Package.
    c. Bind Package, Precompile SQL, Bind Plan.
    d. Bind Plan, Precompile SQL, Bind Package.

11. To end a transaction without making the changes permanent, which DB2 statement should be issued?

    a. COMMIT
    b. BACKOUT
    c. ROLLBACK
    d. NO CHANGE

12. If you want to maximize data concurrency without seeing uncommitted data, which isolation level should you use?

    a. RR
    b. UR
    c. RS
    d. CS

13. To end a transaction and make the changes visible to other processes, which statement should be issued?

    a. ROLLBACK
    b. COMMIT
    c. APPLY
    d. CALL

14. Order the isolation levels, from greatest to least impact on performance.

    a. RR, RS, CS, UR
    b. UR, RR, RS, CS
    c. CS, UR, RR, RS
    d. RS, CS, UR, RR

15. Suppose you have created a test version of a production table, and you want to to use the UNLOAD utility to extract the first 1,000 rows from the production table to load to the test version. Which keyword would you use in the UNLOAD statement?

    a. WHEN
    b. SELECT
    c. SAMPLE
    d. SUBSET

16. Which of the following is NOT a way you could test a DB2 SQL statement?

    a. Running the statement from the DB2 command line processor.
    b. Running the statement from the SPUFI utility.
    c. Running the statement from IBM Data Studio.
    d. All of the above are valid ways to test an SQL statement.

Additional Resources

For additional information check out the **Enterprise PL/I for z/OS Programming Guide**. I also suggest that you download the **Enterprise PL/I for z/OS Language Reference**. You can Google search these for the latest IBM URLs.

For more DB2 information, search and download these documents:

DB2 11 for z/OS Application Programming and SQL Guide

DB2 11 for z/OS SQL Reference

Appendices

Chapter Questions and Answers

Chapter One Review Questions

1. If you are performing PLI arithmetic calculations, which data type usually performs best?

   Use of FIXED BINARY generally has a faster performance than using other numeric types.

2. What is an example of an ON condition and what it is used for?

   An ON condition is a situation in a PLI program that could cause a program interrupt. Examples include unexpected errors such as a fixed variable overflow, or encountering the end of a file when reading. PLI programs can be coded to trap these conditions. In the case of the end of file condition, here is an example of code to turn off a more-records switch when end of file is encountered (to avoid the error of reading past the end of file).

   ```
   ON ENDFILE(TRANS)
       S_MORE_RECORDS = NO;
   ```

3. What verb is used to implement the case control structure in a PL/1 program?

   The SELECT statement implements the CASE structure. The syntax is:

   ```
   SELECT (optional expression);
       WHEN (expression) action 1;
       WHEN (expression) action 2;
       OTHERWISE action 3
   END;
   ```

4. What is the difference between a DO WHILE control structure and a DO UNTIL control structure?

411

DO WHILE checks its loop control condition at the top of the loop, while DO UNTIL checks at the bottom. The DO UNTIL is always executed at least once.

5. How would one use the VERIFY function?

VERIFY examines two strings to verify that each character or bit in the first string is represented in the second string. It returns a 0 if true, otherwise it returns the position of the first character in the first string that is not in the second string.

6. How do you include a copybook?

Use the %INCLUDE verb followed by the member name of the copybook:

```
%INCLUDE FILE1234;
```

7. How do you concatenate two string variables in PLI?

The concatenation symbol is two vertical marks || and is placed between the items to be concatenated. For example you could concatenate first and last names with a space between them:

```
FNAME = 'JOHN';
LNAME = 'SMITH';
FULL_NAME = FNAME || ' ' || LNAME;
```

8. If you want to declare an array of 100 elements of CHAR(04) and call the array TABLE1, how would you code it?

You would code it as follows:

```
DCL    TABLE1 (100)    CHAR(04);
```

9. What does the FETCHABLE attribute mean?

When you want a sub-program to have the ability to be called dynamically at run time, declare that program with OPTIONS (FETCHABLE) instead of OPTIONS (MAIN). The sub-program must then be loaded into memory by the calling program using the FETCH verb. Once loaded, the sub-program can be called normally like any other sub-program.

10. What is the basic syntax to declare a file named TESTFILE for record type input?

```
DCL TESTFILE FILE RECORD INPUT;
```

11. What carriage control character would you use to skip to the top of the next page?

The number "1" carriage control character means to skip to the next page.

12. What are the two ways a procedure can end normally?

The procedure ends normally either by reaching the END statement for the procedure or by a RETURN statement. Either way control is passed back to the calling procedure.

13. What statement specifies the action to be taken in a SELECT statement if none of the WHEN conditions is satisfied?

The OTHERWISE clause (if coded) specifies the action to be taken in a SELECT statement if none of the WHEN conditions is satisfied.

```
SELECT (optional expression);
   WHEN (expression) action 1;
   WHEN (expression) action 2;
   OTHERWISE action 3
END;
```

Chapter Two Review Questions

1. What are the three types of VSAM datasets?

   Entry-sequenced datasets (ESDS), key-sequenced datasets (KSDS) and relative record dataset (RRDS).

2. How are records stored in an ESDS (entry sequenced) dataset?

   They are stored in the order in which they are inserted into the file.

3. What VSAM feature enables you to access the records in a KSDS dataset based on a key that is different than the file's primary key?

   VSAM allows creation of an alternate index which enables you to access the records in a KSDS dataset based on that alternate index rather than the primary key.

4. What is the general purpose utility program that provides services for VSAM files?

   Access Method Services is the utility program that provides services for VSAM files. Often it is referred to as IDCAMS which is the executable program in batch.

5. Which AMS function lists information about datasets?

   The LISTCAT function lists information about datasets. An example is:

   ```
   //STEP1     EXEC PGM=IDCAMS
   //SYSPRINT  DD SYSOUT=X
   //SYSIN     DD *
    LISTCAT GDG ENT('DSNAME.GDGFILE.TEST1') ALL
   ```

6. If you are mostly going to use a KSDS file for sequential access, should you define a larger or smaller control interval when creating the file?

For sequential access a larger control interval is desirable for performance because you maximize the data brought in with each I/O.

7. What is the basic AMS command to create a VSAM file?

   `DEFINE CLUSTER` **is the basic command to create a VSAM file.**

8. To use the REWRITE command in COBOL, the VSAM file must be opened in what mode?

   To use the REWRITE command in COBOL, the VSAM file must be opened for I-O.

9. When you define an alternate index, what is the function of the RELATE parameter?

   The RELATE parameter associates your alternate index with the base cluster that you are creating the alternate index for.

10. When you define a path using DEFINE PATH, what does the PATHENTRY parameter do?

    The PATHENTRY parameter includes the name of the alternate index that you are creating the path for.

11. After you've defined an alternate index and path, what AMS command must you issue to actually populate the alternate index?

    Issue the BLXINDEX command to populate an alternate index.

12. After you've created a VSAM file, if you need to add additional DASD volumes that can be used with that file, what command would you use?

Use an **ALTER** command and specify the keyword **ADDVOLUMES (XXX001 YYY002)** where **XXX001** and **YYY002** are **DASD** volume names.

13. If you want to set a VSAM file to read only status, what command would you use?

    Use the **ALTER** command with the **INHIBIT** keyword. For example:

    ```
    //STEP1 EXEC PGM=IDCAMS
    //SYSPRINT DD SYSOUT=*
    //SYSIN DD *
    ALTER -
    PROD.EMPL.DATA -
    INHIBIT
    ALTER -
    PROD.EMPL.INDEX -
    INHIBIT
    /*
    ```

    To return the file to read/update, use **ALTER** with the **UNINHIBIT** keyword.

14. What are some ways you can improve the performance of a KSDS file?

    - **Ensure that the control interval is optimally sized (smaller for random access and larger for sequential access).**

    - **Allocate additional index buffers to reduce data I/Os by keeping needed records in virtual storage.**

    - **Ensure sufficient free space in control intervals to avoid control interval splits.**

15. Do primary key values in a KSDS have to be unique?

    Yes the primary key has to be unique. However, alternate index values need not be unique. For example if an EMPLOYEE file uses employee number as the primary key, then the employee number must be unique.

However the EMPLOYEE file could be alternately indexed on department. In this case, the department need not be unique.

16. Is there a performance penalty for using an alternate index compared to using the primary key?

Yes because if you access a record through an **ALTERNATE INDEX,** the alternate key must first be located and then it points to the primary key entry which is finally used to locate the actual record.

Chapter Three Review Questions

1. What is the name of the interface program you call from a PLI program to perform IMS operations?

   PLITDLI is the normal interface program for a PLI program to access IMS.

2. Here are some IMS return codes and . Explain briefly what each of them means: blank, GE, GB, II

   > **Blank – successful operation**
   > **GE – segment not found**
   > **GB – end of database**
   > **II – duplicate key, insert failed**

3. What is an SSA?

   Segment Search Argument – it is used to select segments by name and to specify search criteria for specific segments.

4. Briefly explain these entities: DBD, PSB, PCB?

   A Database Description (DBD) specifies characteristics of a database. The name, parent, and length of each segment type in the database.

   A Program Specification Block (PSB) is the program view of one or more IMS databases. The PSB includes one or more program communication blocks (PCB) for each IMS database that the program needs access to.

   A Program Communication Block (PCB) specifies the database to be accessed, the processing options such as read-only or various updating options, and the database segments that can be accessed.

5. What is the use of CMPAT parameter in PSB ?

   It is required if you are going to run your program in Batch Mode Processing (BMP), that is - in the online region. If you always run the program in DL/I

mode, you do not need the CMPAT. If you are going to run BMP, you need the CMPAT=YES specified in the PSB.

6. In IMS, what is the difference between a key field and a search field?

A key field is used to make the record unique and to order the database. A search field is a field that is needed to search the database on but does not have to be unique and does not order the database. For example, an **EMPLOYEE** database might be keyed on unique **EMP-NUMBER**. A search field might be needed on **PHONE-NUMBER** or **ZIP-CODE**. Even though the database is not ordered by these fields, they can be made search fields to query the database.

7. What does PROCOPT mean in a PCB?

The **PROCOPT** parameter specifies *processing options* that are allowed for this **PCB** when operating on a segment.

The different **PROCOPTs** and their meaning are:

    G - Get segment from DB
    I - Insert segment into DB
    R - Replace segment
    D - Delete segment
    A - All the above operations

8. What are the four basic parameters of a DLI retrieval call?

- **Function**
- **PCB mask**
- **SSAs**
- **IO Area**

9. What are Qualified SSA and Unqualified SSA?

   A qualified SSA specifies the segment type and the specific instance (key) of the segment to be returned. An unqualified SSA simply supplies the name of the segment type that you want to operate upon. You could use the latter if you don't care which specific segment you retrieve.

10. Which PSB parameter in a PSBGEN specifies the language in which the application program is written?

   The LANG parameter specifies the language in which the application program is written. Examples:

   ```
   LANG=COBOL
   LANG=PLI
   LANG=ASSEM
   ```

11. What does SENSEG stand for and how is it used in a PCB?

   SENSEG is known as Segment Level Sensitivity. It defines the program's access to parts of the database and it is identified at the segment level. For example, PROCOPT=G on a SENSEG means the segment is read-only by this PCB.

12. What storage mechanism/format is used for IMS index databases?

   IMS index databases must use VSAM KSDS.

13. What are the DL/I commands to add, change and remove a segment?

   The following are the DL/I commands for adding, changing and removing a segment:

   - **ISRT**
   - **REPL**
   - **DLET**

14. What return code will you receive from IMS if the DL/I call was successful?

    IMS returns blanks/spaces in the PCB STATUS-CODE field when the call was successful.

15. If you want to retrieve the last occurrence of a child segment under its parent, what command code could you use?

    Use the L command code to retrieve the last child segment under its parent. Incidentally, IMS ignores the L command code at the root level.

16. When would you use a GU call?

    GU is used to retrieve a segment occurrence based on SSA supplied arguments.

17. When would you use a GHU call?

    GHU (Get Hold Unique) retrieves and locks the record that you intend to update or delete.

18. What is the difference between running an IMS program as DLI and BMP ?

    DLI runs within its own address space. BMP runs under the IMS online control region. The practical difference concerns programs that update the database. If performing updates, DLI requires exclusive use of the database. Running BMP does not require exclusive use because it runs under control of the online region.

19. When would you use a GNP call?

    The GNP call is used for Get Next within Parent. This function is used to retrieve segment occurrences in sequence subordinate to an established parent segment.

20. Which IMS call is used to restart an abended program?

The XRST IMS call is made to restart an abended IMS program. Assuming the program has taken checkpoints during the abended program execution, the XRST call is used to restart from the last checkpoint taken instead of starting the processing all over.

21. How do you establish parentage on a segment occurrence?

By issuing a successful GU or GN (or GHU or GHN) call that retrieves the segment on which the parentage is to be established. IMS normally sets parentage at the lowest level segment retrieved in a call. If you want to establish parentage at a level other than the normal level, use the P command code.

22. What is a checkpoint?

A checkpoint is a stage where the modifications done to a database by an application program are considered complete and are committed to the database with the CHKP IMS call.

23. How do you update the primary key of an IMS segment?

You cannot update the primary key of a segment. If the key on a record must be changed, you can DLET the existing segment and then ISRT a new segment with the new key.

24. Do you need to use a qualified SSA with REPL/DLET calls?

No, you don't need to include an SSA with REPL/DLET calls. This is because the target segment has already been retrieved and held by a get hold call (that is the only way you can update or delete a segment).

Chapter Four Review Questions

1. Which of the following is NOT a valid data type for use as an identity column?

   a. INTEGER
   b. REAL
   c. DECIMAL
   d. SMALLINT

   The correct answer is B. A REAL type cannot be used as an identity field because it is considered an approximation of a number rather than an exact value. Only numeric types that have an exact value can be used as an identity field. INTEGER, DECIMAL, and SMALLINT are all incorrect here because they CAN be used as identity fields.

2. You need to store numeric integer values of up to 5,000,000,000. What data type is appropriate for this?

   a. INTEGER
   b. BIGINT
   c. LARGEINT
   d. DOUBLE

   The correct answer is B. BIGINT is an integer that can hold up to 9,223,372,036,854,775,807. INTEGER is not correct because an INTEGER can only hold up to 2,147,483,647. LARGEINT is an invalid type. DOUBLE could be used but since we are dealing with integer data, the double precision is not needed.

3. Which of the following is NOT a LOB (Large Object) data type?

   a. CLOB
   b. BLOB
   c. DBCLOB
   d. DBBLOB

The correct answer is D. There is no DBBLOB datatype in DB2. The other data types are valid. CLOB is a character large object with maximum length 2,147,483,647 bytes. A BLOB stores binary data and has a maximum size of 2,147,483,647. A DBCLOB stores double character data and has a maximum length of 1,073,741,824.

4. If you want to add an XML column VAR1 to table TBL1, which of the following would accomplish that?

    a. ALTER TABLE TBL1 ADD VAR1 XML
    b. ALTER TABLE TBL1 ADD COLUMN VAR1 XML
    c. ALTER TABLE TBL1 ADD COLUMN VAR1 (XML)
    d. ALTER TABLE TBL1 ADD XML COLUMN VAR1

The correct answer is B. The correct syntax is:

```
ALTER TABLE TBL1
ADD COLUMN VAR1 XML;
```

The other choices would result in a syntax error.

5. If you want rows that have similar key values to be stored physically close to each other, what keyword should you specify when you create an index?

    a. UNIQUE
    b. ASC
    c. INCLUDE
    d. CLUSTER

The correct answer is D - CLUSTER. Specifying a CLUSTER type index means that DB2 will attempt to physically store rows with similar keys close together. This is used for performance reasons when sequential type processing is needed according to the index. UNIQUE is incorrect because this keyword simply guarantees that there can be no more than one row with the same index key. ASC is incorrect because it has to do with the sort order for the index, and does not affect the physical storage of rows. INCLUDE specifies that a non-key field or fields will be stored with the index.

6. Assume a table where certain columns contain sensitive data and you don't want all users to see these columns. Some other columns in the table must be made accessible to all users. What type of object could you create to solve this problem?

    a. INDEX
    b. SEQUENCE
    c. VIEW
    d. TRIGGER

The correct answer is C. A view is a virtual table based upon a SELECT query that can include a subset of the columns in a table. So you can create multiple views against the same base table, and control access to the views based upon userid or group.

The other answers do not address the problem of limiting access to specific columns. An INDEX is an object that stores the physical location of records and is used to improve performance and enforce uniqueness. A SEQUENCE allows for the automatic generation of sequential values, and has nothing to do with limiting access to columns in a table. A TRIGGER is an object that performs some predefined action when it is activated. A trigger is only activated by an INSERT, UPDATE or DELETE of a record in a particular table.

7. To grant a privilege to all users of the database, grant the privilege to whom?

    a. ALL
    b. PUBLIC
    c. ANY
    d. DOMAIN

The correct answer is B. PUBLIC is a special "pseudo" group that means all users of the database. The other answers ALL, ANY, and DOMAIN are incorrect because they are not valid recipients of a grant statement.

8. Tara wants to grant CONTROL of table TBL1 to Bill, and also allow Bill to grant the same privilege to other users. What clause should Tara use on the GRANT statement?

   a. WITH CONTROL OPTION
   b. WITH GRANT OPTION
   c. WITH USE OPTION
   d. WITH REVOKE OPTION

The correct answer is B. Using the WITH GRANT OPTION permits the recipient of the grant to also grant this privilege to other users. The other choices WITH CONTROL OPTION, WITH USE OPTION, and WITH REVOKE OPTION are incorrect because they are not valid clauses on a GRANT statement.

9. Which of the following will generate DB2 SQL data structures for a table or view that can be used in a PLI or COBOL program?

   a. DECLARE
   b. INCLUDE
   c. DCLGEN
   d. None of the above.

The correct answer is C. DCLGEN is an IBM utility that generates SQL data structures (table definition and host variables) for a table or view, stores it in a PDS and then that PDS member can be included in a PL/1 or COBOL program. DECLARE is a verb used to define a temporary table or cursor. INCLUDE can be used to embed the generated structure into the program. Assuming the structure is in member MEMBER1 of the PDS, the statement EXEC SQL INCLUDE MEMBER1 will include it in the program.

10. Assuming you are using a DB2 precompiler, which of the following orders the DB2 program preparation steps correctly?

   a. Precompile SQL, Bind Package, Bind Plan.
   b. Precompile SQL, Bind Plan, Bind Package.
   c. Bind Package, Precompile SQL, Bind Plan.
   d. Bind Plan, Precompile SQL, Bind Package.

The correct answer is A. The DB2 related steps for program preparation are:

- **Precompile SQL which produces a DBRM**

- **Bind package using the DBRM**

- **Bind plan specifying the package(s)**

11. To end a transaction without making the changes permanent, which DB2 statement should be issued?

   a. COMMIT
   b. BACKOUT
   c. ROLLBACK
   d. NO CHANGE

The correct answer is C. Issuing a ROLLBACK statement will end a transaction without making the changes permanent.

12. If you want to maximize data concurrency without seeing uncommitted data, which isolation level should you use?

   a. RR
   b. UR
   c. RS
   d. CS

The correct answer is D (Cursor Stability). CURSOR STABILITY (CS) only locks the row where the cursor is placed, thus maximizing concurrency compared to RR or RS. REPEATABLE READ (RR) ensures that a query issued multiple times within the same unit of work will produce the exact same results. It does this by locking ALL rows that could affect the result, and does not permit any changes to the table that could affect the result. With READ STABILITY(RS), all rows that are returned by the query are locked. UNCOMMITTED READ (UR) is incorrect because it permits reading of uncommitted data and the question specifically disallows that.

13. To end a transaction and make the changes visible to other processes, which statement should be issued?

    a. ROLLBACK
    b. COMMIT
    c. APPLY
    d. CALL

The correct answer is B. The COMMIT statement ends a transaction and makes the changes visible to other processes.

14. Order the isolation levels, from greatest to least impact on performance.

    a. RR, RS, CS, UR
    b. UR, RR, RS, CS
    c. CS, UR, RR, RS
    d. RS, CS, UR, RR

The correct answer is A - RR, RS, CS, UR. Repeatable Read has the greatest impact on performance because it incurs the most overhead and locks the most rows. It ensures that a query issued multiple times within the same unit of work will produce the exact same results. It does this by locking all rows that could affect the result, and does not permit any adds/changes/deletes to the table that could affect the result. Next, READ STABILITY locks for the duration of the transaction those rows that are returned by a query, but it allows additional rows to be added to the table. CURSOR STABILITY only locks the row that the cursor is placed on (and any rows it has updated during

428

the unit of work). **UNCOMMITTED READ** permits reading of uncommitted changes which may never be applied to the database and does not lock any rows at all unless the row(s) is updated during the unit of work.

15. Suppose you have created a test version of a production table, and you want to to use the UNLOAD utility to extract the first 1,000 rows from the production table to load to the test version. Which keyword would you use in the UNLOAD statement?

    a. WHEN
    b. SELECT
    c. SAMPLE
    d. SUBSET

The correct answer is C. You can specify **SAMPLE** n where n is the number of rows to unload. For example you can limit the unloaded rows to the first 5,000 by specifying:

    SAMPLE 1000

WHEN is used to specify rows that meet a criteria such as: **WHEN (EMP_SALARY < 90000)**.

SELECT and **SUBSET** are invalid clauses and would cause an error.

16. Which of the following is NOT a way you could test a DB2 SQL statement?

    a. Running the statement from the DB2 command line processor.
    b. Running the statement from the SPUFI utility.
    c. Running the statement from IBM Data Studio.
    d. All of the above are valid ways to test an SQL statement.

The correct answer is D. Any of these three methods could be used to test a DB2 SQL statement.

Index

AGGREGATE Functions, 311
    AVERAGE, 311
    COUNT, 311
    MAX, 312
    MIN, 312
    SUM, 313
Case Expressions, 285
Common table expression, 296
DATA CONCURRENCY
    COMMIT, 340
    Isolation Level by Situation, 338
    Isolation Level Override, 339
    ROLLBACK, 341
    SAVEPOINT, 341
Data Manipulation Language
    DELETE Statement, 264
    INSERT Statement, 251
    MERGE Statement, 268
    SELECT Statement, 274
    Update Statement, 259
Data Manipulation Language (DML), 250
DB2 Support for XML, 300
DELETE Statement, 264
Error Handling
    Using a Standard Routine, 330
FETCH FIRST X ROWS, 281
GROUP BY, 283
HAVING, 284
IMS
    CBLTDLI, 137
    CHKP Call, 213
    Command Codes, 203, 209
    Committing and Rolling Back Changes, 210
    Database Descriptor (DBD), 132
    Deleting a Segment (GHU/DLET), 160
    IMS calls, 137
    IMS Programming Guidelines, 236
    IMS Status Codes, 139
    Inserting Child Segments, 163
    Loading an IMS Database, 141
    Performing Checkpoint Restart, 223
    Program Status Block (PSB), 135
    Reading a Database Sequentially (GN), 152
    Reading a Segment (GU), 148

    Reading Child Segments Sequentially (GNP), 170
    Retrieve Segments Using Boolean SSAs, 198
    Retrieve Segments Using Searchable Fields, 193
    Updating a Segment (GHU/REPL), 156
    XRST Call, 211
Information Management System (IMS), 129
INSERT Statement, 251
JOINS, 286
    Full Outer Join, 291
    Inner joins, 287
    Left Outer Join, 289
    Right Outer Join, 290
MERGE Statement, 268
ORDER BY, 284
PLI
    Calculations, 45
    Data Structures, 18
    Data Types, 16
    DO UNTIL, 22
    DO WHILE, 22
    Edits and Validation, 51
    File I/O, 25
    IF-THEN, 21
    Programming Format, 15
    Reporting, 33
    SELECT, 22
    Sub Programs, 73
    Tables, 63
SCALAR Functions, 313
    COALESCE, 313
    CONCAT, 315
    LCASE, 315
    Month, 317
    REPEAT, 317
    SPACE, 318
    UCASE, 319
    YEAR, 320
SELECT Statement, 274
SPECIAL REGISTERS
    CURRENT CLIENT_USERID, 307
    CURRENT DATE, 307
    CURRENT MEMBER, 308
    CURRENT OPTIMIZATION HINT, 308
    CURRENT RULES, 308

CURRENT SCHEMA, 308
CURRENT SQLID, 309
CURRENT TEMPORAL BUSINESS TIME, 309
CURRENT TEMPORAL SYSTEM TIME, 309
CURRENT TIME, 309
CURRENT TIMESTAMP, 309
SESSION USER, 310
STORED PROCEDURES
Types of Stored Procedures, 350
SUBQUERY, 282
TEMPORAL TABLES
Bi-Temporal Example, 397
Bitemporal Support, 392
Business Time, 391
Business Time Example, 392
System Time, 391
System time Example, 395
TEMPORARY Tables
CREATED Temporary Table, 402
DECLARED Temporary Table, 403
TRIGGERS
Examples of Triggers, 381
Timings of Triggers, 380
Types of Triggers, 380
UNION and INTERSECT, 292
INTERSECT, 295
UNION, 292
UPDATE Statement, 259
USER DEFINED FUNCTIONS (UDF)
External Scalar Function, 372
External Table Function, 374
Sourced Function, 378
SQL Scalar Function, 369
SQL Table Function, 371

Types of UDF, 369
VSAM
Application Programming with VSAM, 103
Creating and Accessing Alternate Indexes, 115
Creating VSAM Files, 92
Entry Sequence Data Set, 92
File Status Codes, 125
Key Sequence Data Set, 91
Linear Data Set, 92
Loading and Unloading VSAM Files, 94
Relative Record Data Set, 92
WHERE Condition
AND, 275
BETWEEN, 277
DISTINCT, 278
EXCEPT, 277
IN, 276
LIKE, 278
OR, 275
XML Builtin Functions
XMLEXISTS, 304
XMLMODIFY, 306
XMLPARSE, 305
XMLQUERY, 304
XMLTABLE, 305
XML Examples, 300
XML OPERATIONS
DELETE With XML, 302
INSERT With XML, 301
SELECT With XML, 302
UPDATE With XML, 302
XML Related Technologies, 299
XML Structure, 298
XQuery, 300

Other Titles by Robert Wingate

Quick Start Training for IBM z/OS Application Developers, Volume 1

ISBN-13: 978-1986039840

This book will teach you the basic information and skills you need to develop applications on IBM mainframes running z/OS. The instruction, examples and sample programs in this book are a fast track to becoming productive as quickly as possible in JCL, MVS Utilities, COBOL, PLI and DB2. The content is easy to read and digest, well organized and focused on honing real job skills. IBM z/OS Quick Start Training for Application Developers is a key step in the direction of mastering IBM application development so you'll be ready to join a technical team.

Quick Start Training for IBM z/OS Application Developers, Volume 2

ISBN-13: 978-1717284594

This book will teach you the basic information and skills you need to develop applications on IBM mainframes running z/OS. The instruction, examples and sample programs in this book are a fast track to becoming productive as quickly as possible in VSAM, IMS and DB2. The content is easy to read and digest, well organized and focused on honing real job skills. IBM z/OS Quick Start Training for Application Developers is a key step in the direction of mastering IBM application development so you'll be ready to join a technical team.

DB2 Exam C2090-313 Preparation Guide

ISBN 13: 978-1548463052

This book will help you pass IBM Exam C2090-313 and become an IBM Certified Application Developer - DB2 11 for z/OS. The instruction, examples and questions/answers in the book offer you a significant advantage by helping you to gauge your readiness for the exam, to better understand the objectives being tested, and to get a broad exposure to the DB2 11 knowledge you'll be tested on.

DB2 Exam C2090-320 Preparation Guide

ISBN 13: 978-1544852096

This book will help you pass IBM Exam C2090-320 and become an IBM Certified Database Associate - DB2 11 Fundamentals for z/OS. The instruction, examples and questions/answers in the book offer you a significant advantage by helping you to gauge your readiness for the exam, to better understand the objectives being tested, and to get a broad exposure to the DB2 11 knowledge you'll be tested on. The book is also a fine introduction to DB2 for z/OS!

DB2 Exam C2090-313 Practice Questions

ISBN 13: 978-1534992467

This book will help you pass IBM Exam C2090-313 and become an IBM Certified Application Developer - DB2 11 for z/OS. The 180 questions and answers in the book (three full practice exams) offer you a significant advantage by helping you to gauge your readiness for the exam, to better understand the objectives being tested, and to get a broad exposure to the DB2 11 knowledge you'll be tested on.

DB2 Exam C2090-615 Practice Questions

ISBN 13: 978-1535028349

This book will help you pass IBM Exam C2090-615 and become an IBM Certified Database Associate (DB2 10.5 for Linux, Unix and Windows). The questions and answers in the book offer you a significant advantage by helping you to gauge your readiness for the exam, to better understand the objectives being tested, and to get a broad exposure to the knowledge you'll be tested on.

DB2 10.1 Exam 610 Practice Questions

ISBN 13: 978-1-300-07991-0

This book will help you pass IBM Exam 610 and become an IBM Certified Database Associate. The questions and answers in the book offer you a significant advantage by helping you to gauge your readiness for the exam, to better understand the objectives being tested, and to get a broad exposure to the knowledge you'll be tested on.

DB2 10.1 Exam 611 Practice Questions

ISBN 13: 978-1-300-08321-4

This book will help you pass IBM Exam 611 and become an IBM Certified Database Administrator. The questions and answers in the book offer you a significant advantage by helping you to gauge your readiness for the exam, better understand the objectives being tested, and get a broad exposure to the knowledge you'll be tested on.

DB2 9 Exam 730 Practice Questions: Second Edition

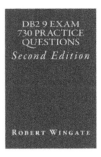

ISBN-13: 978-1463798833

This book will help you pass IBM Exam 730 and become an IBM Certified Database Associate. The questions and answers in the book offer you a significant advantage by helping you to gauge your readiness for the exam, to better understand the objectives being tested, and to get a broad exposure to the knowledge you'll be tested on.

DB2 9 Certification Questions for Exams 730 and 731: Second Edition

ISBN-13: 978-1466219755

This book is targeted for IBM Certified Database Administrator candidates for DB2 9 for Windows, Linux and UNIX. It includes approximately 400 practice questions and answers for IBM Exams 730 and 731 (6 complete practice exams).

About the Author

Robert Wingate is a computer services professional with over 30 years of IBM mainframe programming experience. He holds several IBM certifications, including IBM Certified Application Developer - DB2 11 for z/OS, and IBM Certified Database Administrator for LUW. He lives in Fort Worth, Texas.

www.ingramcontent.com/pod-product-compliance
Lightning Source LLC
Chambersburg PA
CBHW081459050326
40690CB00015B/2862